India and Its Visual Cultures

India and Its Visual Cultures

Community, Class and Gender in a Symbolic Landscape

Edited by

Uwe Skoda

Birgit Lettmann

SAGE

Los Angeles | London | New Delhi
Singapore | Washington DC | Melbourne

First published in 2018 by

SAGE Publications India Pvt Ltd
B1/I-1 Mohan Cooperative Industrial Area
Mathura Road, New Delhi 110 044, India
www.sagepub.in

SAGE Publications Inc
2455 Teller Road
Thousand Oaks, California 91320, USA

SAGE Publications Ltd
1 Oliver's Yard, 55 City Road
London EC1Y 1SP, United Kingdom

SAGE Publications Asia-Pacific Pte Ltd
3 Church Street
#10-04 Samsung Hub
Singapore 049483

Published by Vivek Mehra for SAGE Publications India Pvt Ltd, typeset in 10/12 pt Times New Roman by Diligent Typesetter India Pvt Ltd, Delhi and printed at Chaman Enterprises, New Delhi.

Library of Congress Cataloging-in-Publication Data

Names: Skoda, Uwe, 1973- editor. | Lettmann, Birgit, editor.
Title: India and its visual cultures : community, class and gender in a symbolic landscape / edited by Uwe Skoda and Birgit Lettmann.
Description: New Delhi, India; Thousand Oaks, California : SAGE Publications, 2017. | Includes bibliographical references and index.
Identifiers: LCCN 2017020723| ISBN 9789386446688 (hardback) | ISBN 9789386446701 (ePub) | ISBN 9789386446695 (ebook)
Subjects: LCSH: India—Intellectual life—20th century. | India—Intellectual life—21st century. | Visual communication—India—History. | Art and society—India—History. | Mass media—Social aspects—India—History. | Pictures—Social aspects—India—History. | Material culture—India—History. | Popular culture—India—History.
Classification: LCC DS428.2 .I525 2017 | DDC 954—dc23 LC record available at https://lccn.loc.gov/2017020723

ISBN: 978-93-864-4668-8 (HB)

SAGE Team: Rajesh Dey, Alekha Chandra Jena, Deepti Thapa and Ritu Chopra

Contents

List of Figures

Acknowledgements

This volume brings together a range of scholars, senior and junior, from India, Israel and Europe, who have approached visual culture from various angles including anthropology, sociology or cultural studies. While the idea to this book originated during two workshops—an initial workshop *Visual Cultures in Contemporary India* at Aarhus University, Denmark, followed by a second workshop *Delhi and Urban India in Visual Cultures* at Sri Venkateswara College in Delhi—many chapters were contributed to the volume after and independent of the workshops in order to broaden and deepen the theme.

The editors would like to express their gratitude to the Contemporary India Study Centre Aarhus (CISCA) at Aarhus University, Denmark, which—specifically with funds provided by the European Union through its India-EU Study Centres Programme—hosted the first workshop. We would also like to thank Sri Venkateswara College and especially Nirmal Kumar as colleague and friend for co-hosting the workshops as well as for his input that helped to shape the volume. Furthermore, we would acknowledge our gratitude to Routledge, Taylor & Francis Group for their kind permission to reprint the chapter by Radhika Chopra, first published in 2013 in *Sikh Formations: Religion, Culture, Theory* 9(2): 97–114. Last but not least, we would also like to thank SAGE Publications as our publisher for their encouragement and support throughout this editing process.

Introduction: Mapping Visual Cultures in India

Uwe Skoda and Birgit Lettmann

For more than two decades, the visual has held a fixed place in research in the social sciences, as well as in the humanities and the natural sciences. The visual, visuality, processes of visualisation and visual culture have become a popular field of study in recent years. Research in this area may range from the analysis of historical visual phenomena; observing relations between images and the perception of their consumers; the production and use of images and media in both popular culture and the sciences; the study of iconographies and aesthetics; the relationship between media, power and perception; forms of mediatisation; all the way to the study of how meaning is produced by and through images; the circulation of images in and across cultures; practices of seeing and studies of the social and 'cultural construction of visual experience in daily life, in media, in representations and in the visual arts' (Mitchell 1995: 540). Research, however, is not limited to these individual issues, and the very concept of visual culture and its complexity still challenges scholars engaging with it and (re)interpreting its meaning in various ways. In fact, this vague conceptualisation and varying agendas may actually have contributed to its popularity and made possible multifaceted approaches under this umbrella, as well as a wide range of discourses.

The overwhelming flood of studies in this field over the last 20 years is a consequence of a profound shift within academia, a shift which became famous as the *pictorial* (Mitchell [1992] 1994) or *iconic turn* (Boehm 1994). Interpreting these turns as a replacement for the *linguistic turn* made popular by the philosopher Richard Rorty (1967) would be short-sighted and would only perpetuate the long-standing dichotomy between text and image. While the latter refers to a development starting in the 1960s in the humanities and social sciences that puts textuality, text, discourse and language at the centre of investigations of cultures, society and cultural products, the *pictorial* or *iconic turn* points to the growing scientific interest in images, visuality and visual products and the emergence of an academic environment around these issues from the 1990s onwards. Yet, as Doris Bachmann-Medick (2006) points out, turns are not 'paradigms' in Kuhn's (1962) sense: they 'do not aim at "overthrowing" other theoretical regimes' (Bachmann-Medick 2008: 10). Rather, they question systems of power, challenge canons of values and introduce new kinds of scientific questioning. In this understanding, the *pictorial* or *iconic turn* challenges the long-standing dominance of text and aims not so much at a substitution than at shifting the emphasis so that images and, in a more general way, visuality and visual forms become the focus of interest. Thus, neither text nor image is the sole ruler: within the wider range of the full sensorium, they are both inhabitants of the academic landscape. Such an understanding not only works against an ocular-centrism and acknowledges the problems that segregating the visual from the other senses would entail, it also allows us to move beyond clear-cut boundaries and to analyse intermedial forms and constellations such as complex text–image combinations (see López-Varela, Chapter 6).

Throughout the twentieth century, one might invoke different scholars who were already focusing on and engaging with visual aspects of culture, from Aby Warburg and his *Mnemosyne Atlas* through Walter Benjamin's *Passagenwerk* to Ananda Coomaraswamy's *History of Indian and Indonesian Art*, and on to Erwin Panofsky, Roland Barthes, John Berger or Laura Mulvey. The study of visual culture as a field, however, was centrally inspired by the art historian W.J.T. Mitchell who proclaimed the *pictorial turn* in a seminal article of 1992. Putting pictures at the centre of his theoretical considerations, Mitchell advocated a 'postlinguistic, postsemiotic rediscovery of the picture' ([1992] 1994: 16). This brings to the fore another consequence of the *pictorial* or *iconic turn*: the picture as research object traditionally falls under the authority of art history. With the increasing interest of an ever-growing range of disciplines in specific tangible pictures and, more generally, in images as different kinds of optical appearances, art history lost its interpretational sovereignty over them. This newly emerging field of visual cultural studies started to move beyond the sole focus on art images and placed in question the hierarchical system of high culture versus low or popular culture (Mitchell 1995). However, it is not only about pictures: as Mitchell (2002: 178) himself later conceded, the field of visual culture is a lot more complex and cannot be reduced to either pictures or even images: '[…] even something as broad as the image does not exhaust the field of visuality; […] visual studies is not the same thing as image studies, and […] the study of the visual image is just one component of the larger field'.

One of the strongest influences in the interdisciplinary area of visual culture has come from social and cultural anthropology (Pink 2008: 130). Since the establishment of anthropology as an academic discipline, visuality, the visual and visual methods of research and analysis have played an important role in different respects; one might think, for example, of Bronislaw Malinowski's paradigm of participant *observation*, as well as his early use of the camera. However, these uses remained largely undiscussed and were not addressed in any systematic way until the end of the twentieth century (Banks and Morphy 1997).

Within the framework of the sub-discipline of visual anthropology, Marcus Banks and Howard Morphy (1997: 1) distinguish two key activities: 'on the one hand visual anthropology concerns the use of visual material in anthropological research […] and on the other it is the study of visual systems and visible culture'. Regarding the first focus, the employment of visual recording technologies, photography and film as a tool to document, illustrate, record and collect visual evidence and data for ethnographic research goes back to their inventions in the nineteenth century. However, it was only with the work of Margaret Mead and Gregory Bateson in the early 1940s, who systematically introduced the camera (photography and film) into their fieldwork and already included reflexive elements in the methods they developed, that visual anthropology began to take shape as a sub-discipline (ibid.; see also Bateson and Mead [1942] 2012; Karlekar, Chapter 1). Then, from the middle of the twentieth century onwards, visual anthropology became primarily a synonym for ethnographic film-making under the influence of Jean Rouch, John Marshall and the MacDougalls. David MacDougall in particular advocated a 'radical break with anthropological modes of discourse' by employing 'visual media to describe and analyse culture' (MacDougall 1997: 283). Analogous to the 'writing culture' debate (Clifford and Marcus 1986) of the 1980s, with its self-reflection on ethnographic representation and its critique of the textual construction of culture, this urges the sub-discipline to address the question of 'picturing culture' (Ruby 2000; see also Laister 2008).

Due to not only the strong linguistic bias of academic debate in general, but more particularly as a consequence of the *linguistic turn*, visual anthropology in Banks and Morphy's second understanding was hardly practised until the latter part of the twentieth century. In the course of the alternative *pictorial turn*, which affected several disciplines, the focus in anthropology also shifted towards a renewed interest in and a profound engagement with the visual, thus giving way to new subject areas. Visual anthropology was thus broadened into a sub-discipline that took seriously the endeavour to practise visual anthropology in the sense of an 'anthropology of the visual' (MacDougall 1997: 281), to study the visual aspects of culture and 'visible cultural forms' (Banks and Morphy 1997: 5), as well as the culturally specific understanding, production and consumption of media, and to investigate visual representational systems and the like. It is these issues that form the central field of interest of this volume.

Within this context, research activities in India play a specific role. Not only does the discipline look back on a strong tradition of anthropological research focusing on India: 'India' itself is often described as having a special affinity with the visual (Eck 1981), thus offering diverse research opportunities in the field of visual culture. In recent years, pioneering studies in this area have been conducted by scholars from both India and elsewhere. For instance, *Camera Indica* by Christopher Pinney (1997) examines the changing role of photographic practice in India. In a later study, Pinney puts chromolithographs at the centre of interest with the aim of 'rearrang[ing] Indian history so that a central place can be found for the visual' (Pinney 2004: 8). Kajri Jain, in her book *Gods in the Bazaar* (2007), examines this pivotal dimension of Indian mass culture with a strong focus on the economies and histories of calendar art, while Patricia Uberoi's *Freedom and Destiny: Gender, Family, and Popular Culture in India* (2009) also looks at films and their audiences, and Christiane Brosius, in her book *Empowering Visions: The Politics of Representation in Hindu Nationalism* (2005), scrutinises the role of audiovisual media, specifically videos, in the Hindutva movement.

Despite the steady rise of readers and introductions to visual culture published especially in Britain and North America, overviews and compendia bringing together the diversity of studies on individual visual phenomena in India are surprisingly rare, with the exception of works by, for example, Jyotindra Jain (2007), Gayatri Sinha (2009) and Kaur and Dave-Mukherji (2014). Expanding art-historical approaches, the articles collected in the latter volume *Arts and Aesthetics in a Globalizing World* examine anthropology's interface with artworks. With an emphasis on aesthetics, they scrutinise anthropological understandings of arts, artworks and media, the politics as well as ecologies of aesthetics and challenge the conventional distinction between the arts and sciences (ibid.: xiv, 2ff).

The purpose of the present volume is not to offer an overall introduction to visual culture in India in its entirety; rather, while focusing on this analytical concept, it aims to contribute to a more comprehensive anthropological, rather than art-historical mapping of contemporary empirical visual cultures in India, which is still lacking. The collection of essays explicitly interrogates present-day practices, thus moving forward from previous studies primarily occupied with colonial and early post-colonial India and specifically with nineteenth and twentieth century visions and imaginings of the nation. The central role that anthropology plays in analysing visual culture, according to Sarah Pink (2008), is also reflected by the contributors to this volume. Most of them are scholars trained in social or cultural anthropology or sociology—disciplines closely linked in India. They conduct an in-depth ethnographic research in the second of the fields defined by Banks and Morphy, namely, studying visual systems and visible culture. However, we do not confine the visual to still or moving images. Instead and contrary to conventional understandings, *India and Its Visual Cultures* encompasses other artefacts, especially architectural or monumental, also forming crucial parts of wider image-scapes (in landscapes, cityscapes, etc.). Thus, we argue for broadening the horizon of the visual in India and encourage further research in this field.

The Visual and the Popular

The sphere of visual culture in India introduced in this volume, including cinema, advertisements, *pata* rolls (painted scrolls), newspaper cartoons, etc., overlaps to a large extent, though not completely, with the part of culture that is usually called 'popular' or 'public'. Therefore, it is pertinent to hint at common ground, delineate differences and briefly sketch a realm of 'popular visual culture' as one of the volume's central pillars. However, this excludes neither other sensorial dimensions nor other aspects of everyday visual culture such as photography, which, although also considered a popular practice, may—as in the case of post-mortem images—be combined with a distinctive private or domestic usage. Thus, our broader inclusive approach differs and goes beyond earlier contributions like Sinha's (2009), which located visual culture more firmly in the sphere of art and art history.

Following John Storey's seminal work (2001: 1ff.; see also Parker 2011: 148), popular culture always implies otherness. As he states: 'It is never enough to speak of popular culture; we always have to acknowledge that with which it is being contrasted' (ibid.: 14), that is, what is present and what is absent. Thus, popular culture is defined in opposition to something else, be it folk culture, mass culture, dominant culture and so on, the latter being fairly directly linked to power and ideology, and going beyond entertainment and leisure alone. Similarly, on the one hand, the visual is frequently singled out, yet part of the culturally determined broader sensorium. It may be aligned with, compete with or hierarchically distinguished from other sensorial dimensions such as the aural and olfactory, for example, in ritual contexts. Without advocating any (new) ranking within the wider sensorium, we also acknowledge that, on the other hand, in some contexts it is clearly juxtaposed with text or the 'word', while in others the boundaries are blurred, for instance, in calligraphy in South Asia or billboards and commercials (see Brara, Chapter 7), and we are interested in both processes.

Many visual culture examples considered in this volume, such as cinema (see Kumar, Chapter 2) or newspaper cartoons (see Parciack and Shacham, Chapter 10) may easily be located in a popular culture framework by sharing a quantitative dimension by virtue of being mass-produced, mass-circulated and mass-consumed and therefore tightly linked to industrialisation and urbanisation—though it may not be clear whether there are any thresholds to what actually makes a 'mass'. Looking more critically at the term 'mass', Holt N. Parker (2011: 161–63) made the important observation that popular culture is linked to cultural capital, that is, some forms require fairly little cultural capital either to produce (e.g., dances, painted scrolls) or consume (going to watch movies, sports), while other forms, such as films, require a rather greater level of input in terms of production costs. He thus stresses the distinctions between folk culture (not mass-produced yet mass-consumed), mass culture (mass-produced and mass-consumed) and high culture (neither mass-produced nor mass-consumed).

Examples like the *patas* as painted scrolls (see Chatterji, Chapter 4) may be considered as originating relatively strongly in a distinctive folk culture, as coming from the people and being made for the people, yet negotiating the global and the local. Therefore, though feeding into popular culture as well, folk culture should not simplistically be equated with the authentic (see Storey 2001: 10). The forms of visual culture considered here, however, may rarely qualify as high culture either. In this way, as Parker (2011: 166) argued, popular culture may be just a shorthand for 'unauthorised culture', that is, for something that has not yet been legitimised and authenticated by the art world and its institutions such as museums or galleries (see also Davis 1999). The only relevant authority in this view would be the market or demand, though the state may play a significant role as well.

However, this neglects the fact that despite the continuing performance of storytelling in Bengal, the *patas* do find their way into museums where they would be elevated to the status of ethnographic or art objects. As James Clifford noted in 1996, objects of non-Western origin have often been classified into two main categories (leaving aside tourist kitsch and fakes): cultural artefacts (traditional, collective, presented in ethnographic collections) and art (original, unique, presented in galleries). The two categories are connected with the exchanges that become possible when objects are re-evaluated. For example, 'transformative journeys' may lead from culture to art by elevating 'ethnographica' into 'tribal art'. These processes are currently underway in the case of Sora ritual wall paintings (see Guillaume-Pey, Chapter 5): that is, the paintings of this 'tribal' group from Odisha are increasingly becoming de-contextualised and acquiring an aesthetic value and emblematic cultural status. Losing their powerful divine status, the images are sold to museums and find their ways into exhibitions and the like with stakeholders like NGOs and the Indian government, etc., being involved in this process of 'artification', which changes not only the audience but also questions of production and meaning. Guillaume-Pey, being attentive to ethnographic details like all other authors of this volume, is able to reveal the evolution of these complex object/image biographies.

At the same time, folk artists, as in the case of the *pata* scrolls described by Roma Chatterji (Chapter 4), are actively involved in constant reinterpretations that enrich their repertoire of narratives and incorporate unfolding news events into their practices. Taking such insights into account, the popular, particularly in the perspective of Gramscian-influenced scholars, may be best understood as

> a site of struggle between the 'resistance' of subordinate groups in society and the forces of 'incorporation' operating in the interests of dominant groups in society. Popular culture in this usage is not imposed culture of the mass culture theorists, nor is it an emerging from below, spontaneously oppositional culture of 'the people.' Rather, it is a terrain of exchange and negotiation between the two. (Bennett, in Parker 2011: 155–56)

Though rejecting the term 'popular culture' and preferring 'public culture' instead, Arjun Appadurai and Carol Breckenridge (1995: 5) pointed in the same direction in that they considered public culture as essentially a dynamic 'zone of cultural debate, […] contestation and mutual cannibalization, in which national, mass, and folk culture provide both mill and grist for one another', in effect making of the popular a 'compromise equilibrium' (Storey 2001: 11). As Parker (2011: 155) commented, this might also be seen as a bricolage including the reused, refashioned but also re-appropriated acts and materials of elite culture.

Irrespective of the terminological priorities, what is crucial for us here is that 'high' and 'low'—or 'popular visual' broadly speaking—shifted frequently historically, have been re-evaluated and have never been fixed as practices nor as analytical tools (Storey 2001: 15; see also Clifford 1996). Instead, they have always been linked to available and affordable techniques and to specific, historical conditions in terms of their production, circulation and consumption. Thus, we agree with Jain's definition, which also applies to the visual within popular culture:

> What is popular culture? Often unreflectively seen as situated solely in mass-production and mass-consumption, it is usually linked to the common culture of the street as against the 'classical' or 'traditional' cultures, to subaltern or working-class culture vis-a-vis that of the dominant groups. Although it is entangled in the histories of such oversimplified binaries as 'high' and 'low', 'autonomous' and 'instrumental', 'individual' and 'communal', 'authentic' and 'commodified', it has increasingly become possible to critically analyse its locus and role even though these may be continuously shifting with developments in technology, production, the market, and their cumulative impact on culture and society. (Jain 2007: 7)

Jain's apt summary also refers to the development of new technologies as a crucial variable in the production, circulation and consumption triangle. For example, innovations such as photography have democratised portraiture (Tagg [1988] 2005), while new printing presses such as Ravi Varma's early venture facilitated a vision of the nation through the production of 'penny posters' (Castelli and Aprile 2005). Similarly, the Internet supplemented or replaced earlier forms of matchmaking through newspapers, etc., and led to new visual representations of marriage ideals, such as a stronger emphasis on conjugality, without necessarily doing away with older values such as caste endogamy (see Titzmann, Chapter 8).

Ritual Visuality

'India is a visual and visionary culture, one in which the eyes have a prominent role in the apprehension of the sacred', writes Diana Eck (1981: 7) in her famous treaty on *darśan* (visual exchange with a deity), which ascribes the visual a privileged position over other senses, such as the aural or olfactory senses. She locates the 'imaginative and "image-making"' (ibid.) traditions first and foremost in the religious sphere, that is, within the realm of Hinduism, and argues that the divine is conceived as at least potentially visible—as when the deity is considered to be present in an icon—though not every human may necessarily be capable of seeing it, and some Hindus may argue that the icon is merely a tool for meditation. However, the 'central act of Hindu worship, from the point of view of the lay person, is to stand in the presence of the deity and to behold the image with one's own eyes, to see and be seen by the deity' (ibid.: 3). Or, as Lawrence A. Babb (1981: 396) puts it:

> [A]n important theme of Hindu worship is that of 'closure' between deity and worshipper; the devotee surrenders through intimacy, and establishes identification with the deity by taking something of the deity into himself. [...] the worshipper 'drinks in' the deity, but only [...] from below.

For Eck and Babb, as well as for Cornelia Mallebrein and Heinrich von Stietencron (2008), *darśan* is not simply an auspicious sight, it establishes 'contact with the divine' (ibid.: 109ff.). It is intrinsically linked to the two-way process of taking (perspective of the devotee) and giving (perspective of the deity), the latter being clearly symbolised in the usually very prominent eyes of the deities' respective icons and ceremonies to open the deities' eyes whenever a new icon is consecrated (perceived as infusing the breath of life). As Babb (1981: 388) stresses, supplementing Eck's pioneering work, it is particularly the deity's benevolent gaze that is sought, for example, the 'glance of compassion' among followers of Radhasoami Guru, while the negative, malevolent and potentially destructive impact of glancing, as vividly exemplified in the 1975 film *Jai Santoshi Maa*, is feared.

Though the 'exchange of vision' just mentioned is crucial for any encounter between devotee and deity, this intimate connection goes well beyond the mere act of sight as one might misunderstand it in the Euro-American sense. As Eck points out with reference to the work of the art and film theorist Rudolph Arnheim and the art historian Stella Kramrisch, respectively, seeing needs to be considered more like an active, constructive focusing, and it also overlaps with notions of touching: that is, the divine blessing may entail a physical experience. Devotees may also talk about 'drinking' the divine power with their own eyes as a way of describing an overwhelming divine *darśanic* (*darśan*-like) experience (Babb 1981: 388).

Moreover, the concept of *darśan* is in no way limited to icons in, for example, temples, but includes living persons such as sadhus, gurus and spiritual leaders, as well as kings in notions of *rajdarśan* (*darśan* of a ruler) and political leaders or national figures (see Reese, Chapter 11); accordingly, acts of censorship or the denial of *darśan* may be highly politically charged. This also includes holy places such as *tirthas, dhams* or *pithas*[1] as destinations for pilgrimages that worshippers visit as 'sacred sightseer' (Eck 1981: 4; see also Chopra, Chapter 4). In fact, as Babb (1981: 387) notes, the visual interaction between *darśan*-seeking devotee and deity-guru may also involve all sorts of images leading to the emergence of a 'photo-iconography' in which pictures become omnipresent channels within which to transmit power (see also Skoda and Lettmann, Chapter 3). As a 'gaze in reverence' (Jacob 2009: 227), *darśan* is also intrinsically tied to the domains of popular culture, particularly in the form of 'celluloid deities' (ibid.; Kumar, Chapter 2) and/or of domestic politics, as in the political culture of Tamil Nadu, with its thick nexus between cinema and politics (see Reese, Chapter 11).

While Babb already outlined the idea of *darśan* in relation to different religious movements (Brahma Kumaris, Radhasoami), more recently, John E. Cort (2012: 2) has emphasised the multivalence of *darśanic* experiences and called for *darśan* to be situated in relation to sects, regions, time, gender and place. Treating *darśan* as a South Asian and not primarily a Hindu concept, and noting 'many, if not countless, darśan experiences in South Asia' (ibid.: 31), he questions the relevance of the aspect of touching in combination with seeing in Jain philosophies and—perhaps more to the point here—the importance of the outward-looking devotional gaze. In contrast to the outward-reaching process described by Babb and Eck, the Digambar devotional eye may rather be directed inwards, ultimately negating the very visual act (ibid.: 23), though again this view needs to be carefully contextualised.

Memory and *Memento Mori*

With reference to Sophie Hawkins, Cort (2012: 5) argues that Sai Baba devotees need the physical presence of Sai Baba to have a proper *darśan*, that is, using new media like the Internet in order to have *darśan* would not suffice. While elsewhere a 'digital' *darśan* might be practised (Mallapragada 2010), for Sai Baba followers, an 'Internet *darśan*' would actually reduce the mutual, two-directional interaction that presupposes the powerful presence and gaze of the revered Sai Baba to a simple 'one-directional act of memory' (Hawkins, in Cort: 5), that is, a contemplative remembering of the absentee guru. Independent of the question whether every Hindu would agree with Sai Baba devotees or would be prepared to engage in online interactions, significantly here ritual visuality and memory are linked and hierarchised, even though presence cannot be substituted, and memory or the act of memorising are therefore considered inferior. However, the visual is often implicated in acts of remembering in various ways: for example, visuals elicit memories which open up methodological avenues (see Karlekar, Chapter 1), but which may also risk distorting them.

Our understanding of memory and its various dimensions relies on the pioneering work of Aleida Assmann (2006) and Jan Assmann ([1997] 2005). Both distinguish between various levels of memory: individual, social and political in the case of the former and mimetic, material and communicative in the case of the latter. However, both also consider cultural memory to be the outermost and most encompassing dimension of human memory, while the levels generally overlap and intersect in different ways, as when actions involving specific objects are routinised and potentially ritualised. At the same time, both identify certain thresholds; Aleida Assmann (2006: 215) postulates a distinction between embodied memory (individual and social) and mediated memory (both political and cultural, with visual media forms at the forefront), while Jan Assmann ([1997] 2005: 56) suggests a partly fuzzy dichotomy between communicative and cultural memory. The former expands to a time horizon of a maximum of 80 to 100 years, being grounded in lived experiences, while the latter dimension, in going beyond three to four generations, requires specialists, institutions or other durable carriers of external symbols and material representations.

Perhaps more than any other visual culture media, photography spans the various dimensions of memory through its ability to store and revive individual and private hi/stories as much as social, political or national ones. As Karlekar argues (Chapter 1), the double role of photography as a recording and narrating device plays a fundamental role here. Thus, Karlekar, taking up the example of how the history of women's work in India has been created and chronicled through photographs, 'discusses how the visual adds body—if not soul—to an understanding of the lives of half of India's workforce' (ibid., Chapter 1, page 4). Clearly inspired by Roland Barthes, this intersecting of memories has also been summarised poignantly by Annette Kuhn and Kirsten Emiko McAllister (2006: 1) who argue that

> Above all, the photograph is widely held to be a record, a piece of evidence that something happened at some time, somewhere—in the time and the place in front of the camera. Unlike cinema, the photograph holds this recorded moment in stillness, capturing and offering up for contemplation a trace of something lost, lending it a ghostly quality. In this sense, the photograph confronts us with the fleeting nature of our world and reminds us of our mortality. In seeming to capture times and places lost in the past, the photograph can disturb the present moment and the contemporary landscape with troubling or nostalgic memories and with forgotten, or all too vividly remembered, histories.

Moreover, as Roland Barthes ([1980] 1984: 91) reminds us, photographs are not only agents of death but may also block memories, may even essentially be anti-memory by superimposing memories, particularly individual memories, which in turn are often idiosyncratic, fragmented, distorted and adaptive (Assmann 2006: 212–13). The volume reflects this medial potency of photography by including contributions focusing in various ways on *memento mori*, which, however, are not limited to pictures and may include statues, etc. On the one hand, post-mortem photographs of beloved ones who have just passed away are introduced (Skoda and Lettmann, Chapter 3), post-mortem photography meant primarily for private consumption, being a vibrant tradition across religious and caste communities in eastern India. On the other hand, such images can be highly politically charged, as in case of the post-mortem photograph of J.S. Bhindranwale, leader of the Khalistan movement who was killed during Operation Blue Star conducted by the Indian Army (see Chopra, Chapter 4). Photographs imbued with a specific claim to authenticity, the Barthesian 'it has been' (in front of the camera), may cause a specific punctum, like something pricking individual viewers linked to their specific biographies. However, it may also be tied to wider national 'shards' or traumas, as in the case of the events surrounding the Golden Temple. Here, not only is the way the supposed martyr is depicted and portrayed highly contested—painting versus photo—but also the spatial location of the memorial is entangled in the tension between remembering and forgetting, between memories and counter-memories, between various 'memory activists' or lobbying groups. Chopra's contribution demonstrates how the spatial and the visual mutually inform and constitute each other—a central concern of the volume also illustrated in the section 'Monumental Landscapes'.

Moving on from 'fuzzy bottom-up' to the more 'institutionalised top-down' political memory, or more broadly from *having* memories to *making* them, as Aleida Assmann (2006: 216) argues, we see such processes of creating history exemplified in Mayawati's rather successful attempts to constitute what might be called a monumental memory by setting up spectacular *sthal*s, literally 'memorials' (see Khound, Chapter 13). Mayawati's project of memorialising subaltern or Dalit leaders, first and foremost B.R. Ambedkar, but also herself, goes beyond installing statues of individual politicians by combining them with highly visible divine icons and multivalent symbols such as elephants. She establishes grand politico-religious landscapes that connect Dalit identity with Buddhism, though the collective identifications remain contested. Similar processes of inscribing political ideologies and discourses of history on to an urban landscape—here more specifically also aiming at a 'Hinduisation'—can be detected in the case of *Qila Rai Pithora* as 'a structure which qualifies to be called a "monument" without really being monumental' (Pati, Chapter 12, page 329). Declared a heritage site, this altered cityscape documents the interplay of 'Hindu mytho-history, a modern sense of aesthetic and a neo-liberal form of tourism' (ibid., page 345). Such processes, though on a different scale, are also visible in the late Tamil politician Jayalalithaa's attempt to create an image of herself as Amma or mother and thus to memorialise herself not only through larger than life cut-outs, banners, etc., but in everyday life through mundane products such as water bottles, school bags or cement bags that all carry her image (see Reese, Chapter 11).

Entertainment, Enjoyment, Pleasure

Jayalalithaa's initial fame as heroine of the silver screen predating her political career points at another theme that is intrinsically tied to the visual defined broadly. Emerging from several chapters in the present volume is the whole complex variously labelled entertainment, enjoyment, amusement, pleasure and so on, depending on disciplinary traditions. While, commonly, this field has been linked to or even dominated by cinema—often under the heading of 'scopophilia' or the pleasure of looking at something—it is in no way limited to the silver screen and is equally a key factor in consuming and engaging with other forms of media such as novels and, more relevant here, visual practices such as caricatures (see Parciack and Shacham, Chapter 10), photography (e.g., snapshot photography or through the form of photo albums), *pata* paintings (see Chatterji, Chapter 4) and so on.

In India, as elsewhere, considerable time is actually spent on developing entertainment into significant fan cultures based around the most popular film stars such as M.G. Ramachandran (MGR)—often with a political angle to it—and while the experience of media consumption is ideally enjoyable for the user, s/he might spare fewer thoughts for the entertainment industry behind it, that is, for production, circulation and ultimately consumption (Vorderer, Klimmt and Ritterfeld 2004: 389). An increasing entertainment industry juggernaut driven by globalised capitalism not only expands the reach of media but also leads to cross-media fertilisation and franchises, for example, films being promoted as video games or vice versa, even though crossing from one media form to another (theatre, film, books, music records) and from specific regions to metro-cities and beyond India is hardly new (Hansen [2001] 2004: 77).

Media and communication studies have highlighted the complexity of pleasurable entertainment experiences, including (the intermingling of) the psychological, affective and cognitive dimensions. As Peter Vorderer, Christoph Klimmt and Ute Ritterfeld have convincingly argued (2004: 389) entertainment as a process differs depending on the consumers and their different motives, which vary from the desire to stimulate a mood through media exposure to competition and achievement when it comes to interactive gaming. Other major motives include curiosity, seeking distraction from boredom, or escape from a mundane life, etc. Literature on youth, education and the idea of 'killing time', 'waiting' or simply 'timepass', as it is often referred to in India (Jeffrey 2010a), seems to confirm the latter, showing that the link with entertainment should not be underestimated, particularly if one takes into account the relative spending power even of many youngsters in urban India. As one of Craig Jeffrey's (2010b) young interlocutors puts it: 'Time has no value in India. We are just passing the time: hoping something better is round the corner'. However, enjoyment may not just be superficial and meaningless as it is often considered to be, but may actually be better appreciated if it is combined with information à la 'info-tainment' (see also, Raney 2004) or a 'true story' (Chatterji, Chapter 4) or with earning religious merit while, for example, participating in processions, pilgrimages, *lilas* (plays), etc., which equally create excitement and enjoyment.

In any case, as Vorderer, Klimmt and Ritterfeld (2004) argue, recalling Bourdieu's analyses, entertainment and pleasure differ depending on the users' background (a lower class or caste background may lean towards 'escapism'), on when they are consumed, on media products with their specific technological and visual characteristics, and on whether the contents are both available and affordable. Accordingly, the responses—often rather contradictory sensations—range from suspense to relief, fun to frustration, and delight to depression, and involve positive or negative emotions such as euphoria, thrill, fear and sadness, extending even to catharsis and comprehension, as well as learning. Such effects on the audience or individual media consumer have been debated for centuries in India under the aesthetic concept of *rasa* as an emotional feeling or flavour that is central to many Indian art forms, especially the performing arts. *Rasas* inspired by artistic performances include heroism, laughter, love, horror, compassion, fury or disgust, and tranquillity, and are closely tied to emotions (*bhav*) such as disgust and high glee (Pinney 1997: 186–87). For example, *adbhuta rasa* or the sentiment of wonder, amazement and surprise was a crucial feature of the Parsi theatrical tradition (Hansen [2001] 2004: 100–01) and is equally relevant in cinematographic traditions that focus on emotions and spectacle, glamour and attractions. At times, reactions may even evoke awe among spectators or listeners, an emotion that monuments or museums may arouse (as well as any other of the aforementioned *rasas*), while the opposite process of ridiculing, making fun of somebody—often a higher ranking or more powerful person—and laughter are at the centre of caricaturing (see Parciack and Shacham, Chapter 10).

However, as Vorderer, Klimmt and Ritterfeld (2004: 395) stress, such responses presuppose a certain openness and interest on the part of the users, as well as a 'willingness to suspend disbelief', again primarily with reference to the silver screen experience or other multi-sensorial media like interactive gaming. Subsequently, an affinity with specific characters may evolve from a (dis-)liking for them to the opposite extreme of a full-blown star cult, which may grow into fans adopting a caring attitude towards them. However, media products in India, especially religious or mythological films like the 1975 *Jai Santoshi Maa* (Lutgendorf 2002), may be successful precisely because they appeal to beliefs, as the construction of temples in the aftermath of the film showed. Thus, Mary Beth Oliver and Anne Bartsch poignantly summarise the idea of enjoyment in more general terms:

> Feeling entertained […] is not only a matter of amusement or of simply feeling good in a general sense, but is also one of becoming involved with an important topic, of elaborating on existing thoughts and beliefs, of pleasure and of sadness, of fun and of melancholy, of emotional kicks and of deeper thinking. (Oliver and Bartsch 2010 in Vorderer 2011: 60)

While media and communication studies have mainly looked at enjoyment in terms of the conditions it requires and of how the prerequisites determine the possible outputs, film critics like Laura Mulvey (1975) have pursued psychoanalytical approaches by highlighting scopophilia in a Freudian sense and revealing gendered 'structures of fascination' (ibid.: 10). In India, as Asha Kasbekar ([2001] 2004: 286) argued, scopophilia may take precedence over epistemophilia as a desire to know. That is, content-wise, the most thrilling question may not be what is narrated but how it is presented visually. First, Mulvey considers scopophilia to be a sexual instinct or part of the libido or sexual desire that objectifies other persons, 'subjecting them to a controlling and curious gaze' (Mulvey 1975: 8) and deriving pleasure from the process. While Mulvey discusses cinema from a perspective that is both feminist and Freudian, in passing one may note that Freud also established a close connection between sexuality and food, that is, the satisfaction derived from the consumption of food. In this sense, signboards advertising meat shops (see Brara, Chapter 7) may equally evoke, revive or allude to pleasure of a different yet related sort.

However, coming back to the enjoyment of the big screen, Mulvey (1975: 11) stresses particularly that 'In their traditional exhibitionist role women are simultaneously looked at and displayed, with their appearance coded for strong visual and erotic impact so that they can be said to connote *to-be-looked-at-ness*. Woman displayed as sexual object is the leitmotif of erotic spectacle [...]'—even though in Parsi theatre, for example, many female roles were initially played by men, substituted, after initial resistance, by Anglo-Indian women who were considered less strictly confined to norms of decency (Hansen [2001] 2004: 93).

Second, Mulvey highlights a narcissistic side or ego dimension, that is, identifying oneself with the seen image. This aspect is expressed particularly in the spectacular star system, which offers idealised, yet also sexualised and glamorous, ego models, which may also offer female pleasures of identification with and fantasising around heroines or '*Devis*' (Goddesses) in the Indian context (see Kumar, Chapter 2).

In addition, Kasbekar ([2001] 2004: 289–90) has argued that cinema in India—and we might venture to add other sites of visual culture such as theatre as well—rests to a large extent on contradictions. Particularly, the double role of a woman—being on the one hand a commodity for a male audience, however socially stratified, but also a consumer-customer who might object to an overtly 'erotic spectacle' on the other hand—is a case in point. As Kasbekar (ibid.: 290) emphasises, many cinematographic and broader pictorial pleasures are disguised or hidden, entertainment being essentially controlled and occasionally censored by the state, for example, imposing bans on actual kissing scenes. Therefore, particularly sought-after and pleasurable elements in terms of erotic dance or 'item numbers' (Brara 2010) may be staged in di- or transgressive subplots and locations, presented as amoral and deviant or explained (away) as supreme sacrifices (being morally superior, though being involved in supposedly degrading practices), while the main plot is able to uphold the values of womanhood, marriage, honour and respect. Yet, while women function 'primarily to address the erotic gaze and constitutes an indispensable ingredient in look-soliciting strategies' (Kasbekar [2001] 2004: 286), more recently new globalised consumable heroes have increasingly been forced to flash the flesh in the form of six-packs (Deshpande 2005) that visually express changing gender equations in an ever-changing visual culture.

The chapters in this volume, already referred to while we have been mapping out the broader field of visual culture in India, are grouped in the following five approximate themes that focus on different aspects of visual culture in India: camera works, folk/artistry, market signs, pictorial politics and monumental landscapes.

Camera Works

Malavika Karlekar's chapter 'The Photograph in Social Science Research: A Few Ethical and Practical Questions' looks at the photographic visual as an aid to research, arguing that no viewing is ever 'innocent'. Briefly tracing the various ways in which the photograph can and has been used in social science research, Karlekar concludes that such images are vital to certain kinds of analysis.

The medium of films in its use of images indicates strong similarities to the ways these can function in dreams, imagination, myth and fantasy—in psyche—as understood by Carl Gustav Jung. Images in cinema, as in Jungian psychoanalytical perspectives, are not intended to be factual representations but are figurative and imaginative expressions carrying emotional 'charge' that can directly involve audiences as participatory 'subjects' engaged in creating their image-based 'realities'—'soul-making'. Here, Anu Kumar in her chapter 'Unlikely "Devis": Gender and Imagination On and Off the Silver Screen' offers perspectives on women in early Indian cinema that suggest ways in which they were able to successfully use the medium of films by imagining and imaging 'feminine selves' that verged on myth, symbol and archetype. Pioneering the way for their present-day successors in confronting gender norms, these early actresses, who were given Hindu names with the suffix of '*Devi*' in a bid to facilitate their social acceptance by producers, ended by opening undreamed areas of feminine imagination where women could claim themselves in society as nothing less than goddesses indeed.

Despite a wider visual turn in Indian studies, the links between photography, death and the corpse remain an under-researched field (e.g., in terms of regional patterns), whereas their medial closeness is highlighted in Western photographic theory. The chapter 'Visualising Death and the Corpse: Perspectives on Post-mortem Photographs in Central-Eastern India' by Uwe Skoda and Birgit Lettmann focuses on the (im)possible photographical representations and the (in)visibility of the body after death by taking into account 'private' photographs from India, embedding them in a broader context of indices and discussing ideas about death and the concept of the person.

Folk/Artistry

In chapter '9/11 and the Folk Artists of Bengal', Roma Chatterji discusses the 9/11 attacks as an event that carries the potential not only for story-making but for mythicisation as well. It describes the way in which the 9/11 story has been incorporated into the repertoire of narratives of a community of picture storytellers in Bengal and is actively re-interpreted in terms of their mythic universe, thus showing that the relationship between the global and the local is not one of passive reception. Beyond that, the chapter highlights recent attempts at inter-medium exchange in storytelling by contrasting the narrative scroll paintings with the graphic novel form, hence locating the former within a wider field of popular visual art forms.

Cécile Guillaume-Pey addresses ritual wall paintings made by the Sora, a tribal group from Central-Eastern India, and sketches their transformative journey in her chapter 'From Ritual Images to Animated Movies: The Transformative Journey of the Sora Paintings (Central-Eastern India)'. In Sora villages, these images, in front of which sacrifices are performed, are considered to be houses made for deities. Their designs form part of a complex ritual system which requires close collaboration between a ritual painter and other religious specialists, who, through their songs, invite local deities to inhabit the picture. Visual, aural and physical expressions are interwoven in a unique manner to create 'living' and powerful divine images. However, these 'altar paintings' may be disconnected from the converging agencies that are set in motion by the ritual. Nowadays, Sora paintings are exhibited in museums, sold in local markets or exported abroad, even inspiring the production of animated films. The transformation of these paintings into 'folk art' or 'art' is bringing about major changes in their production, audience and meaning.

Some of the works by the Bengali poet Anjan Sen and illustrations of his poems by several major artists are presented in Asunción López-Varela Azcárate's chapter 'Anjan Sen's Visual Poetry and the Bengal *Uttar-Adhunik* School'. Sen, together with Amitabha Gupta, is perhaps the greatest contributor to the formulation of sharp critique of Euro-American modernity and the Enlightenment as Western cultural domination. The chapter studies Sen's creations in the context of traditional Indic culture, where historical, mythical and folk accounts are viewed as dialogical and fluid intersubjective and intercultural happenings. Furthermore, the chapter seeks to support the idea that cultural and aesthetic influences move in several directions at the same time, not just from West to East but also from East to West.

Market Signs

The 'visual turn' in the social sciences invites attention to recurring public signs of sacredness in contemporary India. Signs of everyday difference in the constitution of the sacred within different faiths are often communicated visually (and linguistically) in the social and public contexts of meat shops. In her chapter 'The Visual Culture of Meat-Shop Signs in Delhi', Rita Brara shows that meat-shop hoardings afford visual and vernacular condensations of class and religious difference.

Matrimonial websites are the topic of Fritzi Titzmann's chapter, 'The Imagery of Indian Matchmaking: Representations of Community, Class and Gender in a Transnational Online Matrimonial Market'. While arranging marriages has a long tradition in South Asia, recent decades have seen the emergence of a growing, highly complex and transnational multimedia Indian matchmaking industry. The market's differentiation and fragmentation continues steadily. To some extent, the parameters are specific to the Indian context, and websites specialising in targeting certain

Indian regions, languages, religions or sociocultural classes make up the majority today. The gradual commercialisation of online networks in the form of dating and matrimonial websites includes the ever-increasing visual perfection of these sites and their commercial promotion and advertisement. However, the use of images is never impartial or without its ideological implications. Analysis of the promotional strategies of different service providers—particularly matrimonial websites and advertisements directly linked to these sites—reveals how format and design convey the concept of an 'Indianness' that consists of a combination of modernity and tradition as well as of globality and regionalism. While promoting images of cosmopolitanism, the visual performance of 'Indianness' is at the same time tied to an increasing emphasis on traditionality and religiosity. One aspect of this is the medial propagation of an ideal Indian femininity as defined by the image of the 'New Indian Woman'.

Pictorial Politics

Histories of dislocation and violence have shaped the politics of Punjab across time and location. In her chapter 'A Museum, a Memorial, and a Martyr', Radhika Chopra analyses the narrowing of what constitutes memories and remembrance of 1984. The prominence given to remembering the 'life and death' of Bhindranwale has literally reshaped spaces within the Darbar Sahib and in the Kendriya Sikh Ajaibghar, the museum in the sacred complex. The insistent emphasis on remembering Bhindranwale has overshadowed the destruction of the *Akal Takht*[2] as a key in narratives of Operation Blue Star. Key ideas of remembering and forgetting are apparent in the visual politics that shape the architecture, museum displays and souvenir posters in the bazaars around Sikhism's most sacred shrine.

Ronie Parciack and Ilanit Loewy Shacham's chapter, 'Divine Order, Social Disorder: Debating the Visual Representations of Lalu Prasad Yadav', addresses the ways in which Indian visual media have created a theological model to rationalise and condone political corruption in sovereign India. This model is examined through the example of the Bihari Rashtriya Janata Dal (RJD) leader Lalu Prasad Yadav and how he was represented in cartoons published between the mid-1990s and the early 2000s. Yadav, formerly Bihar's chief minister, a member of the Lok Sabha and the Minister of Railways in the United Progressive

Alliance (UPA) government, is known to be a highly controversial leader, identified with corruption scams and with a style known as *goonda* (bully) politics. Until late 2013, when a special Central Bureau of Investigation (CBI) court convicted him, Yadav became a living example of political resilience against all the odds. While his resilience was mainly explained in terms of caste politics, Parciack and Shacham offer a perspective deeply rooted in Hindu theology, as expressed through the vernacular plane of visual culture. At the root of Yadav's legitimisation is an association with the Hindu God Kṛṣṇa, particularly as depicted in *purāṇic* traditions. This identification serves to rationalise a theological model that places antinomic conduct within an authoritative and non-democratic framework.

Politics and religion in the Indian state of Tamil Nadu have a complex historical relationship, given the dominance of parties founded on atheistic, anti-Brahman and Dravidian ideologies. Jill Reese's chapter 'Amma Provides for All: Popular Devotional Aesthetics, Material Politics and the *amman* in Tamil Nadu' examines the seeming dichotomy of devotional idioms at work in the political imagery and schemes of late Jayalalithaa Jayaram, leader of the All India Anna Dravida Munnetra Kazhagam (AIADMK) and several times chief minister. Although she is a devout Hindu Brahman and not of Tamil origin, the former Tamil actress asserted herself as heir to the party leadership after the death of its founder (and her former co-star), MGR. Her claim to power was initially articulated in campaign materials perpetuating her image as MGR's divine consort, but her imagery was transformed once her power had been legitimised, Jayalalithaa then being christened 'Amma', a revered *amman* who is either a 'mother goddess' whose children are her devotees or a chaste and childless woman. Reese suggests that Jayalalithaa's introduction of what the author terms 'nutrition schemes'—the results of an enormous expansion of campaign promises to give away 'freebies', as they are glossed by critics, in exchange for votes—is an effort to address the lack of resonance of her 'Amma' persona within the Tamil electorate. Reese's chapter aims to go beyond the aesthetics of transformation in physical form to propose a corporeally based image regime that binds patrons to Jayalalithaa as 'Amma' through the consumption of items dispersed through her nutrition schemes, which are adorned with her image. These government schemes include the distribution of electronic kitchen equipment, new laptops for students, subsidised rice, a statewide chain of government restaurants and other schemes to provide sustenance for the body, mind and soul.

Monumental Landscapes

Sushmita Pati's chapter 'Building "Monuments" in a World Class City: Aesthetics and Politics of Contemporary Delhi' attempts to look at two contemporary forms of 'monuments' in the city of Delhi and tries to locate them in contemporary politics. These two 'monuments', the *Qila Rai Pithora* (the memorial site of Prithviraj Chauhan, built by the state) and the 108-foot Sankatmochan Dham (a temple built on illegal land with a 108-foot-high Hanuman statue and a fake Vaishno Devi Shrine built by a lower-caste community), both erected in the last decade, though seemingly unconnected, point towards a larger conflict over space and its meanings and effects. Together, they throw up a host of questions regarding religiosity, sacrality, urban legends, histories, contemporary forms of urban governance and lower-caste mobilisation in the context of a city which is going 'global' and lead us beyond their apolitical appearances. These two structures symbolise how an ocular field that is being created through the vast, manicured lawns of *Qila Rai Pithora* is simultaneously being disrupted by the kitschy, brightly painted Hanuman. The Prithviraj Chauhan Memorial indicates how the state has come a long way from creating a secular, national culture for the city (built over a Muslim graveyard), while the Hanuman temple takes us to a different narrative of attempts to erect a permanent temple on illegal land.

Upasona Khound's chapter 'Mayawati's Politics of *Sthals*: Spectacle of the Symbolic Landscape' explores the politics of iconography pursued by the erstwhile Dalit chief minister of Uttar Pradesh, Mayawati, who has taken up the task of iconising and memorialising Dalit heroes, leaders and social reformers in the form of statues and memorials. The chapter tries to show how the early phase of Mayawati's 'politics of statues' has expanded, consolidated and regimented itself as the 'politics of *sthal*s' during her recent tenure as chief minister. Given that the *sthal*s occupy large areas in terms of physical space, the broader issue of the reclamation of public space for subalterns is discussed, asking if such iconographic politics through the construction of majestic *sthal*s has been able to (re)-configure the power relations of Dalits symbolically.

Notes

1. *Tirthas* (crossing place), *dhams* (sacred abode of a God, pilgrimage site) or *pithas* (seats of goddesses).

2. *Akal Takht* literally means 'throne of the timeless one', one of the five seats of power of the Sikh community inside the Golden Temple in Amritsar.

References

Appadurai, Arjun, and Carol A. Breckenridge. 1995. 'Public Modernity in India'. In *Consuming Modernity: Public Culture in a South Asian World*, edited by Carol A. Breckenridge, pp. 1–22. Minneapolis: University of Minnesota Press.

Assmann, Aleida. 2006. 'Memory, Individual and Collective'. In *The Oxford Handbook of Contextual Political Analysis*, edited by Robert E. Goodin and Charles Tilly, pp. 210–24. Oxford: Oxford University Press.

Assmann, Jan, trans. (1997) 2005. *Das kulturelle Gedächtnis: Schrift, Erinnerung und politische Identität in frühen Hochkulturen* [*Cultural Memory and Early Civilization. Writing, Remembrance, and Political Imagination*]. München: Beck.

Babb, Lawrence A. 1981. 'Glancing: Visual Interaction in Hinduism'. *Journal of Anthropological Research* 37 (4): 387–401.

Bachmann-Medick, Doris, trans. 2006. *Cultural Turns: Neuorientierungen in den Kulturwissenschaften* [*Cultural Turns: New Orientations in the Study of Culture*]. Reinbek bei Hamburg: Rowohlt.

———. 2008. 'Gegen Worte: Was heißt "Iconic/Visual Turn"?' *Gegenworte* 20 (Autumn): 10–15.

Banks, Marcus, and Howard Morphy. 1997. 'Introduction: Rethinking Visual Anthropology'. In *Rethinking Visual Anthropology*, edited by Marcus Banks and Howard Morphy, pp. 1–35. New Haven and London: Yale University Press.

Barthes, Roland. (1980) 1984. *Camera Lucida: Reflections on Photography*. London: Fontana Paperbacks.

Bateson, Gregory, and Margaret Mead. (1942) 2012. 'Balinese Character: A Photographic Analysis'. In *Ethnographic Fieldwork: An Anthropological Reader*, edited by Antonius C.G.M. Robben and Jeffrey A. Sluka, pp. 450–64. Oxford: Wiley-Blackwell.

Boehm, Gottfried. 1994. *Was ist ein Bild?* [*What Is an Image?*, translated by authors] München: Wilhelm Fink Verlag.

Brara, Rita. 2010. 'The Item Number: Cinesexuality in Bollywood and Social Life'. *Economic and Political Weekly* 45 (23): 67–75.

Brosius, Christiane. 2005. *Empowering Visions: The Politics of Representation in Hindu Nationalism.* London: Anthem Press.

Castelli, Enrico, and Giovanni Aprile. 2005. *Divine Lithography*. New Delhi: Il Tamburo Parlante.

Clifford, James. 1996. 'Ausgestellte Kulturen: Artefakte, Gegenstände, Fetische im "System der Objekte"' [Exhibited Cultures: Artefacts, Objects, Fetishes in "System of Objects", translated by authors]. *Lettre International* 33: 28–31.

Clifford, James, and George E. Marcus. 1986. *Writing Culture: The Poetics and Politics of Ethnography*. Berkeley and Los Angeles: University of California Press.

Cort, John E. 2012. 'Situating *Darśan*: Seeing the Digambar Jina Icon in Eighteenth- and Nineteenth-Century North India'. *International Journal of Hindu Studies* 16 (1): 1–56.

Davis, Richard H. 1999. *Lives of Indian Images*. Princeton: Princeton University Press.

Deshpande, Sudhanva. 2005. 'The Consumable Hero of Globalized India'. In *Bollywood: Popular Indian Cinema Through a Transnational Lens*, edited by Raminder Kaur and Ajay J. Sinha, pp. 186–203. New Delhi: SAGE Publications.

Eck, Diana L. 1981. *Darśan: Seeing the Divine Image in India*. New York, NY: Columbia University Press.

Hansen, Kathryn. (2001) 2004. 'The Indar Sabha Phenomenon: Public Theatre and Consumption in Greater India (1853–1956)'. In *Pleasure and the Nation: The History, Politics and Consumption of Public Culture in India*, edited by Rachel Dwyer and Christopher Pinney, pp. 76–114. Delhi: Oxford University Press.

Jacob, Preminda. 2009. *Celluloid Deities: The Visual Culture of Cinema and Politics in South India*. Hyderabad: Orient BlackSwan.

Jain, Jyotindra. 2007. *India's Popular Culture: Iconic Spaces and Fluid Images*. Mumbai: Marg Publications.

Jain, Kajri. 2007. *Gods in the Bazaar: The Economies of Indian Calendar Art*. Durham: Duke University Press.

Jeffrey, Craig. 2010a. *Timepass: Youth, Class, and the Politics of Waiting in India*. Stanford: Stanford University Press.

———. 2010b. 'The Politics of Waiting'. *The Guardian*, 29 May. Accessed on 6 October 2015 at http://www.theguardian.com/commentisfree/2010/may/29/politics-waiting-social-action

Kasbekar, Asha. (2001) 2004. 'Hidden Pleasures: Negotiating the Myth of the Female Ideal in Popular Hindi Cinema'. In *Pleasure and the Nation: The History, Politics and Consumption of Public Culture in India*, edited by Rachel Dwyer and Christopher Pinney, pp. 286–308. New Delhi: Oxford University Press.

Kaur, Ramindder, and Parul Dave-Mukherji. 2014. *Arts and Aesthetics in a Globalizing World*. London and New Delhi: Bloomsbury.

Kuhn, Annette, and Kirsten Emiko McAllister, eds. 2006. *Locating Memory: Photographic Acts*. New York, NY: Berghahn.

Kuhn, Thomas. 1962. *The Structure of Scientific Revolutions*. Chicago: The University of Chicago Press.

Laister, Judith. 2008. 'Andere Bilder: im Dienste ethnographischer Repräsentationskritik' ['Other Images: In Service of Ethnographic Critique of Representation', translated by authors]. In *Kunst und Ethnographie: zum Verhaeltnis von visueller Kultur und ethnographischem Arbeiten*, edited by Beate Binder, Dagmar Neuland-Kitzerow and Karoline Noack, pp. 20–30. Münster: LIT.

Lutgendorf, Philip A. 2002. 'A Superhit Goddess/A Made-to-Satisfaction Goddess: *Jai Santoshi Maa* Revisited'. *Manushi—A Journal about Women and Society* 131: 10–16, 24–37.

MacDougall, David. 1997. 'The Visual in Anthropology'. In *Rethinking Visual Anthropology*, edited by Marcus Banks and Howard Morphy, pp. 276–95. New Haven and London: Yale University Press.

Mallapragada, Madhavi. 2010. 'Desktop Deities: Hindu Temples, Online Cultures and the Politics of Remediation'. *South Asian Popular Culture* 8 (2): 109–21.

Mallebrein, Cornelia, and Heinrich von Stietencron. 2008. *The Divine Play on Earth: Religious Aesthetics and Ritual in Orissa*. Heidelberg: Synchron Publishers.

Mitchell, William J.T. (1992) 1994. *Picture Theory*. Chicago: The University of Chicago Press.

———. 1995. 'Interdisciplinarity and Visual Culture'. *Art Bulletin* 77 (4): 540–44.

Mitchell, William J.T. 2002. 'Showing Seeing: A Critique of Visual Culture'. *Journal of Visual Culture* 1 (2): 165–81.

Mulvey, Laura. 1975. 'Visual Pleasure and Narrative Cinema'. *Screen* 16 (3): 6–18.

Oliver, M. B., and Bartsch, A. 2010. 'Appreciation as Audience Response: Exploring Entertainment Gratifications beyond Hedonism'. *Human Communication Research* 36 (1): 53–81.

Parker, Holt N. 2011. 'Toward a Definition of Popular Culture'. *History and Theory* 50 (2): 147–70.

Pink, Sarah. 2008. 'Analysing Visual Experience'. In *Research Methods for Cultural Studies*, edited by Michael Pickering, pp. 125–49. Edinburgh: Edinburgh University Press.

Pinney, Christopher. 1997. *Camera Indica: The Social Life of Indian Photographs*. London: Reaction Books.

———. 2004. *'Photos of the Gods': The Printed Image and Political Struggle in India*. London: Reaction Books.

Raney, Arthur A. 2004. 'Expanding Disposition Theory: Reconsidering Character Liking, Moral Evaluations, and Enjoyment'. *Communication Theory* 14 (4): 348–69.

Rorty, Richard. 1967. *The Linguistic Turn: Essays in Philosophical Method*. Chicago: The University of Chicago Press.

Ruby, Jay. 2000. *Picturing Culture: Explorations of Film and Anthropology*. Chicago: The University of Chicago Press.

Sinha, Gayatri. 2009. *Art and Visual Culture in India 1857–2007*. Mumbai: Marg Publications.

Storey, John. 2001. *Cultural Theory and Popular Culture*. London: Pearson.

Tagg, John. (1988) 2005. *The Burden of Representation: Essays on Photographies and Histories*. Minneapolis: University of Minnesota Press.

Uberoi, Patricia. 2009. *Freedom and Destiny: Gender, Family, and Popular Culture in India*. New Delhi: Oxford University Press.

Vorderer, Peter. 2011. 'What's Next? Remarks on the Current Vitalization of Entertainment Theory'. *Journal of Media Psychology* 23 (1): 60–63.

Vorderer, Peter, Christoph Klimmt, and Ute Ritterfeld. 2004. 'Enjoyment: At the Heart of Media Entertainment'. *Communication Theory* 14 (4): 388–408.

Part I

Camera Works

1

The Photograph in Social Science Research: A Few Ethical and Practical Questions

Malavika Karlekar

Introduction

A few years before she died in 1978, Margaret Mead regretted that fieldworkers continued to rely on 'the hopelessly inadequate note-taking of an earlier generation of an earlier age [...] with no equipment beyond a pencil and a notebook'. For Mead, arguments that photography required a certain artistic skill and that the process of filming was expensive were specious, and she added quite unequivocally, 'I think that we must squarely face the fact that we, as a discipline have only ourselves to blame for our gross and dreadful negligence' (Mead [1975] 1995). Imagine, she wrote that film could have 'caught and preserved for centuries (preserved for the joy of the descendants of those who dance a ritual for the last time and for the illumination of future generations of human scientists)' before it all 'disappears—disappears in front of everybody's eyes. Why? What has gone wrong?' she asked accusingly. Margaret Mead was uniquely positioned to chastise her peers and their students: 40 years earlier, in the late 1930s, together with her British anthropologist husband Geoffrey Bateson and other members of the team, a massive study based in and around Bali resulted in thousands of feet of film and 38,000 photographs. Of these, 759 were selected for *Balinese Character*, a joint study with Bateson (Bateson and Mead 1942). Clearly, the publication introduced a unique dimension, that of the visual into the recording and presentation of ethnological data.

Writing in the twenty-first century, Christopher Pinney, the University College, London (UCL)-based social anthropologist well-known for his prodigious and unique work with the colonial photograph, pointed out that Mead and Bateson had taken photographs without asking for permission from their subjects, often using 'an angular viewfinder to record their subjects unaware' (Pinney 2011: 112). While there may be legitimate issues with post-facto debunkings of theories and ideological stances by succeeding generations of authors, researchers and others, Pinney's position helps in arguments that are to follow.

The chapter comprises three sections: the first section looks at the issue of the ethics of the anthropological photograph—Pinney's area of concern too. The second section discusses the photograph as record, as a tool in research and as the creator of an independent narrative. And as an example of the earlier section, the final section looks at some photographs on the history of women's work in India, mainly for a wage, but also unpaid, as in the case of farm labour and political activism. It discusses how the visual adds body—if not soul—to an understanding of the lives of half of India's workforce.

The Ethics of the Anthropological Photograph

In *Photography and Anthropology*, Christopher Pinney's (2011) description of the early anthropological photograph is noteworthy. He encourages us to view the camera as 'an intimate prosthesis of a local cultural practice' and not as an invasive instrument of oppression. The first men in the field (Mead was the first woman to go to the field) were primarily concerned with the physiognomy of those deemed to be savages, there being a not-so-subtle congruence between their interest and that of colonising powers. A fundamental belief in difference influenced the ideology of both, the Lamprey's grid being a suitable invention to bear out the physical difference between races. Subjects were made to stand before a large frame from which hung silk threads formed into two-inch squares and then photographed, often in profile. Comparisons were made between these images and that of strapping six-foot models from the land of the rulers.

However, writes Pinney, a self-conscious shift was around the corner: when anthropology came to be known as E.B. Tylor's science in the late nineteenth century, he was enthusiastically applauding the camera's role, writing that photographs were not 'mere book decorations' but rather 'object lessons' (Pinney 2011: 14). Tylor was among the earliest anthropologists to move from an obsession with the physical body to the wider notion of different cultures, an approach that was soon to be honed through Bronislaw Malinowski's development of fieldwork techniques. Earlier, Sir Everard im Thurn had imperiously declared that he had little time for the mugshot genre so popular then—humans were not to be photographed in a manner not dissimilar to 'badly stuffed birds and animals' (quoted in Pinney 2011: 36), but rather they were to be represented as active, working bodies. His photographs have a certain dynamism, unlike the huge corpus of material developed in the closing years of the century by the hard-working administrator-cum-amateur anthropologist in the Andamans, M.V. Portman. Portman's photographs (incidentally, many of the albums are available in the Anthropological Survey of India's office in Kolkata) reflected what Pinney calls 'an austere colonial sensibility' (Pinney 2011: 41), reflected in an 'objective' representation of the subject people.

Three decades later, Malinowski—regarded as the founder of modern British anthropology—sought to fracture the subject/viewer divide by asking the reader to 'imagine' being on distant islands amidst Trobrianders. He used the camera extensively, often inserting himself into images; as the 'self-mythologizing perfector of "participant-observation"' (Pinney 2011: 52) that has influenced generations of fieldwork-based researchers, he had to be seen to be 'there'. Yet, even his best attempts could not do away with the divide implicit in the colonial enterprise.

In the deftly composed photograph (Figure 1.1), the white male ethnographer stands with his hands on his hips—a favourite posture with countless colonial administrators—his head just that bit tilted downwards as he looks imperiously at the 'man in a wig', a sorcerer of repute. The colour of an overclad Malinowski's skin, his clothes and even his boots are in direct contrast to the natives, their 'undress' and the bored look of some. The photograph has the quality of a theatrical scene, and that clearly was the intention: the outsider engages with the insiders and tries hard to be no longer the superior observer and recorder alone.

That being photographed was not always readily accepted by the subject/'native' is discussed at some length by Pinney, pointing out that recording discomfiture became almost a genre in the photography of

Figure 1.1

Bronislaw Malinowski and Billy Hancock, Ethnographer with a Man in a Wig

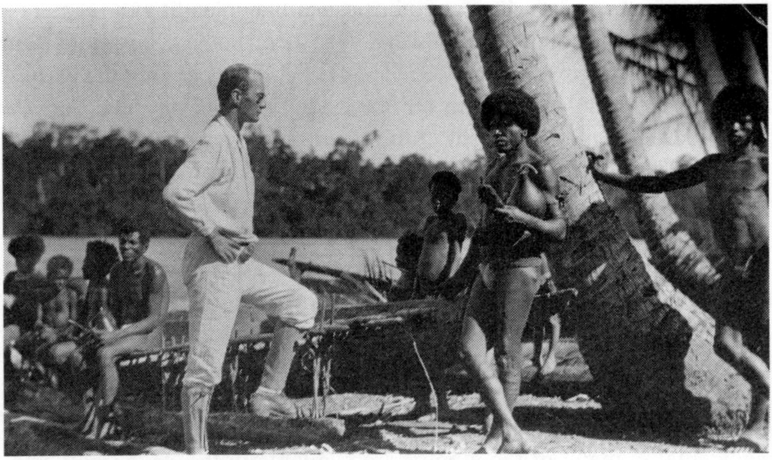

Source: From Bronislaw Malinowski, *The Sexual Life of Savages in North-Western Melanesia* (courtesy of London School of Economics and Political Science; MALINOWSKI/3/SOS/68).

the times. Coercive techniques were not unknown and contemporary anthropological practice self-consciously seeks to distance itself from this lack of sensitivity of its forebears: in a particularly telling image, Australian anthropologist Nicolas Peterson overlays an early twentieth-century image of photographers avidly zeroing in on a secret aboriginal men's ceremony with a black rectangle (Figure 1.2). Thus, we see a group of hungry, paparazzi-like photographers—but are no longer privy to the focus of their interest. The new imaging reflects an acceptance of what Peterson calls a 'changing photographic contract' (quoted in Pinney 2011: 130) where deference to aboriginal sensibilities replaces an earlier autocratic regimen.

Such paradigm shifts in the role of the photograph in anthropology lead us logically to the core of Christopher Pinney's book. Mindful of Paul Rabinow's angst at being the 'rich' American anthropologist living in a 'poor' village hut in Morocco, Pinney carries over this feeling to the domain of the visual. In part, this is overcome by what he calls 'indigenous media'—communities photographing or filming themselves. Interestingly, some years ago, the Ahmedabad Self Employed Women's Association (SEWA) trained a group of documentary film-makers from among its workers; the aim was to see and document their labour and with their own

Figure 1.2

Censored photograph of men's ceremony

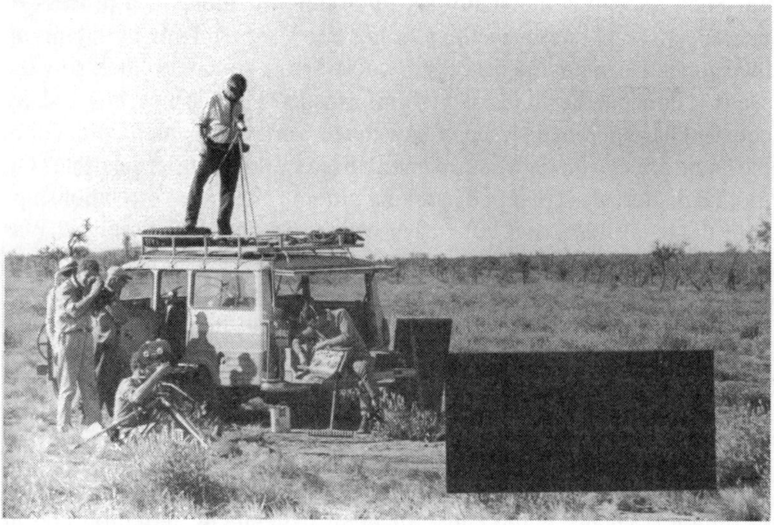

Source: N. Peterson. 2003. 'The Changing Photographic Contract: Aborigines and Image Ethics'. In *Photography's Other Histories* (eds) C. Pinney and N. Peterson. Durham: Duke University Press. pp. 119–45. (See page 134.)

eyes. In such cases too, it became important to distinguish the viewpoint of the trainer from that of the trainee, so to speak.

Rabinow's concern is, of course, shared by many Indian fieldworkers who are often at odds to come to terms with the dilemma of studying subcultures within one's own culture. There is a strong congruence between the ethics of the photograph and the ethics of fieldwork. At the risk of being accused of digressing, I shall nevertheless briefly recount the extreme anxiety and self-doubt that overcame me after I had finished my fieldwork amongst women of the *Balmiki* (sweeper) caste way back in 1975. When, at the end of the fieldwork, I told my respondents that they had been of considerable help to me, they were not impressed with my candour; they only wanted to know what my fieldwork was going to do for them. 'Bibiji, you will write your book—or whatever else it is that you do—but how will it change our lives', they rightly asked. If I would have had a camera with me, and even if they had been willing to be photographed, I am sure they would have asked me the same question; the kids may even have demanded to be paid!

My dilemma was of course not something unique: many a fieldworker is faced with similar situations where questions of one's role keep cropping up. Such questions inevitably set up a chain of thought, a process of introspection: Is one in fact exploiting one's respondents by taking up their time? Does not the process of questioning, sooner or later, sow the seeds of doubt in the minds of one's informants? For instance, how did my constant harping on the issue of how much work men actually did within the home affect women who had internalised exploitation as their fate? Or, for that matter, was I justified in asking probing questions on relationships with the natal home and how often women visited their families? Was I right in asking those at the subsistence level what consumer goods they owned? I knew many years ago that I enjoyed fieldwork; what I did not know—or did not know well enough—was that fieldwork involves a dialogical process, a renegotiation of categories. As I found, it was not easy to adjust to different and, at times, conflicting realities.

If this is a problem with fieldwork, it is compounded when the camera enters the arena—even if it is a phone camera that might be less unobtrusive. Often, the appearance of photographic paraphernalia in remote villages is the cause of great excitement, agitation and at times unease. Generations of colonial photographers and post-colonial fieldworkers may have chosen to overlook the Roland Barthesian notion of the disturbance caused by the photograph, but today it is no longer possible to do so. Responsible fieldworkers need to acknowledge that their work with pen, laptop recorder and camera is often invasive.

The Photograph as Record

In India, soon after the invention of photography in 1839, the camera became a vital part of the colonial state's structures of surveillance and control; photography was identified with veracity and truthful representation. This was clearly vital in a climate of growing distrust particularly after 1857, where the rulers felt that they had to embolden themselves with 'objective' evidence and information about a people so different in race, temperament and inclinations. The imperial gaze that stressed Otherness and the principle of difference rather than of similarity was now emphasised somewhat stridently.

It was perhaps no coincidence then that after the traumatic years of 1857–1858, in 1861, the first Viceroy of India, Lord Canning, issued an official circular with instructions to provincial administrations to collect 'photographic likenesses of characteristic specimens of the more remarkable tribes of India' in large enough format so as to 'exhibit the chief physical peculiarities and distinctive costume of each race'. At the outset, the aim of the project was to have an impressive display for the 1862 London International Exhibition. Wherever possible, descriptive notes were to accompany the visuals. It was a project in which both the Cannings had a deep interest—for though he was perhaps not a photographer like his wife, Charlotte, Charles Canning's partiality to the new medium was palpable. Between 1863 and 1865, the stamp of official sanction led to over 100,000 prints being produced, illustrating 'the various divisions of the Asian family'. The eight volumes consisting of 468 photographs taken by 17 photographers 'of whom seven were army officers and another two each were doctors and clergymen' were put out between 1868 and 1872 (Watson and Kaye 1868–1872).

The introduction noted modestly that though the work did not make any 'claim to scientific research or philosophical investigations', it was hoped that from 'the ethnographic point of view, it will not be without interest and virtue'. Soon the volume of photographs far exceeded what could be displayed at the exhibition, and the extensive *The People of India* photographic project was inaugurated. And there was more than enough for the bereft Lord Canning to take home as memorabilia of his days in India (Charlotte, photographer and artist, died in Calcutta in late 1861). The details in the photographs and the descriptive notes by 19 contributors (10 army officers and 1 clergyman as well as a Mr Krishnaswamy—the only Indian acknowledged in the project) are noteworthy additions to the classificatory discourse of the times. Shortly after its publication, the Political and Secret Department of the Government of India acquired four of the eight-volume set. Racial types were identified through an arduous process in which numerous 'volunteers' were subjected to the unpleasant experience of every aspect of their physiognomy being measured, tabulated and analysed over long hours, often in a tiring if not humiliating fashion. The mugshot was increasingly used to identify criminals, pensioners and prostitutes. As Pinney noted earlier (1997) in *Camera Indica*:

> The state mobilized photography in its attempt to have knowledge over, and control of, diverse and mobile urban workforces, and the power relations constructed through this process came to invest photography with an authority that could not be reduced to its technical and semiotic properties. (Pinney 1997: 23)

Not unexpectedly, the early history of emergent areas of research and study, such as anthropology, archaeology and epigraphy, ran almost parallel to that of photography (Pelizzari 2003: 14; see also Singh 2004). The exoticisation of the Orient through the representation of widely differing ethnic types, often shot in contrived poses and situations, was a part of the incarcerating imperial gaze (Boast, Guha, and Herle 2001), amply aided by the new discipline of anthropology. Physical and cultural anthropology in particular were invaluable in the British rulers' attempts at bringing some order to their understanding of the land and its people (Pinney 1997). As David MacDougall argues, for a general public imbued with ideas of social Darwinism, the visual appearance of exotic peoples was the most obvious way of placing them on a scale between civilised man and animal. Pictures became a substitute for more abstract or esoteric knowledge (MacDougall 1997: 279).

This was the age of positivism and scientific enquiry when it was assumed that the photograph was a source of highly reliable data. However, that the imperial camera was never an innocent recorder—the colonial gaze determined pose, expression and juxtaposition of bodies in a manner that fitted into the wider beliefs of differences and inequalities. Though Sophie Gordon (2004), a British historian who has worked extensively with British colonial photographs, has suggested that in their use of photographs taken in the colonial period, later-day Indian nationalistic historians often change their meanings. I would argue that substituting 'Burmese beauty' or 'African' (a Dravidian so-named!) with a serious ethnographic comment does not negate the notion of the *initial* gaze. At the same time, viewed well over a century and a half later by a researcher engaged in a historical study of, say, the work of *Chamars* (leather workers) in the United Provinces, a relevant visual may well provide data on tools used all those many years ago. Pushing the argument a bit further, photographs that provide a romanticised view of Native Americans such as those of Edward Curtis—ethnologist and photographer of the American West and of Native American peoples—need not be rejected out of hand as being racist and ethnocentric: they can provide important visual information to those present-day Native Indians wishing to reconstruct their cultural identity. The viewer's gaze therefore is determined by her or his context—but this does not do away with the importance of the gaze of the photographer all those many years ago and the fact that he had made a choice on what to represent and what to leave out in his image. The present-day viewer has to factor this into her viewing. She needs to remember that a photograph does not exist in isolation but is a product of a historical worldview that had distinct ideological underpinnings.

The Photograph as a Tool in Research

In theory, the primary function of photographs in the field is that they should serve as aide-memoire, similar to written field notes, to help reconstitute events in the mind of the ethnographer. Here again, I would add, the principles of inclusion and exclusion come into play: What does the fieldworker choose to record? When discussing agricultural labour, who is recorded—the man at the plough or the women bent over in flooded leech-infested paddy fields? A further selection takes place when some images become illustrations for publications, slides for lectures or, even occasionally, the basis for an exhibition. The ultimate fate so far of field notes and photographs has not been a happy one. In rare cases, these are deposited in college and university archives and the occasional conscientious researcher maintains them in personal archives; most are likely to be buried, if not forgotten, amidst the detritus of academic production.

By the last years of the twentieth century, and indeed the present, the role of the photograph in social science research has become increasingly important—though as yet there would only be a modest shelf-full of titles in most libraries on the subject. A photographic technique that has been in vogue for a while is that of photo-interviewing. While studying the culture of the Trobriand Islands, Franz Boas, for instance, would show photographs to key informants in order to initiate a discussion around specific rituals. Clearly, Boas was an early anthropologist who used the camera imaginatively in the field, finding it useful to start off interviews. Generations of later researchers devised ways of making the photograph a part of the process of interaction. As Rosalind Huworth (2003) points out, photo-interviews have been used to analyse the effectiveness or otherwise of shelter housing in an American neighbourhood (Suchar and Rotenberg 1984), and in group discussions, photographs encourage 'picture stories' where many voices are melded to provide a composite analysis. Similarly, Judith Modell and Charlee Brodsky (1994) provided archival photographs to evoke memories about a steel town. Interestingly, these researchers asked informants for accounts first, and only then to respond to the photos and lastly to discuss their own photographs of life in the area. Of course, this was possible in a context where informants had photographs of themselves. In their absence, it becomes important for the researcher to share her photographs with informants and elicit their responses—either archival or contemporary ones.

What does this mean for social science research? Without venturing into the contentious debate on the objective/subjective divide, it can still be argued that the choice, usage and arrangement of visuals in a text can never be 'innocent'. Most importantly, the caption—or indeed its absence—its detail as well as analysis, becomes significant. To go back to the example of the paddy fields: if the two photographs appear as 'side illustrations' in a study of agricultural practices and appear under a common caption such as 'working in a paddy field in Bellary district of Karnataka', then little can be gleaned about the differences in women and men's roles and what it implies for women's health. On the other hand, a caption detailing gender differences in the nature of work—that may well be missing in the text—would provide another dimension to the study. Of course, most fieldworkers may just wish to use photographs as illustrations, thereby limiting the visuals' power to speak. Here, the discourse around the photograph merely adds a visual footnote to the text. Clearly, the researcher did not intend it to act as an independent narrative.

The Photograph as Narrative: Women's Work in India

When the photograph acts as narrative, then photographing persons and their subsequent viewing means a two-way relationship between the subject and the photographer and later between both and the viewer. Today, even though the relationship between the subject and the photographer has become more democratic, it still remains another's vision that determines the presentation of the self in varying formats, sizes and frames. The act of being photographed was not (nor is) merely a 'mechanical record'. Rather, as John Berger (1972) has pointed out, the photographer was exercising a choice and taking a decision on what was worth recording. As soon as it is admitted that the photographic moment is one of making choices, the selectivity of the photograph is evident. Susan Sontag wrote:

> A photograph is not just the result of an encounter between an event and a photographer; picture-taking is an event in itself, and one with ever more peremptory rights—to interfere with, to invade, or to ignore whatever is going on. [...] After the event has ended, the picture will still exist, conferring on the event a kind of immortality (and importance) it would never otherwise have enjoyed. (Sontag 1977: 11)

The argument here is that to add a visual element to a history, context or even relationship that may have been written about, discussed and analysed is not merely to slip in 'pretty or telling' images. Rather, 'reading' photographs, is to introduce another dimension to the experience, in this case, a history of women's work in India. While all photographs can be 'read', some more than others lend themselves to greater narrativisation. Again, the narrative can focus on information on the activity, and/or on the pose, demeanour, and if there is more than one person in the photograph, their relative body languages, gaze and inter-relationships. A reading of the dozen archival photographs that follow will help in understanding significant changes in the Indian economy and women's place in it.

By the middle of the nineteenth century, changes in the agrarian economy of India brought about by colonialism and the drastic de-industrialisation that followed led to the collapse of traditional work opportunities for poor women. Spinning, crafts, grain husking and other ancillary occupations, in which women had been involved for subsistence in rural areas, gradually disappeared. As mobility was limited, domestic service and a few non-agricultural occupations such as petty trade, food processing and home-based industries like weaving became the sole work options for rural women. Large numbers continued to work in agriculture as unskilled labour and some entered prostitution. Most new opportunities in the emerging regulated modern sector mainly benefited men, and some industries attracted large-scale migration of men as well as some family migration. The earliest among these were the coffee, rubber and tea plantations. A considerable number of women entered the coal mines and textile, cotton and jute mills that were set up by the turn of the twentieth century, often working under most exploitative conditions. In many of these sectors, gender distinctions tended to be strong and unskilled seasonal tasks associated with low wages were relegated to women. Furthermore, increased mechanisation and the imposition of labour legislation led to a decline in female paid and unpaid employment.

In 1932, an informal survey estimated that 90 per cent of adult Indian women worked either for a wage or as unpaid family labour. Poor women's contribution to the economy remained unacknowledged as they continued to be seen in the mould of reproducers and nurturers rather than producers. Women's productive roles therefore remained invisible, both within the household and at the workplace. In the latter, they performed underpaid, unskilled and undervalued tasks and were regarded by all—the state, employers, trade unionists and their own families—as supplementary workers. The pervasive notion was that women worked to supplement the family income, which in turn served to justify the low wages paid to them, while in reality they were often their families' principal breadwinners. There was no clear realisation about the widespread and diverse economic participation of the vast majority of Indian women who needed to work to survive and support their families, and the actual number of working women must have been much higher than actually reported.

Although by this time, the leaders of the growing women's movement sought to speak for all Indian women, the issues they pursued—female education, social conditions, legal and political rights—reflected in the main concerns and interests of their own class. Some leaders and organisations were concerned with employment for poor and destitute women of their own milieu. Less than 2 per cent of middle-class women worked for a living and most married women from well-off and elite families did not, for wages obviously—nor were encouraged to seek employment. Interestingly, the growing number of women's organisations did not take notice of the range of problems of women professionals such as doctors and teachers, and much less understood or seriously addressed the condition of ordinary women.

Although the agricultural economy as well as individual familial economies of the majority of Indians were heavily dependent on the unpaid labour of women, their history is characterised by silences, absences of written and visual records. Women of this class did not leave behind any writings for the historical record, nor were movements of working-class women documented in any detail during the early decades of the century—not surprisingly, their appearance in photographs was unusual. Similarly, images of their counterparts in rural areas, as they undertook agricultural or other tasks, remain few and far between. I now look at images of women as workers and argue that a close reading of these changes how we understand ideas of work.

Apart from the needs of Empire, a popular interest in 'native' types led to a growing body of photographs for commercial use—many of which were organised into albums and, after 1899, available also as the more easily sold and disseminated postcard. This pre-1905 postcard of a young girl from Madras Presidency (Figure 1.3) exemplifies the Orientalist vision; it is also possible that she was paid to pose for the photograph. It is likely that she was the daughter of a domestic servant—or may even have been a child prostitute. Her gesture and her slightly bent head would indicate subservience—somewhat belied by her left hand that is akimbo, almost in denial the right side of her body!

Figure 1.4 provides an insight into women's roles in agricultural practices at the close of the nineteenth century. Not only does it give information on changing practices in winnowing but some other questions also come to mind. For instance, the fact that women had to climb up to

Figure 1.3

Salaams *from India*

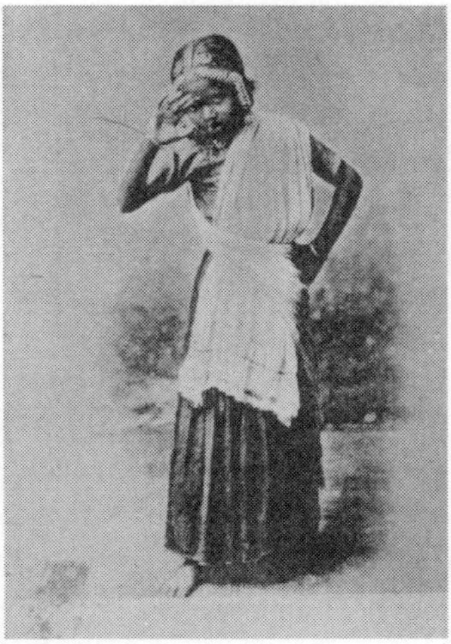

Source: Courtesy of Malavika Karlekar.

Figure 1.4

Women winnowing grain, c. 1890s

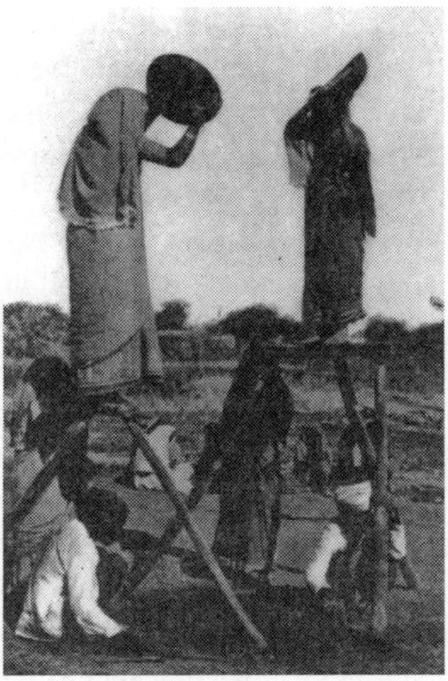

Source: Helen S. Dyer (1900) (courtesy of Uma Chakravarty, New Delhi and India Foundation for the Arts, Bangalore).

Figure 1.5

Women at work in cotton mills, c. 1920s

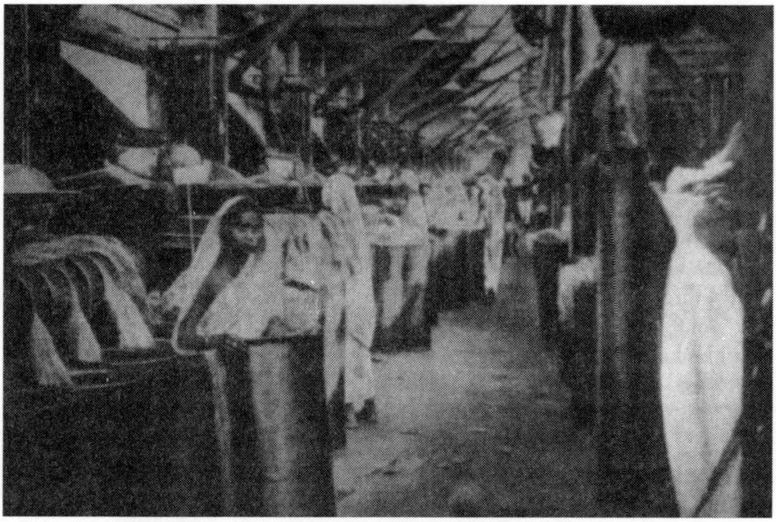

Source: Woman's Outlook in India, June–July 1927.

the platform would suggest that it was a task for relatively young and able-bodied women. While turbaned men in the foreground appear to be removing the leftover chaff from the winnowed grain, women in the background are aged in some other activity. Women started joining the industrial workforce by the 1920s; Figure 1.5 shows them at work in a cotton mill with their heads demurely covered.

In 1882, two Muslim women—Bibi Meherunessa and Bibi Gulabjan—were known to have bought several acres of land in Assam to start a tea company. Not unexpectedly, the enterprise—an unwelcome intrusion into an area dominated by the white male entrepreneur—soon folded up, but the number of women workers in tea plantations continued to grow. In 1905, 40 per cent of the labour force in the Assam Valley tea gardens was female. Historically, planters and colonial administrators encouraged family recruitment of migrants: the presence of women was not only regarded as stabilising but they were also soon indispensable for the dextrous plucking of the delicate 'two leaves and a bud'.

Figure 1.6 of three barefoot women pluckers with tea bushes to the right shows how umbrellas were used to balance the enormous collection baskets. The angle of these seems to indicate that they are empty and the women

Figure 1.6

Tea garden workers, c. 1930s

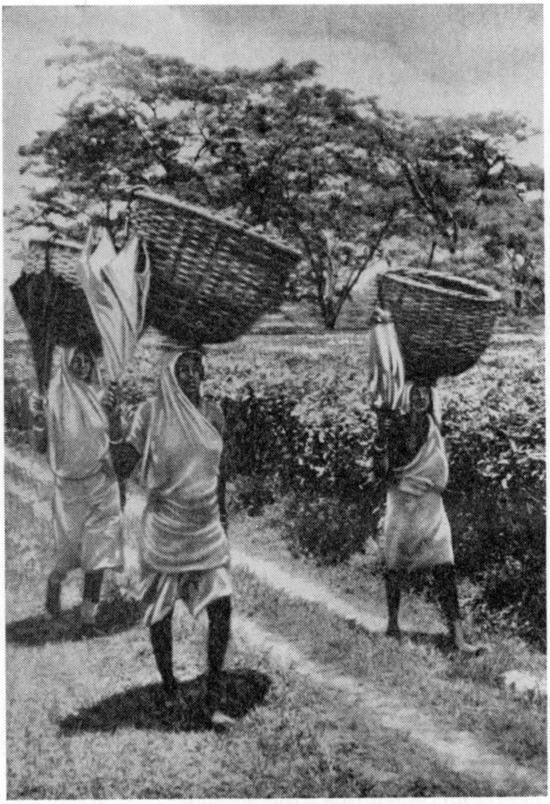

Source: Wonderful India and Three of Her Beautiful Neighbours, c. 1940s.

were probably on their way to work. Saris are hitched up to facilitate easy movement and the woman in front appears to have pulled hers between the legs, a style of draping usual in western India and Madras Presidency.

An introduction of this photograph into a study of tea garden labour, with of course a detailed caption, would help enormously in an understanding of the occupation as well as the gendering of various tasks and what these involved.

Fetching water, often from long distances, continues to be a major preoccupation for a substantial number of women in India. While it is not unusual for young girls to help too, it is not so normal for men to participate

Figure 1.7

Fetching water at the Gangaur Ghat, on the shores of the Pichola Lake, c. 1930s

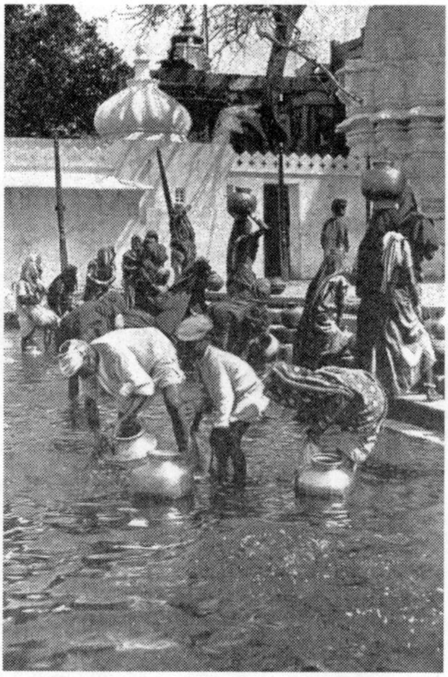

Source: Wonderful India and Three of Her Beautiful Neighbours, c. 1940s.

in the onerous task. In Figure 1.7, however, a couple of men appear to be filling brass vessels that they would then place on the women's heads. Interestingly, women in the back are doing both. It is significant that the photographer—in all probability a man—chose to concentrate on the men on the job, though there is much more 'action' and activity by several women in the background. This visual can be read at many levels—at one, it can be used as a visual illustrating a major preoccupation of working-class Indian women; at another, it can bring into focus the relationship between the photographer and his subjects and his choice of foregrounding men participating in a usually woman-oriented task. In the latter case, the narrative around the photograph can provide a sub-discourse of its own, one that the researcher may or may not wish to recognise/engage with.

By the 1930s, of course, middle-class women were coming out into the public as professionals such as teachers, lawyers and doctors, as well as dancers, musicians, actors and political activists.

Rukmini Devi was born into a traditional Brahmin family. At the age of 16, defying convention, she married George Arundale, Scotsman and

Theosophist. On her travels abroad to promote the goals of Theosophy, she met—and was deeply influenced by—Pavlova and Ruth St. Denis. She learned ballet from Pavlova's soloist Cleo Nordi and dabbled in 'Oriental dance' for a while, becoming very interested in costume and stage design. Later, encouraged by Annie Besant, she interested herself in the revival of *sadir*, a dance form forbidden by the anti-nautch social reform movement of the 1890s and banned by the British government in 1911. Again defying convention, she learnt *sadir* herself from the famed Mylapore Gowri Ammal and gave a debut performance in public in 1935 at Adyar, Madras.

Renaming the dance form Bharatanatyam, she established *Kalakshetra*, an academy for dance and music in 1936, an institution that has enabled the cultural revival of the performing arts of South India.

A careful study of Figure 1.8 by dancers, researchers or even aficionados of Bharatanatyam would help in understanding changing modes of dress, accoutrements, posture and, of course, admire the sheer beauty of Rukmini Devi!

Figure 1.8

Rukmini Devi Arundale, c. 1940s

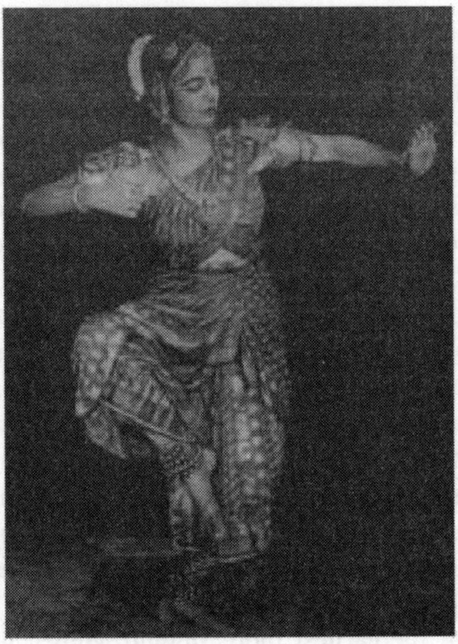

Source: Courtesy of Samudri Archives, Chennai.

Figure 1.9

A still from Achhut Kanya *Starring Ashok Kumar and Devika Rani, 1936*

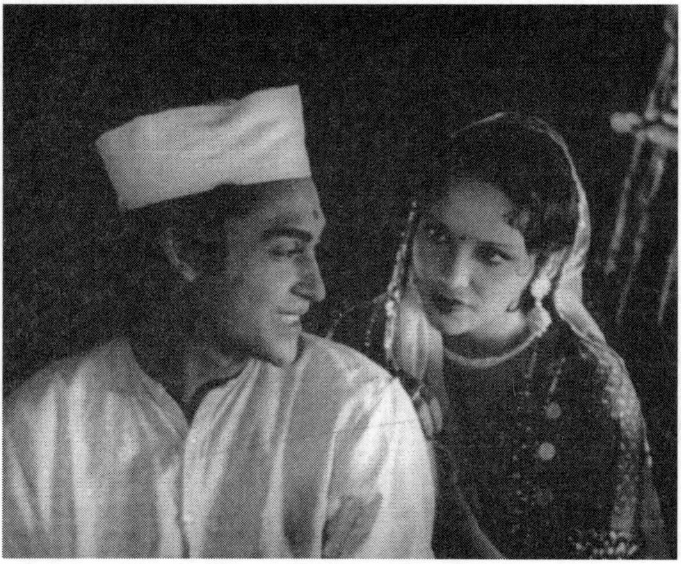

Source: Courtesy of National Film Archive of India, Pune.

Among the early superhits of the Bombay film industry, *Achhut Kanya* is the love story between a Brahmin (Ashok Kumar) and a Dalit girl (Devika Rani) (Figure 1.9). The tragic *Achhut Kanya* was a big hit and started the trend of socially committed films, making the lead couple the most famous on-screen pair of the times. Devika Rani who dominated the first decade of Indian sound films was a grandniece of poet Rabindranath Tagore. In 1929, she married producer Himanshu Rai and together the couple established Bombay Talkies in 1935. After Rai's death in 1941, Devika Rani became Bombay's first woman studio chief, taking responsibility of the management of Bombay Talkies including the business. She later married the expatriate Russian painter Svetoslav Roerich and lived in Bangalore until her death.

Apart from its importance in the emerging Hindi cinema, this visual tells us about the on-screen changing body language between men and women—and of course introduces the viewer to the idea of challenging caste barriers.

Perhaps one of the earliest Indo-Anglian women writers of fiction, Attia Hossain was the first woman to graduate from the feudal *taluqdari*

Figure 1.10

Attia Hossain (R.) with husband and friend, Lucknow, c. 1930s

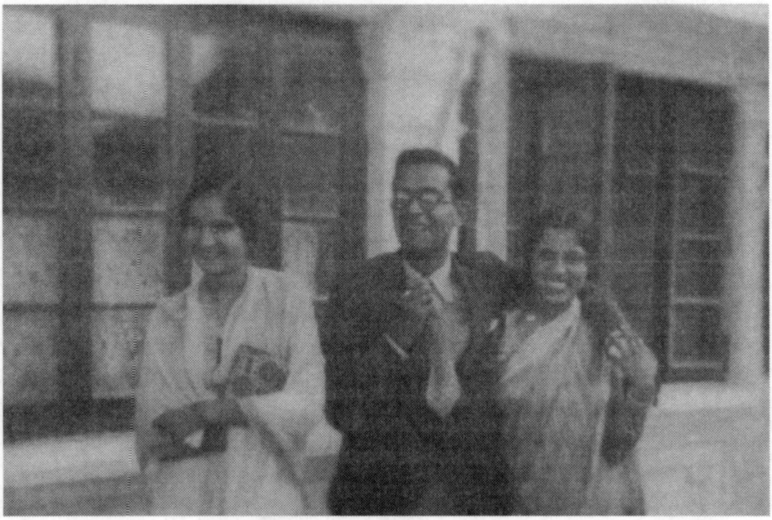

Source: Courtesy of late Dr Mary Badhwar.

(landed) background into which she was born. Her collection of short stories—*Phoenix Fled* (1953)—followed by the novel *Sunlight on a Broken Column* (1961) are sensitive renderings of female seclusion or life behind *parda* or the veil.

The on-location photograph (Figure 1.10) was taken by an amateur, perhaps a friend, and that may explain the informality of the pose. The obvious show of affection between the couple was not unsurprising, given Attia's Anglicised social background. The third person in the photograph stands a little apart, an outsider to happy conjugality—and it is almost possible to cut through the photograph, creating two discrete images! An inclusion of this image in any research either on Attia or on early Indo-Anglian fiction or even changing *taluqdari* families would add to the richness of the discourse.

Born in Budapest in 1913 of a Hungarian mother and a Sikh father, Amrita Sher-Gil worked ceaselessly in her studio in Summer Hill (Shimla), while on the family estate and in Saraya, Gorakhpur as well. Amrita was perhaps the most talented Indian woman artist of the twentieth century. During her brief life Amrita painted a large number of incredibly beautiful canvases using strong brush strokes and vibrant colours.

Figure 1.11

Amrita Sher-Gil in her studio in Shimla photographed by father Umrao Singh Sher-Gil, 1937

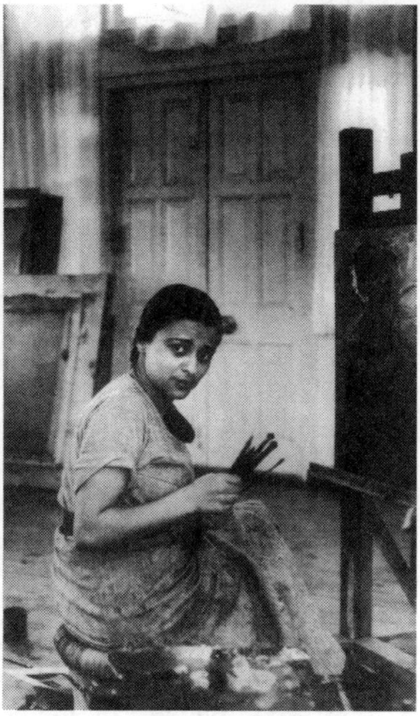

Source: Courtesy of Vivan Sundaram, New Delhi.

Figure 1.11 is one of the very few photographs of Amrita at work—and she has turned back, surprised by her father. It is possible that her father had asked her to 'hold' her pose; remember, it was long before the point-and-shoot days of the digital, and Umrao Singh would have had to spend quite a bit of time in setting up his equint, focusing and then taking the shot.

After her matriculation from Indraprastha College, Delhi, Sarla Thukral joined her husband—a commercial pilot—in Lahore where she took flying lessons. In 1936, she got her pilot's license, becoming the first woman pilot of undivided India. After 10 flying hours, she flew solo. When, in 1948, the Maharani of Alwar advertised for a lady pilot, Sarla applied and got the job.

A self-assured Sarla smiles (Figure 1.12)—and contemporary women pilots can hardly not be impressed that she flew wearing what appears to be a georgette or crepe sari and has bangles on her left hand!

Figure 1.12

Pilot Sarla Sharma (later Thukral), 1936

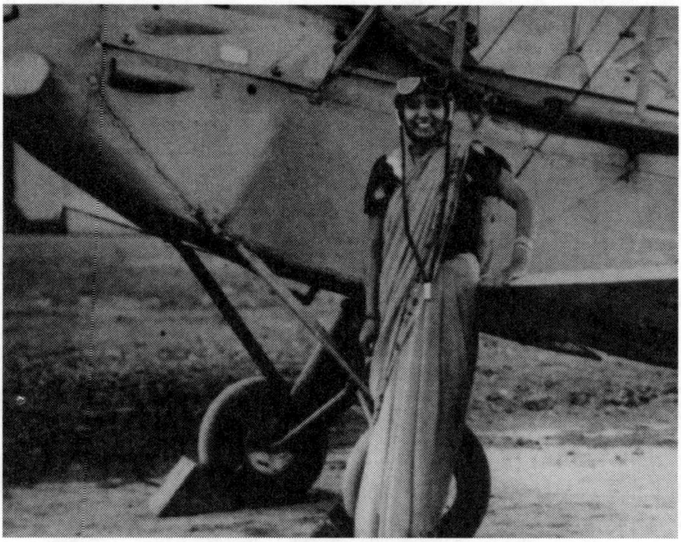

Source: Courtesy of Sarla Thukral, New Delhi.

Figure 1.13

Self-portrait by photographer Annapurna Dutta, c. 1940s

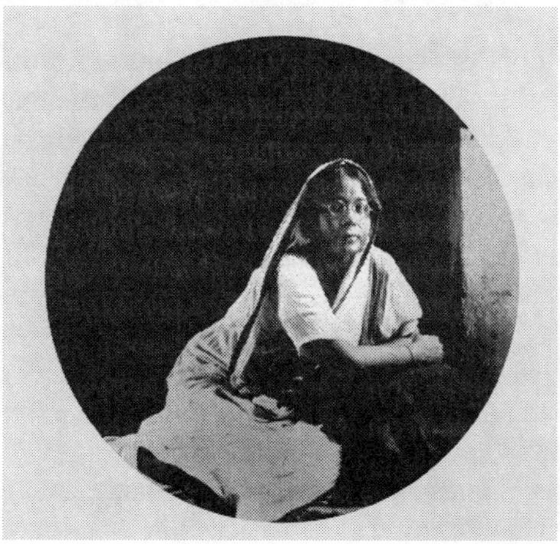

Source: Courtesy of Centre for Studies in Social Sciences, Calcutta, Kolkata.

Better known as Artist Mashima among her younger contemporaries, Annapurna Dutta became a leading professional photographer during the first half of the twentieth century (Figure 1.13). Married at 12 to Upendranath Dutta, Annapurna learned photography and painting, and took up photography as a profession when she was 25. Though she did not own a separate studio establishment, and ran her business from home, she supported herself and her children by earnings from photography. Annapurna had a preference for outdoor assignments and single-handedly did all the developing and printing. Her commissions for photography came mainly from both Hindu and Muslim households of *pardnashins* (those women who observed *parda*).

In the self-portrait (Figure 1.13), Annapurna has positioned herself comfortably and looks, with some concentration, straight at the camera. Though family sources have given the date of the photograph as 1930, she looks clearly older and it is possible that she was in her forties, if not early fifties at the time. I need hardly add that for students of early photography and indeed the self-portrait, this image lends itself to multiple analyses: at one level, it is information, and at another, it opens up an entire discourse on presentation of the self by a photographer.

The communist-led peasant uprising in Telangana (1945–1946) before Independence was as much against repression by landlords as a nationalist

Figure 1.14

Women volunteers at rifle practice, Telangana, c. 1946

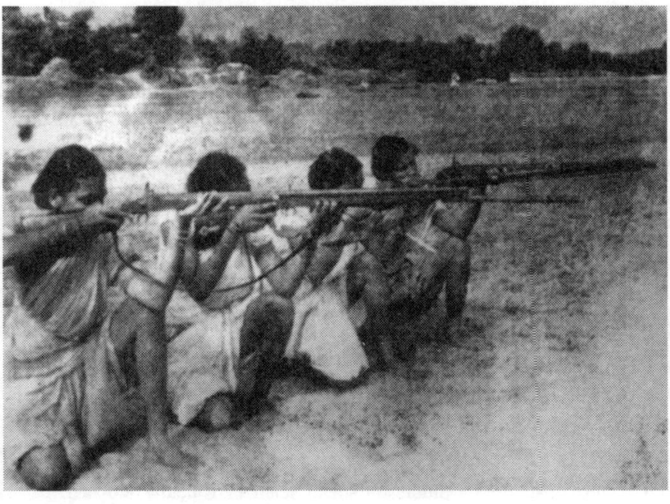

Source: Courtesy of Vidya Munshi, Kolkata.

struggle against the Nizam's rule. During this struggle, women in the fighting squads questioned patriarchal practices. Here, with their saris hitched up, village women hold the cumbersome rifles with ease (Figure 1.14). They are barefoot and concentrate intently at distant targets. This final visual not only provides insights into women's political mobilisation but also shows how gender did not deter women—nor did their traditional dress!

Conclusion

The choice of visuals and their reading reflects the world view of a woman social anthropologist who have been working in the field of gender studies since the 1970s and has, since 2000, chosen to focus on the role of the photograph in understanding social relationships. This has led to some reflection on the role of all those involved in the photographic process. A reading of photographic prints has been/is determined by the position, gender, class and nationality of the viewer. To read a photograph means to read it as one would a footprint or a cardiogram—as a part of a continuum (Berger 1972: 181). Even the uncaptioned photograph 'is invaded by language' and 'traversed by language when it is "read"' (Burgin 1982: 144) as memory, personal histories and association come into play. Like any form of engaged reading, that of a photograph too 'involves a series of problematic, ambiguous and often contradictory meanings' (Clarke 1997: 17). In other words, visual readings may even be subversive, that is, in the case of women's paid work, they may go against the accepted wisdom of roles and expectations. Thus, visual evidence can be quite 'revolutionary' at times.

A viewing/reading of the handful of photographs in the last section shows us the changes in women's employment in India and the nature of work. These not only add ballast to textual readings but also allow the gender-sensitive viewer to analyse the different roles of men and women in particular tasks. Each viewing—and there is an important difference between the reading of a written text that is not likely to be read more than once or perhaps twice and reading a photograph constantly on view—can bring new insights or contradict an earlier reading. It can evoke different responses each time—in different persons or in the same person at different moments. For some, Barthes argues, photographs are regarded as 'good' if the *object speaks* and 'it induces us, vaguely to think' (Barthes 1993: 38). However, there is a danger in this as not all can accept photographs that 'speak too much'. For instance, the pensive, brooding photograph is often viewed as subversive, dangerous to the established order.

There is, therefore, no innocence in the photographic act. Are all the photographs on women's paid and unpaid activities then imbued with a meaning beyond the obvious? Can they not be viewed just as illustrations of an existing reality? They can—yet, at the same time, the onion skin-like layering of a photograph leads to multiple meanings, each determined by the specificities of the viewers' situation, and such viewings may go well beyond the physical blemish, a positioning of the hand or the nature of the task performed by women.

This brings us once again to the question of the relationship between photographs, textual material and issues of 'truth' and verisimilitude. That there are differences of opinion on this point is clear if we look at Stephen Bann's general optimism expressed in his view that 'nowadays we take it for granted that the visual image will not only supplement, but in most cases lend validation to the printed text' (Bann 2003: 62). I would argue that there is tremendous scope for the use of the photograph not only to supplement and validate the written word but often to add new information. In this case, an understanding of the scope of women's employment is enhanced by a viewing and reading of photographs. These not only provide us with visual evidence but also allow a layered and differing understanding of what it has meant historically be a woman working and living in India.

References

Bann, Stephen. 2003. 'Antiquarianism, Visuality, and the Exotic Monument'. In *Traces of India: Photography, Architecture and the Politics of Representation, 1850–1900*, edited by Maria Antonella Pelizzari, pp. 60–85. Montreal: Canadian Centre for Architecture; New Haven: Yale Center for British Art; Ahmedabad: Mapin Publishing.

Barthes, Roland. (1980) 1993. *Camera Lucida: Reflections on Photography*. London: Vintage.

Bateson, G., and Margaret Mead. 1942. *Balinese Character: A Photographic Analysis*. New York: New York Academy of Sciences.

Berger, John, ed. 1972. 'Understanding a Photograph'. In *Selected Essays and Articles: The Look of Things*. Harmondsworth: Penguin Books Ltd.

Boast, Herle, Sudeshna Guha, and Anita Herle, eds. 2001. *Collected Sights: Photographic Collections of the Museum of Archaeology and Anthropology, 1860s–1930s*. Cambridge: University of Cambridge.

Burgin, Victor, ed. 1982. *Thinking Photography*. London: The Macmillan Press.

Clarke, Graham. 1997. *The Photograph*. Oxford: Oxford University Press.

Dyer, Helen S. 1900. *Pandita Ramabai: The Story of her Life.* London: Morgan and Scott.

Gordon, Sophie. 2004. 'Uncovering India: Studies in Nineteenth-century Indian Photography'. *History of Photography* 28 (2): 180–90.

Huworth, Rosalind. 'Photo-interviewing for Research'. Social Research Update 40. Accessed on 31 June 2014 at http://sru.soc.surrey.ac.uk/SRU40.html

MacDougall, David. 1997. 'The Visual in Anthropology'. In *Rethinking Visual Anthropology*, edited by Marcus Banks and Howard Morphy, pp. 276–95. New Haven: Yale University Press.

Mead, Margaret. (1975) 1995. 'Visual Anthropology in a Discipline of Words'. In *Principles of Visual Anthropology*, edited by Paul Hockings, pp. 3–10. Berlin: Mouton.

Modell, Judith A., and Charlee Brodsky. 1994. 'Envisioning Homestead: Using Photographs in Interviewing in Interactive Oral History Interviewing'. In *Interactive Oral History Interviewing*, edited by Eva M. McMahan and Kim Lacy Rogers, pp. 141–61. Hillsdale, NJ: Erlbaum.

Pelizzari, Maria Antonella. 2003. 'Introduction'. In *Traces of India: Photography, Architecture and the Politics of Representation, 1850–1900*, edited by Maria Antonella Pelizzari, pp. 13–18. Montreal: Canadian Centre for Architecture; New Haven: Yale Center for British Art; Ahmedabad: Mapin Publishing.

Pinney, Christopher. 1997. *Camera Indica: The Social Life of Indian Photographs*. London: Reaktion Books.

———. 2011. *Photography and Anthropology*. New Delhi: Oxford University Press.

Singh, Upinder. 2004. *The Discovery of Ancient India*. New Delhi: Permanent Black.

Sontag, Susan. (1973) 1977. *On Photography*. New York, NY: Delta.

Suchar, Charles S., and Robert Rotenberg. 1984. 'Judging the Adequacy of Shelter: A Case from Lincoln Park'. *Journal of Architectural and Planning Research* 11 (2): 149–65.

Watson, J. Forbes, and John William Kaye, eds. 1868–1872. *The People of India: A Series of Photographic Illustrations with Descriptive Letterpress of the Races and Tribes of Hindustan*. London: Indian Museum (W.H. Allen and Co.).

2

Unlikely 'Devis': Gender and Imagination On and Off the Silver Screen

Anusuya Kumar

Introduction: Women in Early Indian Cinema

The year 2013 marked a full century of Indian cinema—a hundred years since Dadasaheb Phalke (1870–1944), a small-town photographer, first ran India's full-feature-length film, *Raja Harishchandra* (1913), to a spellbound audience in a private theatre in Mumbai. For an industry that is now twice as old as the Indian nation itself, this marker of historical time and rite of passage is perhaps not without a measure of irony: for a hundred years, it seems, the Indian film industry has held millions in thrall through the art and manufacture of myths, dreams and fantasies by turning them into popular entertainment. The centennial year, then, seems to have evoked space for some self-reflections and imaginings regarding the interplay of 'reel' with 'real' cinema history and also time for evaluating key roles played by those who were once part of the formative years of the world's largest 'dream' industry.

In this regard, there have appeared more than a few documentary tributes, films and popular articles on the birth of Indian cinema and on personalities like Dadasaheb Phalke, Ardeshir Irani (1886–1969), Jamshedji Framji Madan (1856–1923) and others who were responsible for the first film productions and early cutting-edge innovations in film technology. We have heard at length about Phalke as the Father of Indian

Cinema and his film company, Hindustan Films, producing some 95 full-length and 26 short films in 19 years between 1913 and 1937 (Vatave 2004).[1] Likewise, there has been much shared about Ardeshir Irani, the founder of 'talkies' in India, who produced and directed 158 films in a career spanning 25 years (Ahmed 2012).[2] His contemporary, Jamshedji Madan of Madan Theatres has also been recently rediscovered as a pioneer film-maker and producer who owned 127 theatres nationwide at the peak of his career and controlled half the country's box office in 1930 (Abel 2008: 580).[3] Chandulal Shah (1898–1975) of Ranjit Studios (1929–1975) is estimated to have produced and directed a staggering 220 films between 1929 and 1970, employing an estimated 300 people from actors to studio-hands (Sharma 2012).[4] Similarly, we have heard much about the legendary Himanshu Rai (1892–1940) of Bombay Talkies (1934–1948) studios who produced and directed *The Star of the East* and went on to produce some 102 films between the years 1934 and 1940 (Sharma 2013).[5]

Without diminishing or devaluing these achievements in any way, one can gain the impression from current narratives of Bollywood's early years of a shared film script with a recognisable cast of largely male entrepreneur figures and 'movie moghuls' who made film history, much like the larger-than-life heroes of their own films, by facing indomitable odds. However, as in all imaginings of history—here, written texts, documentaries and films about early Bollywood years—attention may be drawn unerringly towards that which has been rendered invisible or elided and occluded—'cast out' or left 'behind the scenes', as it were.

It is perhaps significant, then, that there exists little, if any, mention in these contemporary accounts of the often extraordinary women who once entered the early Indian film industry—usually from forgotten and extreme margins of Indian society—and played quite important roles, not just in the first films but in the real life story of Indian cinema. These individuals, it turns out, were sometimes not only Bollywood's pioneering actresses facing the arc lights and its first real 'stars' but also worked as film producers, financiers, directors, scriptwriters, set designers, music composers and songwriters, to name but a few. Their entry into Indian cinema and making of film careers at a time when women were invisible in most public areas of society was in fact nothing short of revolutionary: as dramatic performers, singers and dancers in theatre troupes across the country, in film production studios and on radio shows or record labels, women erupted on the stage, as it were, in the first decades of the twentieth century and transformed the fabric of Indian society in ways that we are perhaps just beginning to understand.

In this chapter, I look at the lives and times of some of the film industry's very early women—its unsung 'heroines'—and try to show the ways in which they contributed to defining and shaping the cast, character and visual iconography of modern Indian cinema with their unique stage images. Their on-screen presence—and also off-screen—I will argue, seems to have carried an exceptional mythic, symbolic and archetypal charge, not only because of the kinds of roles and characters they played in early Indian films but also because of who they were in themselves as individual women with very particular histories, cultural backgrounds and the ways in which they were engaged in incarnating unexplored imaginary feminine 'selves' at a critical juncture of the birth of Indian cinema and transformation of early twentieth-century Indian society.

I will show how many women who entered the Indian film industry in its early years often came from the margins of its society—in fact, several had their origins in the *tawaif* or 'courtesan' households (*kothas*) of cities like Lucknow, Agra, Lahore and Delhi or in multicultural and minority communities across the subcontinent like Armenian Jews, Parsis and Anglo-Indians (Sameen 2014).[6] As such, they were often perceived by film-makers and producers as 'outsiders': professional actresses who could take on the challenge of representing women for the first time in a public and visual medium where they would undoubtedly be called upon to engage with emotionally and erotically charged projections of a mostly male audience. In a bid to domesticate the potentially explosive nature of this female appearance on screen, film producers often gave the early film actresses traditional or mythological Hindu names with the classical suffix of 'devi' or 'goddess' (Kinsley 2005).[7] For example, between the years 1920 and 1945, we find a pantheon of 'goddesses' like Sabitha Devi/Irene Gasper (1914–1965), Seeta Devi/Renee Smith (1905–1985), Renuka Devi/Begum Khurshid Mirza (1918–1989), Saraswati Devi/Khorshid Minochar-Homiji (1912–1980) and many others who came to rule the film industry and were adored by millions.

An important part of my argument is to examine the ways in which some of these early actresses were able to contain and to mediate such 'extra human' identifications—intended ironically to make them seem 'respectable' and 'acceptable' to viewers—by projecting images of feminine 'selves' that often verged on poetic symbol, archetype and myth. For their audiences—and perhaps even for themselves—their first screen presences carried an uncanny power and affective charge as if these women had stepped into the arc lights from some fantastic mythological world inhabited by 'multicultural' goddesses or hybrid 'devis'. In their early films, cast often as princesses, gypsy girls, mystery maidens with lost identities, unattainable legendary lovers, inscrutable women—even stunt queens—some of these actresses could catalyse popular imaginaries on deeper psychological levels suggested by the sometimes extraordinary responses of audiences to their appearances on screen. They were a crucial part of the magic and mystique of early Indian cinema and often took centre stage in dramatic roles designed explicitly for them.

This exceptional appeal of some women actresses in early Indian films can hardly be dismissed as an accidental phenomenon. Rather, it suggests that these actresses were able to project feminine selves that seemed relatively free from the limitations of social realities of the time and to inhabit a world that spoke directly to the imagination while also arising from it. Their appearances on screen, although visibly human and often unabashedly sensual, seemed indefinably 'other' and therefore closer to a realm of fantasy, dream, image and symbol than to waking everyday reality. This sense of feminine 'otherness', visually augmented by exotic costumes, make-up, dramatic performances, use of dance and song sequences in dream-like choreography, special camera lighting, all seemed explicitly designed to reach past a consensual and 'awake' or conscious reality and to access or open up deeper imaginaries. Spellbound, as it were, by a stream of images of feminine alterity enshrined up on a living screen, the audience could become uniquely receptive to their own imaginative possibilities—possibilities usually kept well confined within a patriarchal society—and allow them rare avenue for play.

In such a special and ritual context of the rapt 'filmic' gaze, anything could be possible and the unlikely most often likely. In cinema, the rules of game could shift dramatically—even if momentarily—allowing for power and dominion to the oppressed and suppressed. Traditional gender roles and perceptions of women in society could become pliant and even be subtly subverted. Inside a movie theatre, for example, one could well chance upon a rain-soaked Sulochana Devi/Ruby Myers (1907–1983) in *Typist Girl* (1926) or Madhubala in *Chalti Ka Naam Gaadi* (1958) meandering alone in desolate and dimly lit streets and strike up a conversation as between two archetypal strangers in a nocturnal urban landscape. Likewise, a sultry and bejewelled Devika Rani (1908–1994) in *Jawani Ki Hawa* (1935) could easily sabotage her father's plans for marriage and elope on an overnight train with her lover while possibly killing an interloper along the way.

Jung: Fantasy and Film

Such dream-like images and almost surreal sequences in early Indian cinema seem especially significant with regard to its representations of women. They may also help to reinforce more contemporary trends in the field of film studies that have indicated correlations between the medium of film and Jungian, particularly post-Jungian, analytic psychology. It seems that Carl Gustav Jung's ideas regarding the vital role of images, symbols, fantasies and mythic or archetypal forms in the life of psyche bear striking similarities to films and the particular ways that this medium uses images to touch and reach audiences. For Jung, perhaps far more than for Freud, images were the key constituents of psyche and their action was intended, not simply to obscure or to disguise repressed contents in order to adapt to a so-called 'reality principle' but to communicate effectively and to bring vital and life-transformative energy up from a psychic unconscious into waking consciousness (Izod 2001: 25–26).[8] In Jung's writings, fantasy and imagination have been recognised as indispensable to individual growth and serve a critical compensatory function in bringing balance, depth, soul and differentiation into psyche as a whole (Jung [1954] 1970: 226).[9]

In his work *Psychological Types*, for example, Jung writes of imagination and fantasy:

> Imagination is the […] creative activity of the mind in general […] Fantasy as imaginative activity is […] the direct expression of psychic life, of psychic energy which cannot appear in consciousness except in the form of images or contents, just as physical energy cannot manifest itself except as a definite physical state […] We could therefore say that fantasy […] is a definite sum of libido that cannot appear in consciousness in any other way than in the form of an image. A fantasm is an *idée-force* […]. (Jung [1921] 2014a: 433)[10]

The crucial point here, for Jung, is not only that psychic energy incarnates as images for an observing consciousness but also that these are not 'pictures' or simple representations of 'reality' but creative and figurative expressions verging on symbolic activity and are intended precisely to move, stimulate, communicate and to transform consciousness in every possible way. They can carry high emotional energy and are saturated with life. At deeper levels of psyche, images, for Jung, were expressions of archetypal patterns that carried cultural, cross-cultural and even universal content as myths. In this sense, psychic images are more akin to poetic imagination, art and reverie. In films, as in psyche, the flow of image-narratives are charged in just such expressive ways and intended explicitly for eliciting and arousing emotional responses in their audiences. Movies—like dreams—can be quite 'moving' for those who watch them (Izod 2001).[11]

Making just such an analogy, the film director, Luis Buñuel, has remarked:

> The essential element in any work of art is mystery […] a film is like an involuntary imitation of a dream […] on the screen, as within the human being, the nocturnal voyage into the unconscious begins […] Cinema seems to have been invented to express the life of the subconscious, the roots of which penetrate poetry so deeply. (Buñuel cited in Kyrou 1963: 109–11)[12]

These 'poetic' roots of cinema in the 'subconscious' can be traced back perhaps to its constitutive elements—images—which are closer to the fabric of dreams and fantasy than any of the so-called 'objective reality'. Indeed, according to James Hillman, a post-Jungian analyst and founder of school of Archetypal Psychology, it is precisely this imaginal aspect of Jung's formulation of psyche that is significant and can explain our fascination with visual media like film. Taking Jung's ([1931] 2014b: 149) prescription: 'to understand the dream's meaning I must stick as close as possible to the dream images', Hillman advances a full-scale phenomenology of imagination and a 'psychology of soul that is based in a psychology of image' (Hillman 1975: xi).[13] For Hillman, images are not only primary to experience but they also carry a quality of consciousness such that engagement with each one can reveal a living subject and a person or a figure rather than some neutral objectified essence. Psyche, in this post-Jungian view, is radically constituted as an 'inscape' (Polikoff 2011)[14] of personified images which gain an archetypal depth of field upon closer viewing—a field of dreams incarnating as mythic gods and 'devis', so to speak. He writes:

> To live […] means to imagine things […] To be in soul is to experience the fantasy in all realities and the basic reality of fantasy […] In the beginning is the image; first imagination, then perception; first fantasy then reality […] Man is primarily an image maker and our psychic substance consists of images; our experience is imagination. We are indeed such stuff as dreams made on. (Hillman 1975: 23)[15]

Hillman's (1975: x) notion of 'soul' or 'anima'—taken from Jung—is closely linked to image and to fantasy as that 'mode which recognises all realities as primarily symbolic or metaphorical' and constitutes an imaginatively mythic way of seeing itself and the world (Cobb 1992). According to this view, any perspective that we have on the 'anima', or soul, is also its own imaginative self-expression as well so that we are not construed as observers from afar but always active participants in the 'figuring forth' of images. By such means, Hillman brings the Jungian symbolic process closer to a phenomenology of soul as it emerges through images and as an image. Images are self-referential—they do not need evidence through reference to external objects—mythopoetic imagination is the ground necessary for life of soul to be expressed.

It is perhaps clear how Hillman's remarkable 'revisioning' of Jung's notions of myth, fantasy and image as the figurative language of soul pertains to films—and, as we shall see, in special ways to the screen 'devis' of early twentieth-century Indian cinema. Despite the camera's seeming dissimilitude, audiences in film theatres—perhaps more than in live theatre or on stage—seem to be tacitly aware that the characters and events projected on screen are a priori images and constructed in and of themselves rather than 'literal' or positive representations. It is precisely in this way that films, quite like dream psyche, can free us into an imaginal space where we actively participate in the cinematic mythmaking process and draw pleasure from doing so. An audience's response to an image on screen could only be another image, and if such images have the emotional power to fascinate and to draw into depths, they can also be 'archetypal' in the sense of enjoining a shared dimension that brings film viewers close together in an act of 'dreaming' (Avens 1980). The extreme popularity of films as a visual media in our times, aside from their entertainment value, could then be an indication of such imaginative possibilities of play and of an engagement with 'anima' through creative self-expression.

Jung and Hillman's unique understanding of psyche, 'anima' and its imaginal capacities, developed as aforementioned in the context of films, seems especially significant with regard to early Indian film actresses—the unlikely 'devis' of popular cinematic mythology. It offers new perspectives on these now forgotten women in the ways in which they were able to work directly with an imaginal field by bringing to their screen performances an entire phenomenology of mythic characters and personalities. The images these early actresses projected in their films were not intended to replicate 'real' women in Indian society but rather to enhance, heighten, fascinate and to evoke the mythic imagination of their audiences to the fullest extent possible.

In this, they often brought onto early Indian screens an archetypal imagery of a pantheon of devis, *apsaras* or celestial beings, *paris* or fairies—mystery women—from the mythic and symbolic depths of a shared multicultural past. Even more fascinating than this, however, is how each of these actresses chose to give figure, body and form to a shared field of dreams. Their self-expressive personas on screen—or 'anima' in Jung's and Hillman's aforementioned revisionist terms—and a feminine phenomenology of mythmaking is especially revealing for us across this entire length of time. For in these images of feminine persons, once cast as shadows on the film screen, lie the deeper dreams of women who had once brought their own imagining souls into a fabulous sensuality of being.

Tawaif and Other Outsiders: From *Kothas* to Cinema

There is perhaps a correlation between the creativity and effusion of archetypal imagery expressed by actresses in early Indian cinema and another undeniable social fact: many women who entered the Indian film industry in the early decades of the twentieth century came from the margins of its society and were often perceived as 'outcasts'. This is quite true of those women who came to early films from *tawaif* backgrounds in the old cities of Lucknow, Lahore and Delhi. As professional performers with deep roots in the cultural arts such as classical singing, dancing and poetry recitation, or even as popular artisans, the so-called *tawaifs* were obvious choices for film actresses and brought to the revolutionary medium of films their already well-trained abilities to enthral live audiences and invoke a popular imagination. The film screen, in its difference from live stage and its focus on projecting into empty, virtual space, offered a kind of creative autonomy to 'anima' for expression of images that transgressed the bounds of literal or 'waking' reality of women in traditional Indian society.

This liminal quality of early Indian women actors as 'transgressors' who broke through barriers of social convention and morality that would keep women invisible in society also seems to link them closely to films as a special ritual place—an 'underworld', if you will—for a shared expression of unconscious dreams and fantasies. The classic black and white imagery of early Indian films with shades of brooding grey and chiaroscuro is fitting to a subterranean psychic domain of 'anima' figures who seem cast in 'film noir' light. As 'shadow' figures composed of the 'stuff of dreams', these women actors were paradoxical in their 'visible invisibility', straddling the tension lines between public and private, forbidden and sanctioned, history and myth: their personal identities were altered and their social origins deeply shrouded in mystery.

In actual fact, even a cursory glance at the genealogy of several early actresses can reveal their links to *tawaif* cultural contexts. For example, women like Fatma Begum (1895–1983), Zubeida (1911–1990), Sardar Akhtar (1915–1984), Wahidan Bai (1896–1940), Jahanara Kajjan (1915–1945), Gohar Jan (1910–1985), Begum Akhtar (1914–1974), Naseem Banu (1916–2002), Jaddanbai (1892–1949), Nimmi Bano (1933–), and many others, began their performing careers in local feudal courts and old-world 'bazaars' across India before moving into films. More than a few of these actresses had fathers who were *nawabs* or *rajahs* but were brought up in *kothas* to be educated in the traditional performing arts of music, song and dance. These *kothas* were in fact enclaves of feminine power with considerable financial and artistic autonomy from external control, and here women determined not only their own private lives but also often ran successful businesses employing entire orchestras and travelling shows with elaborate entourages to aid their public performances (Oldenburg 1990).[16] In making their entry into films, *tawaif* actresses like Fatma Begum, Zubeida, Sardar Akhtar, Jaddan Bai and Jahanara Kajjan were therefore not simply meeting the demands of a new industry for women actresses, they brought with them backgrounds and living contexts of feminine agency and skilled imagination as well as expertise as singers, actors, dancers, choreographers, costume designers and business women. Almost all of these women, as we shall see, became entrepreneurs and eventually launched their own film production companies.

It is salutary at this point to try and define the term *tawaif* more accurately since it seems overladen with associations with prostitution. According to Mukul Kesavan:

> The 'tawaif' was not […] a prostitute, though she served that purpose […] the 'tawaif' catered comprehensively to the needs of the cultivated man-about-town, she was more the accomplished courtesan, a sort of geisha […] the 'tawaif' […] undertook the social education of the sons of the gentry. She taught them a proper appreciation of the finer things in life: music, dance, conversation and etiquette—the legendary courtliness of 'Awadhi' manners, Lucknow's 'nazakat' and 'tehzeeb' were her stock-in-trade. In this sublimated understanding of the 'tawaif', even her dance, the 'mujra' is not an erotic performance but a choreographed ritual of salutation. The dance floor […] becomes a theatre […] in which the 'tawaif' and her patrons […] stage their little drama of politeness,

> where everyone knows their lines, where every cue finds its rehearsed response. (Kesavan 1994: 253)[17]

This rarified and polite world of feudal courts like Awadh of Wajid Ali Shah in Lucknow has been amply documented by Veena Talwar Oldenburg (1990) in her remarkable work, 'Lifestyle as Resistance: The Case of the Courtesans of Lucknow', where she shows the dismantlement and dislocation of *tawaif* households under British colonial rule in the wake of 1857 rebellions.[18] Under pressure from a new regime, many women were forced to seek jobs in new and emerging markets for their traditional craft as skilled singers, dancers and performers. The dying *tawaif* of a feudal and *nawabi* world found new opportunities for rebirth and transformation in Indian cinema and in the recording industry at the turn of the century. The transition here seems to have come gradually through Urdu and Parsi theatres in new urban environments where women first began performing on public stage and were often spotted by the new film entrepreneurs for contracts in the first silent movies (Pande 2006: 1647).[19]

In a similar vein, there were also several women who entered Indian cinema from multicultural contexts across the subcontinent such as Armenian, Jewish, Anglo-Indian or Parsi communities. Like their *tawaif* counterparts, these women were also looking for work in a rapidly changing urban and economic environment after the First World War. Some had prior experience in public theatres, colonial clubs, as well as in dancing halls, travelling shows and circuses. Others, like Sulochana, Romola and Pramila/Esther Victoria Abraham), were part of an emerging cadre of working women in colonial urban cities like Mumbai, Pune and Calcutta where they worked in hotels or in offices as receptionists, telephone operators, school teachers or secretaries (Weinbaum et al. 2008).[20] The early Indian film industry seemed to offer such new urban working women the enticement of fame and financial success without any stringent requirements of acting experience other than a willingness to change their identities and to assume fantastic film 'personas'. Indeed, in many instances, the very fact of their urban modernity and multiculturalism is what contributed to their popularity on screen as if these women expressed some residual longing and fascination in the popular imagination for an 'otherness' of cultural patterns that were free from traditional images of feminine domesticity. However, this remarkable trend of the 'modern girl' in Indian cinema could only gain momentum by first overcoming strong resistance and only with an a priori condition of assuming a traditional, respectable and almost divine Hindu identity.

Altered Identities and Respectability: Becoming 'Devis'

Khorshed Minocher-Homiji (1912–1980), for example, who joined Himanshu Rai's Bombay Talkies in the late 1930s, changed her name to Saraswati Devi at least in part to assuage the wrath of Mumbai's leading Parsi families who did not wish to have a woman from their own community represented openly on stage. In recounting the circumstances that led to this altered persona many years later, Khorshed (cited in Pande 2006: 1649)[21] observed:

> [...] when I think of those days, my hair stands on end. They (the parsi community) were determined to get us out of films. The newspapers added fuel to the fire [...] the result was that Himanshu Rai and his unit were threatened, even their lives were threatened.

Khorshed went on to become a music director for Bombay Talkies producing popular melodies, or *geets*, that are still considered as classics. Her compositions were inspired by a fusion of *Hindustani sangeet* and Western classical music in which she was trained from childhood, and this new genre soon became a norm for films in later decades. Khorshed is also credited in Indian film history as having invented playback singing by using hidden mikes on studio stages.

It appears that Himanshu Rai learned from this earlier debacle about hiring women with multicultural backgrounds, and when he met a young Anglo-Indian woman in Calcutta, Renee Smith, for a screen test, he convinced her to change her name to Seeta Devi. Renee was a daughter of a successful civil servant in the local colonial administration and she acted as Gautama Buddha's wife, Gopa, in her debut film, *Light of Asia* (1927). Seeta Devi became a national sensation, acting in several Bombay Talkies home productions where she played classical and mythological roles to adoring audiences. Likewise, Rachel Cohen (1917–1976) came from an Armenian Jewish background and left her career as a school teacher to become a hot-selling star in Mumbai's film studios as Ramola. Beryl Claessen (1913–1983) left her Anglo-Indian roots in Nainital for Mumbai in 1929 and rose to fame as Madhuri Devi under the patronage of Ranjit Studios. Perhaps, the most well-known example of an altered persona in early Indian cinema is Ruby Myers who was discovered as a telephone operator in Pune and went on to stellar fame as Sulochana earning a salary bigger than the Governor of Mumbai at the height of her youthful career and owning a fleet of Studebakers.

These altered personas and switched identities, despite all the fame and success involved, certainly suggest the ways in which women in early Indian cinema were shaped and moulded by dominant patriarchal ideas and images of Indian 'womanhood' and divested of their vibrant and real multicultural identities to assume others that were considered more 'respectable'. It is salutary to note that women actresses facing the early camera lights were performing, as Laura Mulvey (1975) notes in her feminist essay, Visual Pleasure and Narrative Cinema, as 'objects of spectacle' for a predominantly 'male gaze' since film spectatorship in India in the first part of the twentieth century, was an irrevocably gendered experience.[22] Their very presence on screen, in a newly invented medium like film, that seemed designed to elicit compelling projections from a psychic unconscious, was considered dangerous and risky by many in contemporary Indian society, and there was serious debate in several quarters if it should be allowed at all.

Film pioneers like Dadasaheb Phalke were openly outspoken in their opposition to women actresses and opinions changed in time only in accordance with the reality of an overwhelming popularity of women on stage. In an interview given to Lokmanya Tilak's Marathi paper *Kesari* on August 1919, Phalke (cited in Pande 2006: 1649) concedes the point but with serious reservations:

> It'd be better if female roles are enacted by women [...] god willing, if one day these prostitutes can be removed and replaced with women from good families, our studios will no longer be compared with whore houses and the prestige of the film-makers and their teams will be salvaged. Then it will no longer be embarrassing to see films accompanied by ones' mother [...] daughter or daughter-in-law [...] If, unfortunately, women with good characters ('charitravaan') [...] find their entry blocked by male wolves, I will request my sisters to stare them down and chase them away. If this is still not enough they should take to carrying sharp knives and use them in an emergency.[23]

And again, reiterating his case, notes the following:

> Women from good 'samskari' families alone should act in films. Brothers, how would you feel if Sita and Draupadi were to be played by someone who is in the habit of making [...] lewd eyes and has [...] a half-revealed bosom [...]? Women from good families will add a glow to the mythical devis and to the atmosphere in and around our studios. (Pande 2006: 1649)[24]

While Dadasaheb Phalke seems a bit short in his awareness of ways in which women in ancient India in fact dressed themselves, excelled in the erotic arts and were represented in their feminine sexuality on temple walls, his point about 'women actresses from good families' being welcomed in Indian cinema may go some ways in explaining why so many early actresses used classical Indian names to gain entry to a medium that was otherwise uniquely suitable in providing scope for their often considerable screen presences and performing talents. These adopted mythical identities were somehow part of the imaginary and fantasy world of Indian films and seemed not to have hindered a more real and undeniable process of multiculturalism underway in the early twentieth-century Indian film industry. Film studios like Bombay Talkies, Minerva Movietone (1936–1958), Wadia Movietone (1933–1941) and Ranjit Movietone, among many others, drew a motley crew of people of extraordinarily varied backgrounds from around the country to the world of film-making and not the least of these were women actresses who were somehow its most alluring and fascinating aspect for millions of new-born film-goers (Manto 2010).[25]

'Devis' as Pioneering Artist and Entrepreneurs in Indian Cinema

The emergence of women from the social margins and into centre stage of early films seems to have brought not only success for them as actresses but it also fuelled in many ambitions and dreams as film entrepreneurs, directors, music composers and art designers. Indeed, several of the earliest generation of actresses like Fatma Begum, Zubeida, Devika Rani, Sulochana, Pramila and Gohar Jan either launched their own film production companies at some point in their careers or partnered with men in production ventures. As early as 1926, Fatma Begum, for example, began producing and directing films under the banner of Fatma Films with unprecedented success. Her daughter, Zubeida, followed with Mahalakshmi Cinetone in partnership with Nanubhai Vakil in 1934 and produced the earliest fantasy films with women playing lead roles. In 1936, Sulochana/Ruby Myers had reached the pinnacle of her success as an actress and began producing independent films under the banner of Ruby Pictures with scripts often revolving around women-picaresque characters in a changing urban Mumbai landscape. Her contemporary, Pramila, launched Silver Productions in the midst of the Second World War and an economic recession in 1942, and went on to sustain the company with a series of 'action films'. After the end of the war, we find that actresses like Gohar Jan, Sardar Akhtar and Naseem Bano partnered successfully with men to form companies—Ranjit Studios, Mehboob Studios in 1950 and Taj Mahal Pictures in 1952.

It appears that film production was not the only area of interest for early actresses-entrepreneurs. Many who entered the new film industry from *tawaif* cultural contexts were already quite well known as singers, composers and musicians, and their decision to take up acting may even have been impelled by this earlier popularity. Some of the first recordings of songs in India were made by women artisans like Rattan Bai, Jaddan Bai, Wahidan Bai, Gohar Jan, Indu Bala, Amirbai Karnataki, Bibbo/Ishraq Sultana (1906–1972), Jahanara Kajjan and Noor Jehan, all of whom also ventured into films. With the advent of 'talkies' and sound technology, these singers/actresses were able to combine their talents and indeed helped launch an era of 'musicals' that soon became a norm for Indian cinema. The first sound films like *Alam Ara* (1931), *Indra Sabha* (1932) and *Laila Majnu* (1935) showcased actresses as singers, some of whom then turned independent music directors and producers. Perhaps, the most celebrated of these singer-entrepreneurs was Jaddan Bai who launched Sangeet Film Company in 1934 and produced *Talash-E-Haq* (1935) for which she wrote the music and also acted. In 1936, she produced, directed, acted and wrote music for *Madame Fashion*, a film that is noteworthy for her daughter, Nargis, as a child actor. Her contemporary, Bibbo/Ishrat Sultana was also an actress as well as singer and music composer and had already composed music for *Adl-E-Jahangir* in 1934 making her the first woman music director and composer in the Indian film industry.

A common feature of these business ventures seems to be that they were launched by women largely for the sake of expanding their possibilities as artists and performers rather than for simple financial opportunity. It was primarily a matter of establishing creative autonomy over a new medium—films—which in many ways was not so different from earlier entertainment industries. Certainly, we learn from Veena Talwar Oldenburg's (1990) research and findings that women from *tawaif* backgrounds in Indian cities were quite accustomed to running their artisan households like well-governed cohesive business ventures or 'companies'. The film industry, despite its obvious control by male entrepreneurs, then, offered these women possibilities for further autonomy as producers and directors in the wake of their often remarkable successes as actresses and performers.

By the same token, actresses like Devika Rani, Sulochana and Pramila, who entered the early film production business, much like their *tawaif* counterparts, were also seeking space for their independent visions of

Indian films and creative scope for their skills as actors, scriptwriters, costume designers and set choreographers. Women with education and working backgrounds represented an emerging modern subcontinental woman who could step across a diverse social field and contain contrasting cultural identities in herself even if at the imaginal and archetypal level of the world of cinema. The potency of this 'anima' archetype to reach out beyond the screen and gradually take shape for women of an emerging post-colonial Indian society is perhaps a sign of deeper imaginaries here at work under the surface of a docile and homogeneous feminine social façade. Certainly, the early actress-turned-producer and entrepreneur could constellate private dreams of Indian women by first casting them into bold reality.

In view of the aforementioned, then, it may be of interest to look briefly into the lives and careers of some of these actress-entrepreneur women in early Indian cinema. By doing so, one may gain a sense of who they were as real women in a changing society and how they came into films or managed to create extraordinary careers at a time when opportunities for women in the working world were virtually non-existent. Perhaps, most significantly for our purposes, bringing light to their individual lives—now almost entirely shrouded in obscurity—could help to illuminate the imagination and mythology of soul which these early actresses once brought to their screen personas. For, as we shall see, the images of women they presented in film—no matter how influenced by directors, producers and the demands of market—remained ultimately self-imaginings and figurative expressions of their own inner fantasy lives. As such, their 'real' lives—often poignant and tragic in experience—provided a field of rich metaphors and symbols for imaging the women characters in their films. Certainly, this would have been more so in cases where such actresses were able to engage directly with their screen roles also as directors, producers, set designers and even as scriptwriters.

It is for this reason that the actresses chosen below for biographical review represent mostly women who did manage to find a degree of creative autonomy and self-expression in early Indian films, albeit against all odds. It may seem unlikely that such enclaves of feminine agency and power could have emerged in a nascent industry—especially, as we have seen, women were perceived as such a threat to the 'respectability' of films from the start. However, even cursory glimpses into the circumstances and lives of early actresses may help account for their unusual rise to fame: each one, in her own way, seemed able to bring to the light of screen an elusive quality of presence without which the emerging cinema in

India could only have remained lifeless and incomplete—its 'anima'. It is this imaginal presence expressed on screen in luminous ways that can be explored in some depth by discovering who these actresses were as individuals and how they shaped their personal destinities in a time and a place when women had little access to their dreaming souls.

On- and Off-screen 'Devis': Entangled Personas and Life Histories

Fatma Begum (1892–1983)

Fatma Begum, like Jahanara Kajjan, also came to early Indian cinema of the 'silent movies' from *tawaif* cultural contexts—here, in the *kothas* of Sachin in Gujarat. Her family roots seem to be embedded in the women performers of this royal court, and she was herself romantically involved with Nawab Sidi Ibrahim Yakut Khan III of Sachin with whom she had three daughters. Fatma and her daughters, Zubeida, Sultana and Shehzadi entered films as part of their professional upbringing as performers, singers and dancers. Fatma began her career, like many other women of her times, in the Urdu theatre industry and entered films in the 1920s (The Cinema Resource Center 2013). She first acted in Ardeshir Irani's silent film *Veer Abhimanyu* (1922), but very soon established her own film production company, Victoria-Fatma Films in 1926 (Khurana 2010)—not unusual as Vikram Sampath's (2010) path-breaking documentation of the life and times of Gauhar Jaan of Calcutta, and Katherine Butler Brown's (2006) historical survey of the development of *tawaif* cultures from the nineteenth century into the modern era, already indicated that women performers ran their own enterprises and only employed men as musicians for their often lavish entourage.

Fatma Begum's multitasking venture into film production, direction, scriptwriting and acting as well as singing was therefore not so radical in the eyes of many, although it certainly set a precedent in the newly born film industry. Her first independent film was *Bulbul-E-Paristan* (1926), a fantasy tale set in a *Paristan*, where a queen must restore order in her world by use of her special magic powers. These include her special ability to charm and spellbind aggressors from other worlds—demons—who know little about refinement of art and culture. The film used special effects showing aerial warfare between fairies and demons and involved some deft camerawork on the part of the director. It was also a significant film for its almost entirely feminine cast and for featuring a fantasy world—*Paristan*—inhabited by women (*Pariyan* [fairies]), where rules and codes are based on freedom from 'earthly' control and on the principle of love. In this feminine society, the solitary male presence is of a *Bulbul* (nightingale) whose longing reaches beyond his mortality and ends in a union of lovers that is also a meeting of realms.

Fatma Begum's choice of a Persian tale for her film instead of the Hindu mythological material used by her male precursors was remarkable for the ways that it first opened up rich imaginal fields from India's multicultural Parsi and Armenian communities and drew them into popular focus on screen. In fact, *Bulbul-E-Paristan* began a new genre of fantasy films such as *Alladin and the Wonderful Lamp* (1931), *Afghan Abla* (1931) and *Alam Ara*, all produced by Fatma Begum's colleague and friend, Ardeshir Irani. Fatma went on to direct and produce nine more films between the years 1926 and 1929. These were hugely successful as fantasy romances in their time and were shot in lavish sets. Perhaps, the most popular of these were *Goddess of Love* (1927), *Shakuntala* (1929), *Heer Ranjha* (1928) and *Chandravali* (1928). A common strain in these films is their lead feminine characters drawn from classical literature and of women as lovers facing trials in a social context that would judge and banish them based on conventional morality. Each character ends by perfectly transcending her fate. It is perhaps easy to see the 'courtesan' archetype emerging here in the imagery of mythic characters and defined as someone with the power to change a soulless, limiting, world with her magical presence and art.

Certainly, Fatma's films were visually crafted to display their leading women in all their erotic charge with exotic costumes and facial close-ups—a feature that Bollywood has incorporated into its films ever since. They are, above all, reflexive in quality—made by courtesans about women like themselves mirrored through the lens of imagination and fantasy as long-lost princesses, fairies and mythic lovers. Through a mesh of intrigues, betrayals and rivalries, the films explore possibilities of feminine love in its sensual and artistic aspects.

Fatma Begum's daughter, Zubeida, also became a successful actress in the 1920s, acting in films like *Veer Abhimanyu*, *Kala Chor* (1925), *Desh Ka Dushman* (1925) and in her mother's films. Her most popular film was *Alam Ara*—India's first 'talkie'—in which she played a gypsy girl, Alam Ara, whose songs enchant a young prince and lead him to win her through several trials and adventures. The story, written by Joseph David, a Parsi playwright, is like a dream sequence cast in forests, where secret lovers meet in caverns and are separated by dark forces. The place of fantasy and imagination is paramount here as aspects of the psychic unconscious are bared to the surface and expressed through images charged with erotic energy. Zubeida is cast boldly in the shadows in gypsy dress with her body leaning into her lover or sitting semi-clothed before a mirror. As she emerges from the shadows into light, like the 'anima', she discovers that her 'real' identity is of a lost princess whose father was cast into prison by a rival queen, Dilbahar. It ends well for this 'gypsy princess' and her prince as it did in real life for Zubeida. She married a prince, Maharaj Dhanrajgir, of Hyderabad and left the film industry in 1949 at the height of her fame and glory.

Ruby Myers/Sulochana (1907–1983)

The rise and fall of Ruby Myers/Sulochana in Indian film history is like a classic Bollywood movie in itself with all the ingredients of high drama, adventure, romantic love, comedy verging on farce and tragic denouement. She came from a Baghdadi Jewish family in Pune and worked as a telephone operator in Mumbai when a film director, Mohan Bhavnani, of Kohinoor Films spotted her and offered a lead role in an action film, *Veer Bala* (1924; Majumdar 2009).[26] Reluctant at first to take on films, Ruby Myers relented and played a daredevil superwoman who could rescue people in distress by jumping off cliffs, flying, riding fast horses and landing on rooftops. This role was about as far as one could get from Dadasaheb Phalke's notions of Indian womanhood, but its daring conception and successful delivery in theatres across India suggests that images of femininity and gender roles were undergoing genuine change with the emerging urban environments of cities like Calcutta, Delhi and Mumbai (Weinbaum et al. 2008).

In many ways, Ruby Myers' film 'persona' in *Veer Bala* and succeeding films resembles her *tawaif* counterpart and contemporary in her independence and subaltern identity. However, it also foreshadows a feminine modernity that would soon enter into Indian cinema and generate tensions between the keenness of nostalgia for a traditional social order as part of a nationalist agenda and anticipation of something quite different ahead in terms of what becoming a nation in a global context could really envision. Interestingly, it is mainly through the imagining lens of feminine identities that Indian cinema seems to conduct this uneasy dialogue with sovereignty and change. An actress like Sulochana could capture the spirit of an upcoming urban and urbane feminine world in colonial India of the 1930s with her sophistication, wit, self-assurance and visibly cross-cultural appearance. She also exuded a sense of ease and sexuality on screen that seemed to exceed the demands of a film script and was at once disconcertingly 'other' and liberating for her captive audiences. This feminine self-presence seemed to draw upon mysterious and hidden reserves of power that verged on the archetypal and extraordinary. As a reviewer of her films noted in 1933: 'She appears to have marched straight out of the classic world of the ancients even to have paced down from the olympian Goddesses themselves' (Majumdar 2009: 101). J.B.H. Wadia describes her in his memoirs as 'easily the most beautiful woman to adorn the Indian screen' with a 'magnetism' and 'seduction' in her eyes (ibid.: 100).[27]

In her next film, *Cinema Queen* (1925), Sulochana plays an imaginary version of herself—a glamorous film actress—who inspires a young painter to return to his art by becoming his muse. We see her through his eyes as the camera lingers and explores a persona who seems charged from within and need do nothing more than be herself to impact and transform others. Her worldly success and cosmopolitan lifestyle are an important part of her appeal, but these are seen as trappings beyond which the 'real' woman emerges as a person who can befriend a suicidal man and bring him back to life. The film plays with the tensions between aspirations for a new and emerging Indian Dream of wealth and dreams of another kind: artistic life, worship of beauty, and love. Sulochana's movie-star persona is larger than life in the ways that she can transgress the moral conventions of her society and rise to power on the strength of ambition—the world of films, the film suggests, makes this fantasy possible for all.

In her next film, *Telephone Girl*, Sulochana played a young modern gal about town with a fantasy life involving bank robbers, heists, cops and a suave lover, played by Dinshaw Billimoria, who could salvage any situation. This urban myth showed the life of a city like Mumbai in the early decades of the twentieth century with its fast-paced action and unusual cast of characters. Perhaps, the most popular film with Sulochana in the lead was *Wild Cat of Bombay* (1927) in which she played eight different parts including a street brat, a banana seller, a European blonde, a sly gardener and a Hyderabadi gentleman. This film was remade as *Bambai Ki Billi* (1936) to full sound effects and songs and had people stamping in the aisles. Sulochana had arrived changing the face of modern Indian women in a global age.

Her last film, *Anarkali* (1928/1932), was a box-office success and shot Sulochana to the height of her fame leading to an extravagant lifestyle that kept her in the news. In 1939, she launched her own film company, Ruby Pictures, and began producing films in alliance with her lover, Dinshaw Billimoria. However, the ventures were risky and as quickly as her star had risen so did it fall. If anything, Sulochana/Ruby Myers may have had almost too much imagination and ambition for her times and could not sustain her dreams. A fact that is revealing and sheds some light on her personal courage is that she continued to produce films even as she had lost her entire fortune. She continued to act in minor roles till the early 1970s but died in isolation and in penury in 1983.

Devika Rani Chaudhri (1908–1994)

Devika Rani may be considered the first superstar of Indian cinema starring in some of its first major and international productions. Her rise to fame, in many ways, paralleled the rise of the film industry itself which, even in early silent films, showed the power of visual images on screen to mesmerise audiences. The camera, under the directorship of Franz Osten, closing in on Devika Rani's face as she leans over Himanshu Rai in a languorous kiss in the film *Karma* (1933), seemed designed for its voyeuristic purpose and to hold the fascinated gaze of thousands upon its object of desire. Devika Rani was quite aware of the new film medium having studied film-making in Berlin with Fritz Lang in 1929 and with Max Reinhardt in Austria, and she used its possibilities to her advantage on screen (Manjapra 2014).[28] Her slow movements, facial expressions, costume and appearance were crafted for maximum visual impact: one could think of Devika as an artiste who developed a conscious methodology for acting in films at a time when others in the Indian film industry were still struggling with their transitions from the worlds of Parsi and other indigenous theatres or careers as live performers.

Devika Rani's entrance into films was quite unusual for her time since she came not from the margins of Indian society like many *tawaif* but from its highest ranks of intellectual elite. Her father, Col Manmatha Nath Chaudhri, was the first Indian Surgeon-General of Madras Presidency, and she was related to the poet Rabindranath Tagore (1861–1941) from her paternal grandmother's side. She spent her childhood and adult years in England and studied acting, music, interior design, architecture and couture in London (Jaikumar 2006).[29] One might think of her as the kind of woman that Dadasaheb Phalke would have approved of as an actress for the early Indian film industry but, family pedigree to the contrary, she broke with every convention of social 'respectability' during her reign in films, deconstructing the image and myth of chaste Indian womanhood, both on- and off-screen.

Devika Rani's screen persona, for example, and the images she projected of women in films, reflected the uneasy ambivalences and paradoxes of her own cross-cultural identity. At once anchored in the old-nineteenth-century aristocratic identities of Bengal and in modern urban London of the early 1900s, she was both Indian and English, with a cosmopolitan European sensibility for the fine arts and a rare passion for film-making. This tension and irony between worlds that Devika carried in her personal life is visible and tangible in all her films like *Karma* (1933), *Jawani Ki Hawa*, *Jeevan Naiya* (1936) and *Achhut Kanya* (1936). In these films, she appears on screen dressed like an Indian woman with traditional costumes, jewellery and attire, but in fact her bearing, make-up, short hair, her crisp dialogue delivery, sexual candour in kissing scenes and erotic charge, all suggest someone quite elusive to the spectator's gaze.

The allure and mystique of Devika Rani's film 'persona' in her vintage films are perhaps reminiscent of Greta Garbo and verges on the archetypal in transcending determined cultural categories, gender boundaries and fixed historical time frames. She seems to embody in her singular screen presence, the emerging complexities of modern Indian women as they straddled the weight of traditional roles and stepped into new possibilities of personal freedom in the increasingly urbanised Indian environments and a global age. In this respect, it seems that Devika Rani's imaginaries foreshadow deeper issues of modernity and identity confronting Indian women later in the twentieth century. In the depth of field of her classic film frames, there seems expressed a feminine individuality—a person as a promise, of someone unknown and mysterious, yet familiar, who may only now in the twenty-first century be coming into accomplishment of fact for many.

Devika Rani's real-life story was in fact as complex and as mysterious as her screen 'persona'. She had met Himanshu Rai, a young rebel with a cause, in London where Rai was exploring film-making. Recently graduated from the Royal Academy of Dramatic Arts (RADA), Devika collaborated with him and Niranjan Pal (1887–1957), an avant-garde playwright in London, on the production of *A Throw of the Dice* (1928). Rai's earlier film, *Light of Asia*, had been a popular success with showings in London, Europe and in India (Saran 2014).[30] Their creative partnership, with Devika as Himanshu Rai's set designer and choreographer, turned into a full-scale relationship and marrying her. Rai launched Bombay Talkies film company with Devika Rani as co-producer and co-actor.

Rai and Rani's Bombay Talkies was in fact India's first real production company with indoor studios and a contracted international staff of artists, writers, music composers, directors and cinematographers (Purohit 1988).[31] The early scripts for Bombay Talkies were clearly written with Devika in mind and showcased her considerable talents as portraying women of substance—often with characters who defy an existing social status quo. In *Karma*, for example, she plays a princess who falls in love with a neighbouring prince but is rejected by her lover's father, a tyrannical king. She wins her lover in a test of strength where she proves herself to the king. In *Achhut Kanya*, she plays a lower-caste woman who falls in love with a Brahmin boy and reveals her moral superiority as a woman to the local villagers. In *Jeevan Prabhat* (1937), she takes on the role of an older upper-caste woman who is accused of marital infidelity with a younger and untouchable man.

Like her character in *Jeevan Prabhat*, Devika entered into a romantic relationship with her lover and co-star, Najm-ul-Hassan, of *Jawani Ki Hawa*. This film, a crime thriller shot on a train about two eloping lovers, had the lead actors eloping in real life to Calcutta and moving into the Grand Hotel until Himanshu Rai was able to persuade Devika to return and salvage Bombay Talkies from near-bankruptcy (Pande 2006: 1648).[32] She agreed but only after signing a contract that would pay her wages as an employed actor and assure her financial independence from Himanshu Rai. When Rai died a few years later in 1940, she assumed the control of Bombay Talkies and went on to produce and act in films like *Anjaan* (1941), *Basant* (1942) and *Kismet* (1943). This last film was hugely successful for its covert nationalist themes and music, but it also featured an anti-hero and conman 'pickpocket' as the central protagonist and dealt openly with themes of illicit love.

Devika's running of Bombay Talkies in 1940 and her artistic control over the company's productions were not without its detractors, and she was often referred to as the Dragon Lady of Indian Cinema (Bhattacharya 2012). However, fellow actresses and women producers like Pramila and Renuka Devi perceived Devika's reign differently. In a letter addressed to Devika discovered recently in the Dietz Family Archives in Australia, Pramila writes:

> I am proud to say that you have shown that a lady in India too can be entirely capable of holding supreme sway. We can now say without hesitation that

> we have a queen in our midst. Devika—women—all women should be proud that you have won your way and [...] that is how it will be in your future struggles too [...] I have always been your admirer and on screen you are still my favorite. (Dietz Family Archives 1998: 8)[33]

A growing factionalism within Bombay Talkies over commercial cinema and art brought things to a head and in 1945, facing opposition from investors and a new generation of film-makers, Devika Rani resigned from her company. She had met Svetoslav Roerich, a painter and son of Nicholas Roerich, and together they moved first to Manali and then to Bangalore (Katz 2014).[34] Like Greta Garbo, Devika Rani chose a self-imposed exile from the world of cinema—a world that she had once helped co-create with Himanshu Rai but which she felt increasingly alienated from for its loss of artistic vision and integrity in changing times. She died almost half a century later in 1994, a forgotten legend.

Jahanara Kajjan Bai: 'Lark of India' (1915–1945)

This actress/singer was Devika Rani's contemporary and enjoyed great popularity across India till her early death. However, unlike Devika, Jahanara Kajjan's origins were in the *tawaif* circles of old India from where many of the early actresses in Indian cinema actually came. It seems that Kajjan was the daughter of a renowned *tawaif* called Suggan who was the mistress of a feudal lord, Nawab Chammi Saheb of Bhagalpur (Pande 2006: 1651).[35] Jahanara Kajjan began her career in the Parsi and Urdu theatres of Patna in the late 1920s when women performers were being first allowed on stage. Prior to this time, these indigenous theatres presented live plays—often of the highest quality—but the actors could only be men as in Elizabethan stage. The advent of women actresses on stage and in early silent movies was nothing short of revolutionary and could cause a stampede. Recognising the potential of women actresses and singers for drawing mass audiences to these theatres, producers began hiring them both individually and in small troupes. Jahanara Kajjan's 'knife dances' during the intermissions of silent movies became regular crowd-pullers and she was hired by Jamshed Madan, heir to his father's film company in Calcutta, to act in his first sound film production *Shirin Farhad* (1931; Neville 2015).

Kajjan's screen presence seems to have been electric and her celebrated beauty brought a mythic quality to *Shirin*, the tragic Persian princess of legend who died unattained by her lover, *Farhad*. In opulent sets, reminiscent of a fantasy homeland imagined by Parsi-Indian movie-makers like J.J. Madan, Jahanara Kajjan seemed to bring a lost world to life in image and song. Her classically trained voice, singing plaintive *thumris* (classical Hindustani short vocal pieces) was a significant part of her film 'persona' and her songs from *Shirin Farhad* were soon being recorded by His Masters' Voice in Calcutta (ibid.).[36] A published Urdu poet herself, Jahanara collaborated with Agha Hashar Kashmiri (1879–1935) on lyrics for this film, which was based on the work of Persian poet, Nizami Ganjavi (1149–1209). In 1932, she acted in *Laila Majnu*, another Madan production of Nizami's famous poem of tragic lovers and sang the classical songs that became so popular that they helped forge the lighter *geet* of later films. In the same year, only 17 years old, she was cast in her most popular film, *Indra Sabha*. This fantasy opera film had over 70 songs and was based on an Urdu play by the renowned playwright Agha Hassan Amanat (1815–1858) (Trivedi 2010).[37] Her performance as Sabz Pari, the celestial fairy who falls in love with a mortal prince and wins his release from a jealous Indra with artful magic of her poetry and song was one of the early blockbusters of Indian cinema.

It seems that Jahanara Kajjan's personal life was no less than the stuff of myth and legend. Like Devika Rani, she lived openly with her partners of choice and moved freely across cultural milieus in cosmopolitan Calcutta of the 1930s. Her proclivity for Western dance and music made her popular at the exclusive Calcutta Club where she performed regularly for the English ruling elite with a fellow artist, Mahjabeen, even as she also recorded classic *thumris* in chaste Urdu for major labels and acted in Hindi films (Neville 2015). In her late twenties, she ventured into film production when one of Calcutta's richest men, Seth Karnani, bought the film company, Madan Theatres, as a personal gift for Jahanara Kajjan in exchange for her love (Adil 2011).[38] At the peak of her career in 1940, she withdrew for a few years to her estate outside of Calcutta in the company of her pet tigers and composed books of Urdu poetry recorded in her legendary singing voice. She returned in 1944 with another popular film, *Bharthari* (1944), followed by *Prarthana* (1943) and *Mumtaz Mahal* in 1945. Both these films remain classics for their songs and *ragas*. She died under mysterious circumstances at the age of 30 in 1945, and her rich patron and lover died soon after in the following year.

Even a brief glance at Jahanara Kajjan's biography suggests a life saturated with poetry, dance, music and song, and a unique cultural environment that could make this possible in the early years of Indian cinema. It seems obvious that her origins in courtly *tawaif* contexts infused early skills in the performing arts as well as a certain feminine mystique that gave a distinctive depth of field to the characters she played on screen. In her films, as in real life, Kajjan remained elusive—a person only seemingly mortal but in fact invested with the life of an archetype. Despite passionate romances with men both on- and off-screen, the quality she embodied in herself was of someone married to a life of art and culture and therefore firmly existing outside the purview of conventional feminine domesticity. This is perhaps most obvious in her performance as Sabz Pari in *Indra Sabha* where she wins a battle of moral superiority over Indra in heaven by singing a succession of classical *thumris* of surpassing beauty (Rosen 1892).

The theme of love and 'eros' as a spiritual aspiration transcending social codes and political power is an important feature of both of Nizami Ganjavi's classics, *Laila and Majnun* and *Shirin and Farhad* (Ganjavi 1997). Over centuries, these entered into popular mythic lore across an entire region extending from Iran to the Indian subcontinent. Here, they became an important part of early twentieth-century Parsi and Urdu theatre repertoire with scriptwriters like Agha Hashar Kashmiri blending a mix of Nizami's Persian poetry and popular literary styles. When J.J. Madan, the owner of Madan Theatres, cast Jahanara Kajjan in film versions of both classics in 1931 and 1932, he knew that she could embody the soul of these female lovers on screen not only with her star presence but also with an imaginal and ethereal quality that verged on myth. This quality that Kajjan brought to *Shirin* and *Laila* gave their film characters a perceptible freedom from lovers, husbands and from the rules of society even as they were portrayed as objects of possession and of erotic desire. Ironically, Kajjan's personal freedom as a woman in early twentieth-century Indian society and her transcendence into a world of lived poetry and music were part and parcel of her *tawaif* lineage: as a child of a royal courtesan, her foremost allegiance was to her art. It is to this goal that she was brought up with diligence in a feminine household and it is art that seems to have brought her real power. The name she adopted for herself, Jahanara (Empress of the World), was perhaps not accidental but reflected a sense of her own unique identity and soul as a woman artist in society.

It is this mysterious identity of the artist as woman, imagined in her films in a cast of royal maidens, celestial fairies, queens and goddesses, that emerges on screen and is captured here both visually and as a song. The mythic, literary and complex romantic storylines, choreography, set designs, even the sophisticated use of camera by directors like Georgio Mannini, Camille Le Grand and Eugenio De Liguoro, seem to be ultimately only foils for another purpose. Through such a mix of cinematic elements, the artist's already charged presence has been underscored and highlighted on screen as visual image and sound. Even the pace and length of films like *Indra Sabha*, *Bharthari* and *Prarthana* seem to be adapted to accommodate Jahanara's langorous physical presence and her meditative renderings of *thumris* and *khayals* with the drama of action serving somewhat as interstice to this soulful main event.

The response of audiences to Jahanara's performance on screen became a measure of her acknowledgment and recognition as an artist in early Indian cinema. She was sought after by leading production houses like Minerva Movietone (*Prarthana*) and helped sustain Madan Theatres during the war years (Joshi 2014). Her decision to withdraw from films at the peak of her career may seem mysterious but it is also consistent with the spirit of the music and art that she embodied in films—commercial success meant little without the time and space to develop her soul-craft. There is evidence that she trained rigorously in music for four years before returning to films in 1943 (Adil 2011). Her popularity in films like *Bharthari* and *Mumtaz Mahal* was stronger than ever, and the songs she sang here remain classics to this day. In light of this, her death at the age of 30 is inexplicable and adds to the mystery of a woman artist who chose to remain an 'outsider' to the end.

Conclusion

The medium of films in its use of images indicates strong similarities to the ways these can function in dreams, imagination, myth and fantasy—in psyche—as understood by Carl Gustav Jung. Images in cinema, as in Jungian psychoanalytical perspectives, are not intended to be factual representations but are figurative and imaginative expressions carrying emotional 'charge' that can directly involve audiences as participatory 'subjects' engaged in creating their image-based 'realities'—'soul-making'. It may be obvious from the very varied, colourful and different actresses of the early Indian cinema treated here that these were not women who conformed to any fixed notions or ideals of femininity, but were able to successfully use the medium of films by imagining and imaging 'feminine selves'.

Their film 'personas' like the identities they forged, both on- and off-screen, certainly reveal a lot about them as women with distinct histories and very discernible roots in an earlier Indian century. This is most obvious, as we have seen, for those women film actresses who came from *tawaif* backgrounds and a dying feudal patriarchal world of courtly entertainments, bearing the treasures of music, dance and finer arts with them. Even so, Indian cinema, like the new century it betokened, represented an open-ended 'future': it brought productive work, economic independence, entrepreneurial opportunities, artistic expression and released a whole force field of desires and imaginaries into society such that things could never be the same again. The actress had arrived, though initially actresses were given Hindu names with the suffix of 'devi' in a bid to facilitate their social acceptance by producers, while at the same time they opened up undreamed areas of feminine imagination where women could claim themselves in society as nothing less than goddesses indeed.

Bollywood's continuing story through the shifting decades of the twentieth century and beyond has certainly kept women actresses in front stage with colourful singing roles, dances and visually fantasy-like impact. Gender roles and stereotypes were reconfigured in various way, for example, juxtaposing supposedly 'good', decent, homely and most importantly marriageable women and lascivious 'item-girls' in the latter part of the twentieth century before more women-centred main-stream films emerged in the early twenty-first century—reflecting changing positions of women in society. However, despite the advances made in the emergence of women in public spheres, new structures of urbanism and post-modernist explorations of gender roles, the questions regarding individual, artistic and economic sovereignty still remain very open-ended. Perhaps, these early women in Indian cinema, unlikely 'devis' and 'divas' as they were, could help illuminate the present by showing what was once made possible.

Notes

1. This biography by Bapu Vatave is most notable for details regarding the first films like *Mohini Bhasmasur* (1913), *Satyavan Savitri* (1914) and lesser known ventures like *Lanka Dahan* (1917) and *Kaliya Mardan* (1919). His analysis of *Raja Harishchandra* (1925) seems rather cryptic focusing more on technical aspects to the exclusion of social and cultural angles important to this first full-length film.

2. Irani's use of sound technology such as hidden mikes and grips and controlled studio environment seem real innovations for the time. As well, Irani's use of songs in generous measure for *Alam Ara* seems to have launched an early trend in Indian cinema.
3. The 'race' for making the first 'talkie' involved J.J. Madan and Ardeshir Irani as contenders across the subcontinent. Madan was influenced by his viewing of *Jazz Singer* in New York and spent some time in Hollywood learning sound technology.
4. According to Sharma (2012), Ranjit Studios had over 700 employees in the 1960s. Actresses like Madhuri and Sulochana, among many others, were under contract to Ranjit. Chandulal Shah, the owner of Ranjit Studios, was in partnership to his wife, Gohar Jan, a singer and actress with origins in Gujarati *tawaif* cultural contexts.
5. The roots of Bombay Talkies in Mumbai seem to have been in faraway places like London and Berlin where Himanshu Rai conceived of a production company with state-of-the-art technology and an international staff of scriptwriters (Niranjan Pal), directors (Franz Osten, J.J. Freer Hunt), camera staff and financial investors (Sir Richard Temple, Governor of Mumbai, Emelka Cojern and others).
6. The infamous *kothas* of cities like Lucknow and Lahore were collective matriarchal establishments, where women ran an alternative society based on shared economy and use of resources. They often employed men as artisans and musicians and paid them generously.
7. Kinsley's understanding of 'goddess traditions' across the Indian subcontinent seems focused primarily on *Shakta tantric* (feminine cosmic power) contexts.
8. Izod's analysis on emotion-laden imagery in films and their psychoanalytic implications as 'dreamscapes' is especially pertinent with regard to early Indian cinema which relied exclusively on strong and theatrical images to communicate with audiences.
9. The role of imagination and fantasy in Jung's formulation of *Psyche* has been well established, but what is of particular interest here is the creative part that fantasy and images play in the process of 'self-individuation'.
10. Jung's emphasis on 'images' as irreducible elements of psychic production is perhaps comparable to the way the films use images as 'semes' in narrative constructs.
11. Izod's understanding of the power of emotions in film discourse is in line with Jungian concepts of 'affect' and 'cathexis'.
12. Buñuel's emphasis on the role of 'symbol' in his films is especially pertinent to the place of myth and archetypal imagery in earlier Indian films.
13. Hillman's project of 'revisioning' psychology by focusing on 'image' takes its inspiration from Jung's basic prescription and seems consistent to the end even when it leads to a 'polymorphic' view of psyche as a domain of many imagined 'gods' and 'goddesses'. Many would argue that this contradicts Jung's focus on the 'monotheistic' 'self' archetype.
14. Polikoff understands the myth of *Orpheus* as 'soul-making' by taking the poetry of images as self-expressive modes.
15. Hillman's emphasis on the primacy of 'images' in *psyche* may endow an inextricable archetypal and mythic constituency to them—'images' are 'gods' in themselves.
16. Oldenburg's ground-breaking study of *tawaif* households in Lucknow traces tax records and documentation in colonial archives that establish the role of these women in enriching the local economies while maintaining their independence from state structures of control.

17. Kesavan's analysis of the role of the *tawaif* in courtly cultures may seem discontinuous with the entry of women into early cinema, but, in fact, strong elements of these courtly contexts remain through the introduction of poetic modes like *geet* (popular songs) or *ghazals* in films.
18. After 1857, it seems that the British civil administration forcefully usurped assets of many *tawaif* households and coerced these women to 'register' as 'prostitutes' for services to local cantonments.
19. A detailed description of the environments of *Parsi* and *Urdu* theatres is provided, and the monopoly during the development of these theatres seems to have been the introduction of real women actresses. The first performances were stormy both for audiences and for the producers who had to contend with challenges that seemed to go to the core of cultural communities.
20. Ramamurthy makes an excellent case for the emergence of the 'city girl' trope in Indian films and urban actresses who played such roles. The case of Sulochana/Ruby Myers is dealt with here in some detail.
21. Pande quotes from an interview where Khorshid describes a whole movement in Parsi communities against the entry of women. The most vociferous voice to this argument was the Parsi paper *Jam-e-Jamshed*, which forced the women entering theatres to change their names and take on Hindu pseudonyms.
22. Mulvey's feminist analysis of how women were viewed as 'objects' is still considered groundbreaking, although it has catalysed decades of debate in Marxist and Jungian circles.
23. Tilak's paper, *Kesari,* was a vehicle for many debates regarding the entry of women into theatres and films.
24. Phalke seems to have been a realist and argued not for banning women from films but for their 'respectability'!
25. Manto documents the entry of actresses, scriptwriters, spot boys and assorted workers into the Indian film industry in great detail. His intimate knowledge of leading actresses in the decades of the 1930s and 1940s and their embroilments in 'scandals' is without parallel.
26. Majumdar devotes a whole chapter to Sulochana and her colourful career in Indian films.
27. Wadia's fascination of Sulochana seems to have had perilous results for his later film productions as her star waned.
28. Manjapra documents the presence of Devika Rani and Himanshu Rai in Germany in the early twentieth century. He also follows the careers of German director, Franz Osten, in Bombay Talkies in India before the Second World War.
29. Devika Rani's entry into films was made easier by her family environment which was decidedly artistic and literary. Tagore's influence seems to have been seminal in her decision to travel to England for film studies.
30. This encyclopaedia gives some basic information about Rani's pursuit of fashion design and couture in the London years while also shedding light on her friendship with Niranjan Pal, the celebrated playwright.
31. Niranjan Pal's involvement with films and theatre in urban London seems to have been decisive in Himanshu Rai and Devika Rani's increased fascination with producing films in India.
32. Pande offers some details of negotiations between Kishore Kumar and Himanshu Rai with regards to Devika Rani's return from Calcutta to Mumbai.

33. A rare compilation of correspondence between Devika Rani and her colleagues that sheds light on the inner climate of Bombay Talkies in the 1930s and 1940s. The letters were claimed by Himanshu Rai's first wife who had moved to Australia and by her son and heir.
34. A brief biography of the artist and painter, Roerich, who lived in India for the better part of his life. His father, Nicholas Roerich, was a painter and influenced by Gurdjieff's philosophy.
35. Pande documents the early life of Jahanara Kajjan and her origins in courtly Patna.
36. Neville claims that Madan saw her perform on Parsi stage and was convinced that she could be in his next 'talkie'. Her command of singing and dancing had a lot to do with this notion.
37. Playwrights like Amanat were a vital part of Awadhi court performances. Wajid Ali Shah, the ruler of Awadh, was himself a reputed singer and poet.
38. Adil's article documents the relationship between Seth Karnani, an important businessman in Calcutta, and Jahanara Kajjan.

References

Adil, Omer. 2011. 'Here Comes the Punjab Mail'. *The Friday Times*, 23 (10). Accessed on 20 December 2015 at http://www.thefridaytimes.com/22042011/page16.shtml

Avens, Robert. 1980. 'James Hillman: Towards a Poetic Psychology'. *Journal of Religion and Health* 19 (3): 186–200.

Bhattacharya, Sayan. 2012. 'Devika Rani: Thunderbird'. *Kindle: Ideas Imagination, Dialectics*. Accessed on 5 January 2016 at http//www.kindlemag.in

Brown, Katherine Butler. 2006. 'If Music Be the Food of Love: Masculinity and Eroticism in the Mughal "Mehfil"'. In *Love in South Asia: A Cultural History*, edited by Francesca Orsini, 61–83. Cambridge: University of Cambridge Oriental Publications.

Cobb, Noel. 1992. *Archetypal Imagination: Glimpses of the Gods in Life and Art*. Hudson, NY: Lindisfarne Press.

Dietz Family Archives. 1998. 'Letter No. 62'. In *Pramila—Esther Victoria Abraham*, edited by Roshan G. Shahani, 135–76. Mumbai: Sound and Picture Archives for Research on Women [SPARROW].

Ganjavi, Nizami. 1997. *Layla and Majnun: The Classic Love Story of Persian Literature by Nizami Ganjavi*. London: John Blake Publications.

Hillman, James. 1975. *Re-Visioning Psychology*. New York, NY: Harper and Row.

Izod, John. 2001. *Myth, Mind and the Screen: Understanding the Heroes of our Times*. Cambridge: Cambridge University Press.

Jaikumar, Priya. 2006. *Cinema at the End of Empire: A Politics of Transition in Britain and India*. North Carolina: Duke University Press.

Joshi, Namrata. 2014. 'Smoke on the Bioscope: Film and Theatre'. Accessed on 20 December 2015 at http//www.outlookindia.com

Jung, Carl Gustav. (1954) 1970. 'On the Nature of the Psyche'. In *The Collected Works of C. G. Jung, Vol. 8: The Structure and Dynamics of the Psyche*, edited by Gerhard Adler and R.F.C. Hull, pp. 159–236 (Bollingen Series XX). Princeton, NJ: Princeton University Press.

Jung, Carl Gustav. (1921) 2014a. 'Definitions', In *The Collected Works of C. G. Jung, Vol. 6: Psychological Types*, edited by Gerhard Adler and R.F.C. Hull, pp. 408–86 (Bollingen Series). Princeton and Oxford: Princeton University Press.

———. (1931) 2014b. 'The Practical Use of Dream Analysis'. In *The Collected Works of C. G. Jung, Vol. 16: The Practice of Psychotherapy*, edited by Gerhard Adler and R.F.C. Hull, pp. 139–62 (Bollingen Series). Princeton and Oxford: Princeton University Press.

Katz, Alexandra. 2014. 'Svetoslav Roerich: A Bridge between Russia and India'. *Rossiyskaya Gazeta*. Accessed on 5 January 2016 at http//www.in.rbth.com

Kesavan, Mukul. 1994. 'Urdu, Awadh, and the Tawaif: the Islamicate Roots of Hindi Cinema'. In *Forging Identities: Gender, Communities and the State*, edited by Zoya Hasan, pp. 245–57. Colorado: Westview Press.

Kinsley, David. 2005. *Hindi Goddesses: Vision of the Divine Feminine in the Hindu Religious Traditions*. Berkeley: University of California Press.

Khurana, Ashleesh. 2010. 'Bollywood's Unforgettable Women'. Accessed on 20 December 2015 at http//www.timesof india.indiatimes.com

Kyrou, Ado. 1963. *Luis Buñuel: An Introduction*. New York, NY: Simon and Schuster.

Majumdar, Neepa. 2009. *Wanted Cultured Ladies Only! Female Stardom and Cinema in India, 1930s–1950s*. Urbana and Chicago: University of Chicago Press.

Manjapra, Kris. 2014. *Age of Entanglement: German and Indian Intellectuals across Empire*. Cambridge, Massachusetts: Harvard University Press.

Manto, Saadat Hasan. 2010. *Stars from Another Sky: The Bombay Film World of the 1940s*. New Delhi: Penguin Books India.

Mulvey, Laura. 1975. 'Visual Pleasure and Narrative Cinema'. *Screen* 16 (3): 6–18.

Neville, Pran. 2015. 'A Gem Called Jahanara Kajjan'. Accessed on 20 January 2015 at http//www.thehindu.com

Oldenburg, Veena Talwar. 1990. 'Lifestyle as Resistance: The Case of Courtesans of Lucknow, India'. *Feminist Studies* 16 (2), Speaking for Others/Speaking for Self: Women of Color: 259–87.

Pande, Mrinal. 2006. 'Moving Beyond Themselves: Women in Hindustani Parsi Theatre and Early Hindi Films'. *Economic and Political Weekly* 41 (17): 1646–53.

Polikoff, Daniel Joseph. 2011. *In the Image of Orpheus: Rilke—A Soul History*. Illinois: Chiron Publications.

Purohit, Vinayak. 1988. *Arts of Transitional India in Twentieth Century*. New Delhi: Popular Prakashan.

Rosen, Friedrich. 1892. *Die Indarsabha des Amanat: neuindisches Singspiel in lithographischen Originaltext* [*The Indrasabha of Amanat: An Artistic Contribution of Hindustani Literature*]. Leipzig: Brockhaus Verlag.

Sameen, Zoya. 2014. 'Prostituting the Tawaif: Nawabi Patronage and Colonial Regulation of Courtesans in Lucknow, 1847–1899'. Accessed on 20 December 2015 at http//www.academia.edu

Sampath, Vikram. 2010. *My Name is Gauhar Jaan! The Life and Times of a Musician*. New Delhi: Rupa Publications.

Saran, Renu. 2014. *Encyclopedia of Bollywood Film Actresses*. New Delhi: Diamond Pocket Books.

Sharma, Shishir Krishna. 2012. 'Bigger than the Sky—Ranjit Studios'. Accessed on 14 June 2012 at http//www.beetehuedin.blogspot.in

———. 2013. 'Ye Raat Phir Na Ayegi—Bombay Talkies'. Accessed on 18 July 2015 at http//www.beetehuedin.blogspot.in

The Cinema Resource Center. 2013. 'The Story of Fatma Begum, India's First Woman Film Director'. Accessed on 20 December 2015 at http//www.tcrcindia.com

Trivedi, Madhu. 2010. *The Making of Awadh Culture*. New Delhi: Primus Books.

Vatave, Bapu. 2004. *Dadasaheb Phalke: The Father of Indian Cinema*. New Delhi: National Book Trust Press.

Weinbaum, Alys Eve, Lynn M. Thomas, Priti Ramamurthy, Uta G. Poiger, Madeleine Yue Dong and Tani E. Barlow, eds. 2008. *The Modern Girl Around the World: Consumption, Modernity, and Globalization*. North Carolina: Duke University Press.

3

Visualising Death and the Corpse: Perspectives on Post-mortem Photographs in Central-Eastern India[1]

Uwe Skoda and Birgit Lettmann

Introduction

Barely two weeks after my arrival in the house of an Aghria landlord (the younger brother of a village headman or *gauntia*) in 2000, the head of the family passed away very suddenly. Having been rushed to a nearby hospital, where he died the very same day, he was carried back to his home. His body was laid in an inner yard of his house, where a son-in-law approached me to take pictures—the first but not the last time I was asked to take post-mortem pictures during my research among Aghria farmers between 2000 and 2002, an experience shared by other anthropologists working in the region (Peter Berger, James Freeman and Eva Reichel, pers. comm.). Shortly afterwards, I also noticed a post-mortem photograph (Figure 3.1) hanging in the former landlord's bedroom, which had been converted into a guest room. The room was located rather close to the entrance, being conveniently situated in order to accommodate less well-known guests as well. Inside the room were five beds, and the room was decorated with two rows of images hanging on the walls. The upper one was a set of chromolithographs collected primarily by the landlord's elder wife, while the lower one consisted of family photographs including portraits and wedding photographs across generations. Thus, the post-mortem picture—the only one of 20-odd photographs on display in this

Figure 3.1

Post-mortem photograph among Aghria farmers, Odisha, c. 1981

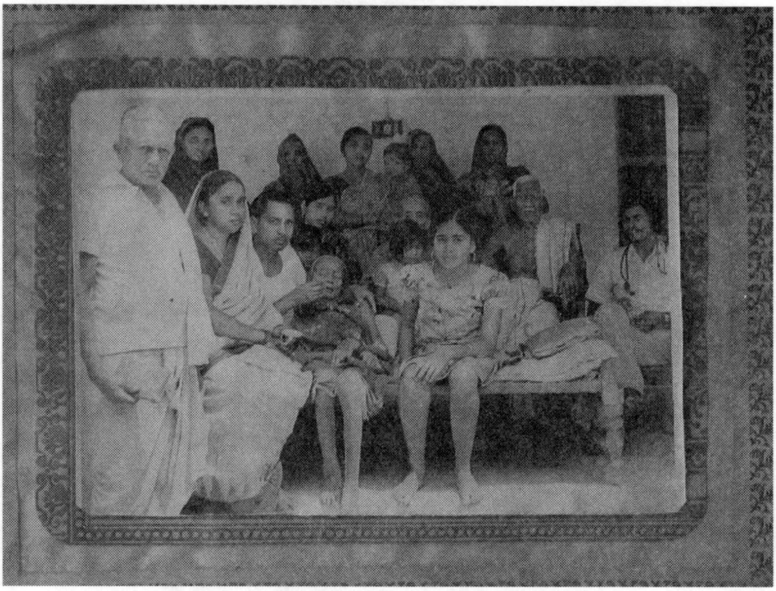

Source: Courtesy of Patel family.

room—was not hidden in any way, and every family member and guest could clearly see it.

Not all the photographs in the room had been taken in the landlord's house: Figure 3.1 was actually taken in the natal house of the landlord's daughter-in-law (son's wife) when grief struck her family in the form of her grandmother (father's mother) passing away around 1981, as she remembers. The photograph was taken by Ayodhya Prasad Naik, known to many older Aghrias simply as Photographer, who, my hosts explained to me, visited Aghria customers and patrons at intervals. On that occasion, he was simply present by chance, when nobody owned a camera in this family, and took a photograph of all those who were present. A copy of this particular photograph was later brought to her conjugal family by the landlord's daughter-in-law and is nowadays placed not far from her own wedding photograph.

The public display of such images in India and their open access contrasts strikingly with widespread perceptions of post-mortem photography in Western Europe and the USA, as, for example, shown in

Figure 3.2

Photograph in Figure 3.1 in situ

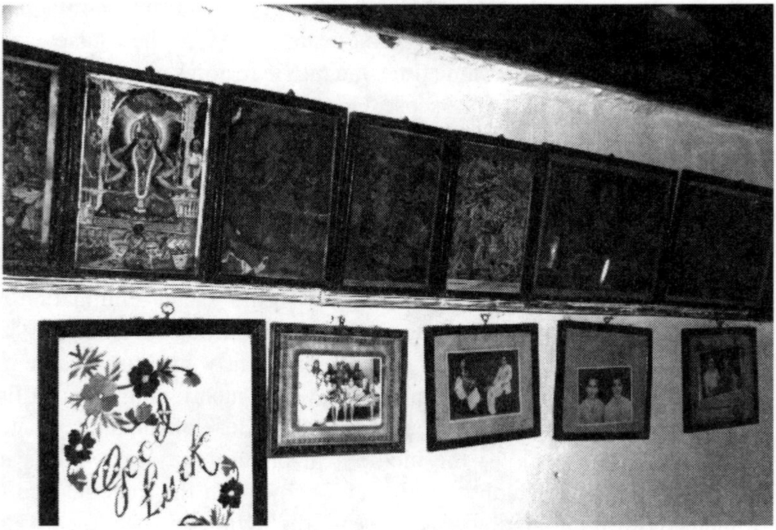

Source: Uwe Skoda.

the film *The Others* (ES, FR, IT 2001, Alejandro Amenábar), set on the Channel Island of Jersey in the aftermath of the Second World War and released in 2001. In a key sequence, Grace Steward (played by Nicole Kidman) finds a photo album with post-mortem images, but not being aware of the tradition of portraying the dead, like the audience in 2001, mistakes those depicted as sleeping.[2] The following dialogue between Grace and the servant Mrs Mills is intriguing. While the former is clueless and appalled, the latter—as we learn later in the movie, a ghost who actually died in 1891—is familiar with the custom, as during her lifetime, taking portraits of the deceased was a flourishing practice.

> Grace: 'Do you have any idea what this might be? […] Look, they are all asleep'.
>
> Mrs Mills: 'They are not asleep Ma'am. They are dead. It is a book of the dead. In the last century I believe they used to take photographs of the dead in the hopes that their souls would go on living through the portraits'.
>
> Grace: 'Oh, it's macabre! How could these people be so superstitious? […] Get rid of it. I don't want it in the house'. (*The Others* 2001, 38′36″–40′16″)

The Others demonstrates that somehow, and at some point, the custom of photographing deceased relatives was withdrawn into a private, invisible, tabooed domain and slowly but surely sank into oblivion in many European as well as Anglo-American contexts in the course of the twentieth century. At the same time, the movie restores our awareness of this historical practice. In this sense, Grace's reaction to the post-mortem photographs reflects an attitude which became common and widespread in the middle of the twentieth century in this primary catchment area of the movie, and it also reflects the current discourse about post-mortem pictures when the movie was released.

Classified as macabre in the film, people feel uncomfortable in the presence of such images, and—analogous to the 'clean' elimination of the decaying and potentially dangerous corpse through cremation—try to dispose of the photographs equally efficiently by burning them.[3] Yet another point from the sequence is worth mentioning: Mrs Mills' understanding of why these pictures were taken. Her explanation resonates with animistic aspects of the medium of photography, as well as its indexical quality. Metaphysical beliefs merge with the material-bodily dimension of photography and thus link the fiction and the hope of an afterlife through the photographic medium, which in turn permits the fantasy of the bereaved being able to touch the departed in and through the portrait.

These two examples indicate the kind of post-mortem photography we will be dealing with in this chapter. With 'post mortem' literally meaning simply 'after death', we focus on post-mortem pictures taken of the departed (private individuals) for the private use of the bereaved.[4] The aim of this chapter is a preliminary regional and comparative mapping of post-mortem photography in both rural and urban settings in central-eastern India—Odisha, Madhya Pradesh, Jharkhand, West Bengal and occasionally Assam, which so far is lacking.[5] While investigating this rather under-researched tradition, we take occasionally inspiration from Western European (using primarily evidence from German-speaking and neighbouring countries) and North American practices of post-mortem photography or rather the existing and relatively extensive body of literature related to as a backdrop for a broader discussion.[6]

A comparative angle of the chapter is not limited to the regional 'central-eastern-India' level, but goes beyond it and helps to shed light on regional specifics. Post-mortem photography in central-eastern India, our evidence suggests, dates back at least to the period around 1910, when it was linked to the richer urban class or nobility, and it has been a continuous, uninterrupted practice since this time.[7] Today, we encounter an even greater increase in the practice of post-mortem photography in central-eastern India due to the easier access to the relevant technology, particularly to mobile phones. We have noticed almost an explosion of images of the deceased in line with the general proliferation of photographs of all genres, having already encountered an earlier tendency in some communities to take not only a single post-mortem picture but rather several shots and even to create albums out of them.[8] Indeed, we found that most people we interviewed in Odisha were familiar with the practice, though they may not have taken such pictures themselves.

To explain the striking difference between our two initial examples (from the Aghria community and from the film *The Others*), we argue that in central-eastern India, death and the corpse have remained visible, permitting their photographibility. There has never been a thorough rupture in the practice in the direction of avoidance. As an Odia Baptist Christian argued in 2013: 'In fact, due to the availability of cameras, the visibility of the corpse has increased these days. Apart from the professional photographers these days, the younger generation has developed the skill of photography, both still and moving'. The visibility and photographibility of death and more precisely of the corpse is linked on the one hand to access to photographic equipment and technology, which has clearly increased in central-eastern India, and on the other hand, and perhaps even more importantly, to social values. As a result, the broader trajectories of post-mortem photography in central-eastern India differ significantly from mainstream photographic practices in Western Europe/North America, where this tradition was relatively popular from the invention of the technology till the 1920s, but was increasingly tabooed and forced into the invisibility of the private sphere from the 1940s onwards. Sometimes it has even been argued that it was not practiced at all any more (Rinhart and Rinhart 1967), which might explain why in the movie Grace is depicted as being unaware of the tradition. While an in-depth research is still missing on this matter in many regions in India, Grace's attitude also appears to resonate with sentiments encountered by the authors in urban areas like Delhi.[9]

The declining acceptance of death and dying had already been analysed by the philosopher Walter Benjamin ([1936] 2002: X) in 1936.[10] Due to the emergence of certain professions and institutions such as the undertaker and mortuaries, the appearance of new bodily concepts, the formation of the idea of the nuclear family, an increasing awareness of issues of hygiene and the growing medicalisation of life in the course of the nineteenth and early twentieth centuries, the corpse has slowly but surely been shifted away from the public view and committed to the care of specialists. These developments have led to an increasing reluctance in many parts of society to handle, touch and, in the late twentieth century, even see the corpse, and they have been responsible for the growing invisibility of the corpse in the visual awareness of certain segments of society. With the gradual shift of dying and death away from private homes to institutions and the parallel innovations in camera technology, the task of taking a last picture was sometimes handed over to the new experts (e.g., the undertakers), or, if at all, photographs were taken by the relatives themselves.

While it has become increasingly common in hospitals since the 1970s to take a last picture of perinatal deceased babies (Lettmann 2010), with parents recently starting to publish such post-mortem pictures—nowadays called 'bereavement photographs'—and some scholars even postulating a 'new visibility of death' in Europe (Macho and Marek 2007), the photographic visibility of the corpse in central-eastern India seems to have been constrained more quantitatively, that is, by relatively more limited access to technology (given, for example, that Figure 3.1 was taken by an itinerant photographer as late as 1981 because no camera was available even in the household of a landlord), rather than qualitatively, that is, by being increasingly tabooed as in the West. The corpse remained largely photographable, and ideas around professionalising and medicalising death appear to have had a limited impact only. Consequently, for central-eastern India, it would hardly be appropriate to speak of a 'new' visibility of death, perhaps rather of a wider visibility.

Apart from proposing such a broader trajectory of post-mortem photography in central-eastern India, the chapter analyses specific post-mortem pictures across caste, class and religious communities, as well as decades. However, given the historical depth of the material and the lack of an anthropological contextualisation as far as several older images are concerned, we focus primarily on an iconographic comparison that allows us to make statements regarding the links between post-mortem photography and the life cycle, including gender and status, as well as those between images, locations and poses.

Privileging such an iconographic angle brings out details in terms of the visibility of the corpse first regarding age groups or individual life histories and the question of a person's relative position within the wider life cycle (Babb 1975); secondly, with reference to poses as 'bodily molding' (Strassler 2010: 26) un-/consciously and un-/willingly chosen as part of a performative or communicative act in line with available cultural models or

Figure 3.3

Bereaved Odia Baptist Christians taking pictures with mobiles, Sambalpur, Odisha

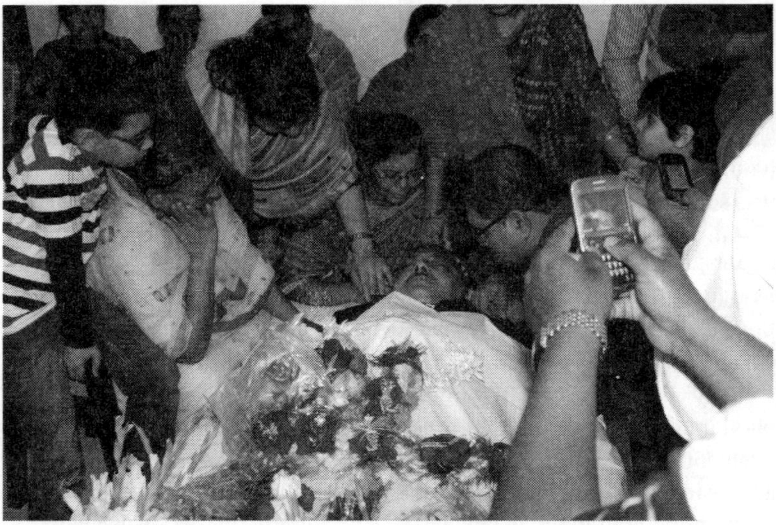

Source: Courtesy of Pramanik family.

'image-repertoires' (Silverman 1996: 179; see also Holschbach 2006), but here employed particularly on the corpse; and thirdly, related to locations and spaces like 'inside'/'outside' as combinations of materiality and relationships emerging through, enabling or prohibiting social practices (Lefebvre [1974] 2011). We bring in information on the social usage of post-mortem photographs as far as possible and hope that this first exercise in multi-layered mapping will lead to a deeper analysis of contemporary post-mortem photography in particular ethnographic contexts.

Photography as the Predestined Medium for Re-presenting the Dead? Theoretical Groundings

Since its emergence in 1839, one of the most consistent definitions of photography and the photograph is that it is a trace, an imprint or an index of the real, thus recalling Charles Sanders Peirce and his theory of signs. In this understanding, the uniqueness of the image derives from the physico-chemical process of its production, that is, and as American art critic Rosalind Krauss puts it: ‘Every photograph is the result of a physical imprint transferred by light reflections onto a sensitive surface. The photograph is thus a type of icon, or visual likeness, which bears an indexical relationship to its object’ (Krauss 1977: 75). Going beyond Krauss, the French philosopher Roland Barthes notes: ‘The photograph is literally an emanation of the referent. From a real body which was there, proceed radiations which ultimately touch me, who am here’ (Barthes [1980] 1984: 80). Thus, Barthes not only emphasises the direct physical relationship, even contact, between the referent, the sensitive surface of the photochemical plate and the subsequent gaze of the spectator, he also brings in the category of time. Due to the index’s demonstrative and intrinsic ‘reference’ to the thing ‘that-has-been’ in front of the lens, Barthes sees the characteristics of photography as lying in its special ability to present or to re-present (in the literal sense) the past and the absent (Barthes [1980] 1984: 76–77). The conception of photography almost as a kind of bodily derivate of the depicted person is matched with the nineteenth-century fantasy and desire that one can hold on to the departed while letting them go. This fantasy of being able to ‘touch’ the absent person through the picture was and still is what is fascinating about the medium and might be considered one explanation for the phenomenon of post-mortem photography (particularly in nineteenth-century Western European and US American contexts).

Barthes also elaborates on the special relationship between photography and death in *Camera Lucida*, arguing that death is the *eidos* or nature of photography:

> In terms of image-repertoire, the Photograph […] represents that very subtle moment when, […] I am neither subject nor object but a subject who feels he is becoming an object: I then experience a micro-version of death […] but when I discover myself in the product of this operation, what I see is that I have become Total-Image, which is to say, Death in person. (Barthes [1980] 1984: 13–14)

For Barthes, the act of being photographed is not only an anticipation of one’s own death: photography also transfers the body into its own image, that is, into its own index. This idea can be transferred to the conception of the corpse: when a person dies, he or she becomes an image that maintains an indexical relationship with the once living human being. French literary theorist Maurice Blanchot argues:

> What we call mortal remains escape common categories. Something is there before us which is not really the living person […]. It is neither the same as

> the person who was alive, nor is it another person, nor is it anything else. […] The cadaver is its own image. (1982 [1955]: 258)

Hence, corpse and photography share a medial closeness: both function as indexical derivates and thus share a close relationship to the referent, despite the distance in time and the paradox of the simultaneous presence and absence in the image. For post-mortem photography this means that, due to the amalgam of bodily and photographic indices, there is a double and thus more intensive trace that refers back from the corpse, or rather the image of the corpse, to the once living person (Sykora 2009: 41).

Other theorists, conversely, do not deduce the specificity of photography from the optic-chemical process of its production. As the 'principle of trace, no matter how essential, only marks a *moment* within the entire photographic process' (Dubois [1990] 1998: 54, translated by authors), these theorists focus more on the culturally coded usages, discourses, receptions and conventions of photographs. For the French sociologist Pierre Bourdieu, photography is both the expression and the symptom of social relations. And as Barry King (2003) adds, the role of family photography can also be understood as a form of visual care and solicitousness, the family increasingly being seen an emotional rather than a structural unit, while the camera serves as tool to express this familial love and affection. Bourdieu investigates not so much the features of photography itself but the features that are attributed to it by society, as well as how this society uses photographs. As he argues:

> Photographs of major ceremonies are possible because—and only because—they capture behaviour that is socially approved and socially regulated, that is, behaviour that has already been solemnized. Nothing *may* be photographed apart from that which *must* be photographed. The ceremony may be photographed because it is outside of the daily routine, and it must be photographed because it realizes the image that the group seeks to give of itself as a group. (Bourdieu [1965] 1990: 23–24)

Thus, we can ask with Bourdieu, who photographs whom, when, where, how and to what end (Sykora 2009: 32)? Regarding, in particular, the poses, film theorist Kaja Silverman (1996: 204, 179, 206) echoes Bourdieu when she describes them as being informed by and limited to what is, as it were, allowed or 'representationally "possible"' at a certain time and within a certain society or its 'cultural image-repertoire', while poses 'generally attest to the aspiration to conform as closely as possible to cultural ideals'. The image-repertoire is perhaps even more explicit when a dead body is photographed and both survivors and photographers have to fulfil carefully the performative act for the deceased, that is, to bring them into a position that protects their integrity and dignity after death.

Recently, this Bourdieuesque approach has been re-emphasised with reference to post-mortem photography by cultural scientist Corinna Caduff. Being concerned with such dignified representations, she altered it slightly by raising the questions: 'Is it allowed to take pictures of deceased people and is it allowed to make these photos accessible for others? Who is allowed to take these pictures and who is not?' (Caduff 2010: 124, translated by authors), while being simultaneously puzzled about the rather unproblematic taking of post-mortem pictures in South Asia.[11]

Approaches to photography in India are in some ways reminiscent of the Barthes–Bourdieu controversy, though they are framed largely in vernacular terms. Here too, debates concerning portrait photography circle around the question of what is visible in or captured by a photograph, as well as what it is desirable to capture in and as an image. Working on central India, visual anthropologist Christopher Pinney (1997) encountered a basic distinction between *vyaktitva* and *charitra*. Locals are only able to see the *vyaktitva*, a person's external, yet also transient and ephemeral characteristics, bodily surface or 'person-ness', in a photo:

> In central Indian photographic portraiture the body (*sharir*) is a ground for the physical and visual aspects of *vyaktitva* (complexion, sharpness of features, dress sense […]) and, of course, these can be captured through photography. What photographs are nearly always completely unable to capture, however, is the internal moral character and biography of a sitter, his *charitra*. *Charitra* reveals itself only through actions (*karma*), through past history and future eventualities. (Pinney 1997: 198)

Although a certain combination of body and soul (*atma*) is discernible in photographs, and although glancing at an image may reveal the 'official-ness' or perhaps even habitus of, let us say, a bureaucrat, the deeper moral quality or *charitra*, for example, 'dacoit-ness', remains hidden from most. However, it is conceded that there are a few specialists who may see beyond *vyaktitva.* While this expertise remains rather vague, visual anthropologist David MacDougall (1992) distinguishes very clearly between different points of view, the sitter's and the photographer's, when it comes to arranging a memorable holiday portrait in Mussoorie, a popular holiday destination for middle-class tourists in North India. He would rather state:

> If the tourists see such photography as dressing up and 'playing' someone else, the photographers often see it otherwise—as a catalyst for the

> release of the true self from the social self. According to one of them, H.S. Chadha, 'all the emotions flow out in photography,' and he has described how he has discovered by taking photographs that a Chief Minister and an astrologer (who looked like a holy man) were both in fact thieves. The process, he maintains, produces an emotional transformation, one which we might compare to a religious experience. For Chadha (as for priests) there may be no clear boundary between religion and science. 'Photography is a psychological, scientific way of bringing out inner feelings, through the use of costumes and objects,' he says. 'You can test anyone with it.' (MacDougall 1992: 104)

One may read this quote—at least in the *photo-wallah's* perspective—as ascribing a Barthesian quality to the photo, and one may wonder about Chadha's take on post-mortem images.

However, while dressing up as a tourist in Mussoorie may actually lead to one's unmasking in the eyes of others, MacDougall (1992: 123) argues that revealing and unmasking are not central to Indian photography (at least not in the same way as they ostensibly are in the images of Félix Nadar or August Sander). Instead, MacDougall (1992: 123; see also Pinney 1997: 108ff) stresses that photography offers additional, potential identities that can be explored or temporarily assumed and that it 'assists in the creation of reality'. Anthropologist Karen Strassler's (2010: 79) insight that Indonesian studio portraiture enables a coupling of 'the actual ("this has been")' with 'the possible ("this might be")'—particularly through the use of backdrops—appears to be applicable to Indian 'chambers of dreams' as well. As Judith Mara Gutman (1982: 46–47) had already pointed out with reference to painted portraits and painted photographs, the image is preferably 'perfected'. This 'improvement' relates to the idea of the person, and accordingly the image of a priest based on the photograph should move closer towards an ideal representation of what a priest should look like. Thus, while 'realistic (*vastavik*) photographs' or those in a 'naturalist' style are hardly preferred (Pinney 1997: 136, 180, 191), in terms of portraiture—including matrimonial photographs, but also memorial images produced after death—a balance is sought between 'ideal and evidential' (MacDougall 1992: 109) or between 'more permanent, truer forms' and 'indexical randomness' (Pinney 1997: 201). The ideal, however—that is, the relatively more timeless form—is crucially linked and specific to the social norms (apart from economic constraints) a group maintains. A case in point for a widespread photographic convention in India is the idea of representing dead ancestors in a frontal, *darśanic* (*darśan*-like) pose for memorialisation and worship, thus enabling a visual exchange between ancestor and descendant. It hints, again, at the social dimension of private photography—that is, 'the group places this practice under its collective rule, so that the most trivial photograph expresses, apart from the explicit intentions of the photographer, the system of schemes of perception, thought and appreciation common to a whole group' (Bourdieu [1965] 1990: 6).

Mapping Post-mortem Images in Eastern India

Since post-mortem photographs in (eastern) India have never been systematically examined, in this section we attempt a preliminary regional mapping. The section is subdivided according to themes we feel emerge from the photographs in a comparative perspective, starting with observations on the links between post-mortem photography and the life cycle, before moving on to the various ways in which the corpse may be positioned and to the social use of these images.

Reflecting the Life Cycle

Starting somehow chronologically with the early stage of the life cycle, one notices the almost complete absence of post-mortem images of children, especially babies.[12] It may in fact be less surprising when we remember the shift in the perception of children and consider, for example, that among the French peasants documented by Bourdieu ([1965] 1990: 21–22), images of children were rarely found before 1939, while after 1945 almost half of all photographs were images of children.

> In the society of former times, the child was never, as now, the centre of attention. The major feasts and ceremonies in the village society were chiefly an adult affair, and it is only since 1945 that children's feasts (such as first communion) have become important; as society comes to place more importance on children [...] (Bourdieu [1965] 1990: 22)

Unlike urban society, French peasants may have replicated, also photographically, wider changes in the concept of childhood rather late, and similar processes of the deferred inclusion of children in the realm of the photographable seem to have occurred in India too, at least among peasant communities like the Aghrias. While photographing children had already become part of representing new conjugal models and ideas of the family in urban Bengal (Karlekar 2005: 107) in the nineteenth century, the availability of the technology, as well as state interventions through, for example, schools, has increasingly led to the photographing of children in rural central-eastern India as well, though somewhat later. For example, early photographs of children encountered in Aghria households were often taken while they were at school (apart from being part of group photographs as discussed earlier—see Figure 3.1). However, this relatively recent proliferation of images of children (roughly from the 1960s onwards) seems to have spilled over into post-mortem photography only quite recently, if at all.

Nonetheless, the relative absence of post-mortem images of children is remarkable in an otherwise fairly vibrant tradition of image-making. Tentatively, we suggest that it may be correlated with concepts of personhood that have assigned an equally subordinate position to children even after 1960. For example, Aghria farmers believe that the individual only reaches the status of a full social person at the time of marriage and is allowed to perform crucial ceremonies only together with a spouse. Accordingly, only after reaching this position will a person receive the complete funerary rites. For unmarried Aghrias, 'short-cut versions' are performed, that is, the funeral reflects one's positioning within the life cycle in relation to attaining full social personhood.[13] Thus, the absence of post-mortem photographs of children may equally indicate their incompleteness as social persons and their subordinate position within the life cycle.

An exception to this more general tendency to exclude children from post-mortem photography seems to be Figure 3.4—the only post-mortem photographs of a child encountered so far, though some Odia Baptist Christians maintained that such images were occasionally taken in their community. Given the relative popularity of post-mortem images of children in various Christian Euro-American traditions with frequent references to baptism (Metken 1984: 77; Sykora 2009: 63; van Gennep [1909] 2004: 153; see also Lettmann 2010), it may not be surprising that Figure 3.4 was taken by Christians too—here specifically in 1954 after the intriguing death of a young boy aged one year and eight months.

Family members came up with a surprising explanation that the boy 'got frightened by the flash of light on his eyes [...] When he was laying on the lap of his mother, a car crossed in front of the house, and the reflection of the sunlight from the glass of the car fell on his eyes, which frightened

Figure 3.4

Death of a small boy, Odia Baptist Christians, Sambalpur, Odisha, 1954

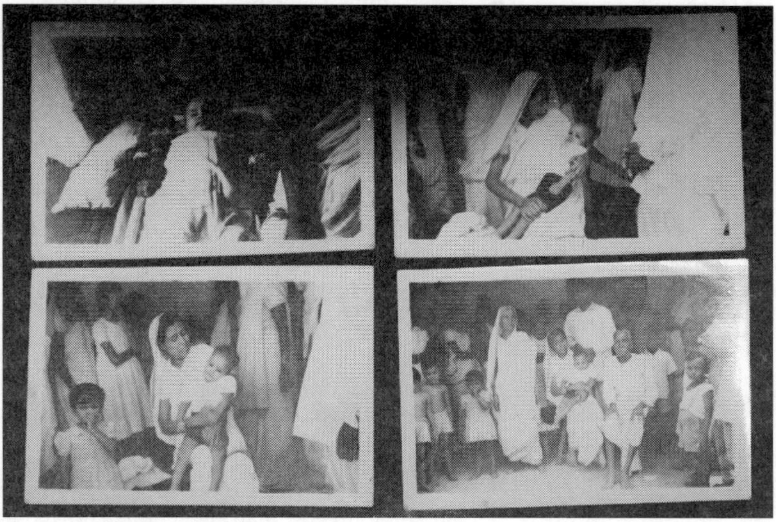

Source: Courtesy of Pramanik family.

him'. This explanation seems to resonate with Christian ideas of children being bathed in radiating brightness and often linked to the omnipresence of white 'that reinforces the notion of innocence and purity, and presages a future home in the effulgent light of heaven' (Linkman 2011: 36). Yet, it remains an exceptional set of images and the special circumstances of the death or those attributed to it may have contributed to the taking of several images. Noteworthy is the number of different images with several poses—lying down alone and sitting on his mother's lap in a pietà-like composition singling out mother and son, or including them in a wider group image (almost an inversion of roles compared to Figure 3.1).

Similarly, the position within the life cycle in relation to marriage—married versus unmarried—is marked in various cases in Odisha, for example, the colour of the cloth covering the coffin among Odia Baptist Christian families in Sambalpur. As interlocutors explained: 'For unmarried the cloth used on the coffin box is white cloth and black cross. For married it is black cloth on the coffin and white cross. White cloth signifies purity and holiness' (see Figures 3.5 and 3.6).

When it comes to dresses, the colour white, for example, the *dhoti* or clothes in Figures 3.11 and 3.14, often also seem to indicate death, but

Figure 3.5

An elderly Odia Baptist Christian lady who passed away of old age in 1993. Note the black cloth wrapping of the coffin

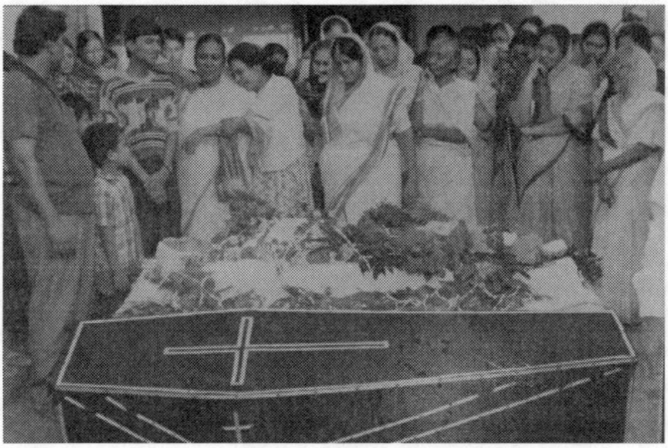

Source: Courtesy of Pramanik family.

Figure 3.6

Death of a young unmarried Odia Baptist Christian man (pictured with his sister) who passed away due to wrong medical treatment in 2002. Note the white cloth wrapping of his coffin

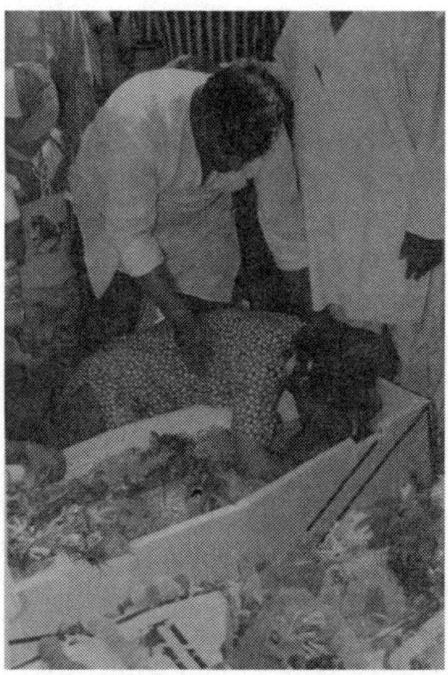

Source: Courtesy of Pramanik family.

irrespective of colour the dress should generally be new. However, a white cloth covering the deceased is sometimes combined with a red sari, as in Figure 3.10 (see also Babb 1975: 93 for these colour preferences in Chhattisgarh), red being a preferred colour for brides in Hindu contexts. Alternatively, men are dressed in more formal dresses like shirt and pants. Some communities like the Odia Baptist Christians also take the individual wishes of the deceased into account if they have already selected clothes before their deaths, for example, if they have instructed family members that they want to be buried in their wedding dress. Individual items used by the deceased like glasses or a walking stick may also be buried with the deceased and captured by the camera. These items will also be on display together with the corpse lying on a bed and therefore equally symbolise death in the picture.

Photographs taken by the Samal family (belonging to the SC/Pana community from coastal Odisha but taken in Sambalpur in 2000 due to the job posting of the head of the family—Swarnalata Samal, pers. comm.) clearly indicate the link between the position of the deceased within the life cycle and the rituals captured by the camera in a Hindu context. Figures 3.7 and 3.8, arranged and taken by the husband's friends, included the deceased's husband and daughter. They portray the deceased

Figure 3.7

Post-mortem photograph, Samal family, Sambalpur, Odisha, 2000

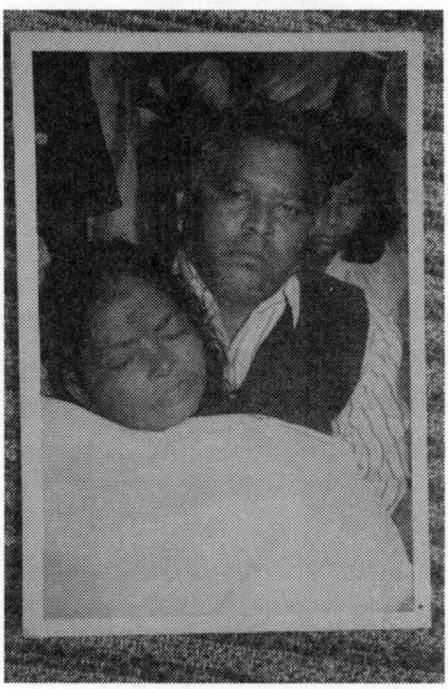

Source: Courtesy of Samal family.

Figure 3.8

Feet of the woman of Figure 3.7 who passed away as suhagin, *Samal family, Sambalpur, Odisha, 2000*

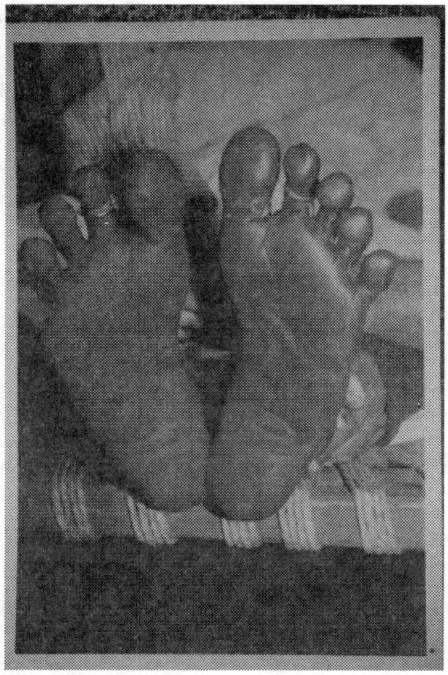

Source: Courtesy of Samal family.

as a *suhagin*, that is, as an auspicious wife. Again, the importance of marriage is stressed, but also the fact, as the daughter emphasises, that her mother did not pass away as widow. Therefore, vermilion (*sindoor*) was applied to her forehead and a red-coloured dye (*aalta*, *lal rang*) to her feet, as is also frequently done at weddings. Besides the new *sindoor* mark, new bangles also indicate her status as married woman, while the new white dress indicates death. This belief that the wife's death shall precede the husband's is shared by many Hindu families and communities, for example, by the high status Bandyopadhyay Brahmin family in Bengal in which women who die before their husbands are considered fortunate (see also Figure 3.18), such a 'timely' death being 'good for the "after-life" of the deceased and a matter of pride for the family' (Abhijit Bhattacharya 2007, pers. comm.).

Apart from depicting the face with the visual markers of a *suhagin*, the Samal family also took a picture of the feet of the wife/mother that reminds one of similar photographs taken of the feet of a guru (e.g., a combination of two photographs, one of a guru coupled with another of the guru's feet garlanded with flowers can be found in Pinney 1997: 166) and the broader idea of touching the feet—not just the guru's feet—as a mark of respect and acceptance of a lower hierarchical position.[14] Moreover, this raises the question of a connection with earlier traditions of keeping footprints in Eastern India (for Bengal, Roma Chatterji, pers. comm.; for Jharkhand, Kiran Sharma, pers. comm.) as another indexical sign of the deceased. At least in some cases, post-mortem photographs were taken together with footprints coloured with *aalta* as in Figure 3.9 (Kiran Sharma, pers. comm.)[15] and sometimes both indices were even jointly displayed in the house (Joachim K. Bautze, pers. comm.)[16] or otherwise jointly retained later on. While in the case of the Samal family no other items (clothes or anything else) were kept apart from the photographs, the practice of the Sharma family (Brahmin by caste) in Jharkhand suggests either a shifting indexicality from 'footprint' to 'photoprint' or perhaps a double/multiple indexicality which is valued.

Figure 3.9

Footprints taken after death, Sharma family, Dhanbad, Jharkhand, 1998

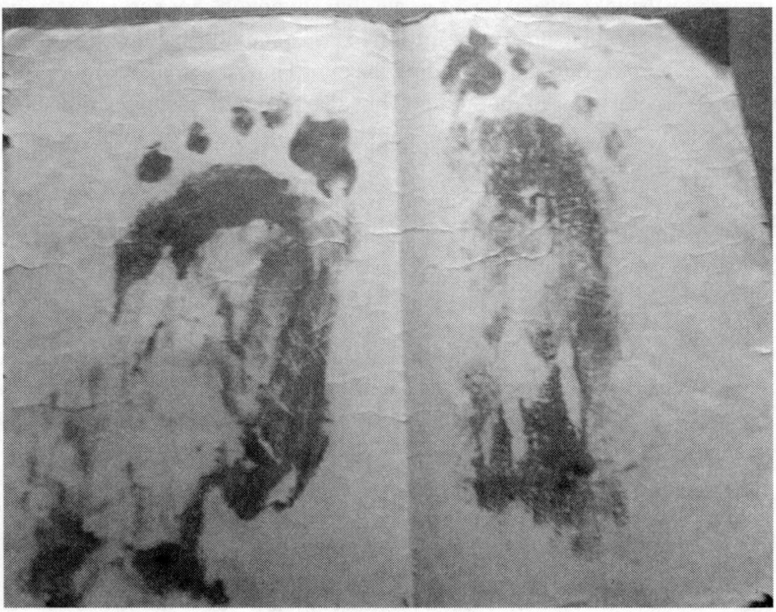

Source: Courtesy of Sharma family.

The images considered here also suggest a certain connection between a type of death considered good or bad and the photographs taken subsequently. A 'good death' either as a *suhagin* and/or having reached a 'blessed age' and being surrounded by children, grandchildren, as in the Aghria image (Figure 3.1), very likely contributes to the taking of pictures. In fact, this Aghria photograph introduced right in the beginning exemplifies this idea by combining a range of remarkable features. First, it is centred on the person who had just passed away reaching a 'blessed age'. Second, the deceased is surrounded by many relatives, men and women as well as their (grand)children—even the doctor and other-caste members are present in an attempt to include as many family members and guests as possible and to show a wealth of relations (see also Figure 3.10). Being surrounded by children, grandchildren and even great-grandchildren at the time of death not only implies a status as a married woman but also seems to indicate a 'good death', that is, a death due to old age after seeing the following generations. As an Aghria explained, a good time to die is after one's duties are over, that is, after the marriages of his/her all children have been arranged and they are well settled financially. It can also be seen that the old lady is still on her bed placed on the veranda of her house—in line with Aghria ideas that one should not die inside a room (where births take place)—and in another inversion, her son is not only holding his mother but, I was informed, was actually feeding her milk, while his wife next to him is holding the cup. Thus, the image conjures up not only crucial ideas of motherhood but also the mother–son relationship, giving birth to a son often being considered of greater importance than giving birth to a daughter.

In contrast, a death by accident, particularly if untimely—that is, if life remains unfulfilled in terms of marriage, having children, etc.—is considered a bad death, in which case the number or types of pictures taken may be limited. As Odia Baptist Christians explained:

> A bad death (death due to any disease, accident, suicide, etc.) has some impact on taking photos. If the face is disfigured, then the entire body and face is covered so that the disfigured state is not captured by taking some snap shots and displaying it to friends and relatives.

Similarly, in Assam, post-mortem photographs may be taken in such cases, for example, after an accident, but the corpse may be covered and may not be shown openly (Mridusmita Mahanta, pers. comm.). In both cases, it seems that the illusion of an 'unscathed' body is being preserved because capturing a 'disfigured' body may cause or revive pain later on.

Figure 3.10

Post-mortem photograph of Srimati Kumari Kamala Priya Devi, Bonaigarh, Odisha, 1990

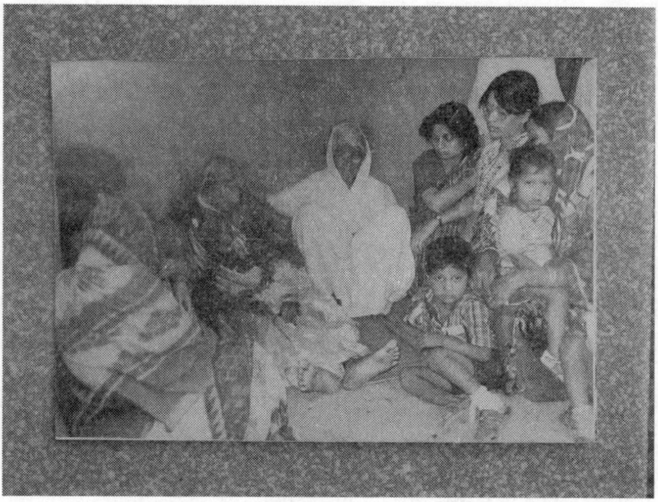

Source: Courtesy of royal family of Bonai.

These cases also indicate the limits of beautifying or aesthetising death or of transforming the corpse into an iconic, photographable body.

While in the Aghria image, men and women are assembled around the loved one, an image from the royal family of Bonai (Figure 3.10, but also Figure 3.11) indicates a gender segregation intrinsically linked to the life cycle and also visible in some post-mortem images. The picture was taken when Kumari Kamala Priya Devi, born in 1898 into the Kera Zamindari (present Jharkhand), passed away in 1990. Kamala Priya Devi, biological mother of the Bonai Raja (the Raja having been adopted by his father's elder brother), is surrounded by female relatives like her granddaughters, with the exception of a young boy who has not yet reached puberty and is therefore acceptable in this situation. She is seated on a veranda in a white and red sari and is garlanded with flowers, while turmeric and sandalwood paste, considered auspicious and purifying, have been applied to her face.

The two images (Figures 3.10 and 3.11) from the royal family of Bonai suggest a clear gender segregation in the 1970s, or even in 1990, which is in line with the architectural structure of most palaces in Odisha—dividing the space into a *Rajmahal* and *Rani Mahal*, with the married women remaining in *purdah* (seclusion) and being removed from the public sphere. However, nowadays, this strict division is no longer maintained in many royal families, and more recent post-mortem images, as when the Raja of Bonai passed away in 2011, show male and female relatives gathered around the deceased. Similarly, in no other case presented here (Aghria, Jadia Parja, Pana, Bauri, Baptist Christians in Odisha, but also, e.g., Nishtha Jain's film on Bengal) is such a separation followed, despite the fact that rules of *purdah* are observed in other contexts.[17]

In almost all the images presented here, the deceased is visibly marked in various ways, thus indicating another transformation within the life cycle and as such separating the deceased from the 'living' relatives. This includes primarily flower garlands and often marigolds, which are preferred across communities, but roses may be used as well. Depending on the community, flower bouquets in the form of a ring or crosses may be added too, clearly linked to religion. This also includes the painting of the feet as done in the Samal family or in the Brahmo Samaj family (Figure 3.17), but not done among Odia Baptist Christians. In communities like the Aghrias and Jadia Parja (Figure 3.14), applying turmeric to the body, particularly the face, is widespread. In addition, an *Om*-sign or the word Ram may be written on the forehead.

Even if one argues that some of the images follow the conventions for portraits of living persons, as in the following case of the Bauris, the garland stands out as a unique feature. Flower garlands often indicate status as a respected and higher being within a wider hierarchical framework that includes the living, the dead and divine beings. Garlands are also used in the veneration of ancestors when (memorial) photographs of ancestors are frequently decorated with them, as in Figure 3.19. However, since there is sometimes a tendency to document all stages of the funeral, including the decoration of the corpse after washing, an elaborate album of post-mortem images may also include initial photographs before flowers are added, first by the family and later by relatives and neighbours.

Status

While one's position within the life cycle is marked or has an impact on post-mortem photography more broadly, status is expressed in the composition of the images in various ways. On the one hand, one's status within a wider ranking of society documents one's wealth and position, class being made visible, for example, in early and costly

Figure 3.11

Post-mortem photograph of Sri Tikayat Keran Keshari Deo Deb, Bonaigarh, Odisha, 1971

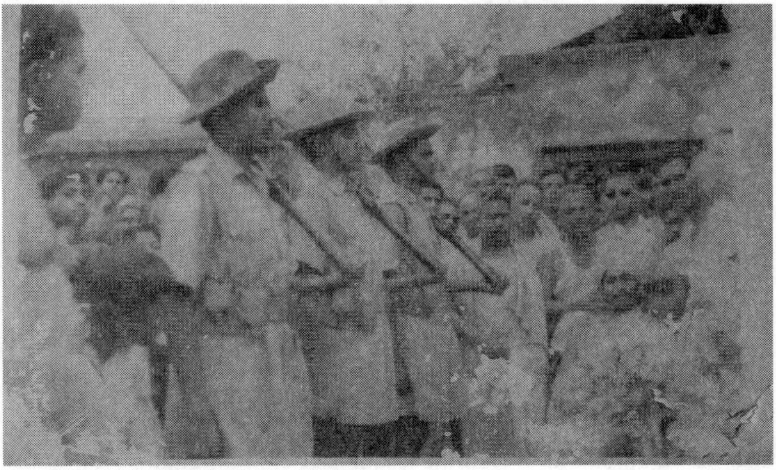

Source: Courtesy of royal family of Bonai.

studio photographs such as that of Shrichandra Mukhopadhyay's wife (Figure 3.18). On the other hand, one may also be depicted as a respected senior relative by demonstrating a multitude of relationships (particularly with juniors). Starting with the first honorific aspect, the image of the *Tikayat* (king's eldest son, a term corresponding to *Yubraj* in other royal families) of Bonai, Keran Keshari Deo Deb, shows his status as the eldest son of a Raja (Figure 3.11). He passed away in 1971 at the age of 22, apparently of sunstroke. His death occurred before the abolition of the privy purses and other royal privileges in 1971/1972 by Indira Gandhi. Therefore, the photograph depicts not only the *Tikayat* in a sitting position held by the relatives and a *Rajpurohit* (royal priest) standing around him but also an armed guard of honour, which is centrally located in the image. The father and Raja of Bonai is seen standing right behind his son (with sunglasses). The *Tikayat* is singled out in the photograph by the flower garlands and the turban he is wearing, as well as by his sitting position.[18] The flowers and this combination more broadly could be understood as marking death. Thus, while the sitting position, as also in the following case of Bauri and Jadia Parja, may contribute to the impression of the person as alive, visual markers like the garlands contradict this impression.

Also, noteworthy is the exclusively male crowd, as well as the location, an inner yard of the palace.

We turn now to the second aspect, the photograph as a figural representation of social relations—almost the idea of a sociogram—and documenting the rich relationality overlapping with the idea of a 'good death'. In the Aghria image (Figure 3.1), every relative present at that moment, even the doctor, was included. This inclusive attempt may be facilitated by an Aghria belief that the people present at the death of a person must have had connections previously. Figure 3.1 not only portrayed the deceased as an individual but also included the following relatives and guests from the perspective of the deceased: son, son's wife, son's daughters, husband of deceased, doctor, son's daughter's daughters, son's daughter's son, distant cousin brothers, *jati* (member of the same caste, but different clan) and son's wife's mother. Applying Erving Goffman's words (1981) freely, one may view such group photographs as a final expression and representation of social blossoming. The inclusion of all the relatives who were present on the occasion may also be interpreted in a Bourdieuesque sense, highlighting the 'family function' of photography, 'namely that of solemnizing and immortalizing the high points of family life, in short, of reinforcing the integration of the family group by reasserting the sense that it has both of itself and of its unity' (Bourdieu [1965] 1990: 19). With reference to Barry King, Strassler (2010: 168) argued that photographing family members may also be understood as 'an act of visual caring'. Thus, a last memento of a kin group or social network around the deceased may simultaneously express affection and care while facilitating social cohesion as well as renewal at the time of death.

Like the idea of photography as a sociogram and visualising family ties, in her documentary on photographic practices in Calcutta, entitled *City of Photos* (2005), Nishtha Jain features a son explaining the post-mortem photograph of his father in Calcutta. As he states:

> So to keep his memory alive the whole family assembled around his dead body, because he was one of us. That's my father [deceased lying down on a bed, surrounded by circa 35 relatives, arches in the background suggest a location outside—authors], that's me [sitting at the foot of the bed touching the father's feet]. My mother's brother, my grand uncles and aunts. (*City of Photos* 2005, 52′50″–54′00″)

The role of photography as an indicator and medium of the family's integration indeed seems striking here. Similarly, Abhijit Bhattacharya (pers. comm.) interviewed a photographer and grocery shopkeeper next to a crematorium in Murshidabad district (about 200 km North of Calcutta) way back in 1996: 'His only photographic assignment was to photograph dead bodies surrounded by the members of the family', according to Bhattacharya. The particular stylistic conventions followed in these photographs taken right at the crematorium showed, for example, the elder son sitting near the head of the deceased, and if the deceased is survived by his wife, as his widow she would be seated next to his legs. Other pictures, however, also show that such conventions were not always followed in Calcutta. For example, in her documentary, Nishtha Jain featured a family photograph with the son sitting at the feet of his deceased father, while other family members stand or sit around the death bed.

The aspects highlighted by Goffman, Bourdieu and Strassler can also be applied to casket and funeral photographs, which, according to anthropologist Jay Ruby (1995), became common especially in the United States by the early twentieth century, where, so the argument goes, the focus shifted increasingly away from the corpse as the primary object of post-mortem photographs towards images of the mourners and the funeral as a social gathering, thus reflecting the shift away from the poses of the corpse towards the *mise-en-scène* of the funeral and the posing of the bereaved. Seldom if ever is any 'interaction' between the bereaved and the dead body captured in these photographs. Rather, the coffin operates as marker of the clear border separating the world of the living from the dead in these pictures. In this sense, the key functions of these photographs are to commemorate and document that the final services have been properly performed by the survivors, as well as the family gathering occasioned by the death of one of its members. The deceased's death has been accepted by the bereaved, and the pictures contribute to the individual and collective last farewell and thus initiate the beginning of the grieving process (Sykora 2009: 146). Moreover, Linkman (2011: 54) stresses that the shift in emphasis from the death of the individual towards including the survivors in its effects turns these pictures into portraits of loss and its consequences.

However, the images from the Aghrias, as well as the example just cited from Calcutta and more recent mobile images, often differ in terms of the missing visual boundary line separating the deceased (inside) from the living standing around (outside), the frequently encountered physical contact between corpse and bereaved and the number of images taken including individual portraits of the deceased and group photographs. Images taken among Christians in the region such as Figure 3.3 show that physical contact is maintained despite the coffin-boundary. The idea of including all relatives is also present among Odia Baptist Christians, but relatives are also often photographed in smaller groups according to the relationship: thus, all brothers are depicted with the deceased, all daughters, all uncles, etc. These photographs are eventually combined in albums often consisting exclusively of post-mortem images. As an Odia Baptist Christian argued: 'Generally when the photos are taken it is taken groupwise. Like all brothers, all sisters, all sister-in-laws, all brother-in-laws, all grandchildren and also familywise. It depicts the relation of the corpse with each group'. In this case, each relationship and the role of each relative in relation to the deceased are stressed rather than an individual mourning process. Figures 3.12 and 3.13 illustrate this idea by arranging groups of relatives around the corpse, and the rather common touching of the corpse, seen in many photographs here (e.g., Figures 3.6 and 3.13), seems to underline the idea of a close relationship and of the deceased 'being one of us', while at least among Odia Baptist Christians, 'one of us' does not refer to the wider kin group but more specifically to 'one person standing in a certain relationship to us'.

Figure 3.12

Elderly Odia Baptist Christian lady together with her nieces (a group of husband's younger brother's daughters), Sambalpur, Odisha, 1993

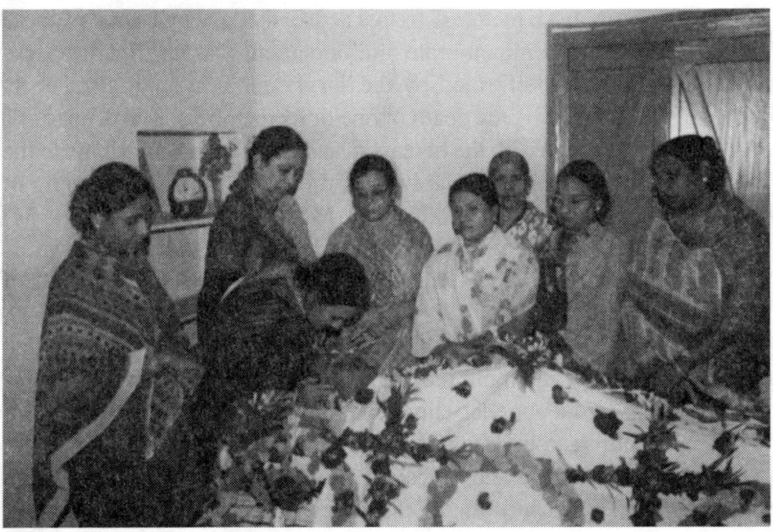

Source: Courtesy of Pramanik family.

Figure 3.13

Odia Baptist Christian unmarried man together with father and uncle (father's younger brother), Sambalpur, Odisha, 2002

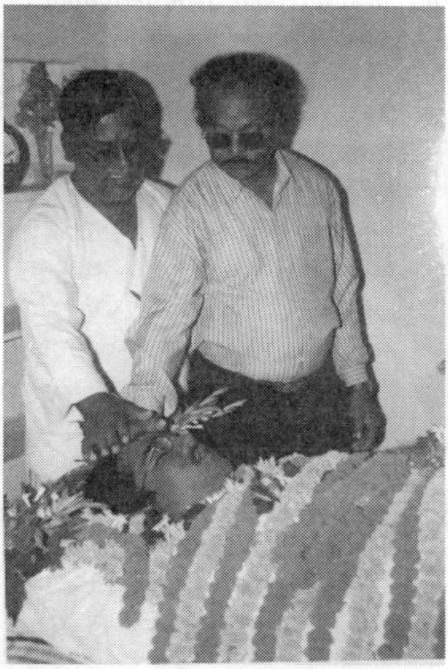

Source: Courtesy of Pramanik family.

Poses and Locations

Let us turn more explicitly to the ways in which the corpse itself is positioned for the picture. Here we can find at least two different poses: (a) a sitting position on a chair and (b) the corpse being laid out on a bed or a stretcher (other pictures, e.g., Figure 3.1 of an Aghria woman sitting on a stretcher or the deceased sitting on the ground as in Figure 3.10 are somewhat in-between these two). However, in both cases there seems to be a clear preference for full-body photographs, though some albums and more recent pictures may also depict only the upper body, face, feet, etc.

To start with the former, we may consider a post-mortem photograph taken by anthropologist Peter Berger (pers. comm.) among the Jaria, classified as Scheduled Tribe, during his field research in southern Odisha in 1996 (Figure 3.14) or of Muli's father taken by James Freeman among the Bauri near Bhubaneswar in 1971 (Figure 3.16)—Muli being the protagonist of Freeman's famous life history *Untouchable* (Freeman

Figure 3.14

Picture of deceased Jadia Parja surrounded by his family, Onukadilli, Odisha, 1996

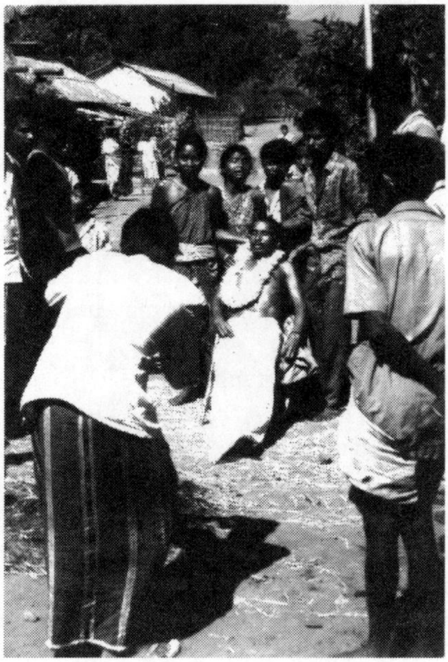

Source: Courtesy of Peter Berger/Kerstin Gudermuth.

[1979] 1993), in which the photograph was also published (ibid.: 9). Though the picture was taken by the fieldworker, it was arranged by Muli's family according to their wishes (James Freeman, pers. comm.). Moreover, Freeman argued that the post-mortem pictures taken by him (two being included in the book) were extensions of a preferred form of portraiture:

> The villagers, much as Americans and other peoples, had definite notions of how a portrait or an official photograph should look. […] For the most part, this meant one or more persons sitting on a chair—something which at that time was unusual for most of them, since they typically sat cross-legged on mats or cushions. They would sit stiffly and unsmiling, with others standing and clustered around them. Some children did not follow this convention but seemed to be more relaxed and smiling—especially when I took portraits of them alone. [Thus] […] the post-mortem photos of Muli's family seemed to follow the official portrait pattern for the living. [...] He [Muli] and his brother set the whole thing up [...]. There

> was no precedent regarding a pattern for post-mortem photos. It seems to me to be simply an extension of photos that people would have while they are living. (ibid.)

Following this line of argument, one may also consider the portrait of the *Tikayat* of Bonai with his guard of honour after he had passed away (Figure 3.11) to be an expression of broader norms for official portraiture. Unlike the Bauri, however, in royal families, this sitting position on chairs was very common, and there are also life portraits (paintings and photographs) in standing positions. It is also noteworthy that the *Tikayat's* grandmother (Figure 3.10) was photographed in a sitting position on the ground and not in a chair, which may or may not be related to gender hierarchies.

Returning to the Bauri photograph (Figure 3.16), we see that Muli is holding his father's hand or arm. According to Freeman, 'it is clear that the brothers are propping up the body—holding hand, head, feet—so it is clear that they were willing to do so, and also that they did it for the purposes of having a photo taken' (Freeman, pers. comm.). This raises the question of how important is contact with the body, including as a pose, between the person who has passed away and the bereaved. In contrast to Freeman's argument, other images seem to suggest that the body is touched, though there was no requirement to hold it in, for example, the Jadia Parja image illustrated earlier or an image of the Sharma family in Dhanbad which depicts the corpse lying with the hands of its relatives touching it. Among Odia Baptist Christians too, relatives often prefer to touch the corpse: 'Some relatives and very dear ones touch the corpse out of affection and respect. They show their last love for him/her' (Rashmi Pramanik, pers. comm.). Similarly, the Sharma family argued that the touching expresses emotions often linked to crying (Kiran Sharma, pers. comm.). One actually finds many images showing close bodily contact in the same album, as is also seen in Figure 3.3, as illustrated earlier. Similarly, in relation to pictures taken in Assam, a colleague, Mridusmita Mahanta (pers. comm.) would exclaim 'all want to touch it!' It is therefore tempting to interpret the touching of the corpse—be it the forehead or feet, etc.—as literally as well as metaphorically 'holding on' to the beloved one while simultaneously letting go. At the same time, climatic conditions, new technical possibilities and hygiene regulations may also limit bodily contact after death, for example, by using glass cooling boxes as temporary coffins, as in Figure 3.15.[19]

Unlike the Bauri around Bhubaneswar, Odia Baptist Christians seem to prefer the corpse to be lying on a bed or in a coffin (the photographs

Figure 3.15

Death of elderly Odia Baptist Christian, Sambalpur, Odisha, 2013

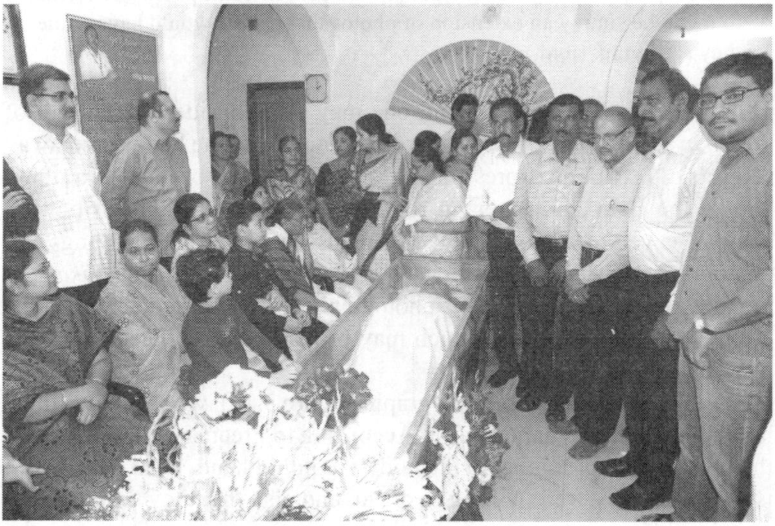

Source: Courtesy of Pramanik family.

Figure 3.16

Post-mortem photograph of Muli's father, Bhubaneswar, Odisha, 1971

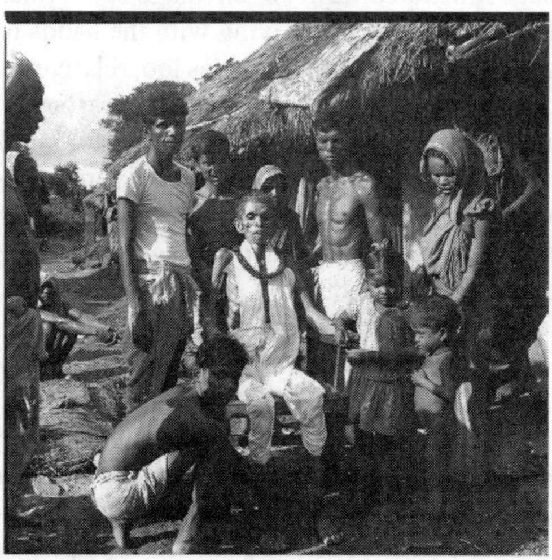

Source: © 1971 James M. Freeman.

of the young boy being an exception rather than the norm). Moreover, in Bengal and particularly Calcutta, we find evidence not only for a relatively common tradition of post-mortem photography from the early twentieth century onwards but also for positioning the corpse so that it is lying or semi-lying. Thus, the following examples, which belong to the collection of the Center for Studies in Social Sciences, Calcutta (CSSSC) and were suggested to us by its archivist, Abhijit Bhattacharya (pers. comm.), add a stronger historical dimension to our discussion concerning post-mortem photography in India. Taking them into consideration, we see early photographs with the corpse in a lying position, followed by images from the 1970s and 1990s with corpses in sitting positions, on to recent examples such as images of the *Rajasahib* of Bonai (2011) in a lying position. One may speculate that images with the corpse in a sitting position, sharing some iconographic features with the so-called 'alive, yet dead' images (Ruby 1995), may slowly disappear, while images in a sitting position are often favoured in memorial images (see Aghria Figure 3.19).

Figure 3.17 was taken in the family of BN De around 1910, the family being famous for having belonged to the first generation of civil servants in Calcutta and to the Hindu reformist movement, the Brahmo Samaj.[20] It is known that the woman died a natural death and that the photograph

Figure 3.17

Post-mortem photograph of a family member of BN De, Calcutta, roughly 1910

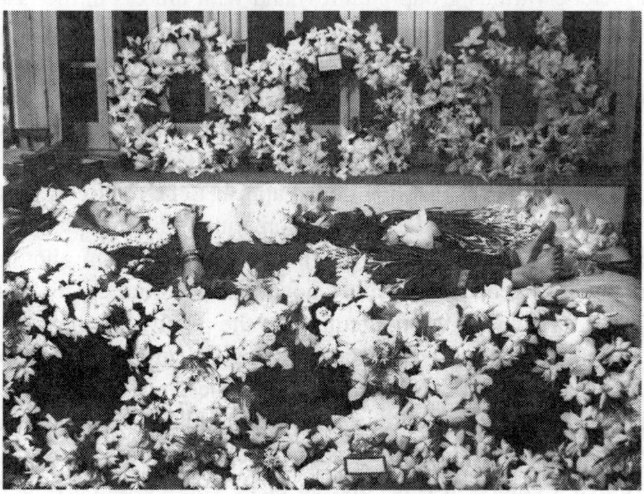

Source: Courtesy of Centre for Studies in Social Sciences, Calcutta, Kolkata.

was taken before the body was carried away from home in order to be cremated. The picture depicts the deceased only, who is covered with flowers, while a darker sari is covering her head. Some bangles and her painted feet are visible too, possibly indicating the status as a married woman, as in Figures 3.7 and 3.8.

According to Bhattacharya (pers. comm.), the image could be considered a 'standard photo from a Brahmo family', a point corroborated by another photograph of Biswanth Kar. According to historian Kailash Chandra Dash (pers. comm.), Kar was not only a famous Brahmo thinker and reformer of Odisha but also an editor (1903–1934) of *Utkala Sahitya*, a popular Odia monthly magazine from Cuttack. The photograph taken by his son Mahanada Kar shows his father, who passed away in 1934, lying on a stretcher covered over with flowers, leaving only his face and folded hands visible. The image was subsequently published as the final page of *Utkala Sahitya* in 1934.[21] Dash (ibid.) suggests that 'according to Brahmo rite he was buried in a sleeping pose, though already dead'. Though Dash makes this point retrospectively, it is significant in light of the pervasive euphemism used in Euro-American contexts of death: the last sleep. This was the only time that this association of death with sleep—both, sleep and death, Hypnos and Thanatos, being brothers in ancient Greek mythology—was mentioned in India, whereas it has a long tradition in the Western culture.

The aforementioned individual Brahmo Samaj image depicting the lavish flower arrangements (with some flower ring-bouquets combined with small texts) has a lot in common iconographically with post-mortem portraits taken by Odia Baptist Christians in Sambalpur (who, however, would include various group pictures) and with images in the last sleep pose, but this is the only time we came across such a statement thus far. However, it is significant that this exception should be linked to the Brahmo Samaj, since, given the intensive intellectual debating of European and Christian ideas in Brahmo Samaj circles in the nineteenth century, the idea of depicting the corpse as if it were asleep might well have emerged then.

While the two poses just mentioned appear to be relatively common, and we encountered several examples, sometimes photographs also show a conjugal couple (e.g., Figure 3.18). Here, post-mortem photography appears to follow general shifts and innovations in portraiture by allocating new spaces for conjugality, particularly in the relatively 'progressive' or 'western-influenced' environment of growing Calcutta in the late colonial era. As Karlekar (2005: 5–6) convincingly argues, 'photographs recorded significant changes in middle- and upper-middle-class urban Bengali society (i.e. men in new professions, the evolution of the nuclear family, [...] women's emergent roles and so on)'. This particularly concerns

Figure 3.18

Post-mortem picture of Shrichandra Mukhopadhyay's wife, Hooghly district, West Bengal, 1930s

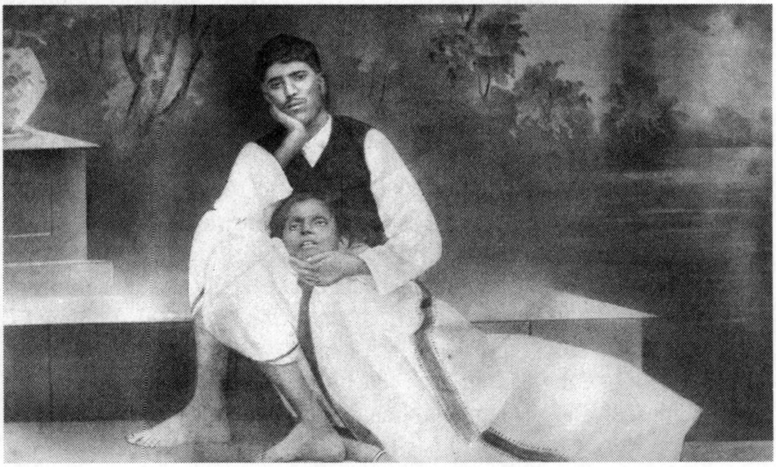

Source: Courtesy of Sibaji Bandyopadhyay and Centre for Studies in Social Sciences, Calcutta, Kolkata.

Brahmo Samaj and Hindu reformist families as well. These transformations, such as a broader tendency to accept separate spaces for couples after marriage, have been reported more recently elsewhere in India too (see, e.g., Wadley [1994] 2010: 23). Accordingly, the 'new family' was increasingly visualised in wedding photographs or other social events and moved into the public sphere, especially if the woman discontinued *purdah* practices (Karlekar 2005: 97ff). Though Karlekar does not focus on post-mortem photographs, it is likely that these societal changes had an impact on them too in the sense that conjugal intimacy was captured here as well, but our sample is too small to make qualified statements in this regard. However, so far, we have only encountered post-mortem photographs depicting the couple with the surviving spouse in Calcutta when just a single photograph was taken or preserved. In more recent cases from Odisha, either such photographs of conjugality beyond death are missing or else couple-centred images like Figure 3.7 of the Samal family (though here with a daughter) form part of albums that include shots from different angles and shots of different groups of relatives, as described earlier.

Figure 3.18, preserved at CSSSC, seems very rare and deserves closer scrutiny. According to Sibaji Bandyopadhyay (pers. comm.), this photograph, taken in the 1930s (possibly around 1932), depicts Shrichandra

Mukhopadhyay (youngest brother of Bandyopadhyay's mother's father) and his wife, whose name is not remembered.[22] Mukhopadhyay belonged to a well-known family based in Hooghly, roughly 60 km from Calcutta and famous for its law court. As an elite and 'educated' Hindu Brahmin family, many members had turned to law as profession since the late nineteenth century. The conjugal couple takes centre stage and it shows a woman in her early 20s who had just passed away, her head with open eyes being in the lap of her husband, in his late 20s. Photographed at a crematorium, a photographic artist from an unknown studio later added a 'theatrical back-drop' (ibid.), possibly proving Pinney's (1997: 161) point that townspeople were more willing to experiment with back-drops or effects than villagers who preferred somewhat more realistic images. With naturalistic landscape elements, but also with architectural features in the back-drop composition, the scene may suggest a cemetery. Instead of including a death bed, a more intimate, semi-sitting/semi-lying position was preferred. As Bandyopadhyay (pers. comm.) explained:

> There is little doubt that the theatricality organized around the dead body was the brainwave of the bereaved husband. [...] taking the (last) photo at the crematorium was a sort of practice then. But, it was not so widespread in the thirties of the twentieth century in moffusil towns—it was yet to become 'customary'.

Though Figure 3.18 was sometimes considered as 'photo of ghost' (Bhattacharya, pers. comm.), it is not hidden, but relatively openly displayed in Bandyopadhyay's maternal grandfather's house at Hooghly. As Bandyopadhyay (pers. comm.) argued:

> [...] this is quite surprising [considering that the family is known to be orthodox—authors]. Any public show of affection between married couples—forget about the unmarried ones—would still be heavily frowned upon there. Yet, this peculiar photo adorns their wall. It illustrates the (cruel) irony involving suppression—you can only come out, display your intimate feelings, only after you are dead. (Here 'you' is the woman, whose name no one remembers.)

Bandyopadhyay also stressed that such a 'play with the *Eros-Thanatos* combine' and the attempt to re-create 'a living proof of conjugal love' is indeed rare, even unique (ibid.). Thus, the time of death may not have led 'only' to the open expression of affection, it may also have enabled such affection to be photographically fixed.[23] One might also note that gestures suggesting or depicting intimacy, such as close bodily contact, were frowned upon not only in India but also in Europe at that time. As Linkman (2011: 62) points out, in those rare cases when, for example, a husband is shown holding the body of his dead wife, sometimes an object like a Bible was included to legitimise the pose and indicate a respectable relationship sanctified by God and going beyond the 'till death do us part'.

And while the display of affection between husband and wife may have been exceptional, at least in the 1930s, other images also captured the affection between mother and son (Figure 3.1). Furthermore, Odia Baptist Christians stated that '[w]hen we look at the images we look at our beloved and recollect our past memories', while a member of the Samal family said, 'sometimes I feel emotions, then I look at it', indicating the link between these photographs and (expressions of) affection. As King (2003: 211) argues, family photographs are used to remember the details of a past event, as well as to revive emotions and feelings in relation to those who are depicted. The latter statement from the Samal family seems to suggest a possible inversion, that is, that emotions are channelled to photographs rather than images being used to release them. However, the post-mortem images may be kept away from children because parents fear they might be shocked (Kiran Sharma, pers. comm.).

In addition to the aforementioned photograph, the husband, as family members remember, in fact also took or arranged to take another one of his wife during the cremation, but, 'given its goriness, others in the family destroyed it' (Bandyopadhyay, pers. comm.). There is no proof of the existence of this second image, but the notion of goriness hints at Grace's reaction in the movie, and, therefore, such notions may have emerged in urban spaces in Calcutta, with the significant difference that another post-mortem picture was still openly displayed. More importantly here, it is worth noticing that Figure 3.18 is openly displayed in the first-floor (inner) veranda of Bandyopadhyay's maternal grandfather's house at Hooghly. We will come back to this point.

While a few photographs like Figures 3.17 and 3.18 were apparently taken in or next to the crematorium, or also inside the house; most of the photographs we came across were actually taken in an outside setting, such as on a veranda or in an inner yard of the house, in front of the house or even on the road (see Figure 3.14—Berger, pers. comm.), with different explanations for this being put forward. Regarding the Bauri, Freeman (pers. comm.) argues that inside or outside did not matter as far as post-mortem photographs are concerned since all places would be polluted anyway. Yet, the Bauri pictures were arranged outside the house. In the case of other communities like the Aghrias, the location clearly mattered. Returning to the photograph of the old Aghria lady (Figure 3.1) on her bed, one can see that it is placed on the veranda of her house. This place is in line with Aghria ideas that one should not die inside a room. Aghrias invert life and death quite clearly by arguing that birth takes place inside, in an inner 'confinement' room, while dying should take place outside.

Ideas about delivery in an inner room at home, such that a birth would never take place on a veranda, are shared by many communities in the region, but unlike the Aghrias, members of the Samal family argued that the post-mortem pictures were taken on the veranda because it was easier for family members to gather there and therefore pictures were not taken inside. A similar reason, that is simply convenience, was suggested by Odia Baptist Christians:

> The pictures are generally taken in the outer veranda. Well, there is no specific restriction, but usually pictures are taken in the outside as it can be taken from different angles with different groups of people (like all sisters, all brothers, all uncles, all aunts). (Rashmi Pramanik, pers. comm.)

At the same time, an increasing shift to hospitals and nursing homes, even emergency rooms, can be observed. Many Aghria and Pana would agree that delivery should take place in hospital, particularly if the mother's condition is critical, and the same holds true for life-threatening conditions and the final stage of life. One may speculate that such a shift may lead to more post-mortem pictures being taken at hospitals, and a recently taken picture of Odia Baptist Christians offers evidences to substantiate this. While access to photography has changed radically with the advent of mobile technology, enabling snapshots to be taken in hospitals, crematoriums have also been considerably modified in recent decades, for example, in changing from open pyres to electrical furnaces, thereby reducing both procedures and 'photo-ops' substantially (Bhattacharya, pers. comm.).

(Post-)Post-mortem Photographs and Their Afterlife: Memory and Social Use

In the following, we move away from a stricter iconographic analysis to link post-mortem images to memory, affection and the wider social use. As Kuhn and McAllister (2006: 1) have already pointed out, photography is a prime memo-technique, and photographs function as a locus for 'shared memory' that

> confronts us with the fleeting nature of our world and reminds us of our mortality. In seeming to capture times and places lost in the past, the photograph can disturb the present moment and the contemporary landscape with troubling or nostalgic memories and with forgotten, or all too vividly remembered, histories. (ibid.)

As Barthes ([1980] 1984: 91) stressed, photographs may also block memory—be anti-memory in this sense—and the post-mortem and memorial images may actually produce a new, selective memory. However, preserving the memory of a beloved one seems to be a strong motive for taking post-mortem pictures, and a common explanation is the need for a photograph when none was taken during the lifetime of the deceased. This reason is clearly articulated by the Calcutta family, already mentioned, who were interviewed in Jain's documentary. Here the son argues:

> No photos were taken during his [the father's—authors] lifetime. So to keep his memory alive the whole family assembled around his dead body, because he was one of us. […] Many of the relatives you see here have passed away. History. That is history. (*City of Photos* 2005, 52′50″–54′00″)

In this way, the photograph stores, combines and revives individual and social memories (Assmann 2006). But the image-making does not stop there. As a Calcutta photographer in the same documentary adds, post-mortem photographs are subsequently used to produce memorial images being over-painted, thus producing quasi post-post-mortem pictures that facilitate a visual exchange:

> When someone who's never been photographed dies, the relatives come and ask us to make a photograph. So we work from the dead person's photo, then we show it to them to ask if it's OK. If they say yes, his cheeks were like this, lips like that, then the photo is complete. Neither you nor I can say what the eyes were like. Only someone close to the person can tell. If they say his eyes were deer-like, or round, that's what I have to go by. In the photo you get the nose, the hair, but not the eyes. It's the eyes which are closed, isn't it? And that's why they come, to have the eyes opened. (*City of Photos* 2005, 51′10″–52′50″)

Jain's film itself documents the process of creating a memorial portrait on the basis of a post-mortem photograph in Bengal, that is, starting from an image of a person laid out on a bed surrounded by seven to eight relatives sitting close around him (apparently with bodily contact).[24] At first glance, the opening of the eyes suggests a parallel to images in the so-called 'alive, yet dead' pose in Europe and North America, where throughout the nineteenth century, photographers discussed techniques for taking post-mortem pictures and keeping customers' wishes in mind, the aim frequently was to produce 'the most life-like picture' (Gihon 1871: 513). One key manipulation made to conceal the death of the portrait subject and to achieve a life-like result was to open his or her eyes. The argument by cultural historian Thomas Macho gives an explanation for the significance of opening the eyes: in the moment of death, eye contact fades away, and 'I can see that I am no longer seen; in that is the deepest injury that can be inflicted on the survivors' (Macho 2009: 142). In trying to overcome this injury and reinstall the gaze by evoking direct contact with the spectator, the opening or better reviving of the eyes was central. Apart from aligning with the living through the gaze, it is in particular the bringing of the body into an upright, often sitting pose through which the fiction of a lively narrative is created.[25]

As discussed earlier with reference to Blanchot, the amalgam of bodily and photographic indices leads to an intensified trace that refers back to the once living person. Therefore, in particular the 'alive, yet dead' pose seems to produce a meaning that exceeds the fact of death and that evokes the material continuity of the deceased person in this world—even if it is the (imagined) materiality of photography that provides the 'body'. This might also be meant when, in the movie *The Others*, Mrs Mills says that 'the souls would go on living through the portraits'.

While opening the eyes may equally be considered the most important part of the retouching of the image in Indian, and particularly Hindu contexts, this transformation is also linked to the concept of *darśan* or visual exchange (Eck 1981). A frontal view with eyes wide open facilitates not only the taking of *darśan* on the part of the survivor but equally importantly the giving of *darśan* from the perspective of the beloved ancestors. Their memorial pictures often possess the same *darśanic* quality that iconic images or idols of gods have, as do gods, saints and kings themselves, all being part of a wider divine hierarchy. Turning post-mortem photographs into memorial images—producing post-post-mortem pictures—appears to be informed by the same ideas about communicating with higher beings, apart from creating an 'as if alive' impression. Jain's film *City of Photos* offers a vivid example of the process.

Thus, the resulting memorial image should not simply be mistaken for an 'alive, yet dead' image of the 'Western' tradition, but rather be considered to be a 'dead to idealised index-icon' transformation. Closely observing and analysing photographic traditions in Madhya Pradesh, Pinney (1997: 201) noticed a desire to produce memorial images, and not always from post-mortem photographs. He also met experts catering to this need. One of the expert's (Joshi's) 'artistry' was 'concerned with perfecting the past, rendering the transient flux recorded in photographic emulsion into more permanent, truer forms'. He worked 'in the space between photography's indexical randomness and [...] clients' demands for images constructed according to a significantly different aesthetic' (ibid.), that is, their desire for 'icons' for ritual commemoration, and not merely the opening of the eyes. We therefore propose to speak of 'index-icons' here. The statement echoes what Gutman (1982: 106) found with reference to painted photographs, that is, '[p]hotographs in their "pure" form, were never as important as the "picture" that finally resulted', but rather a photographic look and a conception of people flow into the image. Thus, the idea of a cherished memorial image differed substantially from Barthes' desire to find a photograph that brought out his mother's essential kindness. Instead, somewhat 'perfectionised', less individualistic and perhaps more timeless images seem to be in demand. However, it remains unclear whether images closer to the death and thus relatively more senior images are preferred as the basis for the photographic negotiation exemplified by Pinney, or relatively more youthful images, if not produced from post-mortem images?

Besides, in the cases we encountered in central-eastern India, post-mortem photographs were often taken despite the family already owning a range of photographs. Thus, a lack of other photographs might be a motivation for some families keen to produce a memorial image as mentioned earlier, but this finding seriously questions any singular explanation for post-mortem photography in India. Similarly, in Pinney's (1997: 139) account, post-mortem pictures, as a photographer from Nagda (Madhya Pradesh) explained to him, were taken 'usually (though not always) because the subject was not photographed during his or her lifetime'.[26] While this may still suggest a certain exceptionality to taking post-mortem pictures, with the increasing proliferation of technology, including mobile phones, there is a clear tendency in central-eastern India nowadays to take post-mortem photographs in addition to or despite the existence of other conventional portraits and/or group photographs taken of a certain individual previously.

A different explanation for post-mortem photographs is put forward by Odia Baptist Christians, who usually take several but prefer to display

Figure 3.19

Ancestor photographs in Aghria household, 2003

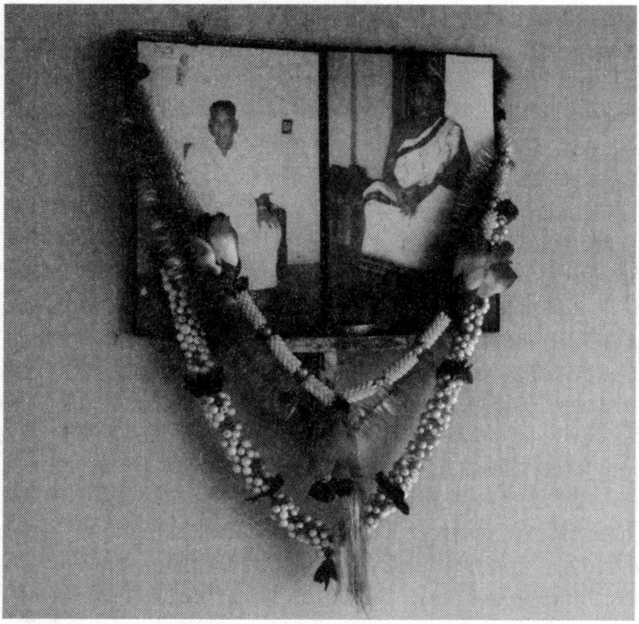

Source: Uwe Skoda.

portraits of ancestors taken during their lifetimes on walls with the eyes looking at the camera, as in Aghria Figure 3.19, though they do not ascribe a *darśanic* quality to the picture, nor do they put any garland on it or venerate it. They argue that post-mortem pictures basically function to inform relatives and friends about the ceremonies. On the one hand, those who cannot make it to the funeral can look at the photographs or album while visiting the house of the deceased. On the other hand, such photographs are sent to relatives residing far away.

> [...] these photos are still even sent to relatives those who stay afar and are unable to come during that period. Not as a proof but to let them know the entire proceedings of the funeral process. A full set of it is sent, so that they can visualize the moments of those days. (Rashmi Pramanik, pers. comm.)

And asked whether the families had other images of those photographed after their death, we received the following reply: 'Yes, the family has other photos of the deceased person also. On occasion of his/her marriage, birthday, marriage anniversary, family get-together, house foundation day, funeral services of other person'. These words not only suggest a multitude of photographs available in relatively richer Christian families but also that all life-cycle rituals and other important occasions are customarily photographed, reminiscent of Bourdieu's argument that photography is essentially linked to the 'domestic cult' (Bourdieu [1965] 1990: 19), with the post-mortem picture being the last of the life-cycle images. Moreover, as Strassler (2010: 204–05) pointed out in relation to Indonesian photography, 'photographs can also move between [...] complementary modes of memory', that is, forms of documentation (*documentasi*) may exist side by side with the idea of 'memory-objects' (*kenangan*) as 'congealed embodiments of past experience imbued with the presence of their absent owners' (ibid.: 204) or rather loved ones.

In mentioning and including two post-mortem images in *Camera Indica* taken in 1975 and 1996, respectively—both deceased being surrounded by family members—Pinney (1997: 139) was told that these pictures were

> [...] an expression of a combination of the love that (Indian) children have for their parents, and the need for grief-stricken relatives to *cling* [emphasis added] to memories of the deceased, just as it was common practice to keep clothes and shoes which had belonged to the deceased. Also significant, perhaps, is the fact that since an individual's *pret* (spirit) is not released from the body until cremation, Hindu death is comparatively slow and inert bodies are able to retain vital qualities.

An important question following this quote for us is: What does it mean here 'to cling'? What does adhere to the image? What do various communities see in the images, given that in Chhattisgarh, for example, '[p]opular [Hindu—authors] conceptions of the fate of the spirit (*jiv*) after death are generally quite vague' (Babb 1975: 91), while the Aghrias state that at the time of death, first a person's life energy (*jiban*) leaves the body and therefore the body does not move any longer, while the soul (*atma*) will leave upon the breaking of the skull during cremation, both being part of the transformation from *pret* (potentially malevolent ghost) to *pitru* (ancestor). Is an ancestor fully visible in a post-mortem image, or is the latter a more limited representation of the beloved linked to a disintegrating social person?

Taking post-mortem photographs when previous images exist may in fact suggest a certain continuity, or at least the absence of a clear rupture as far as the photographibility of the person-body is concerned. This tendency seems to be substantiated by the way photographs are kept, that is, they are often not separated from other photographs. For example, in the Samal family, Figures 3.7 and 3.8 are kept together with other images in an album including images of the father as child in Pondicherry, and the family saw no problem in combining post-mortem pictures with others in a single album. Similarly, Odia Baptist Christians would say 'Yes, they [post-mortem pictures—authors] are kept together with other albums. There is no problem [...] These pictures are kept in Almirah in a common place as with other albums also' (Rashmi Pramanik, pers. comm.). Similarly, the photographs of the Bonai royal family were placed in an album with wedding photographs. Or, the Aghria Figure 3.1 was displayed together with wedding photographs, individual portraits, etc., in a room frequented by guests.

This semi-public display of these photographs also suggests that photographs of the dead are not considered impure, and no interlocutor in any community argued that taking post-mortem photographs, looking at them, etc., would have any polluting impact. Thus, there is no problem involved in keeping them inside the house. In the case of the premature death of a popular peon in her college, M. Mahanta (pers. comm.) narrated that many people, including herself, took pictures of the well-attended funeral and the decorated body with their cameras and mobiles, but no serious pollution was linked to this photographic practice (keeping the image on the mobile or computer here). As with any funeral, she would simply change her dress on arriving home, would take a bath and sprinkle a bit of Ganga water with *tulsi* (basil). Cameras and photographs, however, remain unaffected by death pollution. Therefore, Aghria farmers may not differ much from some families in Calcutta who place such images quite visibly in their drawing rooms, bedrooms or on their verandas. They often combine pre- and post-mortem images in the same pictorial space, whether an album or a drawing room. The continuous display and visibility of death in these images stand in stark contrast to Grace's wish to remove the pictures from her house presented in the film and thus bring us back to the divergent trajectories of post-mortem photography in Euro-American and Indian contexts.

Conclusion

Our investigation into the visibility and photographibility of death and the corpse in central-eastern India started with an example illustrating the almost ubiquitous presence of private post-mortem pictures. Unlike our second example exemplifying the forgotten knowledge of post-mortem pictures in Western Europe and North America, in India, according to our preliminary findings, the production of post-mortem photographs had grown rather steadily in recent decades due to the easier accessibility of technology. In particular, there has been an almost inflationary increase from the beginning of the digital revolution onwards.

Starting by arguing for a distinctive trajectory of post-mortem photography in central-eastern India, we ventured into an iconographic comparison inspired by the two broad traditions of photographic analysis derived from Bourdieu on the one hand and Barthes on the other. Like Barthes, we were interested in what might adhere to an image and why people cling to a post-mortem picture. How important is the tangible quality of the image, and what do people actually see when they look at these images? Are viewers able to see the inner or outer qualities of the sitter, as Barthes and Pinney would both argue with reference to European and Indian photographs, respectively? These questions need to be applied systematically to the specific case of post-mortem photographs, which requires in-depth, multi-sited field research beyond the scope of this preliminary mapping. However, our initial findings suggest, for example, for India, a crucial link to the concept of personhood linked to the stepwise disintegration of social persons in Hindu communities.

Moreover, we not only came across the photographic image as an index in Peircian terms but also other indices in India such as footprints. Perhaps, even more importantly, we found combinations of indices, such as a photograph preserved together with a footprint in India. This double or multiple indexicality suggests a mutual reinforcing of traces of the referent, which is valued and which hints at this Barthesian quality of photography. However, indices may also compete with each other, and the limited historical evidence we have collected so far also indicates a shift from footprints to photoprints in India.

In our analysis, we also followed Bourdieu's approach, yet with special reference to the dead, when we asked who photographed the corpse when and for what purpose. What is not only technologically but also socially photographable and what is not? Thus, going beyond the broader trajectories of whether the corpse has been visible and photographable—or alternatively invisiblised—from the mid-nineteenth century onwards, we investigated the question of how—including when and where—the corpse has been photographed and has been made photographable. This led us to focus on the linkages between post-mortem photography and the life cycle with the status of the deceased within it, and also between post-mortem photography and poses, as well as locations. Based on a largely iconographic analysis, these categories, which emerge from the empirical evidence, appeared as useful starting points for a comparative mapping.

At the same time, all of these angles immediately reveal the ways in which life cycles, poses, locations, social usages, etc., are culturally specific, as well as being determined by gender, class, religion and other factors. A few questions with preliminary findings can be summarised here to indicate possible routes for further research.

1. In which age group is the corpse photographable or invisiblised? Central-eastern Indian contexts—here particularly among peasants—document an emphasis on post-mortem images of full social persons or at least family members closer to marriage (as among Odia Baptists) rather than as babies or infants. In contrast to images of children, post-mortem photographs of elderly deceased have been captured in after-death likenesses. For example, a relative who passed away due to old age, thus dying a 'good death', may commonly be photographed in the midst of a kin group, thus often keeping physical contact by, for example, touching the feet as a mark of respect and signifying a senior position in the life cycle, while other markers of status and wealth might be added too. However, our evidence also suggests that, although old age may be a conducive factor, other aspects such as the role or status within the life cycle—for example, being an auspicious wife rather than a widow—may be equally relevant here.
2. Where is it acceptable to depict the corpse? Linked to the availability of technologies, and specifically the introduction of the Kodak Brownie camera and later models, as well as to the medicalisation of death and the increasing trend to die in hospitals, we came across considerable spatial shifts. That is, photographing the corpse in studios seems to have disappeared, though studios next to crematoriums in Bengal seemed to have served customers till the end of the twentieth century. Earlier photographs also suggest the difference in value attached to spaces, for example, Aghria peasants believed that death, unlike birth, should not occur inside a room, and most images from rural India have been taken outside (verandas or even open streets). Spatial usage is generally, and not only in central-eastern India, linked to available technologies and conditions of exposure (e.g., sufficient light), as well as demands on

the part of the depicted (e.g., limited private space inside to include relatives in the large group photographs that are often sought-after).

3. In what position is the corpse presented to the camera? The poses need to be carefully historicised as well as localised, but our preliminary mapping suggests that poses like the '(last) sleep', popular in Europe and the United States, are predominantly absent in India (with possible exceptions in Calcutta, and here particularly among followers of reform movements). However, one finds greater similarities between the 'alive, yet dead' images and Indian post-mortem images in the sense that many of them can be understood as extensions of official portraiture of the corpse. While open eyes are considered a sign of life across cultures and regions, reasons for opening eyes appear to differ, and a more *darśanic* exchange through eyes is crucial in Indian memorial images. Moreover, physical contact between deceased and bereaved seems very common in Indian contexts, while casket photographs in particular seem to highlight the separation between survivors and the corpse as encapsulated in the coffin as boundary marker. Yet, post-mortem photographs with assembled families are found frequently in eastern India, though the emphasis may range from the aspect of belonging (s/he was one of us) to the idea of commemorating the event with a visual guest list. This may well be interpreted in a Bourdieuesque sense, that is, photography as solemnising and 'immortalising' central episodes of family life or as part of the domestic cult. However, judging from the ethnographic literature on central-eastern India, it is hardly surprising that we also find a larger body of photographs depicting the deceased—often lying down or in a semi-lying position—surrounded by the family or network of kin present, thus stressing the larger extended family, rather than being conceived as individual portraits or nuclear families (parents and children).

Many photographs largely conformed to such acceptable patterns of post-mortem images. However, there are also a few photographs we came across that deviate from these wider patterns. We argued that the liminal position of the dead body, signifying simultaneously absence and presence, enabled or facilitated forms of visualisation that were hardly possible under other circumstances. The expression of conjugal love and affection in an orthodox Hindu family, possible only at the time of death, is a rare case in point here.

While we largely focused on the iconography of individual images, combinations of indices or compilations of images into albums (either exclusively for post-mortem images, as among Odia Baptist Christians and in the film example *The Others*, or placed next to other life-cycle rituals) brought us to consider the social usage of post-mortem images. Though information is often scarce, we tried to include this aspect as far as possible, referring also to the 'post-production' level. Post-mortem images have often been crucial in the production of memorial images linked to ideas of respect, honour and status. A desire to depict a beloved one posthumously in a life-like manner as a respected family member is central to Indian memorial images, as well as constituting a visual exchange with the living.

In other cases, post-mortem images have been taken despite the existence of other portraits taken during the deceased's lifetime, raising the question of the specific value attached to final mementoes, while the production of memorial images as post-post-mortem pictures contradicts the idea of a last memento to some extent. Clearly, the close link between post-mortem photography and memory, as well as the possibility of photography by its very nature blocking memory, needs to be scrutinised in future research. However, the making of memorial images in India already reveals specific processes of negotiation between the ideal and the evidential, between who has been in front of the camera and an improved, perfectionised image of an ancestor, usually in a frontal, *darśanic* pose—quite similar to earlier indigenous traditions of photography in India, namely painted photographs. These processes may or may not be based on post-mortem photographs, perhaps highlighting the fact that, as MacDougall (1992: 123) noted, 'in the end every photograph is that of a missing person'.

Notes

1. This chapter is based on field research and archival work in India. Various periods of field research were conducted among the Aghrias and later among royal families in Odisha, particularly in 2001/2002 and again in 2004/2005, apart from annual visits until 2016 (Uwe Skoda). A recently initiated project in Varanasi has not been taken in account here. We are grateful to various scholars and friends for sharing their extensive knowledge of post-mortem photographs with us, as well as for giving us permission to reprint their photographs here. We would like to thank particularly Sibaji Bandyopadhyay, Abhijit Bhattacharya, Peter Berger, Roma Chatterji, Kailash Chandra

Dash, Sri Bir Kesari Indra Deo (*Rajasahib* of Bonai), James Freeman, Clayton Lewis, Ellen Maas, Mridusmita Mahanta, Rashmi Pramanik, Swarnalata Samal and Kiran Sharma. Diacritic marks are not used in the chapter.

2. Even though relatives who had just passed away were photographed in various poses, director Alejandro Amenábar focuses solely on portraits that depict the deceased as if they were in a deep sleep. It is only because of this that the image-inherent logic of the composition leads to those who are depicted being misinterpreted as sleeping.
3. Visualised by the cross-fade of one of the post-mortem pictures with the cracking flames of the fire place.
4. Thus, we will not discuss pictures that emerged in the fields of forensics, pathology or criminology, nor press or war photography and neither art projects, though we are aware that rich traditions exist in these fields. Pictures of politicians who have just passed away are frequently found in Indian newspapers. Going back to the colonial era, photographs linked to death are occasionally reported, such as photographs of Felice Beato taken after the so-called Indian Mutiny (1857–1858) or Willoughby Wallace Hooper's controversial images of victims of the Madras Famine in 1878. For an account of the scandal of Colonel Hooper photographing the execution of dacoits in Mandalay, see: Geary 1886: 241–43; also http://www.luminous-lint.com/app/photographer/Willoughby_Wallace__Hooper/. Since information on some photographs is rather scarce, we do not distinguish between professional and private photographers, i.e., the photographs we are discussing may have been taken by family members and neighbours interested in photography, or even by anthropologists who allowed the survivors to arrange the photograph themselves.
5. Our rather cursory investigation suggests that post-mortem photography is not evenly popular, neither in India nor in the West. In India, it might be considerably less in vogue in regions like Tamil Nadu or Garhwal. For an unusual case from Punjab, see Chopra, Chapter 9. Looking at the Indian evidence, we came across post-mortem photographs among Hindu, Christian and *Adivasi* communities and families and heard of photographs depicting the mourning process among Muslims.
6. Relating these traditions of image-making—across continents, but also across time and academic disciplines (anthropology and Kulturwissenschaft) raises important questions for the respective fields and comparing the two trajectories of post-mortem photography is productive for scholars working on either region. We believe it is inspiring to think about and make sense of the similarities and striking differences. However, we are painfully aware of risks such an endeavour entails, i.e., projecting findings from one side onto the other or up-/downstreaming respective results as discussed in ethnohistory circles (Axtell 1979; Fenton 1952).
7. This might be an archival problem, since photography arrived in India soon after the Daguerreian process was demonstrated at the Académie des Sciences et des Beaux-Arts in 1839.
8. It can also be assumed for European countries and North America that taking pictures of the recently deceased using a mobile phone is on the rise. Nevertheless, they are often taken quickly and surreptitiously at hospital, capturing 'candid shots of an unprepared still warm body', and thus differing from the thoroughly prepared and staged sceneries of post-mortem or memorial photographs (Burch 2009: 675).
9. A small presentation on the subject during an MA course at the Department of Sociology, University of Delhi, might be indicative here. In the discussion, some

students were clearly not familiar with the practice and rather bewildered by the examples from Odisha, other students coming from UP or Kerala had seen such photographs.

10. He argued that: 'In the course of the nineteenth century bourgeois society has, by means of hygienic and social, private and public institutions, realised a secondary effect which may have been its subconscious main purpose: to make it possible for people to avoid the sight of the dying', and, one might add, to avoid the sight of the corpse.
11. Caduff also noticed the prohibition on taking post-mortem pictures at the burning ghats in Varanasi, which needs to be understood in the context of (Western) tourism and its excessive photographic practices and as such seems to be rather an exception.
12. During a short field trip in 2011, Birgit Lettmann visited four private hospitals, a government hospital and a medical research public university in Delhi. Even though some of the doctors and hospital staff interviewed were aware of the practice of taking photographs of stillborn or perinatal deceased babies in America and Europe to help parents cope with their loss, all of them stressed that this was not practiced in Delhi hospitals.
13. Among the Aghrias, if a child dies before the rituals of the 6th/21st day after birth have been conducted or before the child has been fed the first rice, only a small feast must be served to the *jati* (members of one's own caste), and the barber and washerman have to be called. A Brahmin or priest is only required if death occurs after the 21st day, as most Aghrias say. For all unmarried Aghrias dying later, a relatively basic funeral is performed on the 7th day after death (not between the 9th and 12th day after death). In the case of small children or babies—before the age of one or two years or before five years according to others—no *samadhi* (memorial shrines) is built, and they are usually buried, not cremated.
14. For example, Uwe Skoda also encountered a photograph showing the landlord sitting on a chair with his two wives kneeling down on either side of him and touching his feet in the Aghria household already mentioned.
15. According to Sharma, the footprints were taken by a Bauri neighbour when her father's father passed away in 1998 at the age of 58. The neighbour was also involved in cleaning the body and applying turmeric and sandalwood paste (*chandan*) to it before he took the grandfather's footprint in a lying position. The corpse was later positioned on a construction of bamboo poles, garlanded with marigold flowers and covered with a white and yellow cloth (called *kafan* and *pitambari*, respectively). The latter also had *Jai Shri Ram* (Hail Lord Ram) written on it. It was at this time that a professional photographer known to the family as a family photographer took several pictures, including the full body on the bamboo poles and the upper body surrounded by relatives touching it. Afterwards the corpse was carried to the cremation ground.
16. According to Bautze, he lived in a Bengali family around 40 years ago, where a post-mortem photograph of the recently deceased head of the family was placed inside the house (over the architrave) next to his red-coloured footprint. However, a year later, the photograph had been removed.
17. In an example presented by Pinney (1997: 139), men clearly dominate the picture space, though women can be seen in the background.
18. Though we do not know with certainty whether the turban is a particular marker of respect and implicitly death here, another case of a post-mortem photograph

presented by Pinney (1997: 139), with only the deceased person wearing a turban, may suggest this.

19. Interestingly, it is also reported, for example, from the UK that the bereaved would frequently touch and kiss the physical remains (Linkman 2011: 18), but these touches are rarely captured in the Western post-mortem photographs. Unless parents are photographed with their children or children are depicted together, intimate gestures in Victorian photographic portraiture were considered 'indiscreet' and as 'crossing the boundaries of early photographic convention' in times when, for example, 'physical contact between a man and woman rarely amounted to anything more than a hand resting lightly on the partner's shoulder' (Linkman 2011: 60f)—and not only in case of post-mortem photographs.
20. On the Brahmo Samaj reform movement, see, e.g., Kopf (1979). However, the link between Brahmo Samaj, funeral rites and photography has not been explored in detail thus far. The webpage www.thebrahmosamaj.net offers basic information on life-cycle rituals, including funerals or *antyeshti*. Interestingly, this section http://www.thebrahmosamaj.net/liturgy/funeral.html also contains a post-mortem photograph (face surrounded by flowers) which is not specified.
21. *Utkala Sahitya* 38 (6), October 1934. We are grateful to Dr Kailash C. Dash for the details.
22. Professor Sibaji Bandyopadhyay, himself a renowned scholar in Cultural Studies, has also elaborated on the photograph in Nishtha Jain's documentary *Family Album* (2011).
23. In Nishtha Jain's documentary *Family Album*, Sibaji Bandyopadhyay also discussed this image and argued that:

    > [I]t captured a moment which could not really be found—at least not in my maternal uncle's house. A husband and wife—just themselves—no one around them—they are very intimate and this hangs on the wall of a house where the husband and wife can only meet at night in their bedrooms [...] we would all rush by it [this photograph—authors]—it somehow terrified the kids. [...] and all of us knew that this picture was taken at the burning ghat and the woman we see here is actually a dead woman. This moment of love is staged at the burning ghat. This indeed is a romantic picture. Does it eroticize death or does it inform Eros with a sense of coming death? Whatever happens this much is sure that it strikes a kind of perfect balance and what can be more terrifying than a perfect balance between love and death, Eros and Thanatos. (Bandyopadhyay in *Family Album* 2011, 7′55″–11′01″)

24. The point of taking post-mortem pictures in order to produce an '[a]live portrait' is also confirmed by Bhattacharya, again from a Calcutta perspective:

    > Still, in some families, after death of one of the family members, people often found that either the person [was] never photographed, or the available photograph is an overcrowded group [image], [the] negative of which is missing... so some studios specialised in [...] post-mortem photography, that is, before the body was cremated, they took the deceased to those specialised studios and they took a portrait of the death and later manufacture[d] the image as a live portrait [...]. (Abhijit Bhattacharya, pers. comm. 2007)

25. Jan Assmann (2005: 106) describes an interesting fact concerning the horizontal and upright position:

> The words for 'corpse' (mummy, body) and 'representation' (statue, picture, form, etc.) were determined by one and the same hieroglyph. Standing upright, the sign indicated a 'depiction,' and recumbent, it meant 'corpse'. […] Lift a body up on its own two legs, and it is a representation, lay a statue down on its back, and it is a corpse.

26. This tendency also becomes evident when Pinney mentions that '[p]hotographs are often taken by relatives and studios after death, even when studies from life exist, but are given […] [to the photographer/expert to make a memorial image] only when they are the sole, or the best, image available' (Pinney 1997: 205).

References

Assmann, Alaida. 2006. 'Memory, Individual and Collective'. In *The Oxford Handbook of Contextual Political Analysis*, edited by Robert E. Goodin and Charles Tilly, pp. 211–24. Oxford: Oxford University Press.

Assmann, Jan. 2005. *Death and Salvation in Ancient Egypt*. Ithaca and London: Cornell University Press.

Axtell, James. 1979. 'Ethnohistory: An Historian's Viewpoint'. *Ethnohistory* 26 (1): 1–12.

Babb, Lawrence A. 1975. *The Divine Hierarchy: Popular Hinduism in Central India*. New York, NY: Columbia University Press.

Barthes, Roland. (1980) 1984. *Camera Lucida: Reflections on Photography*. London: Fontana Paperbacks.

Benjamin, Walter. (1936) 2002. 'The Storyteller. Reflections on the Works of Nikolai Leskov'. In *Selected Writings*, edited by Howard Eiland and Michael W. Jennings, *Vol. 3, 1935–1938*, pp. 143–66. London: Harvard University Press.

Blanchot, Maurice. (1955) 1982. 'The two Versions of the Imaginary'. In *The Space of Literature*, edited by Maurice Blanchot, pp. 254–63. Lincoln: University of Nebraska Press.

Bourdieu, Pierre. (1965) 1990. *Photography: A Middle-brow Art*. Stanford: Stanford University Press.

Burch, Patrick B.M. 2009. 'Mobile Phones in Hospital. Resurgence in Memorial Postmortem Photography?'. *British Medical Journal* 338 (b1063): 675.

Caduff, Corinna. 2010. *Kränken und Anerkennen*. Basel: Lenos Verlag.

Dubois, Philippe. (1990) 1998. *Der fotografische Akt: Versuch über ein theoretisches Dispositiv* [*The Photographic Act: Attempt on a Theoretical Dispositive*, translated by authors]. Amsterdam, Dresden: Verlag der Kunst.

Eck, Diana. 1981. *Darśan: Seeing the Divine Image in India*. Chambersburg: Animal Books.

Fenton, William N. 1952. 'The Training of Historical Ethnologists in America'. *American Anthropologist NS* 54 (3): 328–39.

Freeman, James M. (1979) 1993. *Untouchable: An Indian Life History*. New Delhi: Indus.

Geary, Grattan. 1886. *Burma—After the Conquest: Viewed in Its Political, Social, and Commercial Aspects, From Mandalay*. London: Sampson Low, Marston, Searle & Rivington.

Gihon, John L. 1871. 'Curious Photographic Experiences'. *The Photographic News*, 27 October 1871, 512–13.

Goffman, Erving. 1981. 'Bilder-Rahmen'. In *Geschlecht und Werbung*, edited by Erving Goffman, pp. 45–103. Frankfurt am Main: Suhrkamp.

Gutman, Judith Mara. 1982. *Through Indian Eyes: 19th and Early 20th Century Photography from India*. New York, NY: Oxford University Press.

Holschbach, Susanne. 2006. *Vom Ausdruck zur Pose: Theatralität und Weiblichkeit in der Fotografie des 19. Jahrhunderts* [*From Expression to Pose: Theatricality and Womanhood in Photography of the Nineteenth Century*, translated by authors]. Berlin: Dietrich Reimer Verlag.

Karlekar, Malavika. 2005. *Re-visioning the Past: Early Photography in Bengal 1875–1915*. New Delhi: Oxford University Press.

King, Barry. 2003 'Über die Arbeit des Erinnerns. Die Suche nach dem perfekten Moment' ['On the Work of Remembering. The Search for the Perfect Moment', translated by authors]. In *Diskurse der Fotografie. Fotokritik am Ende des fotografischen Zeitalters*, edited by Herta Wolf, pp. 173–214. Frankfurt am Main: Suhrkamp.

Kopf, David. 1979. *The Brahmo Samaj and the Shaping of the Modern India Mind*. Princeton: Princeton University Press.

Krauss, Rosalind. 1977. 'Notes on the Index: Seventies Art in America'. *October* 3 (Spring): 68–81.

Kuhn, Annette, and Kirsten E. McAllister, eds. 2006. *Locating Memory: Photographic Acts*. New York, NY: Berghahn Books.

Lefebvre, Henri. (1974) 2011. *The Production of Space*. Malden: Blackwell.

Lettmann, Birgit. 2010. '"Capturing Little Angels". Postmortemfotografien von Kindern von der Daguerreotypie zum Internet' ['"Capturing Little Angels". Post-mortem Photographs of Children from the Times of the Daguerreotype to the Internet', translated by authors]. Unpublished Magisterarbeit.

Linkman, Audrey. 2011. *Photography and Death*. London: Reaktion Books.

MacDougall, David. 1992. 'Photo Hierarchicus: Signs and Mirrors in Indian Photography'. *Visual Anthropology* 5 (2): 103–29.

Macho, Thomas. 2009. 'Chiara's Farewell or On the Death of Children'. In *Chiara. A Journey into Light*, edited by Elisabeth Zahnd Legnazzi, pp. 135–45. Zürich: Scheidegger & Spiess.

Macho, Thomas, and Kristin Marek, eds. 2007. *Die neue Sichtbarkeit des Todes* [*The New Visibility of Death*, translated by authors]. München: Wilhelm Fink Verlag.

Metken, Sigrid. 1984. 'Zeremonien des Todes. Sterberiten und Trauergepränge in München und Oberbayern' ['Ceremonies of Death. Last Rites and Mourning practices in Munich and Upper Bavaria', translated by authors]. In *Die letzte Reise. Sterben, Tod und Trauersitten in Oberbayern*, edited by Sigrid Metken, pp. 72–96. München: Hugendubel.

Pinney, Christopher. 1997. *Camera Indica: The Social Life of Indian Photographs*. London: Reaction Books.

Rinhart, Floyd, and Marion Rinhart. 1967. 'Rediscovery: An American Way of Death'. *Art in America* 55 (5): 78–81.

Ruby, Jay. 1995. *Secure the Shadow: Death and Photography in America*. Cambridge: MIT Press.

Silverman, Kaja. 1996. *The Threshold of the Visible World*. London: Routledge.

Strassler, Karen. 2010. *Refracted Visions: Popular Photography and National Modernity in Java*. Durham: Duke University Press.

Sykora, Katharina. 2009. *Die Tode der Fotografie. Totenfotografie und ihr sozialer Gebrauch* [*The Deaths of Photography: Death Photography and Its Social Use,* translated by authors]. München: Wilhelm Fink Verlag.

Van Gennep, Arnold. (1909) 2004. *The Rites of Passage*. London: Routledge.

Wadley, Susan S. (1994) 2010. 'One Straw from a Broom Cannot Sweep: The Ideology and Practice of the Joint Family in Rural North India'. In *Everyday Life in South Asia*, edited by Diane P. Mines and Sarah E. Lamb, pp. 14–25. Bloomington: Indiana University Press.

Filmography

City of Photos. 2005. Nishtha Jain. DVD. Raintree Film. India.

Family Album. 2011. Nishtha Jain. DVD. Raintree Film. India.

The Others. 2001. Alejandro Amenabar. DVD. Universal Pictures. Spain, France, Italy, USA.

Part II
Folk/Artistry

4

9/11 and the Folk Artists of Bengal

Roma Chatterji

> *Marvel comics responded to the tragedy in its hometown with a genuinely heartfelt tale in which the superheroes aimlessly assembled at Ground Zero. They were compelled to acknowledge the event as if it had occurred in their own simulated universe, but they hadn't been there to prevent it, which negated their entire raison d'être. If al-Qaeda could do to Marvel Universe New York what Dr Doom, Magneto and Kung the Conqueror had failed to do, surely that meant that the Marvel heroes were ineffectual. September 11 was the biggest challenge yet to the relevance of superhero comics....*
>
> *The disorientation of the time was captured by a single giddy moment wherein Marvel's ultimate evil dictator cum terrorist super villain Dr Doom arrived on the scene at Ground Zero only to be moved to tears by the devastation.... What was real had slipped and become uncertain, fantastic. It would surely serve symmetry if the fantastic could become more real in response.*
>
> —Grant Morrison, *Supergods*

In spite of the fact that the 'news' is one of the 'great political and artistic forms animating our contemporary collective and private lives', events such as the second Gulf War did not produce any images that were truly memorable (Mirzoeff 2005; Seaton 2003: 45). Thus, in spite of the unprecedented scale of image circulation, thanks to 24-hour news channels, the images of war were not able to survive their incarnation as 'breaking news' (Seaton 2003: 45). Nicholas Mirzoeff attributes this to media saturation that leads to the banality of image production as a kind of information (2005: 67). In this chapter, I am not so much interested in the 9/11 strike on the World Trade Centre as news, but as an event that carries the potential not only of story-making as all significant events do but of mythicisation as well. Although we know that even live news has to be organised in terms of a recognisable genre of storytelling to appear as a convincing account of reality, it is myth, a form of storytelling that is both unreal and true, that draws our attention to the extraordinary nature of some events by amplifying them—that is, by using a language to talk about them in a way that distorts through its excess (Barthes 1973; Chatterji 1986). To this end, I describe the way in which the 9/11 story enters the repertoire of narratives of a community of picture storytellers in Bengal and is reinterpreted in terms of their mythic universe. The *Laden story*, as the event is locally termed, is of particular significance in my work on folk culture as not only does it allow me to explore the relationship between the global and the local but also foregrounds folk art as an emergent phenomenon and thus critiques static representations of the folk artist as an unconscious vessel who carries forward an ancient and unbroken tradition across time (Coomaraswamy [1909] 1990).[1] The folk artists' response to the 9/11 strike is not passive but is an active reinterpretation and incorporation in a storytelling tradition that is meaningful to a local audience. But more importantly, the fact that the time period between the event and the composition of the story is short—only two months—allowed the artists to explore the potentiality that the live event offered in terms of its uncertain and contingent unfolding before it got reified and took on the fixed contours of empirical facticity. But before I explain what I mean in greater detail, let me give a brief account of the community itself and the story that I analyse.

The *Chitrakars*

The *Chitrakars* or *patuas*[2] occupy an interstitial position in the caste hierarchy of Bengal, designating themselves as Muslim, following local Hindu customs and displaying *patas* (painted scrolls) that have largely Hindu themes.[3] Also, like many Bengali Muslims, they commonly have two names—a Muslim name and a Bangla name that is more frequently used.[4] Their traditional designation of *patua* was derived from the long scroll paintings—*pata*, from the Sanskrit word for cloth—that they used to tell or sing their stories. The *Chitrakars* are not the only caste of painters in Bengal. Other artisan castes such as the *Kumhars* (potters) or *Shutradhars* (carpenters) also paint similar pictures, but it is only the former who display *patas* and sing the *pata* songs thus making them multimedia performers (Ray 1953). The *Chitrakars* first entered academic discourse through the writings of Gurusaday Dutt (1882–1941) who described them as *shilpi* (craftsmen) and traced their origin to an ancient tradition of picture storytelling mentioned in sacred texts such as the *Brahmavaivarta Purana*. Popular representations tend to characterise them as alms seekers soliciting *dana* (gifts/offerings) by displaying *patas* and singing *pata* songs (Hauser 2002).[5] In the 1930s, when Dutt was researching the art and craft traditions of Bengal, many *Chitrakars* had given up their traditional occupation in an attempt to achieve a higher status. In the early part of the twentieth century, some Hindu nationalist organisations tried to bring lower-caste groups into the Hindu mainstream. 'The Society for the Advancement of the *Chitrakars* of Bengal' (*Bangiya Chitrakar Unnayan Samiti*) was established in this context. But, 're-conversion' did not have much of an impact on their social status and many *Chitrakars* returned to their former religion (Bhattacharjee 1980). (However, the adoption of the title *Chitrakar* by many members of this caste group is probably a result of this earlier mobilisation.) Scholars have identified at least three different styles of *pata* painting in Bengal, viz. the Murshidabad, Birbhum and Medinipur styles. There is also another style restricted to the areas bordering the state of Jharkhand which is different from the aforementioned three styles in that it has ritual significance (Singh 1995a). In Bengal today, apart from the inhabitants of Medinipur, one finds very few active scroll painters and performers. Many *Chitrakars* have given up this occupation altogether while others treat painting as a subsidiary occupation being primarily icon makers. Naya village, in West Medinipur, where I did my fieldwork,[6] is an exception in that it has a vibrant *Chitrakar* community with approximately 45 households actively producing *patas*. However, very few households actually earn their livelihood by displaying *patas* in the traditional way.[7] Instead, their 'craft' has been 'discovered' through both state patronage and new market opportunities so that *patas* are now sold in wider urban markets in India and abroad.

Pata Performance and the Narrative Tradition

The scrolls that one sees in Medinipur today are usually between six- to twelve-feet long and two-and-a-half- to three-feet wide. Most storytellers tend to carry five or six scrolls to give their audience a choice of stories. They usually begin with auspicious themes based on the *mangala kavyas* (auspicious stories) or stories of *pirs* and then go on to display *patas* about local, often sensational, events (Singh 1995a). Even though a *pata* performance today is not considered to be a sacred event, this may not always have been the case. Archival survey reveals that the display of *patas* may have had a sacred character in the past as many old scrolls on sacred themes had inscriptions written at the back with names of donors who had given *dana* to have the *pata* displayed again and again. Such performances were often considered to be rites of atonement for transgression, and the repeated display of the sacred story to the accompaniment of the *pata* song acted as a blessing spread to all the members of the audience (Singh 1995a). Unlike the ritual narrations performed by bards elsewhere in India, *Chitrakars* do not have an established network of patrons, nor are their performances commissioned. They see themselves as entertainers, experimenting with new themes and transforming old ones (Singh 1995b). It is in this spirit that they have included in their repertoire a variety of natural disasters and violent incidents such as the floods in Medinipur, the Gujarat earthquake, the Nandigram violence, the 9/11 strike and the Tsunami. Thanks to recent government patronage, the *Chitrakar* tradition of storytelling is becoming known outside rural Bengal; however, it is not so much the multimedia performance as a whole that circulates but rather the painted scroll that seems to have an exotic appeal for urban audiences both in India and overseas. As a result, the painting carries much of the burden of storytelling. Even though artists still compose the song first because it is the 'poetic language' that anchors the composition as a whole, yet they know that the song will not be widely understood so that the painting must be able to narrate the story on its own.[8]

The 9/11 *Pata*

I now turn to the Laden *pata*, as the scroll painting on the theme of the 9/11 strike is known in Medinipur. It does not belong to the category of sacred *patas* even though it shares some features of the *mangala* stories that are sung by the *Chitrakars*. Its popularity owes more to the new clientele for *pata* painting in cities like Delhi and Philadelphia, where such themes have a certain exotic appeal, rather than to the rural audiences of Bengal. However, as Frank Korom (2006) and Bhaskar Mukhopadhyay (2008) have shown, the immediate inspiration for the Laden *pata* was a *jatra* performance in Naya village by a troupe from Kolkata titled *Amrika Jolchhe* (America is Burning). The play dealt with the events leading up to the Gulf War, and the crash and collapse of the Twin Towers formed the climax of the performance, coming at the end of the play. It was depicted as a cyclorama on a separate stage (Mukhopadhyay 2008). The leader of *Digbijoy Opera*, the troupe that performed this *jatra* in Naya, said in an interview to Bhaskar Mukhopadhyay that the play wove in several themes including a subplot about a middle-class Bengali boy who goes to the United States to study, succumbs to the corrupting influence of a decadent Western life style and dies in the 9/11 crash. The nineteenth-century themes of modern decadence and the corrupting influence of Westernisation are still popular in Bengali films and television serials and were probably added for audience appeal. However, the *pata* renderings of the event are radically different. I have examined 10 versions of the Laden *pata*, and apart from variation in detail such as the manner in which the Twin Towers and the crash are depicted, they reveal a common episodic structure. The pictorial narrative begins with the crash; it then depicts scenes of long-distance communication between Bush and bin Laden and meetings that lead up to the war in Afghanistan, the war and finally bin Laden's escape to the caves in the Tora Bora mountains (Figures 4.1 to 4.6).[9] I have heard three versions of the song that accompanies the *pata*. The songs do not replicate all the activities portrayed in the *pata*. Instead, they serve as a general commentary and it is the storyteller's finger that connects successive images with the song as he slowly unrolls the scroll, frame by frame.

Figure 4.1

Image made by artist Tagar

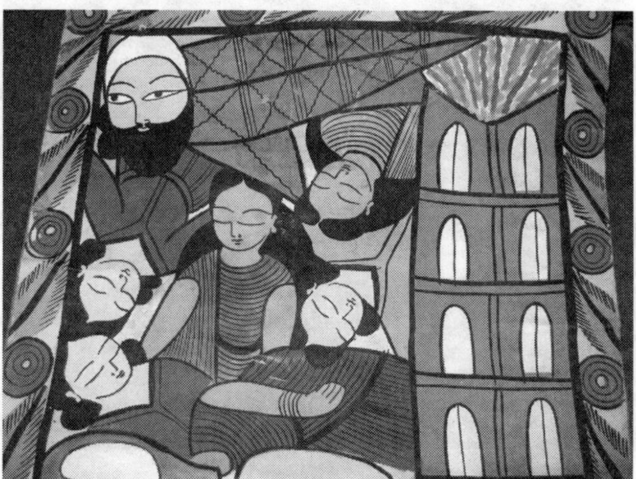

Source: Roma Chatterji.

Figure 4.2

Image made by artist Tagar

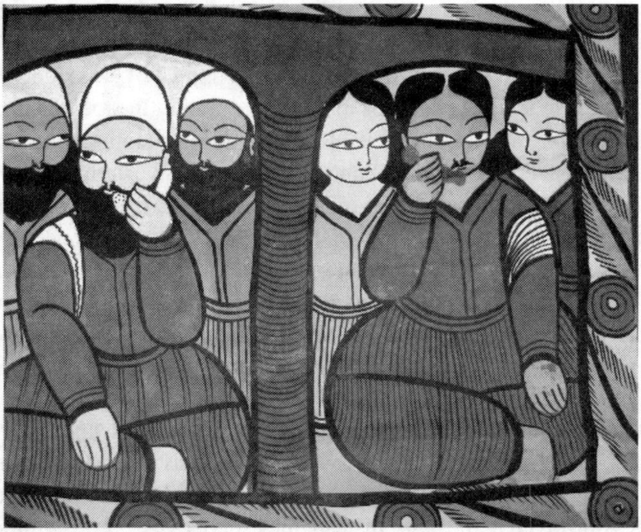

Source: Roma Chatterji.

Figure 4.3

Image made by artist Tagar

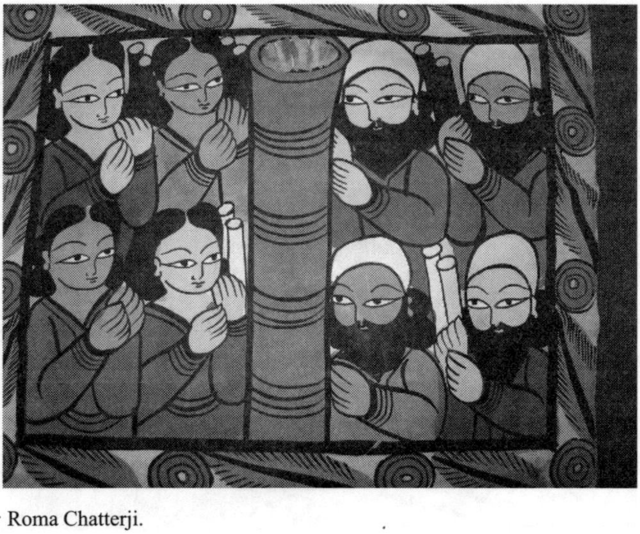

Source: Roma Chatterji.

Figure 4.4

Image made by artist Tagar

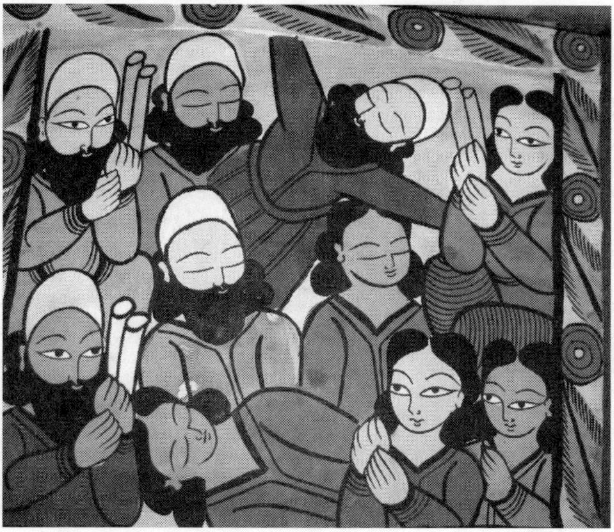

Source: Roma Chatterji.

Figure 4.5

Image made by artist Tagar

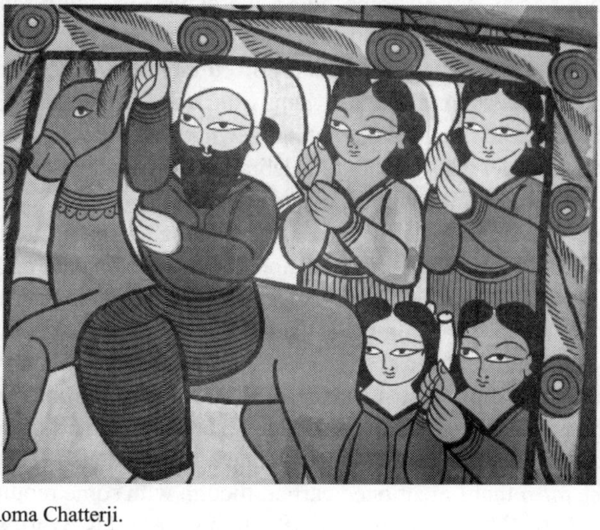

Source: Roma Chatterji.

Figure 4.6

Image made by artist Tagar

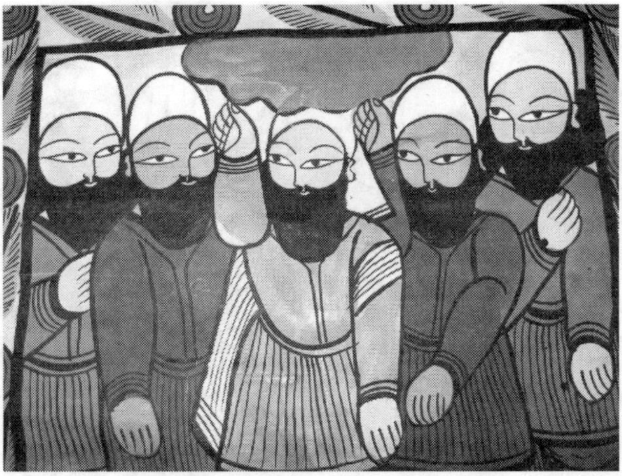

Source: Roma Chatterji.

The *patas* are divided into six frames or more, each frame depicting a different scene in the story.[10] As I have said, all the Laden *patas* begin with the scene of the crash. It is the airplane that is foregrounded in the first register—a swollen fish-shaped form with a bearded face that represents Osama bin Laden, and in some *patas*, the explosion—with tongues of flame opening out like the petals of a flower in bloom.

The first *pata* on the 9/11 theme followed the order of events as they appeared on television. Thus, as Manu Chitrakar, the first composer of the Laden *pata* told me, 'We did not know what was happening, who was behind it. Only later when scenes of celebration were being broadcast from bin Laden's camp did the world came to suspect that it might be him'. The first frame of Manu's *pata* had an ordinary plane crashing into the twin towers followed by scenes of destruction and then revelry in bin Laden's camp (Figures 4.7 and 4.8). It was Swarna Chitrakar, Manu's sister, who first put bin Laden's face on the killer plane (Figure 4.9). But this motif struck a chord and has been absorbed into the painterly vocabulary. (There were other innovations that she made such as anthropomorphic images of the weeping fire engine that did not catch on and are not part of the stable pictorial narrative [see Figure 4.10].) Manu's *pata* had also followed the plot of the *jatra* that I mentioned earlier, though with some modification. A young Bengali boy died in the crash on the eve of his return to India.

Figure 4.7

Image made by artist Manu

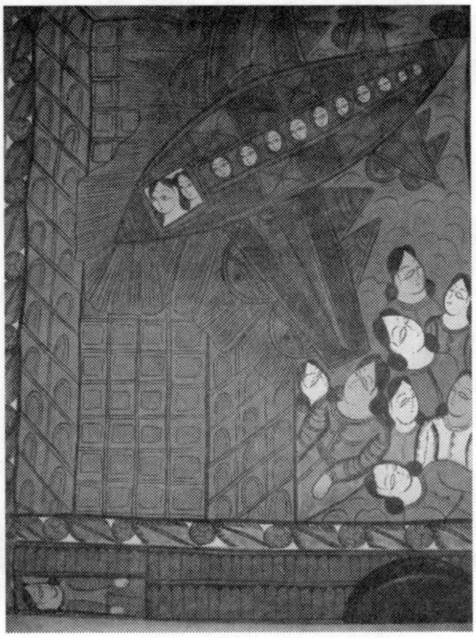

Source: Roma Chatterji.

Figure 4.8

Image made by artist Manu

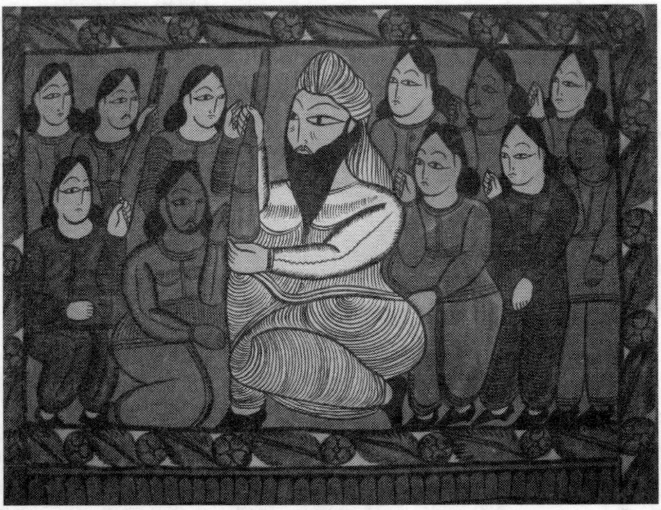

Source: Roma Chatterji.

Figure 4.9

Image made by artist Swarna

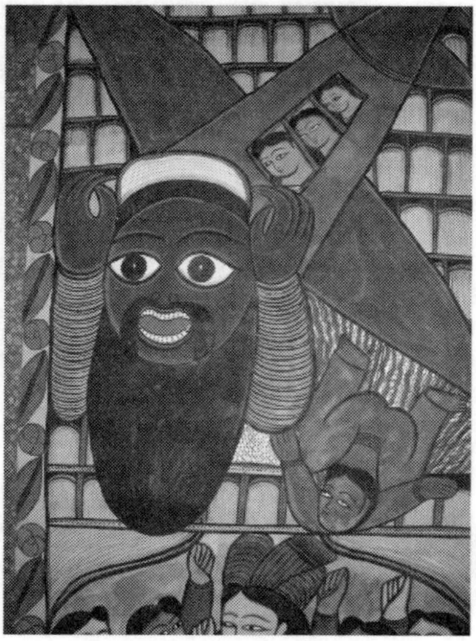

Source: Roma Chatterji.

Figure 4.10

Image made by artist Swarna

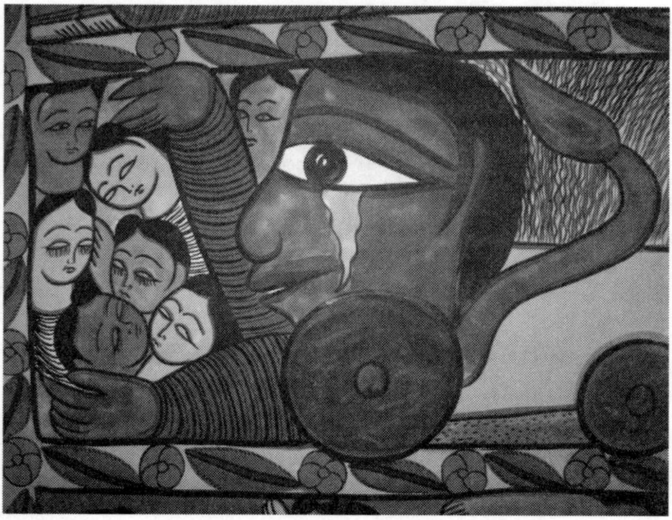

Source: Roma Chatterji.

Scenes of pathos, which showed the parents receiving the news of their son's death by telephone, were included. This theme has not been retained over time, though the telephone motif still occurs but is transformed to signify the Bush–bin Laden relationship as we saw in Tagar's *pata* (Figure 4.2). Manu had tried to bring the event closer to his local audience by including an Indian protagonist. Since the primary audience for the picture scroll is non-local, these elements were soon dropped even by Manu.

In *patas* with sacred themes such as the Satya Pir *patas*,[11] the first scene is usually disjunct from the story (Figure 4.11). It depicts the god or the main protagonist enthroned with a retinue of worshippers and is accompanied by the invocation sung before the actual story is musically rendered. Since the Laden *pata* deals with a historical theme and that to with human tragedy, it cannot begin with an invocation. However, images of the airplane with bin Laden's face and the crash tell us about the subject of the *pata*, as do the invocatory stanzas and the enthroned gods in the traditional *pata* performances.

Tagar Chitrakar's *pata* emphasises the Bush–bin Laden relationship. Only one of the towers is depicted on the right-hand side of the frame.

Figure 4.11
Image made by artist Jomuna

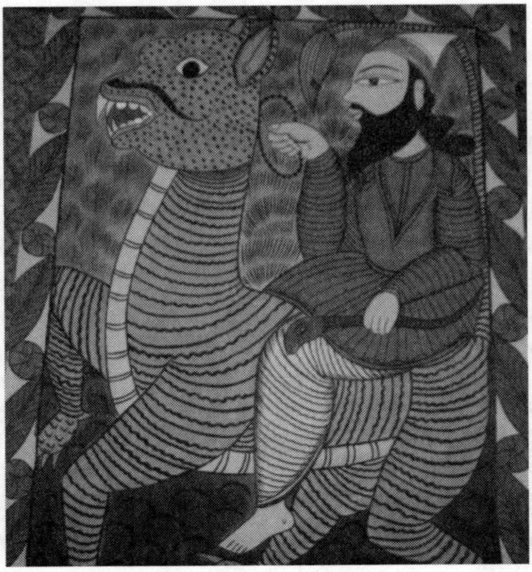

Source: Roma Chatterji.

Flames erupt from the top of the tower and at the bottom of the register in line with the frame, dead bodies lie horizontally with eyes closed (Figure 4.1). It is important to note at this juncture that all the faces are beardless and therefore in marked contrast with the bearded face on the airplane. (Perhaps, viewers who are unfamiliar with the codes of pictorial representation in this genre are likely to see these dead figures as women. Markers of gender are not always highlighted in this tradition. Viewers are expected to fill such details on their own when relevant. However, with respect to this particular frame, it is worth noting that these images could represent young men modelled on the image of the War God *Kartikeya* who is represented as a dandy in popular Bengali culture.) Another point worth noting is the position of the plane vis-à-vis the tower. The plane seems to be flying away from the tower coming towards the left of the frame with the face pointing towards the viewer and seems undamaged, unlike the tower. However, the tower form is repeated in several other frames as we shall see and serves as a motif symbolising the Bush–bin Laden relationship in the narrative (Figure 4.2).

In the second frame of Tagar's *pata*, the tower form becomes a column separating the figures of Bush and bin Laden, seen here talking to each other by telephone. The figures are symmetrically positioned, each one flanked by guards carrying guns. The point of distinction is the presence or absence of the beard, for Bush and his men look young and beardless and bin Laden and his men look old with full beards (Figures 4.2 and 4.3).[12] Bin Laden, a replication of the face on the airplane, is now shown near the right-hand side of the frame. The position of the bearded figure keeps alternating from left to right and again to left in the successive frames. It is only in the last frame that it occupies a position at the centre of the frame (Figures 4.1 to 4.6). Perhaps, these alternating positions of the bearded and beardless faces tell us something about the way the bin Laden–Bush relationship has been conceptualised in this pictorial imagination. A small *pata* on the 9/11 theme, reduced to three frames, drawn by Malek Chitrakar makes the connection between the tower motif and the Bush–bin Laden relationship even more explicit (Figures 4.13 and 4.14). The first two scenes depicted separately in Tagar's *pata* are collapsed in one register (Figures 4.1, 4.2 and 4.12). Two bin Laden-faced airplanes collide with the tower from opposite directions. They form a canopy, supported by the burning tower, over the heads of Bush and bin Laden who are shown standing talking long-distance via telephone. The instruments are attached to the wall very much like the telephones one finds in public call booths (Figure 4.12).

Figure 4.12

Image made by artist Malek

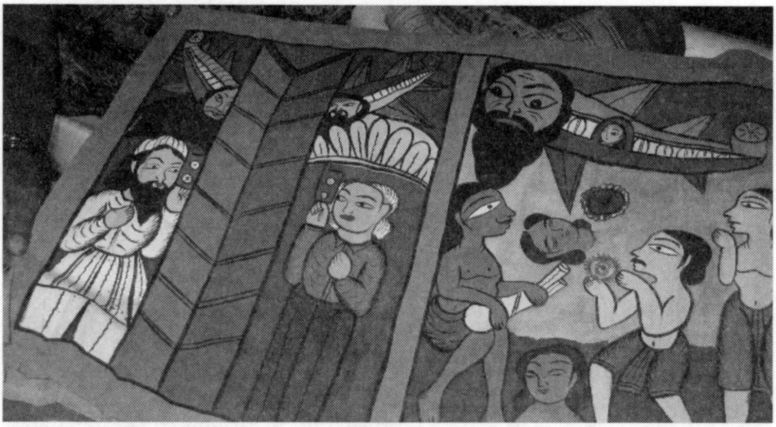

Source: Roma Chatterji.

Figure 4.13

Image made by artist Malek

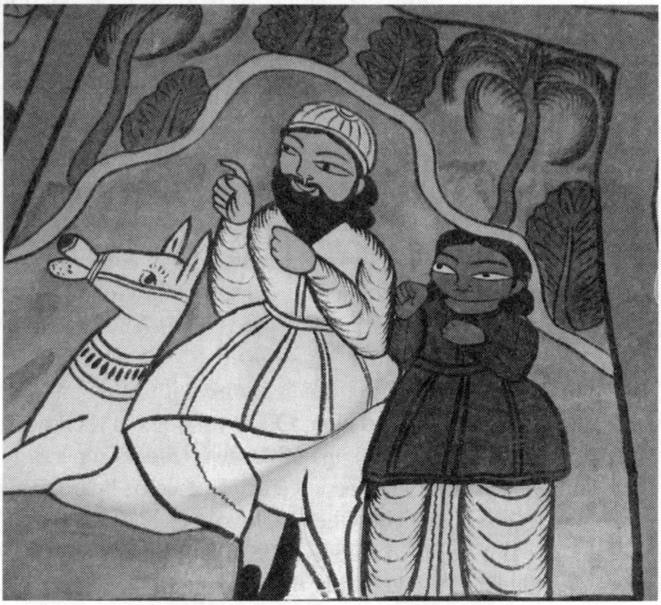

Source: Roma Chatterji.

Figure 4.14

Image made by artist Probir

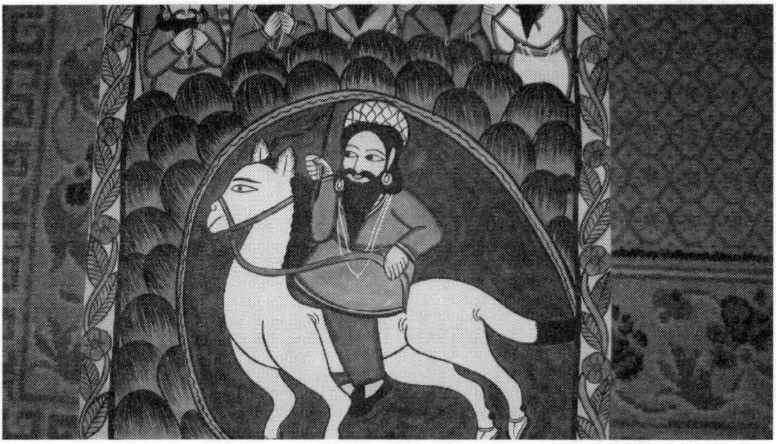

Source: Roma Chatterji.

The song emphasises the relationship between the two leaders. Bush phones bin Laden to ask him what happened to spoil their relationship. 'What led to this terrible catastrophe?'—the storyteller sings in Bush's voice. Bin Laden replies fatalistically, 'What had to happen has come to pass'. Bhaskar Mukhopadhyay (2008) gives a different version. Madhusudan Chitrakar, Mukhopadhyay's main respondent, told him that Bush had once made a derogatory remark about bin Laden that might have sparked the enmity between the two. Bin Laden makes clandestine preparations for the 9/11 strike in Afghanistan and forces his followers to drink the blood of a dog, considered sacrilegious according to their religion, so that they will have to redeem themselves through self-sacrifice. He makes them swear to avenge his honour. This is an unusual variant, and I have never heard it before. Madhusudan is a thoughtful artist, however, and he explicitly draws connections with other motifs from the mythic universe that I discuss later. Other versions of the Laden *pata* depict scenes of round-table meetings of the two leaders separately with their followers—apart from the presence or absence of bearded figures, there is nothing to distinguish between the two scenes. Even when Bush and bin Laden are not depicted side by side in the same frame, there is a remarkable symmetry in the way that they are positioned vis-à-vis their followers. Bush and bin Laden are portrayed as the archetypal rivals—their followers, depicted as replicas of the one or other leader. In fact, in the scene where the US soldiers are chasing bin Laden, his followers are only shown in outline behind his full figure (Figure 4.5). The tower form becomes a canon spouting flames in the third register of Tagar's *pata*, depicting the battle scene—but it acts as a barrier separating the two armies, its mouth points upwards rather than facing the soldiers (Figure 4.3). In only one of the ten Laden *patas* that I have examined, do the guns and canons of the two armies face each other.

The battle scene in Malek Chitrakar's *pata* depicts *dhoti*-clad soldiers who wield cutlasses in addition to guns, juxtaposing figures from the battle scenes in the Ramayana *patas* with scenes of 'modern' warfare (Figure 4.12). American soldiers are depicted in the same way as young 'dandies' in popular theatrical representations and Kalighat prints,[13] sometimes with earrings, moustache and well-groomed hair parted in the middle. The battle scene in Tagar's *pata* shows only corpses, some of which are bearded (Figure 4.4). There are no barriers that separate the soldiers of the two armies, though the bearded figures tend to be concentrated in the upper half of the frame. A bearded Christ-like figure, lying horizontally across the upper half of the frame with his arms outstretched is reminiscent of the crucifixion scene from the *Jishu* (Jesus) *mangala pata.* The last two frames of the Laden *pata* show bin Laden and his followers on horseback, being chased by Bush's men, finally disappearing into the caves in the Tora Bora mountains (Figures 4.5 and 4.6). The last frame of Probir's *pata* is especially interesting. It shows bin Laden on his white horse as an inset set distinctly apart from the mountains in the background. The mouth of the cave is reduced to a border that frames the bin Laden figure and separates it from the action scenes above (Figure 4.14). The first and sometimes the last frames of traditional *patas* are disjunct from the other frames that depict the episodes in the story in that they serve to place the story in the mythic universe so that it resonates with other stories about gods and goddesses. Typically, these stories begin with an invocation to the god who is the subject of the *pata*—describing their attributes and then go on to express the god's desire to receive worship. One person is usually targeted as a potential devotee who will help to spread the god's worship on earth. The *patas* first depict the god/dess as an iconic image and then go on to show us the adventures undertaken by the potential devotees. Some traditional *patas* end with another iconic image of the god/dess, others do not. Compare the last frame of Probir's *pata* that depicts bin Laden, triumphant, on a white horse with the first frame of the Satya Pir *pata* painted by Jomuna Chitrakar, which shows the *pir* sitting on his lion (Figure 4.11). It is their positioning, the first at the end of the narrative and the second at the beginning that makes for a significant difference.[14]

Figure 4.15

Image made by artist Joideb

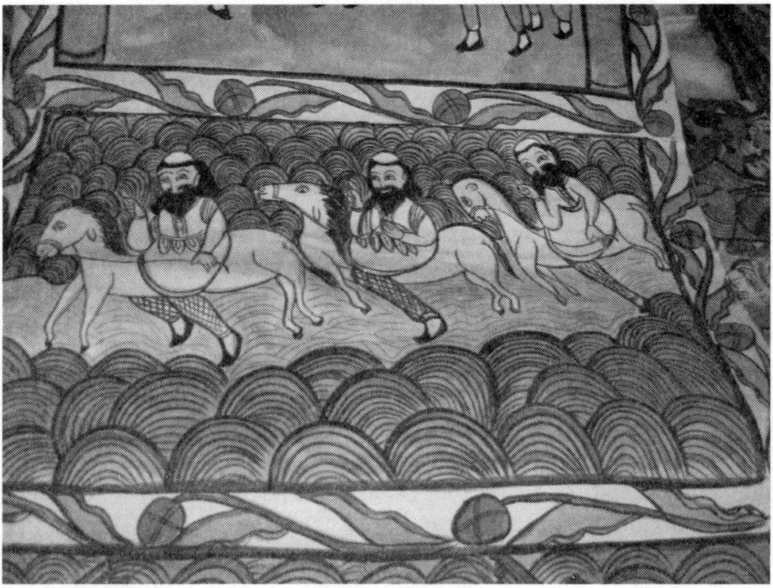

Source: Roma Chatterji.

The Laden story moves between history and myth. In another time and place, it may well have become a story about a *pir*, but the global impact of the 9/11 crash will not allow this to happen.[15]

Much of the creative potential of the 'storyable' event comes from the fact that the ending is deferred. As Alf Hiltebeitel (2001) tells us, myths point to alternate possibilities in the narrative universe by using the technique of 'side shadowing'. A character in a particular story may be constrained by the plot to act in a particular way, but since all stories in a mythic universe are interconnected synchronically, there will be elements in the story that also point to other possibilities that may be deferred and actually be enacted elsewhere. Thus, particular elements in the story of bin Laden as an event in history may also strike a chord with elements in other stories. These elements may not be fragments of plot but could be images or figural types as we just saw in the figures of bin Laden and Satya Pir. But as elements of myth, they have meta-narrative potential so that parts of a story may resonate with other stories in the mythic universe (Lévi-Strauss [1964] 1975). Myths never begin or end in a definitive way. Beginnings always point to events that have already occurred or are taking place in some parallel present, and endings are never definitive, rather they are deferred. The creative possibilities of the 9/11 strike seem to have dried up after bin Laden was discovered in his hideout in Islamabad and killed. There have been attempts at updating the story to take recent events into account. But the attempts are rather weak and involve appending an additional register, almost as an afterthought that shows his bloody corpse lying on the ground surrounded by American soldiers. There has been no attempt to reconstitute the plot in terms of this new and more definite ending. It is as if events in the real world have overtaken the story, and without the possibility of a deferred ending there is little room for creative play within the plot. But the 9/11 story is not quite finished as far as Chitrakar artists are concerned. There has been some attempt to tell the story in another way using a different genre—i.e., the graphic novel—as if to suggest that when the 'storyable' potential offered by the event is no longer available within the formal constraints of one genre, it may be still open to others. The change that must take place in the story to be able to render into another form of narrative is what I discuss in the next section.

The Graphic Novel Experiment and New Forms of Intertextuality

My account of the new rendition of the 9/11 story in the graphic novel form is based on an experimental workshop conducted in 2008 by the Tara Books and Educational Research Society that has been experimenting with picture books based on the diverse folk art styles of India. They had already published a book based on the Chitrakar Tsunami story and were ready to try something more adventurous. Geeta Wolfe, the founder of Tara Books, felt that the *Chitrakar* style of picture storytelling was very close to the graphic novel genre and could easily adapt itself to the form. As she said, 'We try and work within the grammar of the idiom. The stories may be from somewhere else but the style of representation, the text as a combination of words and pictures must never be artificially imposed'.

What do graphic novels have in common with picture scrolls? Time is the first response that comes to mind. Both genres are used to depict sequential narratives and both are cross-discursive. The story is told through a combination of words and images—without, however, blending the two into a unified whole (Imamura 1953). The images are not merely illustrations of the story as it is told in the text, instead they tell a separate story using the verbal or textual story as a 'diegetical horizon'—that is, they gesture towards the text without allowing themselves to be fixed by it (Chute and De Koven 2006: 769). The differences, however, are equally striking. In the *Chitrakar* mode of storytelling, unlike the graphic novel mode in which each story is broken down into many incidents, the action sequences are abbreviated with only the start and climax of the sequence being depicted often in the same frame. Graphic novels usually present stories that are new so that recognisability of the characters and legibility of the episodic structure become major issues for the reader. Characters are built up over successive episodes in the story that are anchored firmly in a plot. This is not the case as far as traditional *Chitrakar* stories are concerned. Traditional stories based on the epics like the Ramayana have an initial legibility as Joanna Williams reminds us—no one ever hears the Ramayana for the first time (1996: 5). The narrator of *Rama katha* is not constrained by the demands of a fixed episodic structure as her audience is already familiar with the plot. Instead, she can select specific events for elaboration depending on her performance style and the emotions (*rasa*) that she wants to convey to her audience. Even in new stories like the 9/11 strike, the storyteller is more interested in conveying particular kinds of emotions to the audience rather than recounting a sequence of episodes. Even though *Chitrakar* stories privilege events, they are not plot-centric. Instead, there is an assumption that there is an empathic connection to the subject that makes the story intelligible without the episodic structure having to be elaborated.

The workshop in Chennai was conducted by Orijit Sen, a well-known graphic novelist. He gave a set of lectures using slides from his own work to show how storytelling was organised in this form and then asked the five *Chitrakar* participants to try and see if they could adapt one of their stories to this form. Most of the other artists turned to traditional stories from the epics but Montu Chitrakar decided to work with the bin Laden story. Inspired by Orijit's story about a machine's past lives, Montu chose the killer plane as his chief protagonist. But having taken that decision, he was unable to situate his main character in a suitable context. Finally, after some prodding, it was decided that the damaged airplane would be placed in a museum where it would tell the story of its adventures to the visitors passing by. But he found it difficult to tell the story from the plane's point of view and kept returning to the iconic figure of the *patua* storyteller that is so popular in contemporary *pata* paintings. The first frame of his series initially showed a plane and below it a storyteller in the midst of his audience, his hand gesturing towards the plane. When it was pointed out to him that the chief protagonist in a story would not need a mediating character, he recomposed the frame, setting the plane in the midst of rectangular cases filled with a variety of figures such as butterflies, tigers and birds. I remarked that these were all figures that Montu loves to paint and includes in all his *patas*. He said a museum should have beautiful and wondrous things—the plane would acquire distinction by being placed in such surroundings. Montu was the only artist present who tried experimenting with the idea of a flexible panel size. He divided the first page of his story into panels of different sizes to show the movement between narrative perspective and modes of address. Thus, while the objects in the background are enframed to indicate the scene in which the narration is set, the plane is not enclosed within a panel and hovers above a group of figures all of whom make the gesture of conversation typical of the *Chitrakar* style. The plane is both the object of the story as well as being the sole narrator. But in spite of this promising beginning, he was not able to develop a story line with a connected sequence of actions in a way that could humanise the airplane. Instead, he showed successive moments of the plane's approach towards the Tower of the World Trade Centre.

Montu is an experienced painter and performer well known for his ability to compose new stories. Then how are we to understand his difficulty in emplotting the 9/11 narrative so that it could tell a coherent story. The story as depicted in the *patua* repertoire is not organised around a plot. Unable to select either Bush or bin Laden as the chief protagonist as the reciprocity in their relationship is the main theme of the *patua* story, he settled on the damaged plane, the one that was hijacked and made to dive into the Tower. But he was unable to humanise the plane. Instead, he communicated his idea to me and I then translated it to the writer who was supposed to help the artists in adding words and dialogue to the images. David, the writer, chose to interpret the narrative in terms of the science fiction genre. He turned the iconic killer plane that wears bin Laden's face, and is really about the anthropomorphic representation of an event, into a humanised subject. The story then became an exploration of the inner life of the airplane and the transformation wrought by the cataclysmic event (Figures 4.16 to 4.20). David's use of text was minimal. Instead, variations in panel size and break ups and slight shifts in the position of the plane on the page were used to suggest shifts in mood and changing points of attention. Thus, the first page shows the plane in a horizontal position, in mid-air as it were, not suggesting any specific direction. The text at the bottom conveys the mood, 'Once I was a happy plane'. From the second page onwards, however, the position of the plane is oriented towards the Tower as if to suggest that its goal has now changed and is focused on destruction. David removed the beard from the face of the plane in the first few panels so as to mark the transformation in personality (Figures 4.16 to 4.18). The bearded plane now signified an evil personality, mirroring bin Laden's face, reinforced by the text in the last panel, 'Something evil was in me that day' (Figure 4.20). The chain of signification set up by the conflation of beard—bin Laden—monstrous act was avoided, however, by the addition of a teardrop to the face of the bearded plane, as it approaches the Tower, at Montu's insistence, as if to suggest that the plane was a victim of circumstance and not a willing participant in this terrible event (Figure 4.19).

Figure 4.16

Image made by artist Montu

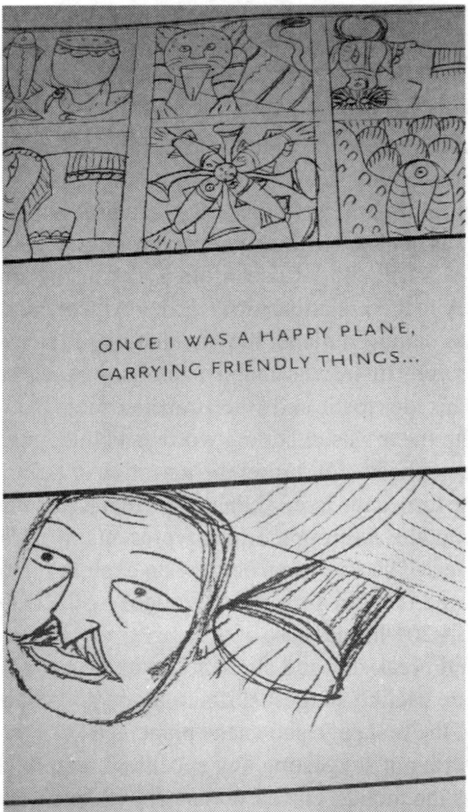

Source: Roma Chatterji.

Figure 4.17

Image made by artist Montu

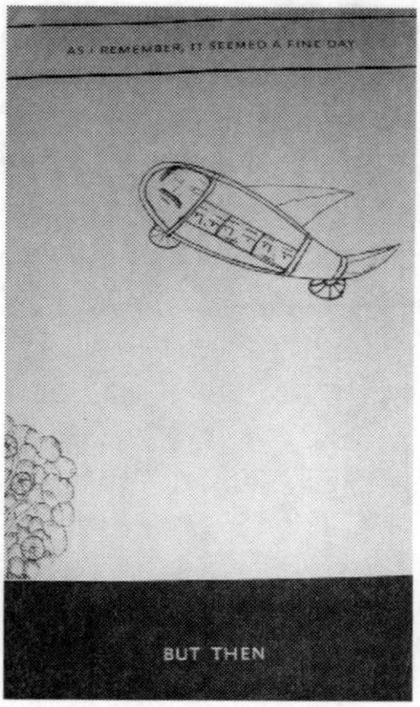

Source: Roma Chatterji.

Figure 4.18

Image made by artist Montu

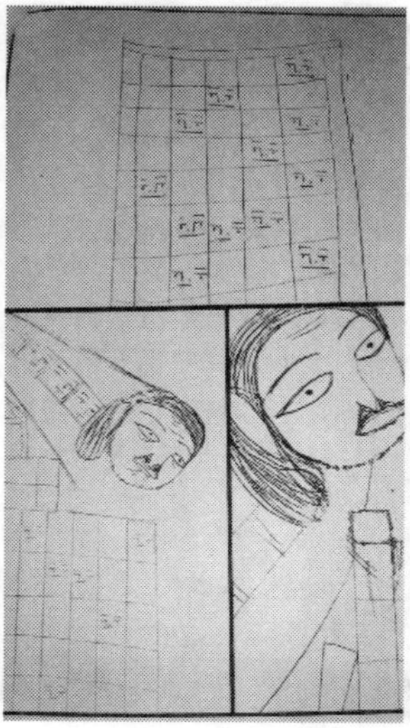

Source: Roma Chatterji.

Figure 4.19

Image made by artist Montu

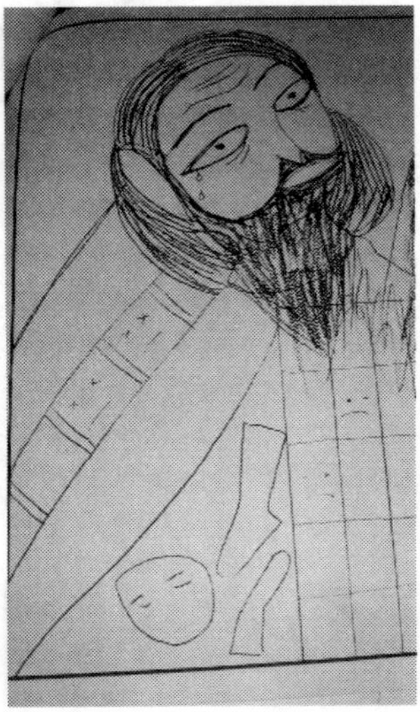

Source: Roma Chatterji.

Figure 4.20

Image made by artist Montu

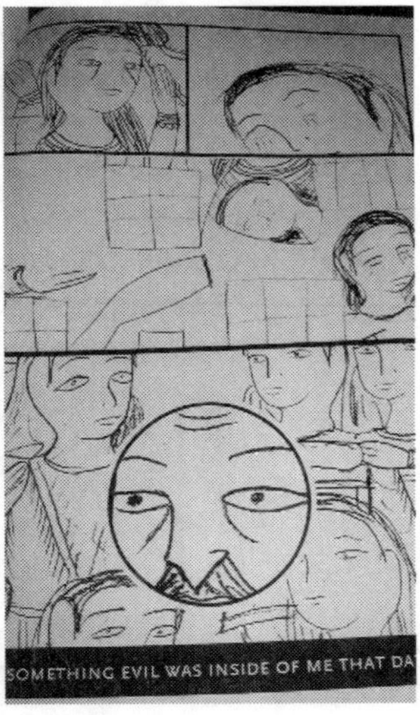

Source: Roma Chatterji.

David used the gutter—the blank spaces between the panels on a page—to shift between different points of view in the narrative. He also positioned the voice-over texts in the gutter on each page to link the different points of view into a coherent plot. In Montu's story, more than that of any of the other *Chitrakars*, the self of the chief protagonist had to be shown changing over time. David used subtle clues to suggest this change, not merely by varying the direction and appearance of the plane as I have described but also by using the expressive potential of the plane's shape. Graphic novels often vary the size and shape of the panels on a page to suggest shifts in time, mood and point of view. The last page of David's reworking of Montu's narrative is especially striking. Thus, a circle, with a close-up of the plane's demonic face, is positioned as an inset within a larger rectangular panel that depicts the scene of destruction (Figure 4.20). Tara has gone on to produce several graphic novels in the *patua* style. Montu's experiment, however, was in the nature of rough work, meant to facilitate familiarity with a new mode of picture storytelling and was not carried forward.

In my first attempt at presenting this material, I was asked if this form of radical makeover was not a violation of a community's rights over its creative production. Apart from a somewhat uncritical acceptance of the category of 'community' which would disallow any consideration of folk art being an emergent phenomenon and a narrow view of ownership, the point of view implied by this question forecloses the possibility of intertextual communication that may lead to the creation of hybrid forms. Ideas of hybridity and intertextuality tend to be associated with the realm of high culture and metropolitan art, while folk art and culture remain within the sphere of authenticity and of tradition (Spielmann and Bolter 2006). However, such questions are valuable because they foreground issues of power and patronage. Are collaborative relationships envisioned by the team at Tara Books possible between actors in such unequal relationships? The *Chitrakars* have been professional performers and painters for many centuries. Their participation in a commodity market may be recent but they are used to orienting their activities according to the demands of their clients. Their performance styles, their compositions, music and painting styles have always coexisted with other performative styles and musical genres in rural Bengal. *Chitrakars* have borrowed popular themes and adapted them to their performative style. In this context of cohabitation of different performative and painterly genres, it makes little sense to speak of the *Chitrakar* tradition as if it was hermetically sealed from outside influences. Let us consider instead if such acts of radical de-contextualisation offer opportunities for creative innovation for traditional artists.

The conventional view of folk tradition assumes that folk artists produce objects whose reception will be confined to a bounded community. However, if we consider the poetic and the symbolic dimension of the folk art forms, then the opposite must be assumed. The symbolic dimension of the art allows the art works to travel in different and sometimes unexpected directions. Symbols combine with other symbols endlessly deferring the destination of the 'true' meaning (Barthes 1985). This is what Walter Benjamin meant by the inherent violence of translation, I think. Translation, Benjamin ([1923] 1968) says, come to be when a work travels outside the area of its birth and tries to engage an audience that does not understand the original. The act of translation de-contextualises the work, detaching certain properties of the original which are then put into circulation. Is this a form of impoverishment? Yes, perhaps, but it can, as I have shown, also be enormously productive.[16]

The Event as Myth vs Television News

The appeal of the bin Laden picture narrative lies in the sense of the uncanny that it creates for its viewers. There is a dissonance between the subject that is familiar to global audiences and a style that is unfamiliar and hence exotic. But there is a deeper structural dissonance within the composition itself that provokes a reflexive engagement with the subject as such. Let us go back to the bin Laden scroll. As the pictorial narrative stabilises overtime, we see a kind of tension building up between the first and the last frames of the scroll. The killer plane with bin Laden's visage—bin Laden as demon—is opposed to the last frame where he is portrayed in the form of a *pir* or a holy man. This kind of dissonance is replicated in the portrayal of the Bush–bin Laden relationship as well where we see close friends becoming mortal enemies. The mythic universe that the *Chitrakars* occupy is replete with stories that deal with the fraught nature of intimacy. Epics like the Mahabharata or the Biblical stories of *Habil and Kabil* (Cain and Abel) portray irreconcilable hostility through the sibling relationship. By portraying the Bush–bin Laden relationship in this canonical way so that it resonates with other stories and using it as the corner stone of the 9/11 story, the event moves from the plane of history to myth. Unlike televised news reporting which presents live events to an audience who is presumed to be in a simultaneous present with its myths render these events as generalities and as primordial, shorn of all historical specificity and contextualisation. In this way, they are able to use the 'what if' mode to present counterfactuals or descriptions of alternate possibilities that could have been real but did not actually happen (McLaughlin 2005). Folktelling of epics like the Ramayana and the Mahabharata uses this mode to refer to time itself as plural—each period with its own way of living out the stories that are part of the everyday world as we know it. These stories are true because even though they may or may not have happened in our time, they have occurred in some other time—in the past or even in an alternate present which is beyond our experiential world.

The way in which the majority of the viewers of the 9/11 strike received the event was as information on live television where the time of the occurrence was presumed to be simultaneous with the time of viewing. Even though we know that there is an element of fabrication and organisation even to news reporting of live events as it is not possible to present a coherent account of an event while it is still occurring, there is an assumption that the audience is an eye witness—co-present in time though not in space, thus turning the event into a dramatic spectacle (Seaton 2003). *Chitrakar* storytellers are quite aware that we live in an increasingly media-saturated world where entertainment, information and social commentary must compete for viewers' attention. Global events like the 9/11 strike are mediatised—available only at one remove as the presence of the television screen in Swarna's Laden *pata* shows us (see Figure 4.21), but the difference between a mediatised event as a form of 'infotainment' and the event as a *Chitrakar* story is the moral message

Figure 4.21

Image made by artist Swarna

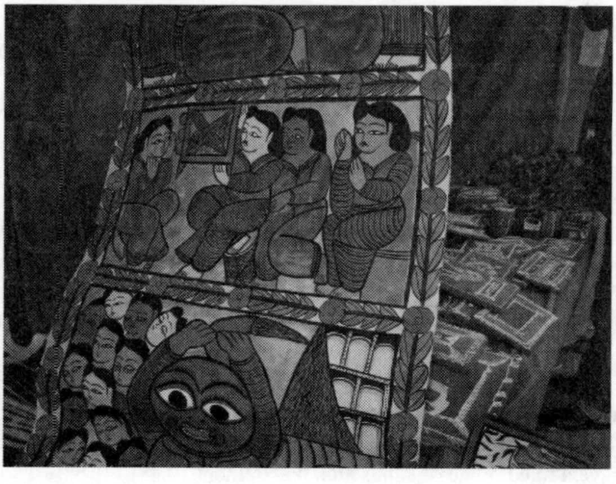

Source: Roma Chatterji.

that it carries. It is only by generalising the event, removing all factual detail so that it can resonate with other stories in the collective memory that it is able to convey a message that can be understood universally and carried forward into the future. I began my essay with an extended quotation from the work of an influential writer of American superhero comic books. In societies which no longer have living myths presented in sophisticated epic form, it is perhaps popular genres such as comics that take their place. By creating a fantasy 'multiverse' where worlds of fiction and reality collide such narratives create 'what if' possibilities where different versions of the world are presented to us as mirrors so that we can reflect and even critique the reality that we live in.

Notes

1. This essay is largely based on an earlier monograph (see Chatterji 2012).
2. The traditional term for designating this community is *patua*. Since Independence, this term has fallen into disfavour as designating low status. Most members prefer to designate themselves as *Chitrakar* in Medinipur at least. *Patua* is still used as a term of self-designation in the district of Birbhum that is adjacent to Medinipur. I use both terms to refer to this community—*Chitrakar* when I refer to the members of the community and *patua* when I speak of them in the context of the performance.
3. Sacred shrines tend to transcend denominational divisions. The shrines of *pirs* (Muslim holy men) are visited by Hindus and Muslims alike. Naya, the village in which I have done fieldwork, houses an important *mazaar* (grave) of a *pir* as well as shrines to Satya Pir (a composite divinity who is worshipped as Satya Narayan by Hindus) and Ola Bibi, a cholera deity who is known as Olai Chandi by Hindus.
4. Some of these names are Hindu such as Radha or Gouranga but others like Khandu or Roopshona do not signify membership in a religious community.
5. In fact, based on the reports of the 1891 census in Bengal, both Risley and Hunter classified the *patuas* and the *chitrakars* as separate castes.
6. I began fieldwork in Naya in 2005 and have been visiting the village ever since.
7. The display of *patas* has always been a seasonal occupation. Some of the other occupations followed by the *Chitrakars* were icon (*murti*) making in clay, snake charming. Some sub-castes of the *Chitrakars* also performed magic tricks, were garland makers, makers of clay dolls (especially women, who often acted as midwives). Some *Chitrakars* have also taken to occupations such as tailoring, bus driving and so on (see Singh 1995a, Ray 1953).
8. The *Chitrakars*, also known as *patua* from the name of the *patas* that they display while singing, are multimedia performers, using pictures to tell or sing their stories. I hesitate to think of the scrolls as illustrations of their songs because the relationship between the pictures and songs are elliptical and indirect. Different singers may interpret the picture scrolls differently. This becomes especially marked in new composition which do not have a fixed range of songs attached to them.

9. Bhaskar Mukhopadhyay (2008) refers to Madhusudhan Chitrakar's *patas* that place the plane crash at the end of the story. His story begins with the telephone conversation between Bush and bin Laden, which leads to a misunderstanding and then to the cataclysmic event. In one of the *patas*, Madhusudhan uses an elephant as a symbol of Bush; in that Bush is seated on an elephant, while bin Laden rides on a tiger very much like Satya Pir.
10. One *pata* only has three registers and is interesting as it describes the essential structure of the story.
11. Muslim warrior saints (*gazis*) and *pirs* deified over the centuries are important mediators between the divine and the earthly realms. Even though most *pir* legends have roots in historical events and biographies, the stories themselves follow the structure of the *mangala kavyas*. *Pirs* are worshipped by both Hindus and Muslims alike. Satya Pir is also worshipped as Satya Narayan by Hindus.
12. This was pointed out to me by Khandu Chitrakar.
13. Kalighat paintings were a form of bazar painting that became popular in the eighteenth and nineteenth centuries. Named after a famous pilgrimage site, the painters at Kalighat migrated from villages in Bengal at a time when Kolkata was developing into an important metropolis. They developed their own folk–urban style of painting, derived from traditional *Chitrakar* styles and popularised the depiction of secular themes. The last Kalighat *patua* died in the 1930s though there has been an attempt to revive this style by Kalam Patua of Birbhum, West Bengal (Jain 1999, 2004).
14. Another way of ending the picture story is to show multiple images of bin Laden in the last frame of the scroll as if to play on the uncanny relationship between the real person who is only available as a video image after the 9/11 strike (see Figure 4.15). The painting plays on the ambivalence of bin Laden's status—between myth and reality.
15. Recent variants of the Laden *pata* have added to the deification of the bin Laden figure by removing his face from the killer plane on the first frame of the *pata* and replacing it with a demonic head. I was told that this substitution was meant to add to the ferocity of the scene—to the impact of the plane as it crashed into the building. Be that as it may, it also dilutes the tension that we see in Probir's *pata* that begins by depicting bin Laden as a demonic figure but ends by portraying him as a *pir*. Chandan's *pata*, however, adds a new motif to the battle scene. The tree of life is stretched across the battle field, separating the two armies. But it appears again above the bin Laden inset in the last frame of the *pata*, offering shade to devotees who have come to pray at the *pir's* shrine—an anticipation of the future perhaps. I have also seen a version of the Laden *pata* by Madhusudan Chitrakar that actually depicts bin Laden on a tiger in the very first frame itself (Brittlebank 1995). Bush who shares the frame with bin Laden is shown riding an elephant—the symbol of the Republican party to which he belongs. Bin Laden's horse sets him apart from the local iconography of the *pir* whose *vahana* (mount) is typically the tiger. This may well be moulded on popular iconography associated with Shiite martyrdom where Hussain is depicted as a warrior saint mounted on a white horse (Chelkowski 1989).
16. Both Manu and Swarna have composed *patas* on the graphic novel themes that they have been commissioned to illustrate. Swarna's project, which is to interpret the Pinocchio story, incorporates the speech balloon as a decorative device. She has also started to experiment with the figurative and gestural aspect of writing. She is, as I have said earlier, unlettered.

References

Barthes, Roland. 1973. *Mythologies*. London: Paladin.

———. 1985. *The Responsibility of Forms: Critical Essays in Music, Art and Representation*. Oxford: Basil Blackwell.

Benjamin, Walter. (1923) 1968. 'The Task of the Translator'. In *Illuminations*, edited by Walter Benjamin, pp. 69–82. New York, NY: Schoken.

Bhattacharjee, Binoy. 1980. *Cultural Oscillation: A Study on Patua Culture*. Calcutta: Naya Prokash Press.

Brittlebank, Kate. 1995. 'Shakti and Barakat: The Power of Tipu's Tiger. An Examination of the Tiger Emblem of Tipu Sultan of Mysore'. *Modern Asian Studies* 29 (2): 257–69.

Chatterji, Roma. 1986. 'The Voyage of the Hero: Self and Other in One Narrative Tradition of Bengal'. In *The Word and the World: Narrative, Symbol and Record*, edited by Veena Das, pp. 95–114. New Delhi: SAGE Publications.

———. 2012. *Speaking with Pictures: Folk Art and the Narrative Tradition in India*. Delhi: Routledge.

Chelkowski, Peter. 1989. 'Narrative Painting and Painting Recitation in Qajar Iran'. *Muqarnas* 6: 98–111.

Chute, Hillary, and Marianne De Koven. 2006. 'Introduction: Graphic Narrative'. *Modern Fiction Studies* 52 (4): 767–82.

Coomaraswamy, Ananda K. (1909) 1990. *The Indian Craftsman*. Delhi: Motilal Banarasidass.

Hauser, Beatrix. 2002. 'From Oral Tradition to "Folk Art"'. *Asian Folklore Studies* 61 (1): 105–22.

Hiltebeitel, Alf. 2001. *Rethinking the Mahabharata: A Reader's Guide to the Education of the Dharma King*. Chicago: University of Chicago Press.

Imamura, Taihei. 1953. 'Japanese Art and the Animated Cartoon'. *The Quarterly Journal of Film, Radio and Television* 7 (3): 217–22.

Jain, Jyotindra. 1999. *Kalighat Painting: Images from a Changing World*. Ahmedabad: Mapin.

———. 2004. *Indian Popular Culture: 'The Conquest of the World as Picture'*. Kolkata: Ajeepay Press.

Korom, Frank. 2006. *Village of Painters: Narrative Scrolls from West Bengal*. Sante Fe: Museum of New Mexico Press.

Lévi-Strauss, Claude. (1964) 1975. *The Raw and the Cooked: Introduction to the Science of Mythology, Vol I*. New York, NY: Harper and Row.

McLaughlin, Jeff. 2005. 'What If? DC's Crisis and Leibnizian Possible Worlds'. In *Comics as Philosophy*, edited by Jeff McLaughlin, pp. 3–14. Jackson: University Press of Mississippi.

Mirzoeff, Nicholas. 2005. *Watching Babylon: The War in Iraq and Global Visual Culture*. New York, NY: Routledge.

Morrison, Grant. 2011. *Supergods*. New York, NY: Speigel and Grau.

Mukhopadhyay, Bhaskar. 2008. 'Dream Kitsch—Folk Art, Indigenous Media and "9/11": The Work of *Pat* in the Era of Electronic Transmission'. *Journal of Material Culture* 13 (1): 5–34.

Ray, Sudhansu Kumar. 1953. 'The Artisan Castes of West Bengal and their Craft', Special Monograph. In *The Tribes and Castes of West Bengal*, edited by Asok Mitra. Alipur: Census 1951, West Bengal, Land and Land Revenue Department.

Seaton, Jean. 2003. 'Understanding not Empathy'. In *War and Media. Reporting Conflict 24/7*, edited by Daya Kishan Thussu and Des Freedman, pp. 45–54. London: SAGE Publications.

Singh, Kavita. 1995a. 'The Pictures of Showmen'. Unpublished PhD thesis, University of Chandigarh.

———. 1995b. 'Stylistic Differences and Narrative Choices in Bengali Pata Paintings'. *Journal of Arts and Ideas* 27–28: 91–104.

Spielmann, Yvonne, and Jay David Bolter. 2006. 'Hybridity: Arts, Sciences and Cultural Effects'. *Leonardo* 30 (2): 106–07.

Williams, Joanna. 1996. *The Two-headed Deer: Illustrations of the Ramayana in Orissa.* Berkeley: The University of California Press.

5

From Ritual Images to Animated Movies: The Transformative Journey of the Sora Paintings (Central-Eastern India)

Cécile Guillaume-Pey

In contemporary India, numerous ritual practices have become disconnected from their original context and have been converted into aesthetic expressions that acquire the status of cultural emblems circulating in museums, markets, festivals and exhibitions organised at regional, national and even global levels. This is notably the case for a spectacular ritual known as the *teyyam* from Kerala (Tarabout 2005) and for a range of painted images: *maithil* paintings from Bihar (Mishra and Owens 1978; Singh 2000), *patta* from Odisha (Bundgaard 1996, 1999) and *patua* from Bengal (Hauser 2002). Recently, various votive objects and ritual images made by painters, sculptors and wood carvers belonging to several tribal groups from India (*Adivasi*)—the Gond, Kondh, Santal, Warli, etc.—were displayed at the Quai Branly Museum (Paris, France) for an exhibition dedicated to the 'Other masters from India'[1] curated by Jyotindra Jain, art historian and former director of the National Craft Museum in New Delhi.

This chapter[2] addresses ritual wall paintings made by the Sora—a tribal group from the Odisha–Andhra Pradesh border[3]—and, adopting Igor Kopytoff's biographical method (1986), sketches their transformative journey. In Sora villages, these images, in front of which sacrifices are performed, are considered to be houses made for deities. The creation of such paintings, which are understood to 'flatter' the spirits, enables the Sora to gain their favours; a ritual action from which villagers expect a result such as good harvests or a recovery from illness. The designing of these images is part of a complex ritual system, which requires the close collaboration between a ritual painter and other religious specialists who, through their songs, invite local deities to inhabit the picture. Visual, aural and physical expressions are interwoven in a unique manner to create 'living' and powerful divine images. But if Indian religious images are alive, as Richard Davis (1997: 13) highlights, it is not only because they embody the divine but because they are animated as well 'by their own histories and by their varied interactions with different human communities'. Less famous in the international art world than the Warli or Gond paintings, those made by the Sora are nevertheless submitted to a process of 'artification' (Heinich and Shapiro 2012; Levanto, Naukkarinen and Vihma 2005) that considerably changes their production, their audience and their meaning. These 'altar-paintings', which are an important means of communication with the divine, may be thus disconnected from the converging agencies set in motion by the ritual to which they belong. Nowadays, the Sora paintings, ephemeral visual traces of a pact with deities whose desires must be satisfied, are exhibited in museums, sold in local markets or exported abroad, even inspiring the production of animated films. The transition of the status and role of these paintings to 'folk art' or to 'art'—a process in which the Indian government, local NGOs, as well as foreign artists, are engaged—results in the transformation of aesthetic categories as well as ontological references of their creators. As ritual images sprayed with blood made for gods and ancestors or as iconic markers of a 'tribal identity' integrated to the regional or the national cultural heritage, the Sora paintings represent valorised medium for the encounter between the self and the other.

Drawing Dreams, Materialising Gods and Fulfilling Their Desires

In the central room of Sora houses, one finds mural paintings made with rice powder, charcoal and vegetable pigments. Among the Sora from Srikakulam district, northern Andhra Pradesh, these paintings are called *idisu'ung*, a word that can be translated as 'painted houses'. In the Sora language, *id* is the radical form of a verb referring to the action of 'painting' or 'writing' and *su'ung* means 'house'.[4] These images are indeed a kind of dwelling for the gods and the ancestors whose presence is thus materialised in the very heart of the domestic space.[5] The prayers chanted by religious specialists, which accompany the gestures of the painter who is sometimes compared to a carpenter (*sapsapmar*)—speak about 'constructing a house within the house' (Mallebrein 2001), a house dedicated to the deities invited to inhabit the image.

What do these images—described as 'icon' by Verrier Elwin (1955: chap. 10), the first ethnographer to study them—look like? Most are rectangular in shape, measuring approximately 1.5 m × 1.2 m. Some of them are pentagonal. In such cases, a triangular pattern depicting the roof of these 'houses' is drawn on the top of the basic rectangle. A band of geometric motifs, often composed of highly stylised dancing silhouettes, defines the outline of the images. The picture's internal structure varies according to the locality. In the paintings from Puttasing Valley, southern Odisha, studied by Elwin and Cornelia Mallebrein, the space inside the frame is often compartmentalised: the painting thus looks like a multilevel building, a kind of dwelling attesting to the high status of its divine owners.[6] Among the Sora from Srikakulam, this kind of composition is quite unusual. In the paintings, there appears always an important geometrical pattern: a rectangular motif filled with triangles. Like the whole painting, this figure called *linguar* refers to the subterranean abode where local gods and ancestors reside. A peacock is often depicted perching at the top, which accentuates the formal similarity between the frames of the *linguar* and the *idisu'ung*, also usually presented with this bird. In some paintings, this process of *mise en abyme* is particularly salient as there is a strict equivalence between the form of the whole painting and the one of the *linguar* traced inside (Figure 5.1).

Whatever the locality, the inner part of these 'houses', composed of a set of patterns juxtaposed without perspective, is always densely filled. Motifs depicting various components of the landscape—hills, trees, celestial bodies[7]—are mixed among numerous white figures with anthropomorphic or zoomorphic contours engaged in all sorts of activities. In the paintings of the Sora villagers, who mainly live from agriculture—shifting cultivation in the hills and rice cultivation in the plains—the agrarian scenes are predominant. Characters ploughing, harvesting rice and carrying crops are therefore depicted. Hunting parties are also numerous. The thematic of the hunter hunted—by a tiger—is frequent. One may also observe some characters engaged into sexual activities (*totomandranji*), a kind of pattern which used to provoke hilarity in my youngest informants. Other groups of characters perform rituals. One may thus see anthropomorphic figures seated, a winnowing fan on her or his lap, evoking religious specialists

Figure 5.1

Painting made in the house of Cécile Guillaume-Pey's hosts (Ondengsung, Andhra Pradesh, 2007)

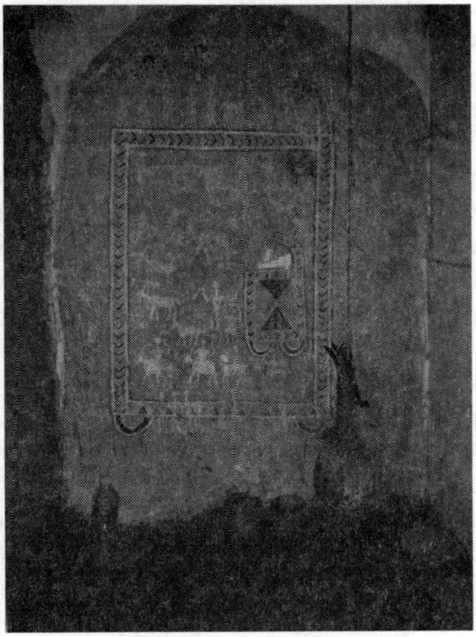

Source: Cécile Guillaume-Pey.

(*kuram*) in trance.[8] The painting thus shows not only what the human actors may see during rituals but also what is at stake on an invisible stage: the metamorphosis of the *kuram's* soul that, in an animal form, reaches the kingdom of gods and ancestors. The image, sometimes mirroring the ritual, may further display some elements referring to myths. Thus, the common motif of the snake swallowing the moon refers to the myth of the eclipse. In Sora society, where myths are rarely narrated, the paintings may thus function as mediums for remembering. At Srikakulam, when the Sora villagers are questioned about the identity of the numerous painted characters, they usually reply that they are *nyonan*, a name given to chthonic deities mainly associated with the hills dedicated to shifting cultivation, or *elda*, the dead pacified by the secondary funeral (*guar*). They are often depicted as raja, kings travelling on horseback and elephant-back, sometimes in palanquin, surrounded by many servants with umbrellas. Kamlesh Guha (1983) puts forward the hypothesis that famous kings and historical events from medieval India are represented in Sora wall paintings. In some paintings, the deities, becoming modernised, are depicted using various means of contemporary transport such as bikes, cars, buses or even planes. Further, in the present day, the figure of the raja is sometimes replaced with more contemporaneous opposite powerful figures[9] such as forest officers and sometimes even the Naxalites present in Srikakulam since the end of the 1960s.[10]

The Sora wall paintings, far from being isolated pictures, are instead integrated into a complex of ritual objects, substances and images. They are not the only medium through which the divine is materialised in the domestic space. It is worth noting that in India, the divine is generally actualised in multiples. Charles Malamoud (1989) employs the word 'polysômie' to evoke the fragmentation of a single divine being into multiple bodies. In Sora houses, near the painting—hung in front or placed on the ground behind—one always finds earthen pots (*danki*)[11] commonly called *sonum-dan*, 'spirit-pot'. Their number depends on the locality considered. In some Sora villages from southern Odisha, it corresponds exactly with the paintings' number. Each pot, filled with crops, ritual miniature objects, vermilion powder and incense is thus hung in front of the very 'house' it is associated with (Figure 5.2). Generally connected to fertility and to the Goddess in India, they are associated with different

Figure 5.2

'Houses' and their pots, Ankarada village, Odisha, 2013

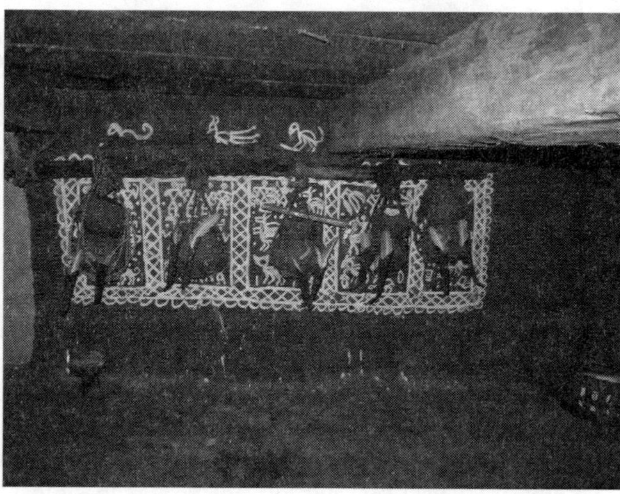

Source: Cécile Guillaume-Pey.

categories of deities—ancestors (*elda*),[12] local chthonic entities (*nyonan/sonum*) and Hindu gods—in Sora houses. Behind the pots dedicated to the latter are placed chromolithographs bought during pilgrimages—or simple visits—to Hindu temples. In the same ritual space, we thus observe a juxtaposition of divine images: on one side, we find images produced at the village level for powerful agents intimately linked to the territory; on the other, we find images bought in cities, dedicated to major deities of Hindu pantheon appropriated by the villagers.[13] In the manner of many ritual objects and pictures that may be called 'effective', 'strong' or 'powerful', we deal here with things that must be concealed and guarded. Aimed at charming invisible deities, these paintings surrounded by pots are not exhibited. In contrast with the divine images worshipped in Hindu temples, where the act of seeing the deity (*darshan*) is crucial (Babb 1981; Eck 1998), the Sora wall paintings are not made to be contemplated by human eyes. Far from being highlighted in the domestic space, they are invariably situated on the northern wall of the central room, where their access is limited to the household members. Sometimes isolated behind a small wall, various profane artefacts—clothes, trunks and cooking vessels—act as protective screens behind which the paintings and other items are hidden.

To understand what confers on the paintings their specific efficacy, we shall focus on their production. The mural paintings are always executed in ritual context. In Srikakulam villages, they are renewed and replaced for a ritual celebrated when the mangos are ripe (*urapur*). During this ritual, the women would go to a sacred grove near the village boundaries to offer fruits to ancestors and to the deities associated with the hills where shifting cultivation is practiced. The paintings drawn during the ritual celebrated at the village level are said to protect members of each household of the village and their fields.[14] The ritual occasion in which wall paintings are done depends on the locality, as well as the function associated with those images. Among the Sora from southern Odisha studied by Elwin, the images can be made for a large variety of purposes. Some paintings are executed before the seasonal feast to regenerate the protection of the village. Others are made to honour the villagers who migrated and died in the tea plantations in Assam and for whom the secondary funeral (*guar*), which could not be celebrated without their bones, have not been performed. This ritual—during which the bones of the dead are exhumed, a stone erected and a buffalo sacrificed—is thus represented in the painting. In such a case, the image replaces the ritual. Other paintings are made in order to heal or to avert illness: they are drawn during a healing ritual or a ceremony celebrated after the birth of a child in order to protect him from the influence of malevolent spirits and witches. Lastly, some images are painted in the house of certain religious specialists (*kuram*) to celebrate their spiritual weddings with their tutelary gods. During the marriage ceremony, the execution of a wall painting dedicated to the deities is accompanied by the consecration of an earthen pot placed near the painting and by a goat sacrifice. The images can be renewed later if a tutelary deity feels neglected by his/her human spouse (Elwin 1955: 429).

The act of painting is considered a religious act in itself. In a myth collected by Elwin (1955: 402), the creation of mural painting is considered as a skill transmitted by the gods to human beings, which are said to be themselves born from a painting spread by divine blood: according to the myth, a god called Kitung drew a man and a woman on the wall of his house. Then, he covered them with leaves, adding blood from his little finger. Some days later, the anthropomorphic figures came to life and out from the wall. The man and the woman born from the god's painting are said to be the ancestors of the Sora. While in the myth, a god shelters human beings, provides them food and clothes and, above all, gives them life by making a picture spread with his own blood; in the ritual, it is humans who draw, invite the gods into their 'house-painting' and feed them with blood sacrifice. Painting, considered a ritual gesture of the utmost importance, is performed by religious specialists called the *idisu'ungmar*—for a man—or *idisu'ungboy*—for a woman. There are usually several persons specialised in the execution of wall paintings in a village, who intervene for their consanguines, affines, as well as their neighbours. In Ondengsung, the Sora village from Srikakulam where I was living during my fieldwork, there are six painters, two women and four men, among 250 inhabitants. They are remunerated with rice, alcohol and pieces of sacrificial meat after the performance. In southern Odisha, according to Dinanath Pathy, the transmission of this skill is patrilineal or avuncular. The access to the status of 'painter' is marked by a ritual during which a buffalo is sacrificed (Pathy 1996: 32). In northern Andhra Pradesh, the access to the status of *idisu'ungmar* is not formalised by a ritual and the modalities of transmission are more flexible: a father, a mother, an uncle or a grandmother can show any member of his lineage how to paint, whatever his or her gender. It is worth noting that simply having technical competences is not sufficient for allowance to paint on the walls. Ritual painters have to follow certain rules. Before drawing an image on the wall, they have to fast. In addition, during the performance, the only substance they can consume is the alcohol offered to the deities.

If the specialist is a woman, she should not be menstruating, as the blood may provoke the wrath of the deities. Finally, painters converted to other cults, however technically competent they may be, are not allowed to continue to draw on the walls.

The painter is far from being the only actor on the ritual scene. The execution of powerful images is not an individual but a collective performance involving other religious specialists: it also involves the village priest (*boya*), who chants invocations, and the medium (*kuram*), who gives his voice to the deities he incorporates during the ritual. The presence and the collaboration of members of the household are also required. The housewife is the first to act: she prepares the place where the house for the deities will be drawn by spreading cow dung on the wall. Then, the priest places rice and alcohol offerings in small leaves, after which the painter can start his work. The painting is made with rice flour mixed with water and traced with a twig on the wall of the central room. The process begins with the creation of the frame, which is then filled with various motives. Other patterns are then added around the perimeter. While the paintings are done to charm invisible beings, very human individuals—the mediums in particular—give their judgement on the painter's work. The painter's skill is thus evaluated during the design process, a semi-private performance whose access is restricted to the ritual officiants and to the beneficiaries of the ritual.

As the designing of a wall painting is accompanied by hymns, prayers, offerings and possession seances, we shall not isolate this visual medium which conveys a divine presence from the web of words, sounds, gestures, looks, desires, intentions and emotions in which it is embedded. The part played by the ritual specialists whose songs accompany the painter's work is crucial in the confection of *idisu'ung*. In the manner of *maithil* paintings from Bihar (Singh 2000), *patua* from Bengal (Hauser 2002) or *kalam* from Kerala (Tarabout 2003), the fulfilment of *idisu'ung* is indeed accompanied by chanting invocations.[15] During the performance, different modes of expression are thus combined. The modes of convergence between visual and aural experiences can be expressed, as Madeleine Leclair (2009) emphasises, in various ways: vision can suggest sound but music can also suggest sight, triggering mental images, provoking a synaesthetic phenomenon or even implying other registers of perception. While in several societies, bursting into—and transmitting—ritual songs implies a visual medium, acting as mnemonic dispositive (Severi 2007), among the Sora, the production of a painting is contemporaneous with the incantation that accompanies its design. Furthermore, the articulation between visual and phonic expression may be connected to the first medium supposed to guide the painter's gestures: mental representations appearing in dreams. Before being traced on the wall, indeed, some Sora affirm that the content of the painting is seen in dreams by the painter himself, by a *kuram*,[16] or by a member of the household (Elwin 1955; Mallebrein 2001). In such a case, the mission of the painter is to make a dream visible, to give it reality.

To be effective, the 'house-paintings' must be shown to the gods who accept to live inside. Such a result is obtained when the interlocutors of the possessed medium manage to convince spirits to focus their attention on the painting and when these powerful agents are satisfied by its content. The latter usually begin by refusing to consider the image. They complain and pretend that the house inhabitants have neglected them, perhaps forgotten to feed them by appropriate sacrifices. Some of them also criticise the content of the paintings dedicated to them. During the performance, a possessed medium may thus intervene to judge the work of the painter, asking him to add here and there some specific 'forgotten' designs, a demand that can explain the saturation of such pictures. Sometimes, the deities to whom the mural paintings are dedicated are not only invited to give their opinion by the mouth of a possessed medium (Elwin 1955: 404), they are said to direct the painter's gestures. Pathy (1996) states that some painters pretend to have been guided—and even possessed—by the spirits themselves, who then appeared as the true authors of the painting dedicated to them. After heated debates, when the gods—and their intermediaries on the ritual stage—are satisfied with the content, the village priest and the medium summon them one last time by their songs to watch and inhabit their house.[17] Then, the priest, with the assistance of the head of the household, sacrifices a goat and spreads the blood on the painting, the pots dedicated to the spirits and the vegetable offerings made in their honour.

What is the status of these images? If the wall paintings may be considered as offerings made for deities, they do not have exactly the same function as the vegetal gifts placed at their feet or the blood and alcohol they are regularly spread with, substances which also contribute to materialise the divine. *Idisu'ung* may be rather considered as a kind of altar: it is in front of them that sacrifices are performed during agrarian ceremonies or village tutelary deity rituals and that, every evening, the housewife deposes cooked rice for the spirits before serving her family members. When, after some years, the *idisu'ung* fade—eventually becoming as invisible as the deities they materialised—they nevertheless play the part of an altar, still regularly spread with blood, until the next renewal ritual updates the pact sealed with the divine.

In these wall paintings which aim at 'less to describe than to institute realities', to borrow an expression from Michel Leiris,[18] a presence undoubtedly takes root. They shall be seen as a 'religious sign' as defined by Jean-Pierre Vernant:

> The religious sign is not simply an instrument of thought. Its purpose is not limited to evoking in men's minds the sacred power to which it refers. Its intention is always also to establish a true means of communication with this power and to really introduce its presence into the human world. (Vernant [1965] 2006: 332)

The operational value of the Sora paintings, inseparable from the web of gestures and the complex menagerie of ritual objects by which they are surrounded, lies in their capacity to embody deities, to personify them by putting them into a medium which enables the Sora to fix them and, thus, to propitiate them. In this matter, the geometrical design called the *linguar*, a crucial component of the paintings, plays a key role. In various regions of India, wall paintings and floor drawings include patterns which condense or captivate the divine. At the centre of the paintings made by Kumaon women from Uttar Pradesh (Hart 1995: 131) and by Mithila women from Bihar (Singh 2000) appears a motive referring to the seat of the deities invited to inhabit the picture. Mani Shekhar Singh, inspired by Alfred Gell's analyses (1998), points out that a geometrical motive like the lotus diagram which spreads out from the vermilion point at the centre of the *maithil* paintings acts as a 'mind-trap'. In the case of the complex non-figurative pattern of the *kolam* made on the floor in southern India, Gell highlights that such designs act as 'demon-trap[s]' (1998: 84–85). Serving as a point of condensation for wandering forces—more or less malevolent—inside the domestic space, the *linguar* figured in the Sora paintings is usually compared to a sanctuary, a temple hosting deities, or to the vehicle carrying the statues of the gods during religious festivals.

The ritual is considered effective especially if the painting—whose 'beauty' may be called 'active', an expression employed by Gilles Tarabout concerning the *kalam* (2003)—meets certain stylistic criteria. 'Realism'—or conformity with the narrative register—is not one of these criteria. Some *idisu'ung/boy* or *kuram* assure that the oneiric images inspiring the production of paintings do not enable them to see the spirits and their underground dwelling as they are but as their divine owners would like them to be (Elwin 1955: 437). The dreams, and the paintings which give them a visibility, would thus allow them to realise spirits' wishes. Besides, the appearance given to the local gods depicted in the picture deeply contrasts with the features these same gods have in the narratives recounted by those who meet them in daytime in the forest. In the paintings, they are depicted as anthropomorphic characters and not as ferocious creatures—half-human, half-beast—that the youngest villagers, sometimes influenced by Hollywood movies, compare to King Kong. In any case, we should consider *idisu'ung* as a mere representation. Like the speech of the possessed medium, often considered as lie (*talu*), painting and dream—which may be a source of inspiration for the painter—are not means of expression which permit to show a static 'reality' or 'truth' (*jarite*). They shall be rather regarded as kinds of decoys inspired by—and dedicated to—deities who are themselves said to be untrustworthy; they are dynamic processes that establish a new order, giving flesh to spirits' desires.

'Divine Houses' for Sale: The Production of De-ritualised Identitarian Emblems

The role conferred on a visual medium dedicated to deities, the techniques employed by the painters to achieve their goals and the modes of knowledge transmission of their skills are currently shifting. We should not consider the execution of 'painting-houses' and the agencies they convey without taking into account the double process of patrimonialisation and commoditisation (Kopytoff 1986), which affects the creation of such images as well as the way the tribal painters perceive their work. What are the implications of this process on the production, the consumption and the circulation of Sora paintings? In what manner is the formal complexity of pictures initially characterised by the entanglement of different modes of expression affected? To what extent does the marketing and the museification of their work offer a new generation of Sora painters a chance to innovate and to divert the images from their original goal? In a society where the spirits' desires are said to guide the painters' gestures and where the art market contemporaneously imposes its rules, the answer is far to be obvious.

Today, *idisu'ung*—on static or mobile mediums—are winning over Indian cities. Pictures which in Sora houses are more or less hidden to the human sight are now displayed in museums, 'tribal markets' and on city walls. At Bhubaneswar, the capital of the Odisha State, Sora paintings are exhibited as ethnographic items inside the Museum of Tribal Arts and Artifacts and decorate the walls on the outside. They may be easily purchased at a relatively cheap price in the Ekamra Haat, a market where 'tribal' artefacts often made and sold by non-tribal craftsmen and artists, and in the exhibition ground of the *Adivasi Mela*, an annual tribal festival. One may also see Sora paintings amongst various artefacts—brass, terracotta, wood carving, etc.—made by different local communities, displayed on the walls of official buildings like the office of the Deputy Commissioner of Police (Figure 5.3). The paintings can even be seen on the walls of hotels, offering a 'picturesque' air to the halls and the rooms. Painted on paper, canvas or clothes, some of these images are also within reach of any Internet surfer in search of exoticism. Indeed, various websites today offer panels largely consisting of Sora paintings at different prices, exportable abroad. Introduced in new places, the style and the content of these paintings evolve. Monochromes designed with rice flour—sometimes highlighted by few touches of red and black—are replaced by brightly coloured canvases made with acrylic and aimed at seducing new clients.

Figure 5.3

On the walls of the Police Station, Bhubaneswar, Odisha

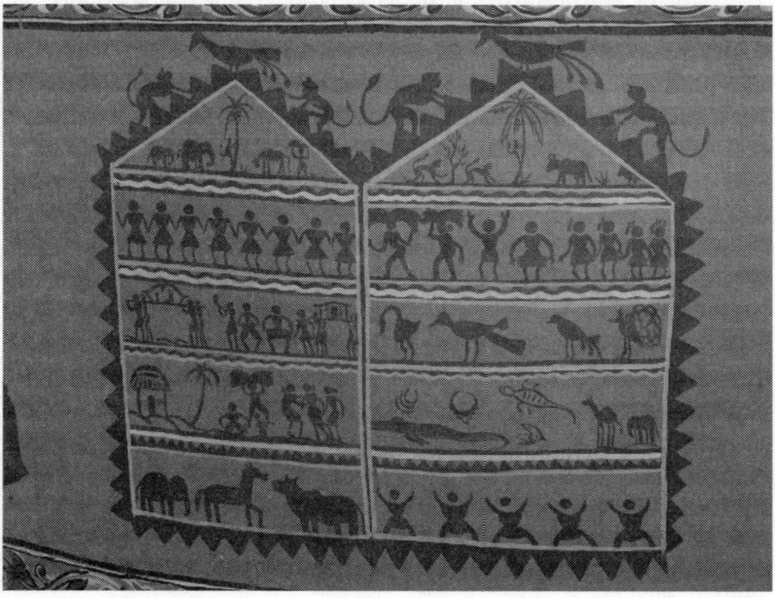

Source: Cécile Guillaume-Pey.

In these changing times, the creation of these Sora paintings is considered an expertise, which, extracted from its ritual context, is recognised by the dominant society and considered a regional cultural emblem. The Indian government, in order to support the integration of a part of a tribal minority culture into the regional heritage, encourages the production and distribution of Sora paintings which it assumes contribute to this conservation. As Tarabout (2003: 46) notes about the *kalam*: 'the announcement of an imminent extinction of these 'arts' is a regular prophecy accompanying their folklorisation'. Trainings in art colleges in Odisha are organised, research projects on paintings are initiated and, last but not least, tribal festivals and exhibitions, in which Sora painters show and sell their productions, are organised (Rousseleau 2014). The two latter processes could be directly linked as some research programmes aim above all else to promote Sora paintings in the framework of exhibitions and other cultural events during which they can be sold.[19] Thus, the Indian government, which is as Ashoke Chatterjee (1988: 6) stresses 'the major client for organised craft activity today', plays a crucial part in the transit and transition of Sora paintings from village ritual images to urban goods and cultural emblems.

Various social actors are involved in this translation and reconfiguration. Tribal Development Agency staff members, local NGO workers and urban educated Sora usually act as mediators between the Sora painters and the coordinators of the various exhibitions, fairs and festivals in which the former are invited to show their work. In Srikakulam, an NGO located near a Tribal Development Agency where most of the Sora living in Andhra Pradesh are concentrated, plays an important part in the transformation of *idisu'ung*. In 2008, this NGO was contacted by the minister of textiles, on behalf of the Government of India, to commercialise Sora paintings. Then, the NGO's director sent members of his staff to nearby Sora villages to search painters judged apt to participate in such a project. Only the youngest villagers—those between 18 and 30 years old—were selected. The director justifies this choice by explaining that the older painters do not possess the required patience to participate in the trainings organised at the NGO's seat and would refuse to obey the instructions given to produce images conforming to criteria defined by their sponsors. In the school[20] dedicated to the education of tribal children—Sora and Jatapu[21]—initiated by this NGO, the designing of *idisu'ung* was strongly encouraged. The most talented students were invited to show their work at regional exhibitions. Mohan, a young man on his twenties and a former student of this school, explains that it was the late director who encouraged him to take interest in the 'Sora traditions', and in the paintings in particular. The young man, whose paintings are still exhibited in the main building of the NGO's seat, has participated in several exhibitions and festivals. He showed me one day, with very clear pride, a photograph taken during an exhibition at Hyderabad where the chief minister of Andhra Pradesh gave him a trophy to reward his talent.

The transition of the Sora paintings and their circulation at the regional or even the national scale has had an impact on how one acquires *idisu'ungmar/boy* status at the village level. Learning to paint, a skill transmitted until recently in certain local patrilineal kin groups within a ritual context, today is instructed in different ways. Nowadays, it is often outside the ritual and outside the bonds of kinship that the youth learn to paint. A new generation of painters is emerging, a group who no longer learn to draw *idisu'ung* on the wall inside the house but instead do so on paper or canvas far from their villages. Thus, in Ondengsung, Tumpi and Rani, girls on their twenties who are the two youngest painters of the village, have learned to paint during the preparation of exhibitions to which the aforementioned director of the NGO and their previous teacher, himself a Sora, invited them. For this tribal master, as for many local Sora teachers, *idisu'ung*—even drained of their ritual component—are considered to be emblematic of 'the Sora culture'. Some of them encourage their pupils or ex-pupils to learn from the elder *idisu'ungmar/boy* of their community what they consider pre-eminently as an 'art'. Thus, it is at school and in an NGO, on paper, and not on the house walls, that Tumpi and Rani started to paint, following the instructions given to them by a Christian painter from a neighbouring village who did not belong to their kin group.

In contemporary society, painting is valued and supported by the government and appears to the young generation as an emblem of Sora identity, of which they are proud and eager to learn and propagate. Their involvement in regional or national exhibitions is moreover greatly praised among the village community. Thus, the painters do not hesitate to display certificates and prizes obtained on such occasions on their veranda, the space which opens to the central allay of the village from where their neighbours can see these honorific distinctions and the photographs which surround them. In Tumpi's house, at the top of the front door, in a frame are thus displayed around 10 shots taken at the State Art Gallery in Hyderabad.[22] One shows Tumpi painting and posing with her drawings, surrounded by a dozen *idisu'ungmar/boy* from the neighbouring villages who participated as well at the last *Girijan Utsav*. This week-long festival has been organised since 2007 in Andhra Pradesh by the Tribal Welfare

Department in collaboration with Integrated Tribal Development Agencies (ITDA), the Tourism Department, the Girijan Cooperative Corporation and the Tribal Cooperative Marketing Development Federation of India Limited (TRIFED). The official aim of this festival is to promote the culture and the art of *Girijan*, a term commonly employed to refer to Scheduled Tribes in this State.[23] On this occasion, more than one hundred stalls are erected, films on tribal culture are screened and a weekly tribal market is organised to show to the numerous visitors—mostly regional and national—the artefacts, dances, forest products, houses, etc., of the various tribal groups of Andhra Pradesh. To participate in such cultural events gives Tumpi and Rani a privileged occasion to escape for some days from the village routine and to discover cities—Srikakulam, Hyderabad, Kolkatta—places that they would never go otherwise. The young girls share their excitement but also their awkwardness (*garoy*) when they perform their paintings in the presence of non-Sora (*yo'oy*). At the outcome of their performances in such cultural events, they gain a certain prestige but not much money. At the present time, no Sora painter from Andhra Pradesh manages to live from their paintings, the profits from which mostly go to non-tribal actors.

Even though 'houses for the gods' are sold today, it doesn't mean at all that the commoditisation of the Sora paintings is necessarily carried out to the detriment of the ritual performance. As in the case of the *maithil* paintings from Bihar (Hart 1995; Mishra and Owens 1978), the arrival of the Sora paintings in the market does not lead to the disappearance of the ritual pictures. The aestheticisation and the transformation of an ephemerous ritual image into a permanent patrimonialised artefact made for exhibition or for sale may be qualified as partial since the Sora *idisu'ungmar/boy*, in the manner of the Mithila painters, commercialise their work without completely ceasing production of wall paintings in a ritual context. Even some younger painters juggle their status as 'tribal artist', granted to them outside the village, and their status as 'ritual specialist', attributed by their kin. At Ondengsung, for instance, the learning process of the youngest painters, lead in a very different context than those of their elders, does not deligitimatise at all the acquisition of their skill and its application during religious events. Thus, for *urapur,* the ritual during which the ritual paintings are renewed, Tumpi and Rani put in application their competences acquired outside the village. They perform in their own house as well as in their neighbours' houses. Then, these new mediators with the divine, who have interiorised aesthetic codes aimed at charming urban customers, introduce some stylistic changes in the paintings made for the deities on the walls. For the ritual painting Tumpi drew upon her house, she has chosen vivid colours: green, red, blue and yellow. Instead of rice flour, today the young girl prefers acrylic. This material gives her a larger palette of tones she considers 'more beautiful' (*boda*). The appropriation of new tools and materials to produce ritual artefacts sometimes brings about crucial changes in their use. In the case of the ritual masks made by the Sulka from New Guinea, Monique Jeudy-Ballini (1999) observes that the use of more sparkling paintings reduces the duration of ritual work and might in fact reinforce the efficacy of the masks in a society where the beautiful is evaluated in terms of radiance and brilliance. We may investigate whether, among the Sora, the use of vivid tints and of more lasting materials to make paintings will have an impact on the frequency of the renewal rituals and, thus, on the duration of the pact established with gods and ancestors.

But not all the Sora painters actively involved in the reconfiguration of ritual images into commercial aestheticised products contribute to the transformation of the wall paintings made for the gods inside the houses. Some of them, indeed, do not officiate anymore in a ritual context. In addition to the young painters whose multiple roles establish them as new guarantors of tradition inside as well as outside the village, the circulation of paintings in markets and museums is led by Sora from all ages who have converted to other religions. These painters who renounce the worship of their ancestors and local deities lose their ritual status and definitively cease to paint on the walls. Among those newly converted to Christianity, the ritual paintings must compete with other sacred pictures and are replaced by mass-produced portraits of Jesus. The paintings are also disappearing among the worshippers of Matharvanam, followers of a new religious movement that condemns the cult of images spread with blood. On the walls of practitioners of this cult based on the adoration of a revealed alphabet the 'spirit-paintings' are replaced by 'spirit-letters' believed to embody the divine[24] (Guillaume-Pey 2014).

The translation from local to regional—or even global—level raises numerous issues concerning the agencies of various actors involved in the production and consumption of Sora paintings. Regarding the practices and beliefs surrounding ritual artefacts, a change of scale often implies a series of ruptures or 'disjunctions', to borrow the expression employed by Fred R. Myers (1991) about the production and the perception of aboriginal visual media in transformation in Australia. Relocation and redisplay of a religious image can 'dramatically alter its significance for new audiences', as Davis (1997) emphasises in the case of a bronze image of Shiva exhibited in an American museum. Continuities can also be observed. In the case of numerous Asian cultural objects, Gérard Toffin (2009) points out that a change of context does not affect necessarily the uses. Thus, in the case of the divine statues exhibited in museums in the Himalayas or on the Indian subcontinent, the museification does not always imply a desacralisation of the objects. The gestures of offerings or respect dispensed to the statues by the visitors (Toffin 2009: 142) attest to this point. The situation differs when those who contemplate or buy objects in transit ignore all of their common use. As Lynn M. Hart (1995: 134) stresses in the case of the *maithil* paintings made for sale, such goods are considered as a 'conversation piece, a provoker of reverie, at worst a curio' by the Western purchasers who have no knowledge of their production context. Similarly, for the Indian middle-class urban consumers who visit tribal museums and buy Sora paintings at tribal exhibitions, such images inspire less devotion than curiosity.[25]

But how are these images perceived by those who produce them? It should be emphasised first of all that marketing, which highlights the painter as the sole agent with valuable expertise, overshadows the work of other traditional religious specialists significant in the creation of ritual paintings. The painter who works for commercial purposes no longer collaborates with other ritual officiants. His gestures are then performed in silence. The intimate links that traditionally bring together words, songs and images, visual signs and sounds, are untied. Deprived of the ritual incantations by the specialists attempting to convince the gods and the ancestors to come into the image, disconnected from the complex of ritual artefacts amongst which they were trapped, are the *idisu'ung* still considered by their creators as powerful objects able to exert any action on their new consumers? The painters who claim that the pictures they sold can enhance prosperity or exert a therapeutic effect on their urban purchasers are rare. Most of them consider that the deities are absent from those images exported far from the village community which can be duplicated at leisure and the content of which is no longer dictated by the spirits' desires. It is worth noting that contrary to the ritual images, the motif called *linguar*—point of condensation of deities inside the painting—is far from being systematically drawn in the pictures made for sale. These pictures nevertheless carry meaning for those who create them. For the painters, especially the younger ones who have acquired their skill in an extra-ritual context, *idisu'ung* are strong identity markers which they are proud to brandish, in opposition to other kinds of ritual knowledge traditionally required for their creation—songs, possession, dialogues with spirits—that do not receive any recognition outside the village community and are considered to already belong to the past.

Thus, one can then be somewhat surprised by the shift that occurs within the content of the paintings for sale: while most are lacking *linguar*, ritual scenes are nevertheless included at a higher frequency than in paintings executed within the religious context. The Sora paintings have shifted from images created in a ritual context to commercial pictures representing ritual performances from which they have been untied. The ritual most represented is the *guar*, the secondary funeral. The celebration of the *guar* is declining in the present day, partly due to the influence of Christianity, but many Sora still consider it the most important of their religious events. The commercial paintings show rituals that appear as crucial emblems for the actors. We have discussed previously that wall paintings may portray the secondary funeral, which would not have occurred without the presence of a corpse. In such cases, the painting functions as a substitute for the funerary ritual. Regarding the painters who have converted to Christianity or to the Matharvanam movement, we then should ask if the designing of 'divine houses' referring to rituals may be a way to keep a link with beliefs and practices which some of them have renounced. Piers Vitebsky (2008) has highlighted the complex emotions held by those Sora who have converted to Christianity regarding their dead parents, for whom they no longer celebrate the secondary funeral. If the ritual paintings materialise an expectation, a wish in the course of its realisation, may not the commercial images function as a kind of simulacrum for the ritual or at least reflecting a certain nostalgia? While the ritual images can be considered as decoys that reveal the desires of tricky deities, the commercial paintings display what is *no more* for some of their creators: the rituals that they have renounced, in particular the one dedicated to their ancestors, with whom they can no longer communicate via the intermediary of a possessed medium.

Disconnected from the ritual field before being integrated, as icons of the regional cultural heritage, in other webs of significations whose stakes often escape to their producers now proclaimed 'tribal artists', the Sora paintings, as numerous tribal ritual artefacts, also inspire non-tribal creators. As Mary-Ann Milford-Lutzker (1999) points out, tribal and village visual media production 'provide a touchstone' for Indian urban artists who, like Jayashree Chakravarty and Arpita Singh, use tribal designs in their works or, like Altaf Navjot, collaborate directly with an *Adivasi* sculptor (Milford-Lutzker 2003).

In Odisha as well as in Andhra Pradesh, the Sora painters must compete with actors already present in the local artistic field. The diffusion of Sora paintings at a national or global level is often operated by non-tribal artists who exploit the label 'tribal art' currently in vogue. Some of them even appropriate the original functions of the Sora wall paintings. Bishnu Prasad Maharana, an Odia artist sensitive to their ritual dimension, claims that his own pictures exert a therapeutic action and favour the happiness of families.[26] The career of this painter who describes himself as a 'tribal artist' started in 1978 when he was doing a study on the tribe.[27] He discovered an artistic vocation while admiring their ritual images and, inspired by them, he made his first acrylics. Serving 'the purpose of urban aesthetics', he asserts to preserve their art through offering insight on their culture with his own creations, which are exhibited in major Indian cities such as Delhi, Madras, Bangalore, etc.

While the Government encourages the marketing of the Sora paintings by various ways, one may be surprised by what is sometimes hidden under the 'Sora Art' label that the Ministry of Culture attributes to artworks. An Odia newspaper reported that during the launch of an exhibition of Sora paintings aimed at 'preserving the heritage of tribal India', the minister of culture and tourism had chosen to showcase paintings made by Susheela Rajendran, the Odisha governor's wife.[28] She had learned Sora painting at home, under the guidance of a non-Sora artist, the principal of an art college introduced to her by Pathy, art historian and author of a book on Sora paintings previously quoted in this chapter who played a key role in the promotion and diffusion of Sora paintings in Odisha (Rousseleau 2014). The laudatory article praises the audacity of Susheela Rajendran, who dares improvise with the choice of colours and patterns, giving a 'new vigour' to the Odia tribal art. Over the past decade, Rajendran has exhibited her canvases in Madras and New Delhi, giving part of the benefit to charity organisations. It is worth noting that the name given to her exhibition at the Lalit Kala Akademi at New Delhi refers to the original context of production of the Sora wall paintings. The Odisha Governor's wife, indeed, has entitled it 'Dreamscapes'.[29]

Thus, it appears that the oneiric experience as well as the therapeutic efficacy of the ritual images, important elements of the pictures made by Sora religious specialists, pass through the 'art sieve', while the agents engaged in the production and the circulation of the paintings called 'Sora art' do not belong to the tribe.

Over the last few years, Sora paintings have also inspired the creation of animated films. Surya Shankar Dash, an Odia activist-film-maker, has used patterns of Sora paintings to denounce the implantation of mining companies in tribal areas. His animated movie, called *Shot Dead for Development* (2008), is a vibrant homage to the tribal men, women and children who have been shot dead by the police for resisting mining and industrial activities on their land at Kashipur in 2001 and at Kalinga Nagar in 2006. The illustrations, accompanied by songs from the Koya and the Bonda, other tribes from southern Odisha, have not been directly inspired by the Sora ritual wall paintings but by their copies, painted on the walls of Bhubaneswar. Dash stresses that his animation is 'a reaction to the wall paintings splashed all over Bhubaneswar city by the government depicting the beauty of Odisha's tribal life, culture and tradition which has been ironically sponsored by the companies for whom the tribals are being displaced and killed'.[30] In the first sequence of the animated movie, white anthropomorphic characters are harvesting rice, ploughing and climbing palm trees to collect the sap; these are scenes that are reminiscent of the patterns central to Sora images. Friezes of dancing figures, similar to those who typically decorate the frames of wall paintings, pass across the screen. Night falls. The second sequence starts with a plane flying over the mountains. Some characters set off to search for uranium, iron, coal and bauxite. Trucks arrive and the mining extraction starts. Other characters depicted as tribals, armed with axes, move towards the trucks blocking their road. The pattern of the dancing figures is then reemployed to represent tribals protesting against the arrival of mining companies while the 'hunter's motif' is used to depict the policemen who circle them. Gunshots blast out and the names 'Kashipur' and 'Kalinga Nagar' appear at each shooting. The animated movie then ends with the message 'Shot Dead for Development'. This short film is part of a movie entitled *60x60secs* produced in 2008 by Motiroti, a London-based creative organisation displaying art in public and open spaces. This movie comprises 60 one-minute films by 60 artists, 20 artists each from Britain, India and Pakistan, who explore notions of identity, home and boundaries 60 years after the Independence of India and the partition that created the republics of Pakistan and India. This film was shown in conventional as well as unconventional settings: it was played on TV, at digital arts and film festivals, and in art galleries, cinemas and public spaces such as shopping malls, cafes and restaurants in UK, India, Pakistan and United States.

In a more poetical vein, Leslie Mackenzie, cartoonist and director of West Highland Animation—a Scottish production house—has also recently been seduced by Sora paintings. Like Surya Shankar Dash, she is member of the Adivasi Art Trust, a London-based organisation working with tribal Indian artists to preserve and promote their art and culture through digital media projects. Involved for more than 20 years in the production of animated movies in Scottish-Gaelic language inspired by Highland myths, Leslie Mackenzie has decided to lead a project dedicated to marginalised languages and cultures of India in collaboration with Tara Douglas, British animator and founding member of the Adivasi Art Trust. This initiative led to the 2006 movie entitled *The Tallest Story Competition*. This film is a collection of five short animations inspired by the art of five tribal groups from Central India: the Ghadwa from Bastar, the Warli from Maharastra, the Gond from Madhya Pradesh, the Santal from Jharkhand and the Sora from Odisha. Tribal painters and sculptors from the first three groups, among whom the aestheticisation process was the most salient, were directly involved in that project. Aiming to promote dialogue between minorities,[31] *The Tallest Story Competition* depicts a famous Gaelic comedian inviting five tribal communities from India to tell their most fantastic story. Each short movie can be seen in the corresponding tribal language, in Hindi or in Gaelic. This collection of animated movies has been shown in Scottish and Indian schools where 12,000 children were invited to vote for their favourite short movie. In India, *The Tallest Story Competition* has also been telecast on Doordarshan National Channel and screened in New Delhi at the British Council, the Indira Gandhi National Centre for the Arts, TRIFED and AISWACS, an Adivasi NGO. Outside of India, the films have also been shown in various places such as the Nehru Centre, SOAS, the Victoria and Albert Museum of Childhood in London, the Radical Book Fair in Edinburgh and a festival organised in the USA by the National Geographic All Roads, one of the sponsors of the movie.[32]

Unlike S.S. Dash, L. Mackenzie was directly inspired by the ritual images drawn in Sora houses she photographed with her team[33] in the Puttasing Valley. Her animated movie, called *Kenkentid*—meaning 'Bird Song' in the Sora language—invites us to travel inside a Sora painting, which has become animated, the medium of the narration. It tells the story of a young girl who asks the help of a female medium (*kuramboy*) to communicate one last time with her dead bird gone to the underground land of the dead. The *kuramboy*, a winnowing fan on her lap, starts to sing and falls into a trance. Her soul separates from her body and, in the form of a monkey, reaches the dead country in search of the bird who has lost his voice since his death. She brings him back to the land of the living; however, a flood of dead people follow the bird as well, frantically searching for everything they had while they were alive. While this story does not belong to the narrative repertoire of the Sora, Mackenzie is nevertheless inspired by their religious practices and beliefs. In this short animated film primarily catering to a young public audience, we still find numerous elements referring to the ritual context of wall painting creation: the ritual song, the ancestors for whom the images are dedicated and the conversation with the dead through the intermediary of a possessed medium, which constitute a privileged way of communication with the ancestors among the Sora (Vitebsky 1993).

Concluding Remarks

Through the journey of these pictures, one now elevated to the rank of regional cultural emblems, the transformation of a ritual into folklore and the consumption of a certain image of alterity is at stake. In this context of reconfiguration of a religious media in a patrimonialised image, the painter's work is no longer submitted to the imperious desires of gods and ancestors nor the critics of religious specialists to whom these invisible agents give their voices. The painter's skill, liberated from the ascendency of local deities and from the tradition's guarantors such as the medium and the priest, is now evaluated by other actors and institutions: organisers of regional cultural events and their intermediaries—NGOs, tribal development agencies, museums and Indian urban consumers wandering through tribal exhibitions and markets. This folklorisation process, which brings about a de-ritualisation of the images, eliminates one of their main features: their multisensoriality. In the manner of the *patua* from Bengal (Hauser 2002) or the *kalam* from Kerala (Tarabout 2003: 42), whose design is traditionally characterised by the connection between sounds and images, the importance given to the visual component of the ritual completely negates the other sensory registers usually implied in the performance.[34]

But the artification of *idisu'ung*, a process in which some Sora villagers are fully involved, could be considered as only partial. We have seen that the mural paintings are still made in a ritual context, and, in addition, that the transformation of the images into Art with a Capital A and their circulation at a global level is not accomplished by the Sora painters themselves. The painters from Srikakulam remain confined to the category 'tribal artists' and stay generally anonymous. In tribal exhibitions, their work, rarely

Figure 5.4

Tumpi and Mangaya, painters from Ondengsung preparing an exhibition at Hyderabad (2008)

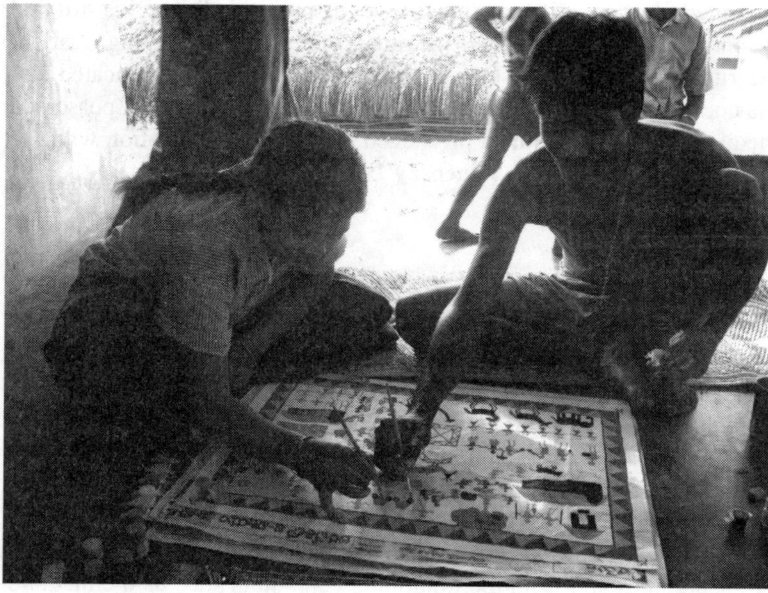

Source: Cécile Guillaume-Pey.

signed and often made collectively (Figure 5.4), is simply labelled 'Sora art' or 'Tribal art', titles sometimes accompanied by the name of their native village. In opposition to other tribal painters—Jivya Soma Mashe (Dalmia 1998) or the tragically famous Jangarh Singh Shyam (Sheikh 1998), whose work, fitting the modern Western criteria for 'high art', is displayed in international art museums and galleries—the Sora painters have not experienced a breakthrough within the contemporary global art world. The folklorisation constitutes an obstacle to their transfiguration into high art; the artification process is, in fact, accomplished by non-tribal actors, Indian as well as foreign.

If the images exhibited or sold far from Sora villages are not produced in a ritual context, we observe, however, a 'return of the ritual' that has infiltrated into the commercial paintings made by the Sora themselves—whose ritual content is enhanced—as well as in some work produced by non-tribal artists inspired by them. Thus, in their paintings, non-tribal Indian artists appropriate the symbolic efficacy and the connection with the oneiric register. Besides, recent animated films reintroduced songs, aural ritual component squeezed out by the folklorisation and the commoditisation. In the film produced by the West Highland Animation, a subtle play is established between the chanting words of the Sora medium and the silence of the bird who will rediscover his voice via the ritual performance. It is through the thematic of the loss of song that takes place the journey of the ritual specialist's soul inside the painted house. At the end of this transition from the wall to the screen, the Sora paintings, whose use has become aesthetic as well as political, find again their multisensoriality.

Notes

1. This exhibition took place at the Quai Branly Museum from 30th of March to 18th of July 2010. Its title echoes an earlier exhibition curated by J. Jain in 1998, held at the National Craft Museum in New Delhi, which showcased five contemporary tribal artists (Jain 1998).
2. This chapter is based on data collected during my PhD fieldwork on Sora ritual practices in northern Andhra Pradesh (2007–2008) and a Post-doctoral project (2012–2013) on Sora paintings (northern Andhra Pradesh and southern Odisha) financed by the Fyssen Foundation. I also would like to thank the two institutions which allowed me to carry out this project: The Study of Religions Department, University College Cork and the Yale Institute of Sacred Music.
3. The Sora, officially classified as a *Scheduled Tribe* by the Indian administration, speak an Austroasiatic language. They are mostly concentrated in Odisha and northern Andhra Pradesh.
4. In South of Odisha, they are also called *idital*, which means 'mural painting' (Elwin 1955).
5. The Warli paintings can also be considered as houses for the spirits (Dalmia 1984).
6. Among the Sora from Puttasing Valley, the deities called *ilda*—a class of spirits which has no equivalent among the Sora from Srikakulam (Guillaume-Pey 2011)—are considered to be beings from a high social status, rich and elegant (Elwin 1955).
7. In the Sora pantheon, the Sun and the Moon also refer to deities.
8. The winnowing fan (*oyer*) is the main tool used by the medium to fall in trance.
9. For an interesting case of the ritual appropriation of powerful figures, *cf.* Michael Taussig's (1993) analysis of the anthropomorphic figurines made by the Kuna and manipulated by the shaman during healing rituals.
10. At the end of the 1960s, the Naxalites achieved great success among tribal groups—i.e., the Sora and Jatapu—who were despoiled from their lands and submitted to restrictions on shifting cultivation imposed by forest officers (Dasgupta 1973; Singh 1995).
11. The pots, dedicated to different classes of deities, are often associated with various mediums which include them and are considered to be kinds of houses, provisional or not. Thus, in the main street of a Sora village, the pot materialising the presence of the village tutelary deity is hung from a wooden pillar erected at the centre of a miniature

Guillaume-Pey, Cécile. 2011. 'Du sang à l'écriture. Les pratiques rituelles des Sora, une tribu du centre-est de l'Inde'. Thèse de doctorat en anthropologie sociale, EHESS, Toulouse. Unpublished MS.

———. 2014. 'From Blood to Scripture. Religious Conversions and the Making of Identity among the Sora (a Scheduled tribe from Orissa-Andhra Pradesh Border)'. In *The Politics of Ethnicity in India, Nepal and China*, edited by Marine Carrin, Gerard Toffin and Pralay Kanungo, pp. 223–39. Delhi: Primus.

Hart, Lynn M. 1995. 'Three Walls: Regional Aesthetics and the International Art World'. In *The Traffic in Culture*, edited by George E. Marcus and Fred R. Myers, pp. 127–51. London: University of California Press.

Hauser, Beatrix. 2002. 'From Oral Tradition to "Folk Art": Reevaluating Bengali Scroll Paintings'. *Asians Folklore Studies* 61 (1): 105–22.

Heinich, Nathalie, and Roberta Shapiro, eds. 2012. *De l'artification. Enquêtes sur le passage à l'art*. Paris: EHESS.

Jain, Jyotindra. 1998. *Other Masters: Five Contemporary Folk and Tribal Artists of India*. New Delhi: The Crafts Museum and Handlooms Export Corporation of India.

Jeudy-Ballini, Monique. 1999. 'Dédommager le désir. Le prix de l'émotion en Nouvelle Bretagne'. *Terrain* 32: 5–20.

Kopytoff, Igor. 1986. 'The Cultural Biography of Things: Commoditization as Process'. In *The Social Life of Things: Commodities in Cultural Perspective*, edited by Arjun Appadurai, pp. 64–91. Cambridge: Cambridge University Press.

Leclair, Madeleine. 2009. 'Voir la musique'. *Voir la musique, Terrain* 53: 4–9.

Leiris, Michel. (1967) 1996. 'La crise nègre dans le monde Occidental'. In *Miroir de l'Afrique*, edited by Michel Leiris, pp. 1125–59. Paris: Gallimard.

Levanto, Yrjana, Ossi Naukkarinen, and Susann Vihma, eds. 2005. *Taiteistuminen*. Helsinki: Taideteollinen korkeakoulu.

Malamoud, Charles. 1989. *Cuire le monde, rite et pensée dans l'Inde ancienne*. Paris: La Découverte.

Malhotra, Anjali. 2001. 'Dying Art Form Finds a Dedicated Votary'. *The Hindu*, 1 October.

Mallebrein, Cornelia. 2001. 'Constructing a "House within the House". Reading the Wall-Paintings of the Lanjia Sora from Recitations'. In *Jagannath Revisited: Studying Society, Religion and the State in Orissa*, edited by Hermann Kulke and Burkhard Schnepel, pp. 93–122. New Delhi: Manohar.

Milford-Lutzkern, Mary-Ann. 1999. 'Intersections: Urban and Village Art in India'. *Art Journal* 58 (3): 22–30.

———. 2003. 'Five Artists from India: Gogi Saroj Pal, Rekha Rodwittiya, Navjot, Anupam Sud, Rummana Hussain'. *Woman's Art Journal* 23 (2): 21–27.

Mishra, Gauri, and Ray Owens. 1978. *Mithila Folk Paintings*. Austin: Huntington Gallery, University of Texas.

Myers, Fred R. 1991. 'Representing Culture: The Production of Discourse(s) for Aboriginal Acrylic Paintings'. *Cultural Anthropology* 6 (I): 26–62.

Pathy, Dinanath. 1996. *The Painted Icons, Wall Paintings of the Sauras of South Asia*. New Delhi: Harman Publishing House.

Pinney, Christopher. 2004. 'Chapter 8: What Pictures Want Now: Rural Consumers of Images, 1980–2000'. In *Photos of the Gods: The Printed Image and Political Struggle in India*, edited by Christopher Pinney, pp. 181–210. London: Reaktion.

Prashanth, G.N. 2002. 'Telling Tales on the Wall'. *The Hindu*, 16 September.

Rousseleau, Raphael. 2014. '"Tribal Artisan" and Artists in Odisha: Between Craft Promotion, "Ethnic Tourism" and Indian Primitivism'. In *The Politics of Ethnicity in*

India, Nepal and China, edited by Marine Carrin, Gérard Toffin and Pralay Kanungo, pp. 121–35. Delhi: Primus.

Satyan, Shweta. 2005. 'Curative Aboriginal Abstracts'. *Metrolife*, 6 June.

Severi, Carlo. 2007. *Le principe de la chimère: une anthropologie de la mémoire*. Paris: Editions rue d'Ulm-musée du quai Branly, coll «Aesthetica».

Sheikh, Gulammohammed. 1998. 'The World of Jangarh Singh Shyam'. In *Other Masters. Five Contemporary Folk and Tribal Artists of India*, edited by Jyotindra Jain, pp. 17–35. New Delhi: The Crafts Museum and Handlooms Export Corporation of India.

Singh, Mani Shekhar. 2000. 'A Journey into Pictorial Space: Poetics of Frame and Field in Maithil Painting'. *Contributions to Indian Sociology* 34 (3): 409–42.

Singh, Prakash. 1995. *The Naxalite Movement in India*. New Delhi: Rupa & Co.

Tarabout, Gilles. 2003. 'Passage à l'art. L'adaptation d'un culte sud-indien au patronage artistique'. In *L'Esthétique: Europe, Chine et ailleurs*, edited by Yolaine Escande and Jean-Marie Schaeffer, pp. 37–60. Paris: Editions You-Feng.

———. 2005. 'Malabar Gods, Nation-Building and Worlds Culture: On Perception of the Local and the Global'. In *Globalizing India. Perspectives from Below*, edited by Jackie Assayag and Christopher J. Fuller, pp. 185–209. London: Anthem Press.

Taussig, Michael. 1993. *Mimesis and Alterity: A Particular History of the Senses*. New York, NY, London: Routledge.

Toffin, Gérard. 2009. 'Exposer/voir: l'image divine dans la religion et l'art néwar'. *L'Homme* 189: 139–64.

Vernant, Jean-Pierre. (1965) 2006. *Myth and Thought among the Greeks*, translated by J. Lloyd and J. Fort. New York, NY: Zone Books. First published in French as *Mythe et pensée chez les Grecs. Etudes de psychologie historique*. Paris: Maspero.

Vitebsky, Piers. 1993. *Dialogues with the Dead: The Discussion of Mortality among the Sora of Eastern India*. Cambridge: Cambridge University Press.

———. 2008. 'Loving and Forgetting: Moments of Inarticulacy in Tribal India'. *The Journal of the Royal Anthropological Institute* 14 (2): 243–61.

Filmography

Shot Dead for Development, in *60 x 60 secs*. 2008. Surya Shankar Dash. London: Moti Roti Production.

The Tallest Story Competition. 2006. MacKenzie, Leslie. Scotland: West Highland Animation.

l'individualisme (1983) remains an important contribution to the contrasts between Eastern holism and Western individualism. Unlike Dumont, McKim Marriott considers interpersonal relations in Hindu culture as irregular and fluid. Persons as both divisible and individual ('dividuals'). To Dumont's opposition of ideologies and notions of 'man in society' and the 'hierarchical' (East) and the 'egalitarian' (West), Marriott opposes the infinite differentiation of 'dividuals', not isolated entities but potentially a relational nexus with all others, family, caste, community and so on. For Marriott, even the rules of purity and pollution cannot be understood without positing this interpenetration of states. In this view, civilisation is the product of infinitely complex and interpersonal exchanges, variously motivated and semiotically codified within biological and sociocultural frames of reference, where historical memory functions as a mediator between individual and collective experiences. Memories are, in fact, the traces of 'webs of significance', to use Max Weber's expression, of the cultural activities of human groups, which include systems of beliefs, symbols, rituals, intellectual and artistic activities (Geertz 1973: 5; see also Halbwachs 1950).

Uttar-Adhunik looks back at Bengal's mythology and folklore, ballads and music, drawings and paintings. It combines individual's idiolect and sociolect following Indian traditions that contemplate authorship as a group and inter-genre activity. The lyrics and rhymes of the *Siddhacharyyas* (Buddhist Saint poets from Eastern India and Bengal between the eighth and twelfth centuries) and the *Mahajans* (Bengali Vhaisnava poets from between fifteenth to seventeenth centuries), as well as *Kalighat* or *Birbhum Drawings*, show early attempts to integrate artistic units in a series of compositions in which groups of artists, sometimes of succeeding generations, participated. Kalighat painting derives its name from these ancient neighbourhoods in Kolkata (Birbhum, Minapore, Bankura, Murshidabad). It developed in late eighteenth century and flourished during the reconstruction of the Kalighat temple in 1809 and later with the development of railway and transport systems brought to the city by the East India Company trade. The prosperity of these nouveau riche families (*babus*) were the object of satire, frequently pictured in carnival-like inversions of the social order and displaying European habits and clothes. Rabindranath Tagore made this *Birbhum* district his home and established his great centre of learning. Artistic works in this area are the result of travelling artists and itinerant scroll painters.[1] When the *pata* was displayed at markets and fairs, vendors would sing the story depicted in it in order to attract potential clients. Ramayana, the most popular of the continuing oral traditions, occupied an important part of the repertoire, both in terms of the paintings as well as the performances.

Figure 6.1

Nineteenth-century Kalighat painting, Calcutta—Woman striking man with a broom

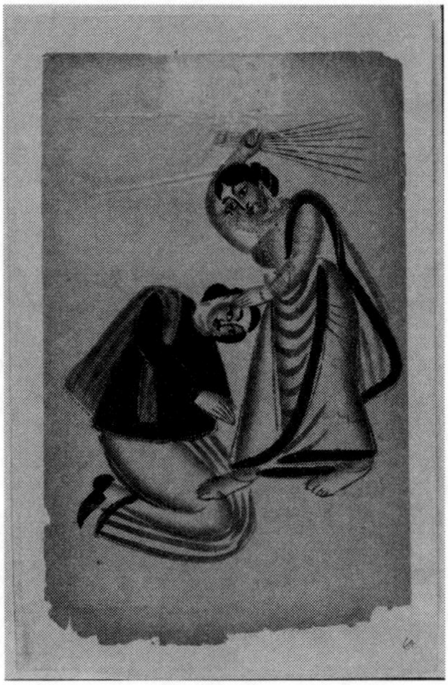

Source: See commons.wikimedia.org; Sinha and Panda (2011).

A member of the group, Bengali poet Anjan Sen has described *Uttar-Adhunik* poetry not as a movement but rather a new stirring, a new tone in old emotion, a puzzle and perhaps an anxiety that attempted to describe a desire to change. Udaya Narayan Singh has similarly referred to the movement as 'attitude, poetic temperament and a technique, and most importantly, as worldview' (1993: 159). Unlike the postmodernists, the school of *Uttar-Adhunik* rebuilds 'the edifice of life on a heightened altar of humanist essence', writes Singh. He also adds that *Uttar-Adhunik* poetry 'remains firmly entrenched in its collective character' (Singh 1993: 158) 'engrossed in the process of making the ineffable dream concrete' (Singh 1993: 161).

Time 'remains the supreme protagonist whose assimilation or negation always determines the ebbs and tides' in *Uttar-Adhunik* poetry, writes Udaya Narayan Singh (1993: 161). Quoting the work of Niharranjan Ray (1968), Anjan Sen points out the notion of social subjectivity represented by the Indian concepts of *Kula* and *Sila*. A person is introduced to his/her social world in terms of his/her *KulaSila*. '*Kula* is heredity, inheritance, which is both biological and cultural, together constituting what we call

Figure 6.2

Stop You Traveler, *illustrated by Diana Magallón. The poem appeared first in* Gaud Bochon *(Sen 1991). It was translated from Bengali by Khandakar Ashraf Hossain (Hossain 2010)*

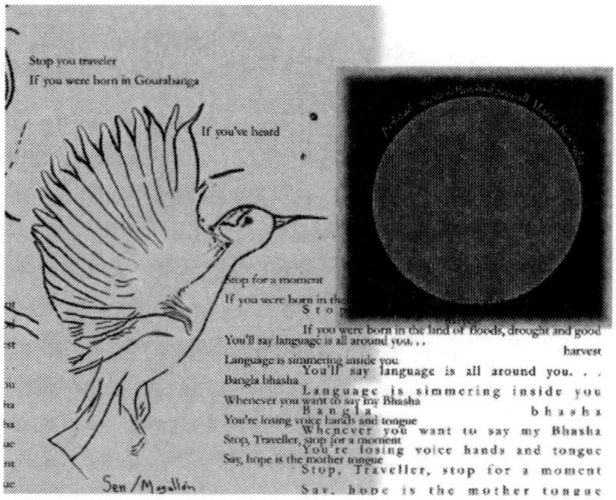

Source: Reproduced with permission of the author.

movement. Madhu are poetic forms from poet M. Madhusudan Dutt (nineteenth century) and Prasadi from poet and Saint Ramprasad Sen (eighteenth century) mentioned later in this chapter.

The poetic subject asks the traveller to 'stop for a moment' and recover his/her 'voice hands and tongue'. The poem/song ends with the line 'say, hope in the mother tongue', emphasising that Indian myths and traditions (mother tongues) are a source of hope and freedom for *Uttar-Adhunik* poets. Figure 6.2 of the poem also refers to this fact by depicting a bird of heavy plumage flying into the sky.

Anjan Sen's poem also refers to the 'travelling across' (time and space) of certain elements in Bangladeshi poetry, which were first spotted not by Bangladeshi critics but by those from West Bengal and Assam. Indian poet-critics were desperately looking for similarities and parallels of their own poetic beliefs and practices in the writings of their counterparts, fellow travellers in Bangladesh. Sen's essay Ashir Kabita, Grihey Pherey Bhramonik Chokh which appeared in *Ekobingsho* (March 1992) graphically showed the similarities between the writings of poets on both sides of the border:

> What a striking unity between Lalon Fakir and Ramprasad Sen! Although as poets they belong to two different religious and social classes. Actually

> what makes them attractive is their love of man which is not to be found in modern poetry. Similarly, there are affinities between the poetic languages of Shah Muhammad Sagir, Chandidas and the *padavali* poetry, though their subjects are different. Sufi-*Sahajia* literature also is a great treasure of Bangla literature: in it there has been a synthesis of various religions. (Sen 1992: 10)

The similarities also appear in Magallón's illustration, where words seem to double and are overlaid by the image of a kind of grain sieve tray in the form of the sun, the words *padavali mangala Panchali prasadi Madhu Rabindra* circle the top of the sieve, as if 'inevitably bound within the periphery of country, time and word' (Chakrabarty 1991: 62). For Professor Birenda Chakraborty (Rabindra Bharati University), 'Everybody lives in a specific country and time, and expresses his mind through words—the thoughts and attitudes of his countrymen are always there in his conscious and unconscious self. Tradition is created in this way' (Chakrabarty 1991: 62). He also refers to tradition as a cage, where the *achin pakhi* (unknown bird) may transcend the cage. *Achin pakhi* refers to a famous song by the mystic and rebel of the eighteenth century Lalon Fakir, who sang of the sufferings of the peasant folk of Bengal and of the heart's yearning for oneness with the Infinite. Lalon is a key figure in the Baul tradition of Bengal, constituting both a religious sect and a musical tradition, a great influence on Rabindranath Tagore and Allen Ginsberg. Lalon did not believe in classes or castes and took a stand against racism. Baul culture seems to have passed down entirely in oral form until very recently, so there are no historical records of their origins and influence. Bauls are found in the Indian state of West Bengal and the country of Bangladesh.

Khachar bhitor achin pakhi kemne ashe jay (the unknown bird in the cage, how does it fly in and out?) is a phrase from a song by Lalon. The image expresses the journeying beyond all things material, longing for oneness with the divine. The texts of Lalon's songs follow Tantric forms of meditation and engage philosophical positions emanating from Hindu, Jainist, Buddhist and Islamic traditions. He sustains a discourse based on the power of music to alter the intellectual and emotional states that lead to a great appreciation of life itself. This syncretism is reflected in the image of the grain sieve in Magallón's painting.

Sadhak Rāmprasād Sen, the eighteenth-century Shakta poet and saint aforementioned by Anjan Sen, wrote *bhakti* poems known as *Ramprasadi*, usually addressed to the Hindu goddess Kāli. He is credited with a new compositional form that combined the Bengali folk style of Baul music,

Figure 6.1

Figure 6.3

Journey, illustrated by Diana Magallón in 1989. Translated from Bengali by Amlan Dasgupta in 1993

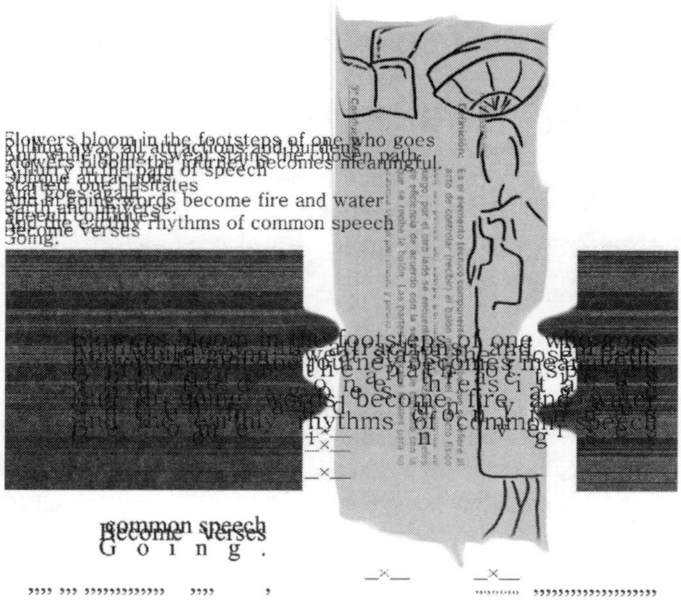

Source: Reproduced with permission of the artist.

Anjan Sen has illustrated many of his poems and invited artists from diverse cultures to put images to his words, crossing the border between text and image and employing different formats, not just illustrations but also digital art forms (used for instance by the Mexican Diana Magallón) and bas-relief (as seen in his poem Imagination illustrated by sculptor Bimal Kundu). This is a direct way of involving other artists into co-creation, making his work more open, public and intersubjective and less private and individual, perhaps, embodying McKim Marriott's notion of 'dividuality', the individual as a relational nexus with all others.

Magallón's illustration of Journey reminds us of a jigsaw puzzle of interlocking pieces that include both text and image. Frequently, her rendering of Anjan Sen's texts are superimposed, creating a doubling that encourages an ambiguous reading. In this case, the doubling contributes to the illusion of movement, with the word 'going' attracting attention.

Puzzles, like life itself, require an ongoing process of inquiry and discovery, and their solution frequently lies in the recognition of patterns in a particular order. Although puzzles are now used as forms of entertainment, they originate in divination practices in ancient religions as a way to bridge present, past and future, material and immaterial or spiritual life. Magallón's illustration also shows a woman balancing a basket of fruit or cereals on her head, a practice that has existed since ancient times and is still common in many parts of the world.

There are many references to rural life in Anjan Sen's poems. In Krishir (Of Agriculture), the use of vernacular terms such as *anno* (food) and *dhan* (paddy) are reminiscent of folk life in West Bengal. They are found, for instance, in an old spell about *dhenki* (a wooden pedal used in husking rice). These expressions enhance the awareness of the native soil in Sen's poems.

Krishir (Of Agriculture)

So many seeds grew into plants
So much gold was reaped
The farmer's daughters walk round the heaps of paddy
Making the shrill 'uloo' sound
The festival continues all morning
The dream of more anno
After that dry soil again
No seed no water. (Sen 1988b)

In Shravan, Anjan Sen uses metaphors of harvest and fertility and puts them in relation with creativity, as he does in many other poems. Shravan is a mythological character in the ancient Sanskrit epic Ramayana, notable for the devotion towards his parents. Old as they were, they could not walk in pilgrimage to the sacred places, and Shravan carried them with the help of a bamboo stick on his shoulders and two baskets balanced at each end, where his parents were placed.

Many festivals are celebrated during the month of *Śrāvaṇa,* the fifth month of the Hindu year which begins in late July and ends in the third week of August, and is considered a holy month. During *Kanwar Yatra,* a large number of people perform a ritual (*pooja*) in which they carry water from River Ganges on their shoulders and travel for around 50 km to offer this water to Lord Shiva in the local temples. The term *Kanwar*

Yatra comes from *kānvar* (काँवर), a pole, usually made of bamboo, with two roughly equal loads fastened or dangling from opposite ends. The *kānvar* is carried by balancing the middle of the pole on one or both shoulders, as Shravan did with his parents. *Amrita* or *Amrit* (Sanskrit: अमृत) refers to the holy water which is poured, in the manner of baptism, over Shiva for purification, thus uplifting a persons' physical and spiritual consciousness to a state of immortality (Sikhism and Buddhism have similar traditions).

Shiva is considered in certain regions as the god of fertility and harvest. His image is often represented shaped in the form of a penis, in a black stone called *linga*. Sen suggests that grain hardens and takes the form of stone, becoming *linga*. Thus, he posits a clear relation between fertility, harvest, reproduction and creativity.

In *The Myth of the Eternal Retour,* Romanian historian of religion, fiction writer and philosopher Mircea Eliade explains how many of these ancient agricultural and fertility rituals may have travelled from their original contexts, being translated and interpreted in new cultures. Interestingly, Eliade studied in Calcutta in the late 1920s under the guidance of Surendranath Dasgupta.

According to Eliade, rituals around the world have many resemblances, possibly not just due to the fact of mutual influence but also owing to the basic structures needed to maintain human life in Neolithic times. Grains stand as sources of food and energy and as symbols of new life and creativity, to the point of becoming the bread used in Christian Communion, for example. Water stands for the cleanliness (baptism into new life in some religions) that helps grain to grow properly on the land, just as food helps human physical and spiritual growth. Echoes of these rituals can also be found in the Egyptian *Book of the Dead* and in ancient Celtic fertility rituals (see *The Golden Bough* by Sir James Frazer, and *From Ritual to Romance,* by Jessie L. Weston).

These myths are related to a cyclic conception of time in which the ritual is used at the end of the cycle in order to clean and prepare the land for a new start (also in a metaphoric sense where the land stands for the physical and spiritual human body). As Eliade explains, the cyclic ritualistic (*illo tempore*) conception of time (still welcomed in contemporary societies every New Year) provides a sense of relief against the linear flux that ends in death. In most religions, after the 'apocalyptic' moment of the end of physical time (life), there would be a possibility of return (either in the form of metempsychoses or reincarnation in those religions believing in the separation of body and soul, or by means of a kind of final judgement day that would enable, those who during their physical life have behaved well, to reach heaven in resurrection).

Shravan

The sky shivers with the swing of rains
the rain drip-dropdrenching the visionary world
O grace. O thunderous grace, quench the cosmic thirst
In the rice field, the festival song is on
In the roots, the swing of the rains
Towards their rock the pilgrims move
their shoulders heavy with the sacrosanct water
Pouring water—Sravan takes a shower
Once again the song of desire for grain
The rock has been washed by many monsoons. (Sen 1993b)

ভাষা

দাঁড়াও পথিক
যদি তোমার জন্ম হয় এই গৌড়বঙ্গে
যদি তুমি শুনে থাকো পদাবলী   মঙ্গল
পাঁচালী   প্রসাদী   মধু   রবীন্দ্র
তিলেক দাঁড়াও
বন্যা সুফলা খরা দেশে তোমার জন্ম যদি হয়
তুমি বলবে   ভাষা আমার চতুর্দিকে
তবু
তোমার কণ্ঠরোধ করা হচ্ছে
যেহেতু তুমি বলতে পার না   ভাষা আমার
আমাকে বলতে দাও
তুমি বলতে পার না তবু
তোমার মধ্যে আউলে উঠছে ভাষা
বাংলা ভাষা
যখনই তুমি বলতে যাচ্ছ   ভাষা আমার
তুমি হারিয়ে ফেলছ কণ্ঠ   বাহু   জিভ
দাঁড়াও পথিক   দাঁড়াও তিলেক
বলো আশাই তো মাতৃভাষা।

১৯৭

Figure 6.4

Shravan, *illustrated by Diana Magallón in 1989. Translated from Bengali by Amlan Dasgupta (Dasgupta 1993)*

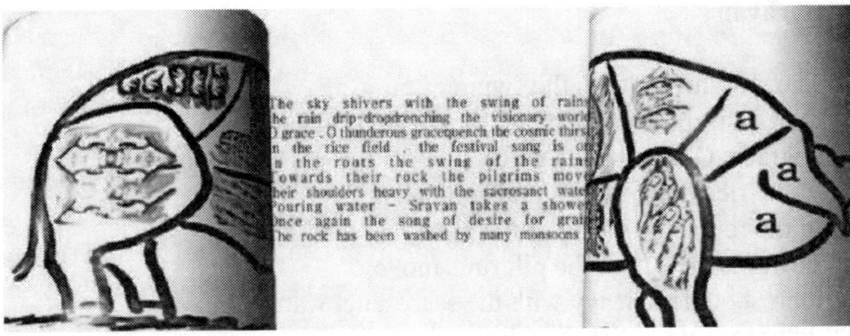

Source: Reproduced with permission of the artist.

The entire month of *Śrāvaṇa* is observed as one of fasting or eating non-vegetarian food. Heavy digestion is considered polluting and sluggish during this season, which takes place in the middle of the monsoon. The month of *Śrāvaṇa* also coincides with the Jain festival of Paryushana Parva. Jainism emphasises the decree of non-violence to various forms of life. Fasting has traditionally been a penance, a process of physical, emotional and mental purification and is accompanied by pursuing good thoughts, good words and good deeds. Diet restrictions include the proscription of root vegetables like potatoes, because eating them entails killing the entire plant, green leafy vegetables (because they might harbour insect life) and sprouted seeds (because they are germinating life). There are many songs on *Śrāvaṇa*, classical, folk and modern, some of them have continued for ages and some are part of rituals. The illustration captures different aspects of *Śrāvaṇa* festival, the praying hands on the bottom right.

Tanushree Bhattacharya (1996) has indicated that *Uttar-Adhunikata* recognises cultural continuity in its philosophical grounding and, thus, it does not see distinct cultures as detached realities but rather as a system of interrelations in continuum influx. The description reminds us again of Marriott's 'dividuals'. The dynamic conception of *Uttar-Adhunikata* poetry, unlike the nostalgic modernist use of myth to capture the past in the present moment, understands temporal happenings as eternal recurrences; a continuous wave of states of being which include past, present and future simultaneously (see Gupta 1992; Nikam

1967). Therefore, the question of seizing a moment of recollection as if suspended in the linear movement of time, present in William Wordsworth's romantic poetry, in James Joyce's notion of 'epiphanies' or in Virginia Woolf's 'moments of being' does not arise in *Uttar-Adhunikata*. Here, time is experienced both in its linearity but also in its circularity, engaging the past (in the form of folklore, ancient myths, vernacular language and so on) with the present moment, and projecting it into the future by means of performative action (happenings is the term we have used in the abstract) since many of these poems are designed to be sung and even danced. Linear time does not exist in Indian thought. The individual moment is contemplated in relation to eternity or timelessness. And since the 'reality' of time is always set on the background of space, timeless time can only be thought within spaceless space, that is, infinity. Both eternity (the temporal dimension) and infinity (the spatial dimension) of humanity are, according to Indian traditions, in perpetual flux or change. Within this movement, the rhythmic, song-like flow of time, the interrelatedness of the substances of which life is made of, material (Sen's poem uses the mythical basic symbolism of earth, water, air/sky) and psychological (affective and aesthetic). The feelings that such a vision enables are captured in the metaphor of the flowing and cleansing waters in Sen's poems and in the illustrations:

Ganga (Flow)

And flows goes on
Standing rock-deep in the holy river, the hibiscus sky
Where hast thou come O river
The flowing locks of the destroyer, in mountains
When the fire of the skies cool, water
Drenches the soil and soothes the eyes
Life flows on through the rain,
And men discuss it as hope
And sing its praises
Call the river their mother,
Sing hymns
In their primal, magical belief
Sky rain mountain river water
Flowing. (Sen 1993c)

Figures 6.5 and 6.6

Ganga (flow). They appeared in Anjan Sen's book Paath/Bharatbarsha *(Reading/India) in 1981. Pyne grew up listening to his grandmother's folktales. His early work was deeply influenced by the Bengal school and especially Abanindranath Tagore, nephew of Rabindranath Tagore. Further, he added the influences of Frans Hals, Rembrandt's handling of chiaroscuro, Paul Klee's simplicity and cubism in developing his own melancholic style of 'poetic surrealism'.*

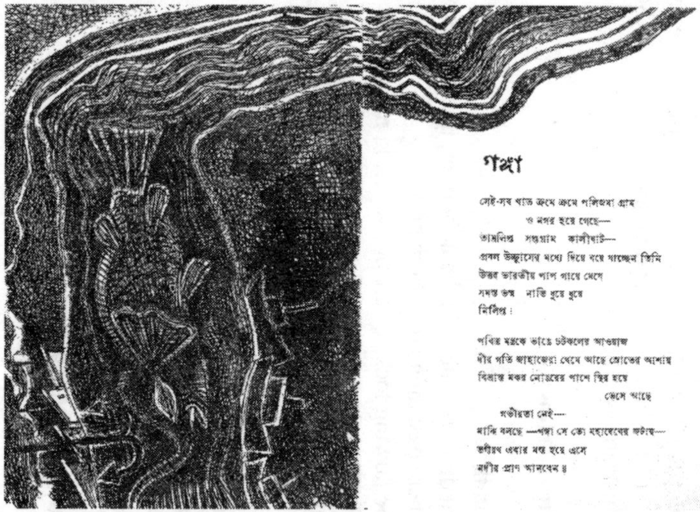

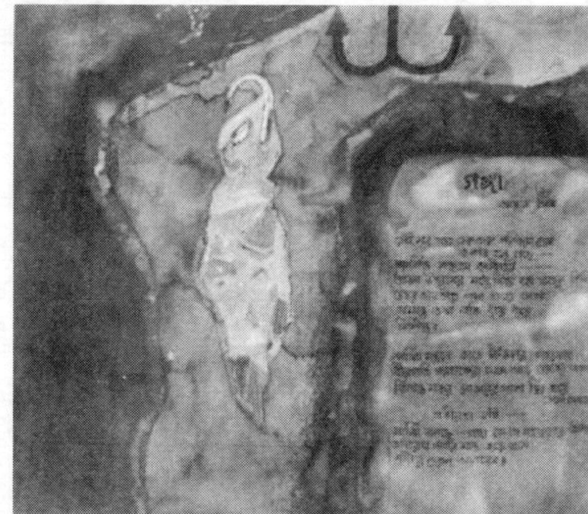

Source: Both illustrations are by Ganesh Pyne (1987).

Figure 6.7

Ganesh Pyne, Shymal Duttaroy and Anjan Sen, 1983

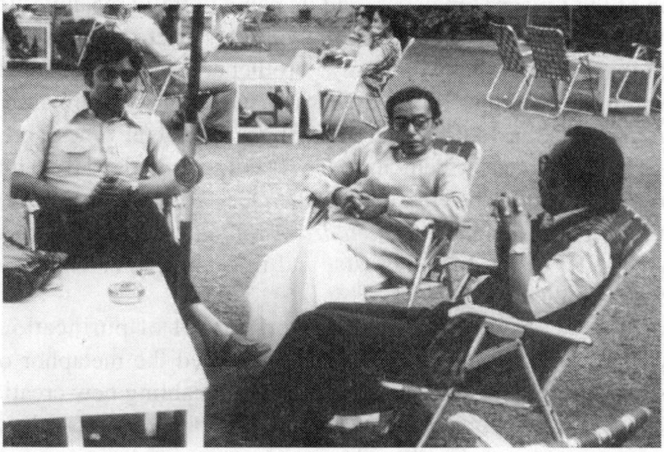

Source: Photo courtesy of Anjan Sen.

Joler (Of the Water)

I don't know what is afloat
A corpse?
The canoe sails on
It has become a skeleton
Having drifted in the dark Yamuna.
His heart distraught, the boatman tows on
It keeps floating walks the water.
The river water swells
It stucks water
And swigs all that it contains

In our three-fourths of water
this one-fourth land is visible
The water swirls around it.
The sky, hills, farmland twirl and become seas
Deluge-
We are floating like fishes.
Propitiate us, O water! Satiate!
It sucks and swigs water.
The dark sea has a low tide now. (Sen 1988c)

The Yamuna is the largest tributary of the Ganges (Ganga) in northern India. It originates from the Yamunotri Glacier, in the uppermost region of the Lower Himalayas, and its name literally meaning 'twins' in Sanskrit, as it runs parallel to the Ganges. There are many Vedic stories that speak of the two rivers as brother and sister and of Yamuna descending to meet her beloved Krishna and to purify the world. Her waters are dark blue like Lord Krishna/Shiva, who at the time of creation and the fight between the demons (*asuras*) and semi-gods (devas) inhaled a poison that had been released into the Ocean of Milk or Milky Way during the period known as *Samudra manthan*. The story appears in Section XVIII of the Mahabharata, and in Canto XLV, The Quest of the Amrit, in the Ramayana.

Together with water, fire is another symbol of purification and renewal. In *Embers of Time* (2004), I have used the metaphor of the ashes that return to physical matter (the soil) enabling new creation as part of the ever flowing circle of life. I deliberately employed a trope that emphasises the materiality of time, a trope present in many cultures (for instance, in the image of the Phoenix rising from its ashes in Greek mythology). It appears in another of Sen's poem where the presence of fire, pyres and 'dormant burial ground' indicate the circle of both life and creativity.

Kshra o Jamunar Bharatbarsha (India of Draught and Yamuna)

Are the days pallid or you can see only hazily?
The enormous India
As much draught she begets
So much do her Yamuna inundate
As many scorching days it has
That many gloomy nights it has
Those who wanted the God of Fire
Could see thousands of pyres
A dormant burial ground
A huge India
Huge is her social information, very many soils oppositions
I do not know any metaphor
O India, write for us a few new poems
I want nothing more than
The boon to remain in the folkground. (Sen 1988d)

The union of opposites, water/fire, death/life, are very much present in Sen's poems. In *Kalpana* (Imagination), he uses the Indian concept of *Kalpa*,[2] which refers to the endless fulfilment of desire related to the mythical cycle of creation and destruction. The poem points back to Kalidasa's Sanskrit epic in its desire to establish an interrelationship between myths, history and poetry. The *Kalpadruma* or *kalpa*-tree roots the future firmly into the past, but the dynamism of the circular time is achieved in the poem through various metaphors that emphasise floating up and down ('a grey cloud floated down') and falling ('dust kept falling'; 'diamond coals ... falling'), the oscillation of bright ('diamonds') and dark ('coal', evening, etc.), and transformation (cutting wood, 'the eyelid flickered'; 'one bird ... become Bihag'). Bihag is an Indian evening melody or rāga (in Sanskrit, it means 'colour', 'hue', but also 'beauty', 'melody'). A rāga uses a series of five or more musical notes upon which a melody is constructed, and it is meant to be performed for a particular time of a day or a season, and transmitted orally. In Sen's poem, grey turns to silver then to diamonds falling from the sky. Colours turn into imagination just as the bird turns into music.

Kalpana (Imagination)

From the Kalpa began imagination
From the leaves of the Meghduta, a grey cloud
Floated down in front of us.
The Kalpadruma shuddered
Gold Silver dust kept falling
Diamonds coals mud kept falling
The eyelid flickered
One bird is flying become Bihag
A woodcutter was gathering wood from Kalpadruma. (Sen 1988e)

The *Kalpadruma* refers to the mythological, *Kalpataru* (or *Kalpavriksha*), one of the five trees of Heaven or Indra's paradise that is supposed to fulfil desires. The other four are Mandaram, Santanam, Harichandanam and Parijatam. In some areas, the tree is identified with the Banyan, a fig tree whose seeds germinate in the cracks and crevices of another host tree, creating plant structures that grow on another plant like bridges between them. The image is interesting in relation to our discussion of 'dividuality', but also because it represents eternal life in its seemingly ever-expanding branches. The cutting of wood or branches from Kalpadruma refers to

Figure 6.8

Kalpana—*relief work by sculptor Bimal Kundu*

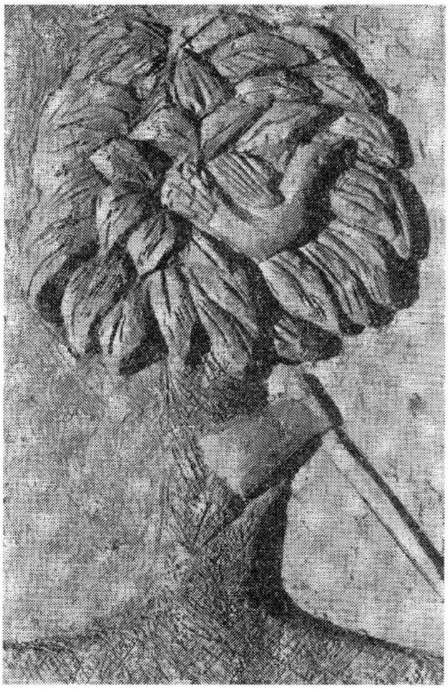

কল্পনা

কল্প থেকে শুরু হয়ে গেল কল্পনা
মেঘদূতের পাতা থেকে খুব ধূসর একটা মেঘ
ভেসে গেল সামনে দিয়ে
কেঁপে উঠল চোখের পাতা
নড়ে উঠল কল্পদ্রুম
পড়তে লাগল সোনা রুপো ধুলো
পড়তে লাগল হীরে কয়লা কাদা
কেঁপে উঠল চোখের পাতা
বিহঙ্গ এক উড়তে উড়তেবেহাগ হয়ে গেল

একজন কাঠুরে কল্পদ্রুমের কাঠ কাটছিল

Source: Reproduced with permission of the artist.

the story of a famous Sanskrit poet who was not very intelligent in his young age, but he acquired knowledge once he began to cut some of the wood. Anjan Sen imagines this poem as a series of continuous images almost like eye flickers, birds flying in Indian *Puranas* (myths), Brahma eyelid flickering in a million years, which is a second to him. It is the end of a *Yuga* or time. These are all dreams, imaginations, paths for the poet.

Similarly, in *Meghrup* (cloud form), Anjan Sen uses the image of the cloud as a messenger, already present in the work of the classical Sanskrit writer *Kālidāsa* (servant of Kāli). 'The cloud forms and it transforms', so *Meghanåd* also refers to the sound of the cloud, and brings echoes of Ravana, king of *Rakshasa* (Sri Lanka) in the Ramayana. Ravana's literal translation from Sanskrit is 'crying' or 'causing to cry'. Krishna is the eighth incarnation of Lord Vishnu. He was a young Prince, often portrait as Radha's lover. The principal scriptures discussing Krishna's story are the Mahabharata, the *Harivamsa*, the *Bhagavata Purana* and the *Vishnu Purana*. Krishna's disappearance marks the end of the previous

Yuga (time) and the start of *Kali Yuga* (present age), which is dated to February 17/18, 3102 BCE. Worship of Krishna (*Kṛṣṇa* = black/dark and protector of the cows) arose in the Middle Ages in the context of the *bhakti* movement. In the Mahabharata and the *Bhagavata Purana*, Krishna spends his childhood among young cow-herd girls (*Gopis*) in the village of Madhuvan, one of them is Radha, who becomes his friend and lover in a sort of divine sense. Radha is almost contemplated as the soul of Krishna. *Yakṣa* are benevolent nature spirits hidden in the earth and the roots of trees. In Kālidāsa's poem *Meghadūta*, the *yakṣa* narrator is a romantic figure, pining with love for his missing beloved. Clouds are also associated to Krishna's colour. He is black but generally painted as blue, similar to Kāli.

Meghrup (Cloud Form)

The cloud went after a cloud;
Meghanåd also cried like a cloud when he was born;
The tired cloud rest on a mountain's breast.
A nervous yakßa said 'go and carry my news';
The cloud went stepping over the sky's undertow.
Seeing the black cloud
I thought of my dark Krishna ...
Lady you got wet in the corner of the courtyard
And your dress oozes and oozes
Pitter patter pitter patter
I thought of my dark Kali ...
On the cloud, my heart,
and on a tender stage, her frightening face sways.
The cloud forms and it transforms. (Sen 2007b)

The goddess of time, change and destruction, Kālī means black, time and death. Shiva is called Kāla (eternal time related to matter) and Kālī is his consort (*Shakti* or cosmic energy). Kālī is a central figure in late medieval Bengali devotional literature, with such devotees as Ramprasad Sen. The goddess is described in Mahabharata 10.8.64 as follows: The warriors in the Pandava camp beheld that Death-Night in her embodied form, a black image, of bloody mouth and bloody eyes, wearing crimson garlands and smeared with crimson unguents, attired in a single piece of red cloth, with a noose in hand, and resembling an elderly lady, employed in chanting a dismal note and standing full before their eyes, and about to lead away men and steeds and elephants all tied in a stout cord. She seemed to take away diverse kinds of spirits, with dishevelled hair and tied together in a cord, as also, O king, many mighty car-warriors divested of their weapons. In Kālī's most famous legend, Devi Durga, she destroys the demon Raktabija by sucking the blood from his body, hence she often appears with blood shot eyes, open mouth and a drooping tongue (see McDaniel 2004). Lord Shiva beneath her feet represents matter, and Kālī is undoubtedly the primeval energy. During the battle against the demons, Shiva tries to stop her and falls among the corpses in the battlefield; she fails to see his body and steps on his chest. The depiction of Kālī on Shiva shows that without energy, matter lies dead. In tantric contexts, the tongue denotes the element of energy and action, possibly related to sexual aspects as well. In tantra, the human body is a symbol for the microcosm of the universe; therefore, the sexual process is responsible for the creation of the world. Kālī is portrayed mostly in four-armed and ten-armed form. Two of these hands, usually the left, hold a sword and a severed head. The sword signifies divine knowledge and the human head signifies human ego which must be slain by divine knowledge in order to attain *moksha*, that is, liberation from *saṃsāra* or the cycle of death and rebirth.

The poem, AkorOn (Structure) is included in Anjan Sen's *Tin bisshe din ratri* (*Days and Nights in the three Worlds*), a volume that can be divided into three parts: (a) poems on days and nights, (b) poems on heaven and (c) poems on earth. Some poems are in narrative style where, like in fiction, the last line summarises the entire message. AkorOn belongs to the second category and reflects on the creation of signs and words. The poet invokes the spirit of *Vak*. In the early Rigveda (books two to seven), *vāc* or *Vāk* is the Sanskrit word for 'speech' and 'voice', particularly the voice of the priest raised in sacrifice. *Vāk* is personified in the Goddess Vāk 'mother of the Vedas', procreator of words and wife of Indra, leader of *devas* (gods or semi-gods). Like Thor or Zeus, in Germanic and Greek mythology, respectively, Indra is the god of rain and lightning, and is presented as wielding a thunderbolt and riding on a white elephant. He is a great warrior and a symbol of courage and strength. The poem reminds of the biblical myth of Babel (Genesis 11: 1–9). The story explains how in the beginning of creation, all peoples on earth spoke the same language. As people migrated from the east, they settled in the land of Shinar and built a city and a tower that reached the sky. When God saw the vices in the city, he confounded the speech of the people so that they could not understand each other and scattered them over the face of the earth.

AkorOn (Structure)

Discourses tear asunder
What shall they speak
Air pollutes Smells of atoms
Sentences infected
Sentences get terribly stiffened
Die stillborn grisly
Now is a drought-epidemic of words now
And putrid becomes the borrowed culture
What will they speak
Words galore have already been said long ago
Slender life and words
Ascend O *Vak*
I celebrate a large plosion. (Sen 1988f)

Figure 6.9

Sorrow, *illustrated by Diana Magallón*

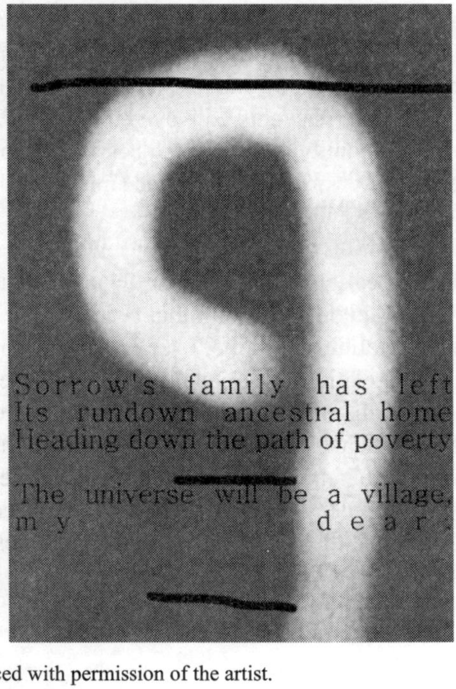

Source: Reproduced with permission of the artist.

Anjan Sen's poems capture a combination of myth, history, folklore and contemporary affairs that often feels as a nostalgic encounter. Sorrow is a short poem about the sadness of migration. Between 2000 and 2005, the Indian government evolved a legal framework that opened the way for private companies to create hyper-liberalised export enclaves on the Chinese model. Many fertile agricultural lands in India are being taken over by the state and industrialists as Special Economic Zones (SEZ). In March 2007, 14 people were killed and many more raped and injured by police in Nandigram, West Bengal, for refusing to give their land for a petrochemical promoted by an Indonesian company. The uproar that followed shook the state and the central government contributing to their eventual downfall and leading to the cancellation of the project and a temporary moratorium on SEZs. Farmers across the country began to rise against government's use of 'eminent domain' to acquire their lands at low price and transfer them to private companies. Land speculation amplifies class and caste inequalities, marginalises women and impoverishes the rural poor, forced to abandon their houses and their previous lives and head into poverty.

When I was asked by Anjan Sen to comment on the poem and its illustration, I imagined the white cloud as a kind of letter, a walking stick or a kind of inverted path. Its ghostly quality contrasted strongly with the colour red, associated with blood and passion in many cultures. The two black lines that cut across unevenly conveyed the idea of fragmentation, but also three-dimensionality, just as the black typography of the text. The irony behind the last word 'dear' reminded me of McLuhan's famous reference on the world as Global Village.

In my unstable position of a reader/listener who tries to understand, a critic who tries to speak/write and a semiotician who tries to discover, I encountered Anjan Sen on a visit to India. His desire to be both author and object of interpretation struck me. I see him as crossing not just the limits of author/critic relationships, but also the boundaries of inter-texts and of intermedial forms of representation. The dialogue between Sen and his illustrators, with his readers and critics, and with me, seems to be pregnant with a desire to innovate and cut across intersubjective positions and intercultural differences. He has helped me to discover the India beyond tourist locations; the rich diversity and friendliness of a country that was once the cradle of Western civilisations.

Figure 6.10

Anjan Sen painted by Ganesh Pyne

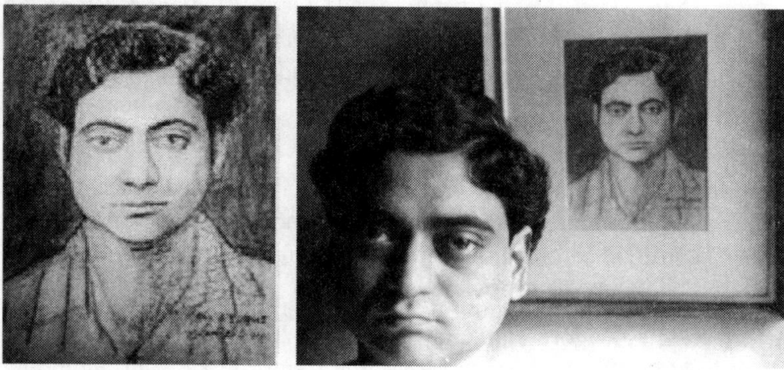

Source: Courtesy of Anjan Sen.

Acknowledgements

Amlan Das Gupta. Professor of English at Jadavpur University, Kolkata, and a noted scholar of classical and biblical studies, English renaissance literature and an authority on Miltonic studies in India. For more information, see http://en.wikipedia.org/wiki/Amlan_Das_Gupta

Khandokar Ashraf Hossain. Professor of English at Dhaka University and one of the leading literary figures in Bangladesh. He has translated many of Anjan Sen's poems. For more information, see http://en.wikipedia.org/wiki/Khondakar_Ashraf_Hossain

Bimal Kundu. A sculptor who has illustrated some of Anjan Sen's poems. For more information, see http://bimalkundu.blogspot.com.es/2008/09/bimal-kundus-arts-work.html

Diana Magallón. An experimental artist, author of visual poetry books: *Del oiseau et del ogre*, *Largos cabellos flotantes*, *Pheromones*, *Oxygenation* and *Phellipe in wolf*. For more information, see http://cipollinaaaaa.blogspot.com

Udaya Narayan Singh. Pro-Vice Chancellor, Viswa Bharati University, poet, critic and a major linguist, translator, lexicographer and creative writer who has translated many of Anjan Sen's poems. He has edited collections of essays in Bengali jointly with Anjan Sen: *Kobitaar*

Bhaashaa (The Language of Poetry) 1987, 2nd edition 2012; *Uponyaaser Sahityatatwa* (The Poetics of Novel) 1989, 2nd edition 2010; *Myth, Sahitya o Samaskriti*, (Myth, Literature and Culture) 1990; *Eurokendrikata o Silpo Samaskriti* (Eurocentrism and Art, Culture) 1992; *Baanglaar Uttaraadhunik Saahityachinta* (The Urraradhunik Literary Ideas of Bengal) 2004. For more information, see http://www.visva-bharati.ac.in/at_a_glance/unscv.pdf

Ganesh Pyne. One of Anjan Sen's personal friends. He has illustrated some of his poems and was one of India's foremost contemporary painters. Pyne died in 2013 before this chapter went to press. For more information, see http://en.wikipedia.org/wiki/Ganesh_Pyne

Anjan Sen. A Tagore National Scholar in 2013. He is the president of Little Magazine Library and Research Centre in Kolkata. Founding member (with Amitabha Gupta) *Uttar-adhunik* School of Poetry and Literary Consciousness, he is a poet and a specialist in Indian and Bengali literary theory, art and folk music, and an art collector. In the last three of four years he has concentrated his research on medieval art, culture and literature as well as cultural intertextuality. He has publish twenty books, seven on Literary Theory (with Udaya Narayan Singh), five on art (his latest *Art Chaitanyadeb* and *the Art of Bengal* is getting published soon), one on folk music as well as seven collections of poems. He edits jointly with Udaya Narayana Singh a Bengali Journal *Gangeyo Patra* on Literary Theory. He has also published around 80 essays on Literary Theory. He was the Writer and Painter in Campus at Assam University, Silchar, where he delivered special lectures in Visual Arts. He has delivered special lectures in various places and universities in Kolkata, Jadavpur, Dhaka, Chittaong and South Gujarat and participated in various seminars of Sahitya Academi, Bharat Bhavan, Bhupal and Center of Cultural Studies at Dhaka. A lawyer by profession, Anjan Sen does not have any academic degree in Literature and Art. For more information, see his CV at https://www.ucm.es/siim/anjan-sen-poems

Notes

1. For the examples of these *patas* made by scroll painters, see the chapter by Roma Chatterji.
2. As Anjan Sen explained: *kalpa* = with the flickering of eyelids of Brahma, a *kalpa* starts. I feel various continuous images are coming in the poem like eyelid flickers,

birds flying in Indian *Puranas* or myths. Brahma's eyelid flickers in some million years, which is a second to him and it is end of a *yuga* or time (era). Meghduta is the famous Sanskrit verse of Kalidasa. *Megh* = cloud; in his verse cloud is carrying the message of the lover. And then birds are flying getting related to raga, music. These are all imaginations.

Comments from his friend Hatto Fischer: Sen retains the wish to be able to bring these ancient meanings into the present. Thus, it is interesting how he describes the role of the imagination as it is derived from *kalpa* standing for the infinite: the source of creativity but also of destruction. This double meaning should not be forgotten for auspices are needed when the *kalpadrum* shudders and things keep falling. One example he gives: the woodcutter gathering wood from the forest of *kalpa* trees—path for the poet.

References

Bhattacharya, Tanushree, ed. 1996. *The Uttar-Adhunik: An Anthology of Creative and Critical Articles.* Ohio: Worthington.

Boethius. *The Consolation of Philosophy*. Translated into English Prose and Verse by H.R. James. Oxford University, Book III, part III, page 105. Accessed on 16 July 2017 at https://www.gutenberg.org/files/14328/14328-h/14328-h.htm#Page_105

Chakraborty, Birendra, ed. 1991. *Bangla Kabitar Prakritayan* (Craving for Legacy of the Roots in Bengali Poetry). Kolkata: Granthalay.

Chatterjee, Partha. 2012. *The Black Hole of Empire: History of a Global Practice of Power*. Princeton: Princeton University Press.

Chitre, Dilip, ed. 1967. *An Anthology of Marathi Poetry 1945–65*. Mumbai: Nirmala Sadananda Publications.

Choudhury, Malay Roy. 2001. *Overview: Postmodern Bangla Poetry*. Kolkata: Haowa Publishers.

Dasgupta, Amlan, ed. 1993. *Goudbochon Kothon Bisswa*. Kolkata: GaNgeo pOttro.

Dumont, Louis. 1967. *Homo hierarchicus. Essai sur le système des castes [The Caste System and Its Implications*]. Paris: Gallimard.

———. 1983. *Essais sur l'individualisme. Une perspective anthropologique sur l'idėologie modern [Essays on Individualism: Modern Ideology in Anthropological Perspective*]. Paris: Le Seuil.

Eliade, Mircea. 1971. *The Myth of the Eternal Return*: *Cosmos and History*. *Princeton: Princeton* University Press.

Frazer, James George. 1890. *The Golden Bough: A Study in Comparative Religion*. London: Macmillan and Company.

Geertz, Clifford. 1973. *The Interpretation of Cultures: Selected Essays*. New York, NY: Basic Books.

Gupta, Amitabha, ed. 1991. *Uttar Adhunik Kavita* [*Post Modern Poetry*]. Kolkata: Alochana Chakra.

———. 1991. *Movements in Infinity.* Kolkata: D.N. Publications.

———. 1992. *Uttar Adhunik Chetanar Bhumika* (Introduction to Transcendent Modern Consciousness). Kolkata: Triratna.

Halbwachs, Maurice. 1950. 'La mémoire collective'. Accessed on 7 July 2014 at http://classiques.uqac.ca/classiques/Halbwachs_maurice/memoire_collective/memoire_collective.html

Helleman, Wendy Elgersma. 2009. *The Feminine Personification of Wisdom: A Study of Homer's Penelope, Cappadocian Macrina, Boethius' Philosophia and Dante's Beatrice*. Lewiston, NY and Lampeter, Wales: Edwin Mellen Press.

Hossain, Khandakar Ashraf. 2010. *Modernism and Beyond Western Influences on Bangladeshi Poetry*. Dhaka: University of Dhaka.

Ittzés, Gábor. 2012. 'The Shape and Unity of the World in Paradise Lost'. In *Milton Through the Centuries*, edited by Gábor Ittzés and Miklós Péti, pp. 34–55. Budapest: Károli Gáspár Református Egyetem; L'Harmattan Kiadó.

Khare, Ravindra. 2006. *Caste, Hierarchy, and Individualism: Indian Critiques of Louis Dumont's Contributions*. New Delhi: Oxford University Press.

King James Bible Online. Chapter 11. https://www.kingjamesbibleonline.org/Genesis-Chapter-11/.

López-Varela Azcárate, Asunción. 2004. Embers of Time: A Pluridisciplinary Exploration of the Crisis of the Representation of Time in Science and Literature. Doctoral Dissertation. Universidad Complutense Madrid, Spain. Summary in Spanish at http://eprints.ucm.es/4660/

Marriott, McKim. 1990. *India Through Hindu Categories*. Delhi: SAGE Publications.

McDaniel, June. 2004. *Offering Flowers, Feeding Skulls: Popular Goddess Worship in West Bengal*. New York: Oxford University Press.

McGill, V.T.J., and Parry, W.T. "The Unity of Opposites: A Dialectical Principle." Guilford Press, Science & Society, 12.4: 418–44. Accessed on 16 July 2017 at http://www.jstor.org/stable/40399913

Midnapore Little Magazine Library—A Digital Library for Little Magazines of East and West from the year 1870 to Now. Accessed on 7 July 2014 at http://midnapore.in/littlemagazine/index.php

Moore, Michael. 1993. '"Wise Women" or Wisdom Woman? A Biblical Study of Women's Roles.' *Restoration Quarterly* 35.3: 147–58. Accessed on 16 July 2017 at https://faculty.gordon.edu/hu/bi/ted_hildebrandt/otesources/20-proverbs/text/articles/moore-womanwisdom-rq.pdf

Nikam, Narayanrao Appurao. 1967. *Some Concepts of Indian Culture*. Shimla: *Indian* Institute of Advanced Study.

Nitai, Jana. 2001. *Uttar-Adhunik Bangla Kabita Parichay* (Treatise on Postmodern and Transcendent Bengali Poetry). Kolkata: Banishilpa.

Ray, Niharranjan. 1968. 'Inaugural Address'. In *Modernity and Contemporary Indian Literature. Proceedings of a Seminar*, edited by Punya Sloka Ray, pp. 3–16. Shimla: *Indian* Institute of Advanced Study.

Sen, Anjan. 1988a. 'Kshudar' (The Hunger). In *Tin bisshe din ratri* (*Days and Nights in the Three Worlds*), translated from Bengali by Udaya Narayana Singh. Kolkata: GaNgeo pOttra.

———. 1988b. 'Krishir' (Of Agriculture). In *Tin bisshe din ratri* (*Days and nights in the three worlds*), translated from Bengali by K.A. Hossain. Kolkata: GaNgeo pOttra.

———. 1988c. 'Joler' (Of the Water). In *Tin bisshe din ratri* (*Days and Nights in the three Worlds*), translated from Bengali by Udaya Narayana Singh. Kolkata: GaNgeo pOttra.

———. 1988d. 'Kshra o Jamunar Bharatbarsha' (India of Draught and Yamuna). In *Tin bisshe din ratri* (*Days and Nights in the three Worlds*), translated from Bengali by Udaya Narayana Singh. Kolkata: GaNgeo pOttra.

Sen, Anjan. 1988e. 'Kalpana' (Imagination). In *Tin bisshe din ratri* (*Days and Nights in the three Worlds*), translated from Bengali by Amlan Dasgupta. Kolkata: GaNgeo pOttra.

———. 1988f. 'AkorOn' (Structure). In *Tin bisshe din ratri* (*Days and Nights in the three Worlds*), translated by Udaya Narayana Singh. Kolkata: GaNgeo pOttra.

———. 1991. 'Darao Pathik' (Stop you Traveller).In *Modernism and Beyond Western Influences on Bangladeshi Poetry*, translated by K.A. Hossain. Dhaka: University of Dhaka. Originally in *Gaud Bochon*. Siliguri: Samproto.

———. 1992. 'Ashir Kabita, Grihey Pherey Bhramonik Chokh'. In *Ekobingsho* (The Twenty-First), edited by Khondakar Ashraf Hossain. Bangladesh: Dhaka University. http://www.foundationsaarcwriters.com/literature/saarc-writers-intellectual/poets/bangladesh/257-khondakar-ashraf-hossain

———. 1993a. 'Chola' (Journey). In Amlan Dasgupta, ed., *Goudbochon Kothon Bisswa*, translated from Bengali by Amlan Dasgupta. Kolkata: GaNgeo pOttro.

———. 1993b. 'Shravan'. In Amlan Dasgupta, ed., *Goudbochon Kothon Bisswa*, translated from Bengali by Amlan Dasgupta. Kolkata: GaNgeo pOttro.

———. 1993c. 'Ganga' (Flow). In Amlan Dasgupta, ed., *Goudbochon Kothon Bisswa*, translated from Bengali by Amlan Dasgupta. Kolkata: GaNgeo pOttro.

———. 2007a. 'Graam' (Village). In *Austric Special Issue on Anjan Sen*, translated by Jesse Knutson. Austric, Tamluk.

———. 2007b. 'Meghrup' (Cloud Form). In *Austric Special Issue on Anjan Sen*, translated by Jesse Kuntson. Austric, Tamluk.

Singh, Udaya Narayan. 1993. 'Toward an Indigenous Post-Modernism: The Bengali Poetic Scene Today'. *Indian Literature* 36 (6): 156–61.

Sinha, Suhashini, and C. Panda, eds. 2011. Kalighat Paintings. Ahmedabad: Mapin Publishing.

Spengler, Oswald. 1918–1922. *Der Untergang des Abendlandes: Umrisse einer Morphologie der Weltgeschichte* (*The Decline of the West: Outlines of a Morphology of World History*), translated by F. Atkinson. Gestalt und Wirklichkeit: Welthistorische Perspektiven.

The Mahabharata. Book 10: Sauptika Parva. Translation by Kisari Mohan Ganguli [1883–1896]. Accessed on 16 July 2017 at http://www.sacred-texts.com/hin/m10/m10008.htm

Weston, Jessie L. 1920. *From Ritual to Romance*. London: Cambridge University Press.

Part III

Market Signs

7

The Visual Culture of Meat-shop Signs in Delhi

Rita Brara

> *Something in the world forces us to think. This something is an object not of recognition but of a fundamental* encounter.... *In whichever tone, its primary characteristic is that it can only be sensed.... It is not a quality but a sign.... It is not the given but that by which the given is given.*
>
> —Deleuze (1994)

As a city dweller, I am a consumer of shop signs. Often in city commutes, what catches the eye is a sea of signs, especially along market-lined roads. Recurring aspects of the hoardings leave an impress—the goods being sold and shop signs, including proper names and images.

What I was struck by in my commute from the University to South Delhi were shop signs that stood out in certain aspects. These were meat-shop signs and what set them apart was the use of the terms *halal* and *jhatka*. These terms were not translated from the vernacular. An agglomeration of hoardings of mostly *halal* shops was often located cheek by jowl with a hoarding announcing a *jhatka* shop. Meat seemed to be a commodity imprinted with these signs. To an onlooker, these terms suggested a metalanguage of difference that was part and parcel of the visual inter-faith milieu of the city. These hoardings aroused my interest and I followed it up with a fieldwork.

Enabled by the visual turn in the social sciences, attention can now be focused on aspects of everyday religiosity that may be missed otherwise (Freitag 2007; Jain 2007). While it is not easy to delimit the field of 'religion', I maintain that the use of the distinctive vernacular terms—*halal* and *jhatka*—which are preserved as non-translatable in the city of Delhi signpost the domain of the sacred.

Right through this chapter, I draw on aspects of the French philosopher Gilles Deleuze's method in *Difference and Repetition* (1994) for an understanding of signs in the ethnographic context of Delhi, albeit with a caveat. While Deleuze writes as a contemporary philosopher in a post-Christian age, I reorient his insights to engage with a social arena where daily life is marked by signs of faith. Borrowing Deleuze's idea, I argue that meat production in the city has two faces—one stemming from habitus or embodied techniques that form 'the life of the present' and the other that grows from memory which conveys 'the being of the past'. In relation to butchers and meat-shop signs discussed later, both acts of habitus and memory are animated by religious faith, depicted and articulated in an inter-faith milieu.

The term *halal* in its widest religious sense denotes all that is considered permitted or lawful by the Quran or the Hadith (Al-Qaradawi 1990). The prohibition on pork and the slaughtering of animals by a prescribed technique are only some of its facets for a believer. In the context of meat-shops in Delhi, however, the word *halal* stands as a visual sign of a Muslim butcher's shop and indicates that the meat sold there has been slaughtered in the correct and ordained manner.

The word *jhatka,* by contrast, has scarce textual genealogy. It is a more recent coinage and as a sign on a hoarding connotes a Sikh/Hindu shop. It is associated with the Hindu Goddess Kali, as she accepts animal sacrifice and meat as food (Caldwell 2003). Among Sikhs, it was Guru Gobind Singh who advised Sikhs to refrain from eating meat produced the *halal* way (Mansukhani 1989).

As habitus, *halal* and *jhatka* entail distinct slaughter practices that are adhered to by Muslim and Sikh/Hindu believers, respectively. The enactment of *halal* is preceded by an invocation to Allah before the slaughter. The animal's throat is slit gradually to allow it to bleed. By contrast, *jhatka* requires execution in a single fell stroke. The word *jhatka,* in fact, suggests a reverse ekphrasis, moving from image to word. This slaughter technique decapitates the animal.[1] The instruments for *halal* and *jhatka* are distinctive since the slaughter methods are different.

The slaughter practices that the terms *halal* and *jhatka* denote are regarded as embodiments and enactments of faith. These signs of everyday difference in the constitution of the sacred within different faiths are communicated visually (and linguistically) in the social and public contexts of buying and selling meat as well.

If one aspect of meat production and meat-shop signs relates to habitus, its other facet shows up hoardings as reflections of memory traces and reimaginings. During the colonial rule, the Roman script and English adjectives began to be affixed to meat-shop names. While Delhi had had Muslim butchers mainly through Mughal rule,[2] it was during the colonial period that the Sikhs asserted their right to slaughter animals the *jhatka* way[3] as a symbol of resistance to the imposition of Muslim slaughter practices on non-Muslims. They pleaded this cause with British authorities repeatedly and the city's slaughter house came to have separate *halal* and *jhatka* enclosures.

Again, in the wake of the Partition of India in 1947, there was an influx of Sikh/Hindu refugees into Delhi and the names of the new entrants made an appearance in the shop titles, as we shall learn later. Muslim butchers who stayed back in the city sometimes reoriented their hoardings to an altered situation where the patriotism of the Muslim could no longer be assumed. The gradual shift from Urdu to Hindi in the hoarding scripts also became apparent in the post-Independence period.

Sikh and Hindu butchers espouse the same slaughter technique. However, meat-eating Hindus consume both *halal* and *jhatka* meat and are therefore wooed by Muslim and Hindu/Sikh butchers. They are referred to as all-rounders (a term from cricket that describes a player who can bat and bowl), and here consumption tells a story that is different from production.

I turn to the presentation and analysis of the meat-shop signs that I encountered in the markets of the city next.

Local Shop-signs Are Invested with Semiotic Care

Differences between meat shops, expressed in words and images, are invested with semiotic care, looking to meanings that are to be conveyed. Visual signs both repeat and differ simultaneously such that alongside habitus and memory, the Deleuzean emphasis on simultaneous difference and repetition is valuable in apprehending this visual culture (Deleuze 1994). Differences—local, multiple and visual—are encased within the repetitions.

A meat-shop hoarding is a public enactment aimed primarily at attracting customers (Figure 7.1). It is a synthesis (that I would tend to break up by divisions such as the religious, the economic and the political)

Figure 7.1

A typical meat-shop hoarding in two scripts

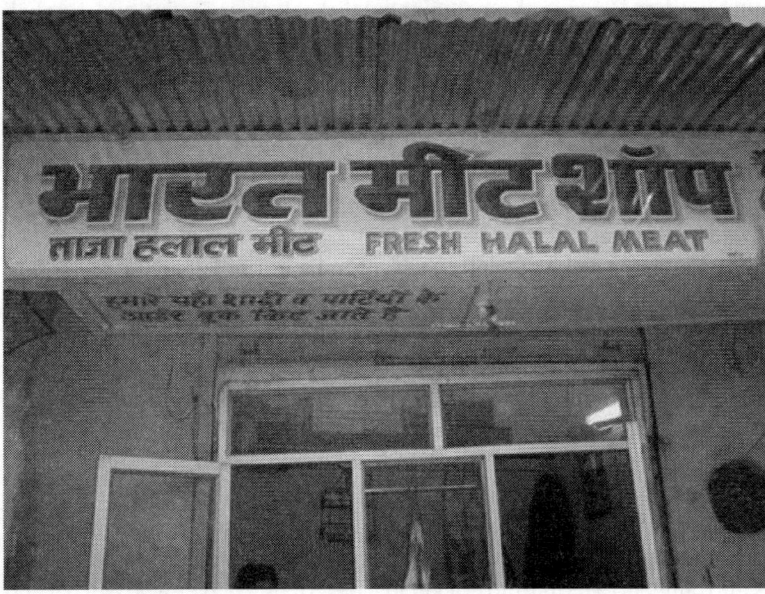

Source: Rita Brara.

that is perceived by the seller as relevant to the inter-faith and local context within which the sale of meat occurs. The scripts and languages evident in the hoardings too, are deployed as diverging social, visual and local practices. Variations of script (uni- or multi-) in the hoarding, for instance, grow from the perception of the spoken and/or reading characteristics of an actual and a prospective clientele.

The accompanying pictures are intended to convey a flavour of the hoardings. I analysed about 106 meat-shop hoardings and looked into shops without billboards as well (about ten that I encountered). This number is arbitrary, but from my point of view here it is enough to yield some of the elements that make up a hoarding. Of the hoardings studied, 79 shops sold *halal* meat, 22 sold *jhatka* and 5 shops left the type of meat unspecified in the hoarding itself.

Meat-shop hoardings shared certain elements with other hoardings in the city such as the name of the shop, the script/s put to use in the hoarding, the type of goods being sold and their pictorial depiction as well as the address of the shop and its telephone number. Other information that recurred in the hoardings spelled out commercial details such as 'orders for weddings/parties are booked here' or 'free home delivery'. Such statements indicated that these hoardings carried multiple marketing messages.

Through this analysis, I have tried to move along the visual 'path' of the hoarding reading it as though it were 'filmed in slow motion [...] to follow the structuration of reading' along with an interpretation of the accompanying pictures (Barthes 1985: 85–86). My idea was to fathom the value assigned to *halal* or *jhatka* as nominal terms by treating the hoardings as a sign system, looking more at what Roland Barthes (1985) describes as 'departures' rather than 'arrivals' of meaning.

Since *halal* and *jhatka* are marked words, their placement in the frame, the font size and the script used could express difference. The term *halal* or *jhatka* could be foregrounded or downplayed and so I thought that I would get some idea of the differential value accorded to them as meat signs within the demarcated frame of a hoarding. I tried to lend fullness to these inscriptions by conversations with shopkeepers about their practices in this regard.

Naming Shops

The name of the shop, more often than not, was painted in the largest font size apparent in the hoarding. Like the flags of nations, it made it possible to distinguish one shop from another in a market.

While the names of shops differed, the proper names that formed a part of meat-shop hoardings fell into certain identifiable series. One sort of series incorporated an adjective as an attributive before the term 'meat shop'. For instance, the adjectives Standard and Quality preceding the phrase '*halal* meat-shop' suggested that what was sold here conformed to a certain standard, while Popular and Famous proclaimed that they were favoured by the many. Fancy, Novel and Royal staked a claim to the extraordinary. The adjective Indian stressed belongingness to the country. A shop called Fresh *Halal* Chicken and Meat indicated the contrast with canned meats in an elite market, which was established during the colonial era. The Empire Store in the same market changed its name as recently as 2012. The different adjectives that formed a part of this series were taken from the English language, and English words were often deployed to connote quality.

Other first terms of hoardings privileged a word from the vernacular. *Bharat* (a term for India this time with vernacular associations), for instance, was followed by the phrase '*halal* meat shop' in English. *Janta* (meaning common folk) and *ajanta* (or unique) formed a competing and opposed verbal set of two meat shops in the same market. *Desi* (indigenous) and *pardesi* (foreign) constituted a similar duo. *Bhai saheb ki dukan* (brother's shop) and *kale bhai saheb* (black brother) called attention to another correlative posturing. Some adjectives, such as Royal and Standard that I found in the *halal* shops, were now apparent in the *jhatka* shops as well.

A meat shop was named Madina[4] after the sacred city. *Pakeezah* (pure) and *Lazeez* (delicious in Urdu) were first names of shops that derived from Urdu. M.S. and Sons and Mirajuddin and Sons preferred the form favoured by private, commercial companies.

Other shop signages espoused person names before the term 'meat shop'. Barthes (1985: 88) calls a proper name the 'Prince of signifiers' and notes that its connotations should 'always be examined carefully' since these are 'rich, social and symbolic'. Liaquat, Nasir, Arif, Kamil, Shamim, Hikmat, to cite some examples, were names that could be easily identified as Muslim by the city's residents. Often these were the names of shop founders. The surname Qureshi, too, figured frequently and butchers in Delhi, by and large, belonged to this social group. Shopkeepers did not use the ascribed group and occupational identity—*kasai* or butcher—as shop signs but preferred to embrace the name Qureshi, which suggested an assumption of descent from the Quresh tribe in the Middle East (Ahmad 2013; Ali 2002).

Recently, the surname Sonkar[5] has been espoused by a group of Hindu butchers and is growing in prominence. Oberoi, Jernail, Gulati and Chawla, again, were identifiable as Punjabi names, mainly Sikh and less often Hindu, by local inhabitants. Like the *pardesi* shop referred to earlier, Lahore Meat Shop drew attention to the presence of Punjabi refugees in the city. Other shops, too, showed regional affiliations—Rajasthani, Bijnori and Bihari—and were frequent in new and still unauthorised markets.

These shop titles certainly afforded a view of the social, visual and cultural history of butchers in the city.[6] Hoardings alluded to the wider social groups of butchers, their patronymics and first names. The religious attachments of the shopkeeper could often be read correctly into these names.

After the Partition in 1947, a few Muslim shop signs espoused indigenous terms that suggested filiation to the nation, while others showed a preference for Urdu titles. Strategically paired terms (*desi/pardesi; janta/ ajanta*) drew their relevance from a micro-context of rivalry between shopkeepers. Differences in the class of clientele of meat shops in city neighbourhoods were also inserted in the course of visualising these signs.

From my point of departure here, shop titles invariably encased the terms *halal* or *jhatka* with first names, adjectives connoting quality, class as locally conceived and so on. In a nutshell, even while the terms *halal* and *jhatka* were recurrent in the hoardings, these did not cease to be prefaced, suffixed or clothed in local differences that were relevant to shop owners.

To recapitulate, my attempt in this section has been 'to locate and to classify [...] not meanings [...] but the forms, the codes which make meanings possible', as Barthes (1985: 84) puts it, in a local context. A series with first names, such as Nasir, Arif, etc., suggested a religious affiliation even as it individuated, or a series with surnames again, connoted caste/religion here. The visual inscriptions in a third series were perhaps adjectival, or a fourth series communicated provincial origins within the country or competitive visual posturing.

These series are certainly not meant to be exhaustive. My idea is simply to draw attention to these codes that build up the social and the visual in the hoardings, bottom-up and diversely in the here-and-now. While these series unfolded at the same time, and could move along different trajectories, my argument in the following section is that these were also shot through with the interpenetrating term *halal* or *jhatka* within the frame of the hoarding. Series that seem to be on disparate frequencies, as it were, then begin to resonate together along these root metaphors.

Repetition and Difference in the Incarnation of *Halal* and *Jhatka* as Terms in the Hoardings

The words *halal* or *jhatka* were incarnated in almost every meat-shop hoarding. Shopkeepers invariably took it on themselves to declare that the shop sold *halal* meat as a part of the shop sign, even where the presence of a first name may have implied a religious affiliation. *Jhatka* shops, too, put the word *jhatka* up front as the first term in the shop sign, except in some upper-end markets. Instead of just reckoning with the preponderance of these signs, I tried to come to terms with both their prevalence and the differences that were folded into these repetitions.

Sometimes a shop title started out, say with Popular, Avon or Standard but was followed by the phrase *Halal* Meat Shop. Often, the term *halal* formed a part of the second phrase of the hoarding as in 'M.S. and Sons/ *Halal* meat shop' or it said, '*Halal* meat is sold here' (*yahan par halal meat milta hai*). An apparent de-centring of the term *halal* occurred when it was painted on the shop's shutters or incorporated as the second word or as a part of the second statement on the hoarding.

On the rare occasion where I did not see a *halal* or *jhatka* sign at once, I explored its missing dimension. Deliberation in such matters, I assumed, was semiotically suggestive. Extracts of conversations with shopkeepers on the de-centring or absence of the *halal* sign from their hoardings are presented here:

1. A middle-aged butcher told me: 'People can tell from my countenance that *halal* meat is sold here' (*mere chehere se hee log pehchan lete hain*). The persona of this shopkeeper was replete with the skullcap and beard even though his shop, in a middle-class market, had the *halal* sign tucked away in a corner.
2. A 25-year-old youngster in a shop that surprisingly did not have the *halal* sign said: 'My name is itself *halal* and that is written on the hoarding' (*mera to naam hi halal hai aur woh to likha hai na*).
3. On two occasions I was told, 'the painter forgot to write it'.
4. In a predominantly Muslim neighbourhood, a butcher said: 'People who come to this market know that the butchers here are Muslim'.

In other words, a name on a shop sign or an appearance could double up as a sign of *halal* on the rare occasion where it was omitted in its written form. The sign was considered, if exceptionally, self-evident in a Muslim neighbourhood. I continue with the following analysis of hoardings.

Meat Shop: The term 'meat shop' was often the second term in the shop title, which I break up below into 'meat' and 'shop'. As a reading unit, the hoarding would read, Famous *Halal* Meat Shop for instance.

The Term 'Meat': Now what did the term 'meat' convey here. The English term was preferred again. I looked around for telltale signs in the hoarding. The vernacular terms—*gosht* and *maas*—were strikingly absent in both *halal* and *jhatka* shops. It was called 'meat', but whether it was goat meat or mutton (sheep meat) was left unspecified or disguised in these 'meat shops'.[7]

Both *halal* and *jhatka* meat shops sold goat meat or mutton and/ or chicken. The shopkeeper's own faith, by and large, generated the combinations offered by a shopkeeper. Except in a few upper-class colonies, pork, chicken and meat were not sold together.

Muslim butchers observed the prohibition on the sale and consumption of pork while Hindus and Sikhs refrained from eating and selling beef. Pork shops in the slums often did not have shop signs and catered primarily to a local clientele. Shops that sold buffalo meat, too, did not advertise their fare through hoardings and were located in alleys away from the central markets. Since the slaughter of cows was banned by the state, the sale of beef in the city was an underground operation.

The Term 'Shop': Again, the English word 'shop' was repeated most often. Fresh, unrefrigerated meat—both *halal* and *jhatka*—was sold, predominantly, in 'meat shops'. Some of these now had refrigeration, but given the vagaries of the power supply and the local palate, fresh 'meat' was still popular. The two hoardings that inscribed the term *dukan*—the vernacular term for a shop—did not have refrigeration.

However, the absence of the term *halal* or *jhatka* was most striking in shops that had ceased to call themselves 'shops'. These 'department stores' sold a combination of chicken, pork and meat. There was a visible difference between the regular 'meat shops' that spelled out the word *halal* or *jhatka* in the hoarding and emphatically refrained from selling pork and these department stores. These stores had names like Pig-Po, Modern Bazaar, Jernail's, Le Marche and the Oberoi's Charcuterie. The terms Charcuterie and Le Marche had a French resonance and their espousal placed them in a class apart from the familiar meat shops in the city (Stewart and Fawcett 2004). These hoardings did not carry the *halal* or *jhatka* sign.

Yet, my enquiries revealed that the Oberoi's charcuterie, Jernail's and Pig Po sold *jhatka* meat. The Muslim butchers I met claimed that they could have told me so with just a little attention to the surname, the name of the shop and whether it sold a combination that comprised chicken, meat and pork. Modern Bazaar and Le Marche had to be Hindu stores if they were selling both pork and *halal* meat.

Chatting with the shopkeepers in the less well-to-do neighbourhoods indicated that the insistence on displaying the *halal* and *jhatka* signs was an aspect of the shopkeeper's faith and his attempt to ensure that the religious consumer was not misled. In a market with a mixed population of Sikh/Hindu and Muslim butchers, I gathered that if a customer bought *halal* meat unwittingly, the shopkeeper took it back and the adjoining *jhatka* shop did likewise.

By contrast with the signs of *halal* and *jhatka*, the script of the hoarding was taken to be a relatively flexible matter as I will discuss next.

The Script of the Hoardings

The script of the hoardings varied with the market and the clientele. The script was mostly Roman or what the shopkeepers and I preferred to call English. Bi-lingual shop signs, in Hindi and English, were most frequent in *halal* meat shops though some tri-lingual shop signs included Urdu as well. Uni-script usages (Hindi or English) were also deployed.

Hoardings that showed the term *jhatka,* almost invariably, had shop signs that were inscribed in Hindi. Again, it was also possible to tell shops that were 'classy' by the exclusive use of the English script, and the composition as well as lettering style of the hoarding. *Lazeez* and Jernail's, for instance, were stand-alone shop titles that had no clutter in the first statement of the hoarding. *Lazeez* was written in English but in calligraphic lettering that drew on the Arabic script. Nevertheless, in contrast to Jernail's, it carried the term *halal* in the second statement of the hoarding.

Remarkably, no *halal* shop had hoardings inscribed solely in Urdu, except in the wholesale market at Ghazipur. I gathered that the older Muslim butchers who came to buy here could read only Urdu though their youngsters had learned Hindi and English. In Jama Masjid, again, just outside the mosque and off what is known as Urdu Bazaar, the shop signs were exclusively in English. This extensive market catered to bulk orders, and the interface of the shopkeeper with his clients was, largely, through another text—a visiting card—that was printed in English and circulated.

The attempt at interpreting hoardings as visual signage practices was motivated by the encounter with both the insistence on the words *halal* and *jhatka* and the manner in which local differences were inserted in the hoardings. The terms *halal* and *jhatka* recurred among the 'meat shops' despite the kaleidoscope of changing scripts and clientele. While the terms *halal* and *jhatka* nearly always marked butcher shops, the words were not in evidence at the upper end of shopping experiences in department stores and shopping malls.

Jacques Derrida (2002) avers that it is not easy to delimit the field of 'religion' for religions that are not Latinised. Religious believers and butchers, however, contrived to signpost the domain of the religious through repetition of the marked words—*halal* and *jhatka*. The use of these vernacular terms brought in a metalanguage that connoted religious difference in an inter-faith milieu.

Pictorial Signs

Apart from written words, pictorial signs on the billboards aimed directly at the customers. Accompanying the hoardings of meat shops were illustrations of cocks and chickens and, occasionally, goats. While pictorial signs form a part of advertising everywhere, these signs assumed an additional importance in the context of limited literacy.

Here, art had a practical horizon and paint attempted to accomplish what mere alphabets could not deliver. Yet butchers, too, imagined an artistic life and I was told, for instance: 'This hoarding is ordinary. You'll come across better painting in Jama Masjid'.

The variety in the depictions was striking as different artists executed these portrayals. Images of chickens had a lively and ubiquitous presence in the hoardings and it was the sign par excellence of a butcher shop. I reproduce extracts from my conversations with four painters on their depictions next:

1. Some painted cocks were a visual delight. The colourful plumage was quite unlike the live, white chickens in coops. Why? The painter remarked: 'The idea is to attract. The customer will be lured into believing that what you see in the hoarding is what will be delivered in the shop'. (*Khareednewale ko bulana hai. Woh ye sochega ki jo main dekh raha hoon wohi milega.*)
2. Another painter declared: 'I try to show live chickens to distract the customer from the dismembered portions that you see in the shop otherwise'. (*Main zinda murgi dikhane ki koshish karta hoon kyonki aap kate hue hisse bhool jayenge.*)
3. A third gentleman commented: 'I have to reduce costs and so I deliver the going thing'. (*Woh karta hoon jo running mein hai.*)
4. Was depicting animals frowned upon by religiously inclined Muslims? The painter replied: 'Not at all. These chickens are being sold in a meat shop. They are going to be killed not idolised'. (*Bilkul nahin! Yeh murge to meat shop mein bik rahe hain! Inko to mara jayega, poojen ge nahin.*)

Figure 7.2

Painted meat-shop hoarding depicting jhatka *visually*

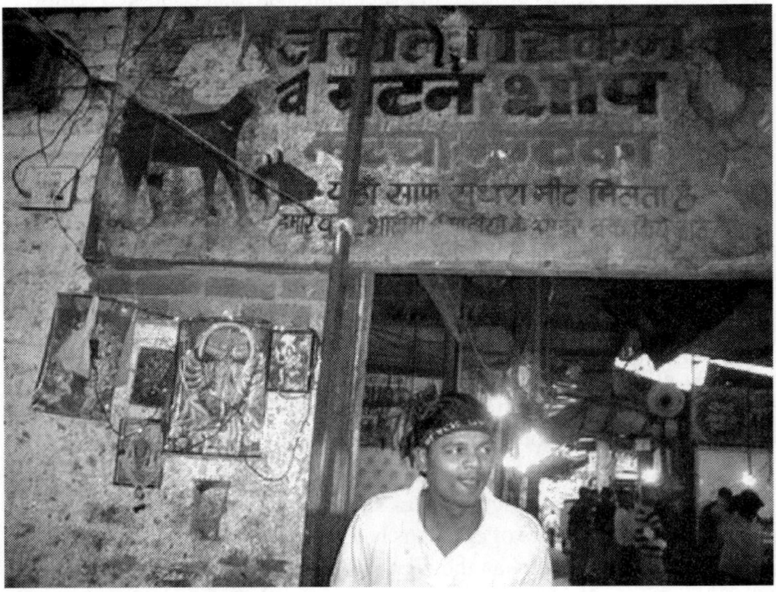

Source: Rita Brara.

While chicken was a culinary favourite, the local palate preferred goat meat to mutton. I did not come across any illustrations of sheep, unlike goats, depicted in the hoardings though mutton was commonly sold. The omission of sheep from the hoardings showed up the extent to which pictorial signs were oriented to the clientele.

Again, the pictorial styles of hoardings in markets frequented by the middle classes were distinct from those apparent in affluent locales. I came across two shops that showed the portions of the goat that were available for sale, graphically, in a middle-class colony. Hoardings depicted the practice of *jhatka* visually as well (Figure 7.2).

The pictorial composition in the signage of the charcuterie, by contrast, was fancy and highly crafted. Here, class spoke through elaborate visuals—a picture of a hen laying eggs in a nest and wallscapes that depicted plump, exotic bakers (Figure 7.3). This shop did not carry a *halal* or *jhatka* sign. In the main, however, the presence of *halal* and *jhatka* as words insisted their presence alongside the pictorial dimension. The latter existed as a parallel language, side by side or beneath the surface.

Figure 7.3
Shop sign outside the upper-class Oberoi charcuterie

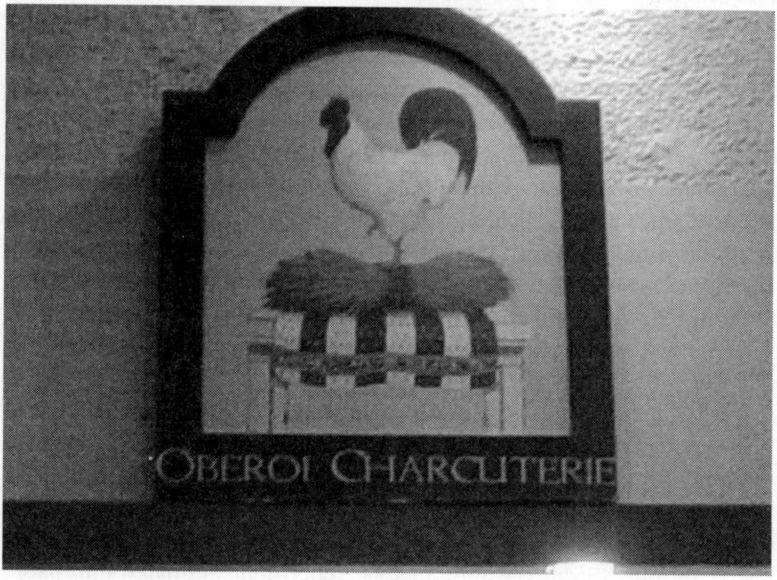

Source: Rita Brara.

The striking incorporation of the words *halal* and *jhatka* in the hoardings of meat shops afforded a glimpse into the local intertwinement and separation of the commercial and the sacred. While the production of meat was imbued with faith-based practices and signs, the dimension of class was co-produced by the self of the shopkeeper and his imagined clientele. It was apprehensible in the varying class-based terms for 'meat shop', in the scripts and lettering styles chosen and in the accompanying visuals. By contrast with the unambiguous, objective meaning of traffic signs, for instance, such shop signs allowed for a combination of objective and subjective dimensions from the perspective of the meat seller.

Signs, Simulacra and Symbols

As I shifted from the visual to spoken words about hoardings, conversations were spontaneously in the colloquial Hindustani—an admixture of Hindi, Urdu and occasional English words. Like the bilingual signs of the hoardings, the city-speech of admixture contrasted with exclusively Hindi or English signs. These spoken words were spontaneous 'airings' that seemed to me to speak about and beyond terrains marked out by *halal* and *jhatka*.

Conversations with butchers convinced me that the sign-value of *halal* and *jhatka* did not end with the hoardings. The hoarding which I had taken to be a detachable, self-contained frame, now folded over to become a part of a larger sign system. As I shifted from the liminal space of the street to the interior of the shop, the words *halal* and *jhatka* that I had taken to be mere signs communicating religious difference transformed into the symbols of faith.[8] Here, I felt that I was at a threshold as I moved from external to internal difference. The visual inscriptions of shop titles and the signs of *halal* and *jhatka* that I have explored this far, then, had to be seen in conjunction with both the linguistic and the non-linguistic signs of *halal* and *jhatka* in the margins and interior of the shops.

Now, the hoarding was described as the exterior aspect of the shop. It was perceived as the commercial or false (*naqli*) self that carried a minimal presentation of the faith. By contrast, the interior of the shop was envisaged as the space for the expression of 'one's heart' and the true or religious self. For the single word *halal*, here there were several visual signifiers. Many 'simultaneous' repetitions animated the 'bare' repetition[9] denoted in the written word *halal*—a landscape of Mecca and/or Medina,[10] often accompanied with an image of Ajmer Sharif, a pilgrimage site in India; a framed verse or a prayer (*dua*) in the Arabic script or a calendar, for instance, indicating festivals and the *rozas* (days of fasting).

The interior of the shop was a miniature faithscape. A crescent moon and star, a sacred word that looked like the number 786, verses such as the Surya Yasin or the Aayat al-Kursi, Suras of the Koran depicted by numerals, and shorter verses (*kuls*) from the Koran that were believed to bring prosperity (*barakat*) abounded in different measure and arrangement in these shops (Figure 7.4). From this angle, the necessity of displaying the term *halal* seemed to dissolve. The profusion of signs and the feeling that any one of them could connote *halal* communicated its affective sense.

Yet, this apparent dissolution of *halal* within a sea of Muslim signs, I thought, was still unwarranted. Each of these signs could indeed summon another story and trace a different path where it would shine or be eclipsed. I simply noted that in the absence of *halal* as a written word, these elements could substitute and repeat in other modes the fact of its being a *halal* shop. Practical reasons for these signs were also palpable. A woman, who

Figure 7.4

Posters in a halal *meat shop displaying popular charts and verses*

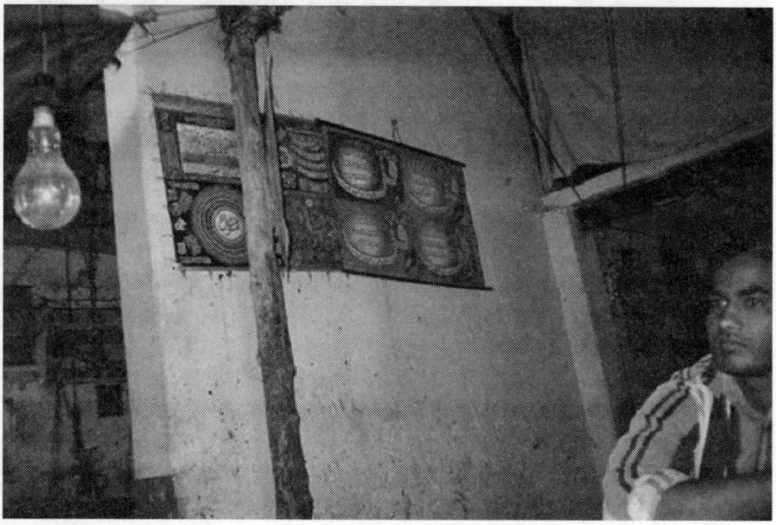

Source: Rita Brara.

could not 'read', read that this was a *halal* shop from the framed verse in Urdu. But what occasioned this plethora of religious signs?

'In the end, we have to return to Allah' was how a shopkeeper put it. These signs were placed in the person's heart and that was signified by the faithscape in the interior of the shop where they resonated together.

In the *jhatka* shops, too, there were pictures of Kali along with Guru Gobind Singh, very often. In the Sikh *jhatka* shops, portraits of Guru Nanak and, sometimes, the founder of the shop, recurred side by side with Kali. The Hindu stalls often combined photographs of Guru Gobind Singh with the Hindu goddesses Durga and Lakshmi, the symbol 'Om' and/or a sticker spelling out the words *Shubh Labh* (auspicious profit) in varying arrangements (Figure 7.5). A string of lemons and chillies hanging from an outer edge of the shop also doubled up as a *jhatka* marker. A circular sign with a double-edged sword, the *khanda,* symbolised the Khalsa or Sikh faith and, once I was alerted to it, I noted its presence in other *jhatka* shops.

What were the motivations for such display? Hindu butchers declared that they prayed to the deity Kali (who accepted meat as an offering) every morning. They also offered an animal sacrifice on the occasion

Figure 7.5

Interior of a jhatka *meat shop showing sacred Sikh and Hindu figures and symbols*

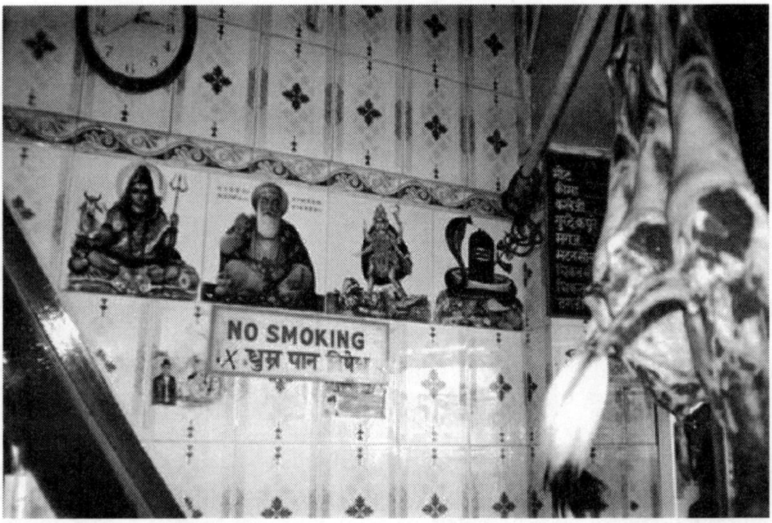

Source: Rita Brara.

of Navaratri (a nine-day auspicious period among the Hindus) in the shape of a severed head of an animal. The Sikh butchers told me that it was Guru Gobind Singh who had asked the Sikhs to refrain from eating meat slaughtered in a way that caused pain to the animal and so his portrait was forefronted. They kept Kali's image as well because as some of them put it, people in eastern India who believed in her formed part of their clientele.

These contemporary juxtapositions of Sikh Gurus and Hindu goddesses were an inventive synthesis intended to draw customers from among both Sikhs and Hindus in the city. It was remarkable because these two faiths that were growing apart in other aspects in the city came together in this domain, united in their espousal of *jhatka* as a slaughter technique.

Affordable posters with religious images or sacred sites and stickers emblazoned with religious signs had certainly given a fillip to the visual and public displays of faith. But how might scholars view this proliferation of religious signs? Were these signs like smiles without the cat, as Alice's story depicts it, diminishing God from being 'a ruler' to just 'fading smiles' (Huxley 1957: 58)?

Writing on simulacra, Jean Baudrillard (1988: 167) puts it thus: 'What if God himself can be simulated, that is to say, reduced to signs which attest his existence? Then the whole system becomes weightless; it is no longer anything but a gigantic simulacrum [...]'. For Baudrillard, simulacra succeed in 'substituting the signs of the real for the real' (Baudrillard 1994: 4). From Deleuze's (1994) perspective, simulacra question both the model and the copy and should therefore be envisaged as new entities. Each simulacrum, in Deleuze's view, affirms difference by diverging from both a model and a copy.

Envisaged as simulacra, the visual signs of sacredness in meat shops may reveal how these tiny foci become the means by which different believers of the same faith, and those of different faiths, relate to each other through neither model nor copy but by expressions of local and adjacent difference. Commenting on the circulation of printed pictures in India, Stephen Inglis (1995) argues that these religious images seem to enhance the power of the sacred while Daniel Smith (1995) talks of a new 'omnipraxy' that now bypasses religious specialists.

Conversations with butchers revealed the densities in which *halal* and *jhatka* materialised as signs of neighbourly difference articulated in local contexts. By contrast with the hardness or formal status of what was visual and written, these spoken words made up the ephemeral, everyday talk that lent meaning to the visual shop signs. I recall fragments of this discourse below.

I casually asked a young boy who worked in a meat shop what *halal* meant and he expressed surprise: 'You don't know that! Like there are Muslims and Hindus, there is *halal* and *jhatka*'. (*Aap ko maloom nahin! Jaise Mussalman hote hain aur Hindu hote hain waise hi halal aur jhatka hota hai.*) When I asked him, about what was happening in a poster on display, he told me: 'They are reading the Quran; it is like your Gita'. (*Woh Quran par rahen hain; jaise aap ki Gita hoti hai.*) Another man described the Kalima (which is a declaration that 'I believe in Allah and Muhammad as his Prophet') as being like their *mantra.* A third butcher said, 'Like you have castes, we have *phirkas* (groupings)'. (*Jaise aap mein jaat hoti hai, hum mein phirke hote hain.*) And another example: 'Our *rozas* are like your religious fasts'. (*Hamare roze aap ke brat ki tarah hain.*)

In ordinary conversations, analogies proliferated, juxtapositions easily turned into verbal duels and similarities were tempered by the acknowledgement of material differences between beliefs (Deleuze 1994). There was a strain towards parallelism, in the context of religious pluralism, apparent for instance, in the equivalence of the Quran and the Gita as holy texts or indeed *halal* and *jhatka* as slaughter techniques.

Were these analogies/homologies attempts at representing difference? Gabriel Tarde (1895/1969) argues that when social life is juxtaposed in pairs, it does not suggest an increase in difference but, rather like dual organisation, is an attempt at containing it. The effort at forming what I may call 'limited equivalences' in an inter-religious milieu enabled residents to talk about the religious in terms of the other's embodied, visual and readily apprehensible dimensions.

On the one hand, Deleuze's (1994) perspective would suggest that such analogies do not enable an understanding of aspects of difference that lie outside this ambit. However, communication on the ground took many turns, and butchers often used the vocabulary of one faith to communicate the same and different sense of another as well, a novel endeavour at a remove from the straitjacketing of analogies. On the other hand, the 'excess' in the ideas of religious difference that could not be contained in this manner bubbled over in talk of continuing difference.

A knot of butchers, who I spoke with, denied the difference between *halal* and *jhatka* contending, 'meat is meat. It has to be produced as a food'. However, how it was produced was 'ultimately, a matter of faith (*iman*; dharma)'. Here, the similarity between *halal* and *jhatka* was noted but the materiality of religious difference was acknowledged.

A third mode of talking about the difference was by casting it as opposed (and not merely juxtaposed) practices existing cheek by jowl. I did not come across a single instance where the two practices were considered identical in the discourse of the butchers.

On being asked what *halal* or *jhatka* was, most butchers enacted it in a gestural language but the matter was never left at that. Almost immediately, what followed was a defence of specific practice. Often, Hindu and Sikh butchers immediately averred that *jhatka* caused less pain to the animal than *halal* in a spirit of one-upmanship. The fear glands, I was told, could not secrete poison into the animal's blood stream if this technique was followed.

Muslim butchers clarified that once the animal's throat was slit, on the other hand, it was, in fact, lifeless and subsequent muscular contractions were involuntary. The animal's 'brain is dead' is how one shopkeeper put it. A Muslim meat seller contended that *halal* ensured that an animal was slaughtered only after Allah's name had been invoked and anyone should know that to have God's name pronounced over the animal's body was better than unsanctified slaughter. An onlooker added that *halal* was also tastier and it had more vitamins. Another Muslim averred that a Muslim shopkeeper would sell only *halal* meat because that was a non-substitutable tenet of his faith.

What was striking in the streets of Delhi was the refusal to give the lack of faith a place. This everyday context contrasts, for instance, with the milieu of post-Christian France where Lefebvre (1984) would speak approvingly of the Nietzschean notion that 'God is dead' to make way for new beginnings. In the context of butchering here, by contrast, distinctive religious practices and visual signs of faith, in the varying combinations attested in each shop, positively constituted Muslims, Sikhs and Hindus as believers.

It may be valuable to distinguish religious signs, which often appear to be free-floating from religious symbols that espouse the specific perspective of a believer. For a religious being, each *n*th enactment of faith and its signifiers partake in the power of its first enactment (Deleuze 1994; Eliade 1959). A sign or an assemblage of signs, invoked by the faith of the practitioner, can transform into a sacred symbol. From the religious perspective, symbols appear as disembodied signs only to casual onlookers and the irreligious.

More to Meat-shop Signs than Meets the Eye

Starting out as a spectator of meat-shop signs in the city, my encounter with differences in the repetition of signs showed that there was more to meat-shop signs than meets the eye. On the one hand, I sensed a rupture as *halal* and *jhatka* ceased to be shop signs and transformed into religious symbols as I crossed from the exterior of the shop to its interior. On the other, the different senses of *halal* and *jhatka* as bodily practices laden with memories of historical events (during the Muslim, British and post-Independence regimes) circulated as a material and live presence in the city (Freitag 2007).

How far do I get by thinking about *halal* and *jhatka* as 'bare' repetitions that are grounded, as it were, by the practices of habitus and the selections of memory (Deleuze 1994)? I can travel considerable distance with the thought but it stops short of enabling me to apprehend the sacred aspects of their meaning for the city's inhabitants.

Firstly, 'bare' visual, religious signs on billboards here attempt to speak to the conjoined concern with morality and ethics that is voiced in the idiom of the religious. Second, even when *halal* and *jhatka* as shop signs are revealed to arise from a combination of commercial interests and religious concerns, they do not lose their religious valences. Third, in an inter-faith context, it is often tiny, visual signs that mark the everyday enactment of difference between religious faiths. And finally, the emergence and salience of relatively new local and sacred signs, such as *jhatka,* shows that signs are not merely repetitions but attempts at coming to terms with religious difference and similarity in contexts of religious pluralism.

Moreover, religious signs appear as such only from the standpoint of an outsider; for the believer, these are symbols invested with sacred powers. Visual signs of one's own faith, even those that may be viewed as subordinate or simulacra by the literati, can resonate with an intensity reserved for symbols; at the same time, what is another's symbol can become a shop sign or more if it allows for a dialogue between residents of different faiths.

What is evident in Delhi is the creation and re-creation of a local language of signs and symbols that inscribes and reinscribes religious difference in a manner that is sensed by believers and residents even though its meanings may not be entirely disclosed in the visual realm. The ongoing inscription of differences between *halal* and *jhatka* on meat-shop hoardings, then, circulates as the visual becomings of religion (as also of commerce or politics) in this inter-religious milieu and sometimes as just disembodied shop signs.

Notes

1. Jhatka is an onamopotoeic sound that mirrors the image/action of one-stroke slaughter, like say the word 'snap' may describe an action and the sound.
2. Information on the social affiliations of butchers is gleaned from the oral accounts of Muslim, Sikh and Hindu butchers at the old Idgah slaughterhouse that was established in the 1940s. See also Ahmad (2013).
3. See, for instance, the Sikh Encyclopedia that documents Sikh resistance to the practice of serving *halal* meat in the Army and its revocation in 1942—www.thesikhencyclopedia.com/martial-heritage/jhatka (accessed 6 January 2013).
4. I follow here the spelling that the shopkeeper provided.
5. Etymologically, *Sonkar* derives from *Shankar*, a name for Lord Shiva, the male deity least likely to be averse to meat-eaters.

6. Three expositions on shop signs that I found useful are Minton (1950) on New York, Stewart and Fawcett (2004) on small towns in Portugal and MacGregor (2003) on Tokyo.
7. I gathered that the hinterland that supplies live goats and sheep now prefers to rear sheep rather than goats because of the latter's attractive returns on wool and meat.
8. The shift from the word 'sign' in the discourse of semiotics to 'symbol' in the sociology of religion is remarkable.
9. Here, again, I am borrowing the idea of 'simultaneous' and 'bare' repetitions from Deleuze (1994).
10. The various spellings of Medina in the chapter reflect different local and global usages.

References

Ahmad, Zarin. 2013. 'Marginal Occupations and Modernising Cities: Muslim Butchers in Urban India'. *Economic and Political Weekly* 47 (32): 121–31.

Ali, Syed. 2002. 'Collective and Elective Ethnicity: Caste among Muslims in India'. *Sociological Forum* 17 (4): 593–620.

Al-Qaradawi, Yusuf. 1990. *The Lawful and the Prohibited in Islam.* India: Hindustan Publications.

Barthes, Roland. 1985. 'Textual Analysis of a Tale of Poe'. In *On Signs*, edited by Marshall Blonsky, 84–97. Baltimore: Johns Hopkins University.

Baudrillard, Jean. 1988. *Selected Writings*, edited by Mark Poster. Stanford: Stanford University Press.

———. 1994. *Simulacra and Simulation*. Ann Arbor: University of Michigan.

Caldwell, Sarah. 2003. 'Margins at the Centre: Tracing Kali through Time, Space and Culture'. In *Encountering Kali: In the Margins, at the Center*, edited by Rachel Fell McDermott and Jeffrey John Kripal, pp. 249–72. Berkeley: University of California Press.

Deleuze, Gilles. 1994. *Difference and Repetition*. London: The Athlone Press.

Derrida, Jacques. 2002. *Acts of Religion.* New York, NY: Routledge.

Eliade, Mircea. 1957. *The Sacred and the Profane.* Florida: Harcourt Books.

Freitag, Sandra. 2007. 'South Asian ways of seeing: Muslim ways of knowing: The Indian Muslim Niche Market in Posters'. *Indian Economic Social History Review* 44 (3): 297–331.

Huxley, Julian. 1957. *Religion without Revelation*. London: Max Parrish.

Inglis, Stephen R. 1995. 'Suitable for Framing: The Work of a Modern Master'. In *Media and the Transformation of Religion in South Asia*, edited by Lawrence A. Babb and Susan S. Wadley, pp. 51–75. Delhi: Motilal Banarsidass Publishers.

Jain, Kajri. 2007. *Gods in the Bazaar: The Economies of Indian Calendar Art.* Durham: Duke University Press.

Lefebvre, Henri. 1984. *Everyday Life in the Modern World.* New Brunswick & London: Transaction Publishers.

MacGregor, Laura. 2003. 'The Language of Shop Signs in Tokyo'. *English Today* 73 (1): 18–23.

Mansukhani, Gobind Singh. 1989. 'Sikh Rehat Maryada and Sikh Symbols'. In *Advanced Studies in Sikhism*, edited by Jasbir Singh Mann and Harbans Singh Saraon, pp. 174–94. Patiala: Western Printer.

Minton, Arthur. 1950. 'A Form of Class Epigraphy'. *Social Forces* 28 (3): 250–62.

Smith, H. Daniel. 1995. 'Impact of "God Posters" on Hindus and their Devotional Traditions'. In *Media and the Transformation of Religion in South Asia*, edited by Lawrence A. Babb and Susan S. Wadley, pp. 24–50. Delhi: Motilal Banarsidass Publishers.

Stewart, Penny, and Richard Fawcett. 2004. 'Shop Signs in Small Towns in Northern Portugal'. *English Today* 20 (1): 56–58.

Tarde, Gabriel. (1895) 1969. *On Communication and Social Influence. Selected Papers*, edited by Terry N. Clark. Chicago: University of Chicago Press.

8

The Imagery of Indian Matchmaking: Representations of Community, Class and Gender in a Transnational Online Matrimonial Market

Fritzi-Marie Titzmann

Introduction

The Internet as a new space has enormously increased the scope of possibilities to meet potential life partners, not only in India but all over the world. According to Monica Whitty (2007: 1), 74 per cent of single US Americans use the Internet for their partner search. Since the launch of the first web browser in 1993, millions of people all over the world have made use of this new technology. They have employed it to communicate and to establish relationships. Naturally, the gradual commercialisation of online networks in the form of dating and matrimonial websites includes an ever-increasing visual perfection of these sites and their commercial promotion and advertisement. But as the following analysis of the Indian case exemplifies, the use of images in a multimedia matchmaking industry is never impartial or without ideological implications. The Indian online matrimonial market consists of thousands of websites, which are basically databases of eligible candidates. The main attention is understandably drawn towards the user profiles and their photographs, but the visual landscape of the matrimonial market also involves the design of these sites. An interpretation of this combination of images and text requires an examination with particular reference to India's sociocultural situation.

While resembling their prototypes (e.g., Match.com) from the USA, Indian matrimonial websites emphasise not relationship but marriage as their purpose of matchmaking. In most other aspects, the basic idea of an online database connecting singles with each other is rather identical. Notably, the clientele is recruited from similar socio-economic backgrounds in North America and India. Most users of the leading US-based website Match.com declared to be college graduates and to live in bigger cities and suburbs.

> Most users claim that their motivations for using dating sites had to do with the very particular working conditions that this class faces. Increased career and time pressures and higher rates of geographical mobility combine to decrease the opportunities available to meet partners offline, or to have a social life in general. (Arvidsson 2006: 686)

Although, I look at the development and dynamics of the Indian market, the aforementioned clientele, their social realities and motivations to go online in order to find a partner apply equally well to Indian urban and diasporic contexts. Thus, I examine a local phenomenon, which is nevertheless global with culturally specific peculiarities.

India's Online Matrimonial Market

Professional marriage bureaus and newspaper advertisements have proved to be successful in the Indian matchmaking context for decades. The introduction of matrimonial websites from the late 1990s onwards is simply the most recent innovation within a thriving multimedia marriage industry. Their emergence is part of a general media boom since the beginning of India's economic liberalisation and the related successive privatisation of media companies (Munshi 2001: 79; Schneider 2007). The number of actual matrimonial websites is unclear, but a Google search for the keyword 'matrimonial website' results today in approximately 22 million pages. As from September 2012 onwards, the majority evidently targets users of South Asian origin.[1] This is not surprising. Marriage arrangements through newspaper advertisements, marriage bureaus and family networks have a long-lasting tradition in South Asia. The Internet is only one more medium used to simplify the search of an eligible partner. Secondly, India is not called the new IT nation for no reason. The growing number of young educated computer users fluent in English explains the overwhelming response matrimonial websites are getting. Overall, India's more than 100 million Internet users make up the world's third largest group of online users after China and the USA (Internet and Mobile Association of India [IAMAI] 2012).[2] According to an earlier study conducted by the IAMAI, about 80 per cent of the users of matrimonial websites are between 18 and 35 years old, have at least one college degree and live in one of India's megacities.[3] The study finds a rapid and continuous rise in user numbers since 2005. The IAMAI researchers estimate that there were about 7 million users of matrimonial websites in 2006 and 2007 (IAMAI 2006: 2).

The online matrimonial market is led by three dominating websites: Shaadi.com, BharatMatrimony.com and Jeevansathi.com[4] of which Shaadi.com claims the highest number of users and successful matches. Shaadi.com's biggest competitor is BharatMatrimony.com, which has developed a different business strategy by going mainly with regional affiliations. The portal consists of 15 regional sub-sites, called TamilMatrimony, BengalMatrimony, MarathiMatrimony, etc. BharatMatrimony.com has a stronger hold in South India (Pepper 2007).[5] In comparison to Shaadi.com, Jeevansathi.com seems to attract fewer Non-Resident Indians (NRI) and educated urban candidates, and is consequently rated as less effective by many of my interviewees.[6] Apart from these big websites, there exist a vast number of small sites which attract plenty of subscribers: Indianmatrimonials.com, Pyar.org, Lifepartnerindia.com, Matrisearch.com, Merasathi.com. New sites are constantly being created. For example, the recently launched SimplyMarry.com, 'India's only metro-monial site', addresses explicitly an urban clientele. Furthermore, there are countless websites that cater to specific communities or customers. Examples include Sikhingyou.com for Sikhs, Nikah.com for Muslims, TrinityMatrimony for Keralite Christians. I have come across several Gujarati websites such as Glagna.com and some which even specialise in distinct castes such as the Patels,[7] Kutchi Lohanas[8] or BrahmKshatriya Sorathiya Vaishnavs.[9]

In 2007, the creators of Shaadi.com bridged another gap in the market by launching the website SecondShaadi.com, which is promoted as the 'No.1 re-marriage site for Indians'. The site now operates independently from its mother-site Shaadi.com. By creating a marriage market for seekers of a second marriage, i.e., for divorcees and widowed people, the founders broke with traditional resentments since remarriage, at least for traditional Hindus, has long been a taboo and is still not accepted all over the subcontinent. Even the general matrimonial sites contain the profiles of a significant percentage of widowed and divorced seekers, although the overwhelming majority of users has never been married (IAMAI 2006: 3). CommunityMatrimony.com invests with its sub-site '40plus matrimony' in a similar niche by targeting elderly singles.

The market's differentiation and fragmentation continues steadily and websites specialising in targeting certain regions, languages, religions or sociocultural classes make up for the majority today. 'The market is flooded with matrimonial services. You think of any word around matrimony or marriage, in India, there is a dot.com that exists' (Vishal Shah, personal interview, 28 January 2011), explained an entrepreneur who operates a marriage bureau and a matrimonial website for Gujaratis in Mumbai. In spite of the strong fragmentation, the industry is highly competitive in terms of professionalism and technological progress in the matchmaking process. Professional appearance results in higher credibility in the eyes of potential subscribers. The race for maximum technological innovation leads to an encompassing technologisation of the entire process. SimplyMarry.com announced to be the first website to introduce Match Tech, a computer-based system to calculate two potential partners' compatibility.

> Match Tech blends astrological principals, physical attributes and socio economic standards, to create a score using a scientific process called ICRS (Intelligent Cross Reference Scoring), which performs numerous complex calculations to shortlist the special few.[10]

The structure of most Indian websites is almost identical, a fact that may be due to the mentioned constant competition. Mohammed Zakir Shaikh, who operates a Muslim marriage bureau in Ahmedabad, describes his relationship to the 'big' providers like Shaadi.com with the following words:

> I am doing this today, so I am lagging behind ten years. They started on a big scale, whereas we have started on a small scale. So there will be a difference amongst us. As for the website, in our site most features are inducted after seeing their website. (Mohammed Zakir Shaikh, personal interview, 7 February 2011)[11]

The emergence and development of matrimonial websites thus continues trends of commercialisation and professionalisation that started with the inception of commercial newspaper advertisements for wanted brides and grooms in the early twentieth century (Majumdar 2004). Jiban Pal (2010: 55) draws a comparison to social networking sites like Facebook and Orkut. He argues that Indian matrimonial websites are inspired by their inherent idea of networking. I would rather contextualise social networking sites as well as matrimonial media within the general process of medialisation[12] and increasing connectivity. The idea of a network is—with regard to marriage matchmaking—far from new for the Indian context. Matrimonial websites avail of the same network principles that family networks and caste association have used for centuries.

Analysing the Visual: Researching Public Relations (PR) and Advertisement Material

The title of this chapter, The Imagery of Matchmaking, refers to a multi-layered understanding of the term imagery. The word itself describes the use of vivid or figurative language to represent objects, actions or ideas, but also the use of expressive and evocative images. Lastly, I understand imagery on a meta-level as the entire set of related (textual and figurative) images. Hence, I employ the term broadly to analyse the visual language of online-based matrimonial services and the inherent ideological representations.

Before looking into select examples of visual depiction within the online matrimonial market, it is important to note that structure and design of commercial matrimonial websites are never coincidental. They are strongly influenced by marketing and PR strategies aimed at obtaining a maximum number of clicks and users. The inherent interrelation of design and PR manifests itself in television and YouTube spots linked to the websites, in prominently placed success stories sent in by satisfied users and in testimonials like the True Stories on Shaadi.com which should not be confused with the supposedly real success stories.

PR in its various forms including advertisement belongs to the daily processes of social construction. PR material is essentially a cultural production that is often perceived as a privileged representation. Therefore, Mickey (2003: vii) emphasises deconstruction as an important approach to challenge the apparent authority of PR and advertisement messages.

In particular, the companies' and organisations' self-advertisement requires verification.

> Deconstructing means to see ideas that rest under the surface of the material we have produced—to peel away the layers that are in front of us but often hidden until we look. This is especially important for public relations, because its reason for being is to promote a client, an organization, a product, or a service. (Mickey 2003: 1)

Thomas Mickey's approach to deconstruct PR is based on the critical theory of the Cultural Studies that focuses on the production of meaning and the codification of values within society (Mickey 2003: 6).[13] For critical media analysis, advertisement campaigns offer rich and highly significant data. Videos, speeches, press releases, brochures and other formats represent important aspects of social construction. 'All of it, however, is colored by some kind of theory about values like society, self, gender, power, and race' (Mickey 2003: 2). The material's deconstruction can be carried out in multiple ways. One may interview the producers, one may examine the material itself or one may explore the target group's reception. I have implemented all three approaches for an extensive analysis of the Indian online matrimonial market in varying degrees of intensity.[14] In order to deconstruct design and self-advertisement of matrimonial websites, I focus primarily on the material level, the analysis of images and their corresponding texts. Hence, representation and deconstruction are intimately connected with each other:

> Public relations materials have a particular view that is constructed with self-interest at heart. Any representation, however, is limited, and frequently limiting in a democratic environment. Soon, however, it often becomes part of the culture's thinking and being: We think this is the way it is when it is really one person's or one organization's view. (Mickey 2003: 3)

Media texts also need to be viewed as expressions of political and economic hierarchies and power positions. It is the context that is decisive. Every symbol represented in a media text or image is ideologically connoted. Cultural Studies, thus, not simply ask for the content but discuss who benefits at whose expense. All ideology becomes material as soon as it appears coded within a product or image. Dominant ideologies tend to constantly repeat its message in varying forms (Mickey 2003: 11f).

In the following paragraph, I will analyse the design and promotional strategies of different service providers within a highly complex and transnational multimedia Indian matchmaking industry. My focus lies primarily on matrimonial websites and advertisements directly linked to these sites.

An Indian Design?

Most international dating websites are structured somewhat identically; the Indian marriage market merely deviates from the usual patterns. In comparison to standardised matchmaking sites like the ones operated by Cupid Media[15]—whose profiles consists of around a dozen categories—Indian websites like Shaadi.com offer around 40 search and dozens of filter options. Dana Diminescu and Matthieu Renault (2011: 687) argue that their design correlates with the highly stratified Indian social system's specificity. One could also interpret these characteristics simply as an Indian variation or with Marshall Sahlin's words as an 'indigenization of modernity' (1999: ix).

Most Indian websites are structured along similar patterns. The user profiles are organised along traditionally decisive factors with regards to partner search like religion, caste, language, horoscope, body measures, profession and income. Shaadi.com additionally includes a section on 'lifestyle' (dietary, drinking and smoking habits) as well as a section on Hobbies, Interests & More, which offer a list of optional answers. Most websites also include a field to freely phrase a text about one's personality and family. A typical user profile ends with an optional section titled Partner Preferences which is filled in by the majority of subscribers.

All matrimonial Internet portals require registration and a personal profile to access other people's profiles. Members can be searched by a quick search or filtered via an advanced search. Shaadi.com's quick search includes gender, marital status (single, divorced, widowed), age, community[16] and country. An advanced search on Shaadi.com works via a function titled Smart Search which filters 24 criteria pertaining to almost all the information contained in a user's profile. Furthermore, the website offers special search options under City Search, Profession Search and AstroSoulMate Search. A noteworthy feature is the possibility to search for Special Cases including physical and mental handicaps as well as HIV-positive candidates. Thus, online matchmaking opens up new avenues and a global marriage market for hitherto disadvantaged sections of society. Through a few clicks, Shaadi.com creates a global marriage market for divorced, widowed and HIV-positive people who due to persistent stigmatisation suffer from discrimination and commonly face severe difficulties when trying to find marriage partners at all.[17] Linking people in similar situations to each other and thus enlarging the pool of suitable candidates comes close to a revolutionary innovation.

However, these forms of differentiation are not the only ones. The rapid growth of the online matrimonial market forces companies to identify ever more market gaps and distinguish their portals from competing providers. Religion-, region- and language-specific websites as well as websites catering to the vast diaspora contribute significantly to the increasing fragmentation.[18] The visual language of these sites corresponds to their target groups and thus conveys at times highly differing messages. Images of gender-specific ideal 'Indianness' are on the other hand—despite of regional or religious variations—surprisingly consistent. The next section explores regional, religious and sociocultural fragmentation within the marriage market and their visual manifestations.

Regional, Religious and Sociocultural Differentiation

As already mentioned, today the majority of India's online marriage market consists of websites catering to particular clienteles like Sikhingyou.com for Sikhs or Glagna.com for Gujaratis. Even more specific are sites that concentrate on a particular caste.[19] They are often part of larger transnational networks. Online community portals that connect a regionally specific local population with their diaspora and vice versa generally offer community-specific marriage advertisements.[20] The website Uttaranchal.ws serves as such a community portal for the North Indian region Uttarakhand, formerly called Uttaranchal.[21]

Under the motto 'community on the web', the portal creates a transnational community of Kumaonis and Garhwalis who traditionally hail from that region. Uttarakhand Forum operates in a similar way, describing its goal as 'connecting Uttarakhand worldwide'.[22] Both portals contain links to corresponding matrimonials. The Internet offers countless such community portals of diverse Indian regional and religious communities, e.g., Odia Khatti, 'The first social networking site of Odisha' or BangaliNET, 'a home away from home'. The more globally widespread a community is, the more differentiated according to locality (Columbus Tamil Sangam, Gujarati Arya Association—Leicester, Punjabi Community Halle e.V.) or activities (Tamil Community Housing Association, UK) are their websites.[23]

An often observed Indian trend towards media regionalisation and religious differentiation manifests itself in the rapidly growing number of such specialised online activities. While the first online matchmaking sites were more general 'Indian' and primarily targeted at the South Asian diaspora, more and more companies started to follow BharatMatrimony.com's example and began to restructure their websites, invent sub-sites or refined their search criteria. Jeevansathi.com divides its sub-sites according to language, not only in Hindi, Urdu, Tamil, etc., but even further into Hindi-Delhi, Hindi-UP, Hindi-MP and Bihari. India's notorious political and cultural regionalism influences these online spaces too. Regional and language differentiation is far from being neutral or free of value. It is striking that Shaadi.com and SimplyMarry.com alike illustrate their Urdu Matrimonials or Muslim Matrimonials with traditionally dressed women, while both websites choose images of women in Western clothes for their Hindu Matrimonials and Hindi Matrimonials, respectively (Figures 8.1 and 8.2).[24] Subliminal prejudices and stereotypes pertaining to religion are strongly reinforced through these images. Through their visual representation, both websites ascribe a progressive and modern lifestyle to their Hindi (or Hindu) users, while the Muslim counterpart is depicted with a conservative connotation. Regional belonging is equally

Figure 8.1
Shaadi.com, Urdu Matrimonials

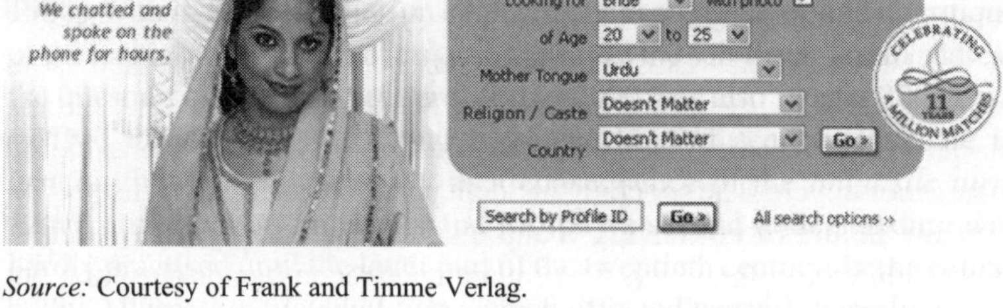

Source: Courtesy of Frank and Timme Verlag.

Figure 8.2
Shaadi.com, Hindi Matrimonials

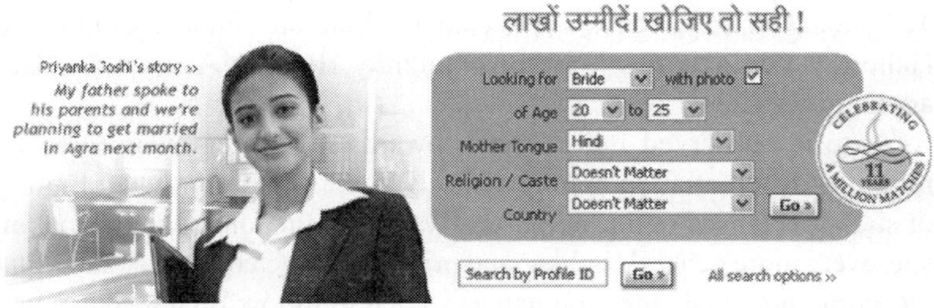

Source: Courtesy of Frank and Timme Verlag.

stereotyped in the websites' discourse. For instance, SimplyMarry.com uses the photograph of a young woman dressed in a folkloristic costume and dancing *Dandiya Raas*, Gujarat's traditional stick dance, to illustrate its Gujarati Matrimonials.

Websites like CommunityMatrimony.com utilise India's accelerated social differentiation as its business model and invest in community as the strongest identity marker.[25] In Indian English, the term community is commonly used not only for a group of people somehow linked to each other but also as a synonym for caste. The term caste is negatively connoted through its long history of discrimination, and among certain classes rather avoided for reasons of 'political correctness'. But eventually CommunityMatrimony.com does not offer anything else than caste-based marriage advertisement:

> In India it is still believed that marriage within the community is healthy, happy and strengthens the bond within the community. CommunityMatrimony.com is a union of over 350 community matrimony sites catering to the unique needs of various communities.[26]

A television commercial additionally suggests that the website's business model targets parents as their prime audience. The TV spot shows an Indian couple living in an unidentified Western country. The parents observe how their daughter passes by, sitting on a young, long-haired man's motorcycle. The shocking incident provokes an agitated discussion over the failure of not having found a suitable groom for the daughter from within the community. An acquaintance recommends checking out CommunityMatrimony.com for that matter.[27] The theme of threatening Westernisation can be found throughout different media formats. Popular

Hindi cinema has extensively portrayed and to some extent probably even amplified the intergenerational tensions occurring between first and second generation migrants. The motif of saving diasporic Indian girls' morality through the 'right' marriage with a partner from the same community has been central to the wave of films set in diasporic contexts since the early 1990s (Athique 2011; Bhatia and Ram 2012). One might even argue that the CommunityMatrimony.com TV spot quotes the scene from one of the popular Hindi films. This indicates a level of intermediality where content is transferred from one medium to another.[28]

Differentiation on linguistic, regional and religious grounds[29] is further complemented by matrimonial websites focusing on sociocultural class. For example, the Ahmedabad-based website Klassicmatch.com proudly announces its services as Marriage Bureau for the Class. SimplyMarry.com, the only 'metro-monial sites' in its own words, uses cosmopolitanism as defining feature. The sites' orientation is emphasised by images that visually transport the inherent message. SimplyMarry.com stands out for its non-traditional front-page picture. It does not, as it is rather common, depict a couple or bride in traditional marriage attire but a flirting, cuddling couple dressed in Western outfits. A portal called Elitematrimony.com is BharatMatrimony.com's Premium Matchmaking Service targeting a clientele consisting of celebrities, business elite, aristocracy and the rest of the 'upper crust of society'.[30] The website pictures its ideal clientele and their approach towards matchmaking in a perfectly designed TV spot.[31] The opening scene shows an evidently upper-class Hindu family having a luxurious dinner in the garden of their palace-like mansion. The daughter then starts into a Happy Birthday Dad—speech and recounts all the incidents when her 'super hero' came to help her. She cites examples from when she and her mom went to a yoga class and her dad put up a cell phone tower in the Himalayas or when he flew a helicopter to come to her rescue. 'He can do anything', she concludes proudly. Rubbish, retorts an elderly female relative and points out her father's duty to find her an eligible groom, which he has not fulfilled so far. The elegant guitar music in the background stops abruptly and the entire table turns silent until a male family member comes up with the recommendation to try out Elitematrimony.com. The last scene shows the girl boarding a helicopter with her newly-wed husband after ostentatious wedding celebrations.[32] The ad is as glossy and smooth as the context requires. Interesting to note is not only the overt, almost snobbish elitism that is meant to attract the wanted audience but also the sublime message that it is self-evidently the father's duty to find a partner of the same class for his well-educated and grown-up daughter. Nobody challenges this notion and it is generally expected of him. Furthermore, the discussion about the daughter's marriage occurs in an extended family setting including aunts and uncles who exercise their say. Thus, in this TV commercial of hardly 50 seconds, the producers touch upon several integral components of a conservative image of supposed 'Indianness': the father as the decision-maker and head of an extended family, the general importance of the familial influence and the function of marriage in perpetuating socio-economic endogamy. Of course, the polished English spoken and the helicopter scenes add a taste of cosmopolitanism to the otherwise traditional orchestration. Again, the TV spot resembles the ways in which popular Hindi cinema portrays its wealthy and globally oriented protagonists. In blockbusters like *Kabhi Khushi Kabhi Gham* (Sometimes Happy, Sometimes Sad, 2001, Karan Johar), the theme of the joint family that struggles to balance tradition, social status and cosmopolitanism is realised in very similar settings.

The professed urban cosmopolitanism of SimplyMarry.com's 'metro-monial' approach manifests itself even stronger in a cooperative project with *The Times of India.* In March 2010, they jointly launched a new column under the name *HUM = TUM* (Me = You) for Equality Matrimonials. According to the print edition in *the Sunday Times*, matrimonials and the cooperating websites, the offer is directed towards 'prospective brides and grooms who have declared their belief in an egalitarian or equal marriage'.[33] The new advertisement category was introduced in *The Times of India* with the caption 'Because marriage is an equal vow between two individuals. Not two families'.[34] Soulmates. Speaking Tree Matrimonials, another cooperation between SimplyMarry.com and *The Times of India*, is a variation of *HUM = TUM*. Initially, Speaking Tree was a spiritual column in the print edition, and since December 2010 it has existed with a separate website.[35] Soulmates matrimonials are accordingly directed towards spiritually inclined readers of a 'modern' urban background. The site advertises with slogans like 'meeting with minds and souls' and anonymous testimonials:

> Whenever I think of a life partner, compatibility is the first thing that comes to my mind. But it would be even better, if I get a life partner who is my companion on a spiritual journey ... Someone who will understand my urge for self realization.... Someone who can accompany me on this path.[36]

HUM = TUM and Soulmates employ an increasing individualisation as working capital. They distance their online portals from traditionally oriented markets that target collectively defined categories of belonging. Nevertheless do they propagate socially endogamous marriage under the label of 'modern' matchmaking. Matrimonial websites of all kinds contribute towards projecting certain values and ideal conceptions. They explicitly promote the use of their websites through success stories, images, testimonials and videos but implicitly also promote certain world views and their preservation through marriage within the 'community'. Shaadi.com or SimplyMarry.com foreground the individual and apply terms like 'soulmates', love, compatibility and individual happiness in their marketing strategies.[37] The start page of the mentioned *HUM = TUM* section exemplifies the visual depiction of these keywords: it shows a hugging couple in Western clothes and reads 'have a happy married life'. Caste- and religion-based websites aim at a different customer segment. Their target groups are parents and families that emphasise caste endogamy and traditional criteria in partner selection. The CommunityMatrimony.com TV commercial is a vivid example.

Images of 'Indianness' and Regionalism in a Transnational Matchmaking Industry

Talking of the Indian online matrimonial market automatically covers more than the Indian subcontinent and refers to processes of deterritorialisation. The translocal aspect inherent in the Internet holds great importance for online matrimonials. But, at the same time, processes of reterritorialisation take place (Schneider and Gräf 2010). Media transgress territorial boundaries but, as the example of the Indian diaspora shows, also cause a return to territory as an identification point. Globally accessible matrimonial websites serve the Indian diaspora all over the world and provide it with the opportunity to connect with a transnational 'Indian' media and marriage market. To be Indian or 'marry the Indian way', one does not need to live in India or hold Indian citizenship. The Indian diaspora's medial and thus social integration involves an advancing dissociation of 'nation' from 'territory'. The online matrimonial market thus helps to promote something which can be termed as Global Indianness because the market is simultaneously a global as well as national media product. Through this kind of medial integration, the concept of 'national' or 'Indianness' is being 'transnationalised' itself (Schneider 2005: 76). The successful and popular matrimonial companies target so-called NRI with directed promotional campaigns. Shaadi.com advertises in the London metro with posters reading 'We were miles apart, but Shaadi.com brought

Figure 8.3

Shaadi.com advertisement in the London metro

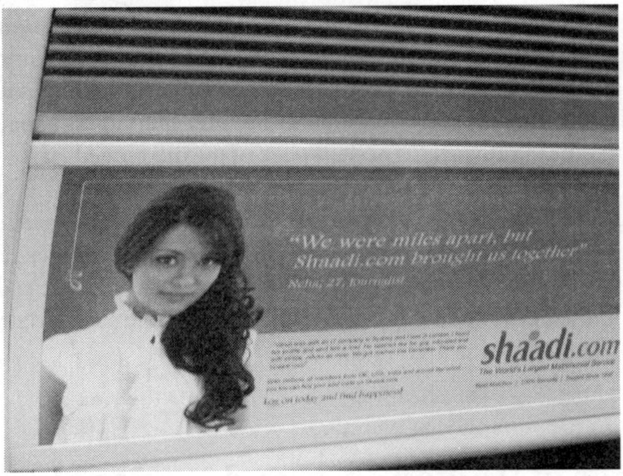

Source: Fritzi Titzmann.

Figure 8.4

Shaadi.com, True Stories

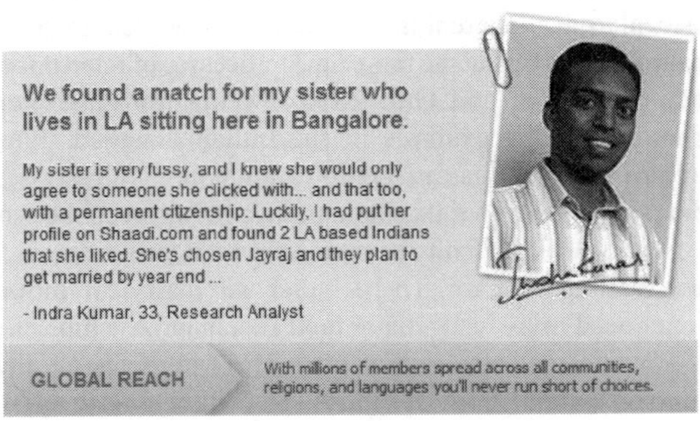

Source: Courtesy of Frank and Timme Verlag.

us together' (Figure 8.3). The so-called 'true stories' of the same website are conceptualised as quality certificates, and they present seven fictional users who speak with their success stories for the website. One section advertises the site's 'Global Reach—With millions of members spread across all communities, religions, and languages you'll never run short of choices' with Indra Kumar from Bangalore: 'We found a match for my sister who lives in LA sitting here in Bangalore' (Figure 8.4) and Yasmin (28) from London: 'Looked all over the world, but I found my man in Essex'. The stories and corresponding photographs show young modern Indians who completely conform to the image of the Globo-Indian who is perfectly at home in the global world while preserving his or her essential 'Indianness'.

Despite such images of Global Indianness, the earlier explained fragmentation and regionalisation does not represent an antagonism to the transnational nature of the phenomenon. The complex dynamics of the Indian marriage market accommodate seemingly diverging tendencies and the diaspora rather contributes towards transnationalising trends of differentiation. Due to limited choice within India or the respective countries of residence, members of regionally or religiously defined communities that attach importance to endogamy activate transnational matchmaking networks exceedingly often.

However, even transnational flows are changing. The older trend of Indian migrant workers looking for brides from 'back home' has reversed and well-to-do urban Indian men are much sought after in today's marriage market. Although, still many Indians abroad prefer partners with similar cultural backgrounds, the growing markets are intra-diasporic marriage markets. This is strongly reflected in advertising strategies and their visual language. For example, the company BharatMatrimony.com conceptualised a promotional campaign targeted explicitly at the Gujarati and Punjabi diaspora. In two separate television commercials, the respective websites GujaratiMatrimony.com and PunjabiMatrimony.com are recommended to find marriage candidates from within the community in a local environment outside India.[38]

The Gujarati TV spot shows a happily married NRI Gujarati who recommends the website to his unmarried friend. The friend asks unbelievingly whether the 'Gujju bride' is really from 'here', whereupon the other one reassures him that this is actually the case: 'For Gujarati go to a Gujarati'. A voice-over explains at the end of the spot: 'GujaratiMatrimony, exclusively for Gujaratis like us!' The advertisement corresponds with my finding from an in-depth analysis of 20 female profiles from outside India on the website BharatMatrimony.com[39] that most users prefer to marry within the diaspora sphere, preferably within their respective countries of residence. At the same time, the Gujarati TV spot illustrates that the emphasis on community is very strong within the diasporic marriage market.

The TV spot for PunjabiMatrimony.com was commissioned by BharatMatrimony.com as well and shows a wedding celebration. An older man, presumably the groom's father, announces proudly, 'he is a loving boy and an Indian at heart', while the older women of the family in view of the bride note approvingly, 'though she is born here, she is pure Punjabi.' The statement implies on the one hand the importance to marry within one's community (Punjabi) and is on the other hand pejorative towards the bride's country of residence (probably Great Britain, USA or Canada). These two simple spots allow us to retrace the changing image of the NRI from an alienated outsider into a desirable cosmopolitan with visible Indian roots.[40] The often expressed fear of Westernisation has been implemented as advertisement strategy by BharatMatrimony.com, and the second spot serves the already existing image of the New Indian Woman dating back to colonial times who resists Western lure and preserves her 'Indianness'. The remark that the groom is 'an Indian at heart' is equally paradigmatic for the image of the Globo-Indian, the male counterpart of the New Indian Woman. I will elaborate on the female role model and its appropriation later.

BharatMatrimony.com expresses anti-Western criticism and a glorification of Indian culture even stronger in another TV commercial. The spot shows a scene where the son of a supposedly NRI family introduces his fiancée 'Amy' to his parents and grandparents. The grandparents are particularly wary and dismissive. The atmosphere finally relaxes when 'Amy' introduces herself as Amritha Khanna and common (Indian) points of reference are identified. The ad was aired with high frequency on Willow TV, a television channel in the USA specialised in broadcasting cricket matches and hence very popular among Indians living in North America. It sparked off a heated debate on the Internet. In blogs and forums, viewers have discussed and criticised the ad as being racist. Many state the spot implies that only an Indian bride would be accepted by the boy's family. A blogger named Lekhni adds to this a criticism of the entire underlying message:

> Okay, I can understand the part on the proposal to marry 'Amy' meeting with stiff resentment while 'Amritha Khanna' is much more acceptable. Fine, we Indians like our children to marry people of Indian origin. You can take objection to this too, but I'll give it a pass, it's understandable—for shared values, culture and all those reasons.
>
> Though, Amritha's own 'Indianness' is a little open to question, given she feels the need to rename herself Amy when she has a perfectly pronounceable name. [...]
>
> But what's much more interesting [than the racist undertone] is how Ms. Khanna introduces herself. She says nothing about herself, or what she

> does, but her first words are 'My father is a doctor in New York'. This piece of information apparently results in instant acceptance by the boy's family. Since doctors in NYC don't exactly live in penury, apparently all we need to know to make her a perfectly acceptable bride is that she is of Indian origin and has a rich father. (Lekhni 2011)

Accordingly, deterritorialisation and a mediated ideal of Global Indianness do not inevitably result in a less traditional approach towards marriage. The assumption that matchmaking can reinforce conventional criteria like caste, ethnicity and community gains relevance with regard to the diaspora. The examples of transnationally oriented media production illustrate that matrimonial media may contribute to the preservation of endogamous and exogamous partner selection criteria. Undesirable candidates can be filtered point-and-click. At the same time, Indian media companies like BharatMatrimony.com and CommunityMatrimony.com produce commercials that directly correlate to ideas of an imagined and definable community.

Based on the analysis of ideal 'Indianness', in my last paragraph, I will explore the explicit and implicit gendered norms inscribed in the imagery of the Indian matrimonial market.

Gendered Images and Ideal Relationships

In my previous work, I have explored the representation of women and female agency in the Indian online matrimonial market (Titzmann 2011b). There I have discussed users' reception of the analysed images and self-representation in user profiles in detail. In this chapter, I focus more on the visual images and their inherent messages. What is striking is the constant attempt of female users to combine seemingly contrasting aspects. While describing career ambitions and adventurous outdoor hobbies, many term themselves as 'simple girls' who respect traditions. Typical sentences read: 'I am a smart, urban woman with traditional values', 'I would call myself a good mix of East and West' or 'thinks rationally still values traditions'. These narratives of self-perception lead to the concept of the New Indian Woman who pursues a global lifestyle but sticks to 'Indian values' (Fernandes 2000; Munshi 2001; Rajan 1993). The concept of the New Indian Woman was constructed and has been increasingly referred to by the media since the 1980s (Mankekar 1999, 2009; Schneider 2005: 52). The online matrimonial market is also influenced by such medial constructions of femininity. Portraits of successful users and their stories are published by almost all websites as part of promotion strategies for proving success. Most of the advertisement illustrations or representatives of True Stories are either female or show happily married couples. The constant attempt to combine 'modern' and 'traditional' elements in these depictions is a dominant tendency. Priyanka Joshi's True Story, which was published by Shaadi.com on Hindi Matrimonials (Figure 8.2), shows a career woman with a laptop dressed in Western clothes, but also tells us that she included her parents in the process of her marriage arrangement and thus holds on to Indian traditions: 'My father spoke to his parents and we are planning to get married next month in Agra'. The inclusion of her parents stands for 'family values' which in many discourses form an integral part of 'Indian cultural identity' (Fernandes 2000; Mankekar 2004: 427; Sonawat 2001; Uberoi 2001: 323, 327). The 'face' for the already mentioned Urdu Matrimonials on Shaadi.com conveys a similar message but in a reverse way. She is dressed in traditional Indo-Muslim clothing, but the attached message tells us 'Heena Khan's story': 'We chatted and spoke on the phone for hours' (Figure 8.1), thus implicating agency, independent communication, the use of technology and therewith 'modernity'. A third, completely visual, example is the image of SimplyMarry.com's Tamil Matrimonials (Figure 8.5) showing a young

Figure 8.5

SimplyMarry.com, Tamil Matrimonials

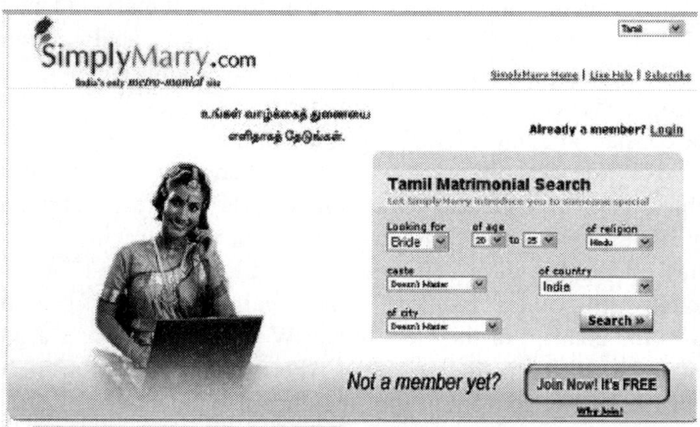

Source: Courtesy of Frank and Timme Verlag.

woman wearing a South Indian sari and further traditional attributes such as flowers in her hair, a bindi on her forehead and jewellery. At the same time, she wears a headset, holds a phone in her hand and is sitting in front of a laptop. Again, she represents a combination of symbols depicting traditional 'Indianness' and progressive, global technology, signifiers for medial mobility. These are but few examples of many which demonstrate how the matrimonial media promote the image of a New Indian Woman and thus represent an ideal 'Indian' who is global and local at the same time.

The same applies for matrimonial media as a market. As I have shown earlier, the whole idea of dating websites has been taken and transformed for the Indian market by including features, which seem to be typically 'Indian'. This tendency has been termed as 'nationalizing the global' by Leela Fernandes (2000). Media producers are well aware of these developments. Advertisement, film and television producers have actively appropriated the trend in view of the increasing profits: 'They have consequently begun to enlarge the range of feminine subjectivities which will increase consumption' (Munshi 2001: 81). New concepts are then transported far beyond urban centres due to the contemporary changes in India's media landscape towards localisation and linguistic differentiation. Thus, the image of the New Indian Woman is 'shining' beyond the middle and upper classes, where it is primarily located, generating desire and longing in other segments of Indian society as well. Mass-media products such as matrimonial websites are continuously permeated by advertising messages such as Shaadi.com's True Stories, thus defining what is perceived as the norm and as a desirable existence (Dörner 2001: 42). An analysis of 100 female profiles on Shaadi.com showed that these medially constructed images and their inherent messages do have an impact on the users' self-representation. Many of the analysed profiles included statements which point towards a subjectivity that bears strong resemblance to the concept of the New Indian Woman (Titzmann 2011b). Mae identifies women as biological and cultural reproducers of the nation which applies to the Indian context very well (Mae 2007: 43). The field of gender is where notions of 'Indianness' are negotiated (Chaudhuri 2001; Fernandes 2000; Puri 1999; Runkle 2004).

The Gujarati matrimonial website Glagna.com chose a different display format with a sequence of images on its welcome page.[41] The first photograph shows a young woman and an arrow assigning the label 'modern thinking' to her. In the next picture, we see an elderly woman, presumably a mother, whose label reads 'traditional thinking'. The last picture shows both women arm and arm, and features a link to the video 'Message from Sarita Joshi & Ridhhi Dhave' where they elucidate the advantages of Glagna.com for modern as well as traditionally thinking users. Glagna.com chose a more conservative depiction in which modernity is associated with youth and traditionalism with old age. The effect is nevertheless similar as online matchmaking is construed as the optimal combination of tradition and modernity. The harmonious unison with which the two women of different generations promote the website is in line with Rajeswari Sunder Rajan's (1993: 131) interpretation of a conflict-free modernity that avoids confrontation and disrupture with traditional values. Against this background, it should not surprise that Glagna.com as a community-specific matrimonial website emphasises a conflict-free modernity in harmony with the parental generation.

But a second look at self-declared urban and progressive websites like SimplyMarry.com reveals similar tendencies. The start page shows a Western-style dressed hugging couple provoking associations of modernity, mutual attraction, love and urbanity. But the search functions mainly via filter options like religion, caste and language. It redirects users to sub-sites that without exception feature images of couples in corresponding regional or religious wedding attire. Although I have concluded earlier in this chapter that 'progressive' formats serve similarly to maintain social endogamy, this second look reveals that they also emphasise regional and religious differentiation and the preservation of these communities.

Further, noteworthy is the fact that SimplyMarry.com used the same photograph of a bridal pair posing in white wedding gown and black suit for its Christian Matrimonial as well as its NIR Matrimonial. The subliminal accusation of Westernisation seems to be medially persistent here despite the previously described changing positive image of the NRI.

Conclusion

The cited examples illustrate how format and design transport the concept of an 'Indianness' consisting of a combination of modernity and tradition, as well as co-existing globalism and regionalism. Part of it is the medial propagation of an ideal Indian femininity as defined by the image of the

New Indian Woman. In addition to my own research findings, I want to refer to Sonora Jha and Mara Adelman's research on skin colour as an important aspect in the Indian online matrimonial market. With their analysis of users' profile photographs, they highlight the impact advertisement messages have on the users' perception, and they emphasise the intensification of existing preferences and prejudices through media technologies:

> [T]he powerful profile 'menu' options and the visual imagery of predominantly light-skinned, 'successful' brides illustrated on current websites visually reinforce the invalidation of dark skinned women. (Jha and Adelman 2009: 65)

Last but not least, particularly the so-called True Stories mediate conceptions of ideal relationships in post-colonial India without discrediting traditional channels of marriage arrangement. Images of hugging couples symbolise the ideal of companionate marriage and mutual understanding, while photographs of couples performing religious rituals in regional wedding costumes reinforce tradition and community as key components. Regionalisation continues to be one of the core marketing strategies in the Indian media landscape and is very visible in the online marriage market. As I have shown with the depiction of women on the respective Hindi and Urdu sub-sites of prominent matrimonial websites, regional and religious identity is often stereotyped.

On the other hand, emerging niche markets with filter options for divorced, widowed, handicapped or HIV-positive candidates offer potential spaces for empowerment. A networked online sphere provides opportunities to diminish stigmatisation and create internal networks. Such cases deserve attention although they represent only a minimal share of a giant differentiated matchmaking industry that focuses predominantly on regional and religious communities.

Individualisation and retraditionalisation represent another pair of seemingly conflicting poles. Although a constellation of tension, both are integral components of the marriage market's medial development. While Shaadi.com and SimplyMarry.com foreground the individual with terms like 'soulmate' and compatibility to market their websites, caste- and religion-based websites target parents and families. Common to all is the inherent network character that manifests itself in different visual imageries and sublime ideological messages. Even the most 'modern' matrimonial websites like the 'metro-monial site' SimplyMarry.com reveal a kind of endogamous marriage network—within a cosmopolitan urban middle class. Networking as a characteristic trait also includes growing connectivity and refers to the broader context of medialisation, the increasing permeation of daily life by media. This is where observations about the transnationality of the Indian marriage market gain importance. The analysis of different television commercials commissioned by BharatMatrimony.com has illustrated the attempt of medially integrating the diaspora. Recurring motifs include negotiations of 'Indianness' and the condemnation of Westernisation. The analysed TV spots further exemplify how the performance of 'Indianness' is tied to an increasing emphasis on traditionality and religiosity. Deterritorialisation and the mediated ideal of Global Indianness do not necessarily result in less or more traditional approaches towards marriage matchmaking. The imagery of the Indian online matrimonial market rather shows an eclectic amalgamation of contrasting tendencies and hence the tensions of post-colonial India in a transitional phase. Promotional images of young women and couples visually represent the—at times starkly conflicting—individual desires and social expectations that are tied to the process of partner selection in a globalising India.

Notes

1. Apart from explicitly Indian websites, transregional Muslim matchmaking websites represent a noticeable percentage.
2. See also Internet World Stats.
3. Most users are located in Mumbai (17 per cent), followed by Delhi (16 per cent) and Chennai, Kolkata and Bangalore (5–6 per cent). See: IAMAI (2006: 3–4).
4. *Shaadi* (Hindi): Marriage; Bharat (Hindi): India; *Jeevansathi* (Hindi): Life Partner.
5. The founder and CEO of the company, Murugavel Janakiraman, hails from Chennai and started his business in the city. His prime target region was initially South India and the respective diaspora but it soon expanded. Today, BharatMatrimony.com's stronghold in South India is evidenced by the higher differentiation in South Indian community affiliations candidates can choose from in the search engine and a higher number of registered users from non-Hindi-speaking regions.
6. My research on the Indian online matrimonial market included around 30 interviews with users and media professionals in India between 2008 and 2010.
7. www.patelvivah.com
8. www.kutchilohana.com
9. http://shaadi.brahmakshatriya.com
10. Match Tech: www.SimplyMarry.com/matchtech (accessed on 2 September 2011).
11. Original interview translated from Hindi by Rohit Bhatia.

12. Medialisation is a theory that describes how media increasingly shape and frame all social, political and economic processes. It means a growing permeation of daily life by media. See Hepp (2010, 2012), Krotz (2007), Meyen (2009) and Schneider (2012).
13. For a research overview on critical theory and public relations, see Mickey (2003: 7–10).
14. See Titzmann (2011a, 2011b) for an in-depth analysis of interviews with users and producers.
15. Cupid Media is one of the leading companies offering online dating. It operates dating sites specialised along ethnic, religious, lifestyle and other preferences: www.cupidmedia.com (accessed on 11 June 2012).
16. Here, the website offers a choice of religious and regional categories as well as the option 'doesn't matter' that also exists for the categories marital status and country.
17. BharatMatrimony.com too operates a sub-site 'for People With Special Needs': www.abilitymatrimony.com (accessed on 5 April 2012).
18. See www.USAshaadi.com, NRI Gujarati Marriage Bureau, Toronto, Canada/ New Jersey, USA (www.nrigujarati.com/matrimonial/index.php), 'Canada's Matrimonial Website specialising in Punjabi Marriages', Vancouver, Canada (www.vichola.com).
19. See www.rastogiworld.com (Rastogi: North Indian Hindu Caste), www.kapumatrimony.com (Kapu caste, prevalent in Andhra Pradesh) and www.patelvivah.org (Patel caste, prevalent in Gujarat).
20. Community portals have been researched primarily in contexts of diasporic media use (see Bernal 2010; Mitra 2005). Though they do not represent a pure 'diaspora medium', but usually include the 'region of origin' and its local population too. Parham (2004) demonstrates these dynamics taking the example of the Global Haiti Village forums.
21. Uttaranchal.ws: community on the web.
22. Uttarakhand.org.in: connecting uttarakhand worldwide.
23. See the list of online community portals under references.
24. The True Stories for Hindi Matrimonials and Urdu Matrimonials were derived from http://www.shaadi.com in December 2009. They are not online anymore.
25. See www.communitymatrimony.com (accessed on 23 October 2013).
26. Main page CommunityMatrimony.com (accessed on 12 December 2012).
27. Community Matrimony TV Commercial.
28. Intermediality refers to the interconnectedness of modern media. An intermedia product describes the usage of two or more media forms within the same context. It includes mixed and hybrid media, media transfer (e.g., film adaptations of literature) and intermedia references (Rajewsky 2002).
29. Religious and regional criteria are often combined: parivarthan.com (South Indian Brahmins); TrinityMatrimony.com (Keralite Christians); kapumatrimony.com (Kapu caste from Andhra Pradesh); rastogiworld.com (North Indian Rastogi caste).
30. www.elitematrimony.com (accessed on 5 September 2011).
31. Elitematrimony.com TV commercial.
32. See Elite Matrimony TV Commercial, https://www.youtube.com/watch?v=EfauOhHtyo4 (accessed on 2 March 2017).
33. www.SimplyMarry.com/matrimonial/humtum
34. The *Sunday Times*, Mumbai, 7 March 2010, 12.
35. Techie Buzz (2010). Website: www.speakingtree.in

36. www.SimplyMarry.com/matrimonial/soulmate
37. See *HUM = TUM*: Equality in heart, equality in marriage! http://www.simplymarry.com/matrimonial/humtum (accessed on 2 March 2017).
38. TV Spots GujaratiMatrimony and PunjabiMatrimony.
39. The analysed profiles were created by women of Indian origin from: USA (6), United Arab Emirates (3), Great Britain (2), Saudi Arabia (2), Singapore (2), Malaysia, Canada, New Zealand, Australia and Switzerland.
40. Popular Hindi cinema plays an important role in the image construction of the NRI as desirable Globo-Indian. The movie *Dilwale Dulhaniya Le Jayenge* (1995, Aditya Chopra) marked the beginning of a positive depiction of Indian migrants in Bollywood cinema (Athique 2011: 5; Bhatia and Ram 2012: 85). Essential motifs include the protagonists' longing for their homeland, the fear of losing their cultural values and the wish to preserve their 'Indianness'.
41. The images were online in October 2010. Glagna.com ceased to exist in late 2011.

References

Arvidsson, Adam. 2006. '"Quality Singles": Internet Dating and the Work of Fantasy'. *New Media & Society* 8 (4): 671–90.

Athique, Adrian. 2011. 'Diasporic Audiences and Non-Resident Media: The Case of Indian Film'. *Participations: Journal of Audience & Reception Studies* 8 (2): 1–23.

Bernal, Victoria. 2010. 'Diasporas and Cyberspace'. In *Diasporas: Concepts, Intersections, Identities*, edited by Kim Knott and Sean McLoughlin, pp. 167–71. London: Zed.

Bhatia, Sunil, and Anjali Ram. 2012. 'Destiny's Children: Mediated Selves and Ambiguous Identities in the Indian Diaspora in the U.S.'. In *India in the World since 1947: National and Transnational Perspectives*, edited by Andreas Hilger and Corinna R. Unger, pp. 77–98. Frankfurt am Main: Peter Lang.

Chaudhuri, Maitrayee. 2001. 'Gender and Advertisements. The Rhetoric of Globalization'. *Women's Studies International Forum* 24 (3–4): 373–85.

Diminescu, Dana, and Matthieu Renault. 2011. 'The Matrimonial Web of Migrants: The Economics of Profiling as a New Form of Ethnic Business'. *Social Science Information* 50 (3–4): 678–704.

Dörner, Andreas. 2001. *Politainment: Politik in der medialen Erlebnisgesellschaft* [*Politainment. Politics in the Medialised Thrill-Seeking Society*]. Frankfurt am Main: Suhrkamp.

Fernandes, Leela. 2000. 'Nationalizing "the Global". Media Images, Cultural Politics and the Middle Class in India'. *Media, Culture & So*ciety 22 (5): 611–28.

Hepp, Andreas. 2010. 'Mediatisierung und Kulturwandel: Kulturelle Kontextfelder und die Prägkräfte der Medien' ['Mediatisation and Cultural Change: Cultural Context Fields and the Moulding Forces of Media]. In *Die Mediatisierung der Alltagswelt: Festschrift zu Ehren von Friedrich Krotz* [*The Mediatisation of the Every Day World. Festschrift in Honour of Friedrich Krotz*], edited by Maren Hartmann and Andreas Hepp, pp. 65–84. Wiesbaden: Verlag für Sozialwissenschaften.

———. 2012. 'Mediatization and the "Molding Force" of the Media'. *Communications—The European Journal of Communication Research* 37 (1): 1–28.

Internet and Mobile Association of India (IAMAI). 2006. 'IAMAI's Report on Matrimonial Search "2006"'. *Report Submitted by the Internet & Mobile Association of India*. Accessed on 20 October 2009 at http://www.iamai.in/Research.aspx?Fileid=r11_home.htm

———. 2012. 'Internet in Urban India'. *Report Submitted by the Internet & Mobile Association of India*. Accessed on 14 January 2013 at http://www.iamai.in/rsh_pay.aspx?rid=HYyJvKsox0I=

Internet World Stats. 2012. *Usage and Population Statistics (2012): Top 20 Internet Countries by Users—2012 Q2*. Accessed on 12 December 2012 at http://www.internetworldstats.com/top20.htm

Jha, Sonora, and Mara Adelman. 2009. 'Looking for Love in All the White Places: A Study of Skin Color Preferences on Indian Matrimonial and Mate-Seeking Websites'. *Studies in South Asian Film and Media* 1 (1): 65–83.

Krotz, Friedrich. 2007. *Mediatisierung. Fallstudien zum Wandel von Kommunikation* [*Mediatisation. Case Studies on Changing Communication*]. Wiesbaden: VS Verlag.

Lekhni. 2011. 'Why I dislike the Bharat Matrimony Ad'. *The Imagined Universe*. Accessed on 3 October 2012 at http://elekhni.com/2011/02/why-i-dislike-the-bharat-matrimony-ad

Mae, Michiko. 2007. 'Auf dem Weg zu einer transkulturellen Genderforschung' ['En Route to Transcultural Gender Research']. In *Transkulturelle Genderforschung. Ein Studienbuch zum Verhältnis von Kultur und Geschlecht* [*Transcultural Gender Research. A Study Book on the Relation of Culture and Gender*], edited by Michiko Mae and Britta Saal, pp. 37–51. Wiesbaden: Verlag für Sozialwissenschaften.

Majumdar, Rochona. 2004. 'Looking for Brides and Grooms. *Ghataks*, Matrimonials, and the Marriage Market in Colonial Calcutta, circa 1875–1940'. *The Journal of Asian Studies* 63 (4): 911–35.

Mankekar, Purnima. 1999. *Screening Culture, Viewing Politics. An Ethnography of Television, Womanhood, and Nation in Postcolonial India*. Durham, NC: Duke University Press.

———. 2004. 'Dangerous Desires: Television and Erotics in Late Twentieth-Century India'. *The Journal of Asian Studies* 63 (2): 403–31.

———. 2009. '"Women-Oriented" Narratives and the New Indian Woman'. In *The Indian Public Sphere. Readings in Media History*, edited by Arvind Rajagopal, pp. 135–50. New Delhi: Oxford University Press.

Meyen, Michael. 2009. 'Medialisierung' ['Medialisation']. *Medien & Kommunikationswissenschaft* [*Media and Communication Science*], 57 (1): 23–38.

Mickey, Thomas J. 2003. *Deconstructing Public Relations: Public Relations Criticism*. Mahwah, London: LEA.

Mitra, Ananda. 2005. 'Creating Immigrant Identities in Cybernetic Space: Examples from a Non-Resident Indian Website'. *Media, Culture & Society* 27 (3): 371–90.

Munshi, Shoma. 2001. 'Marvellous Me: The Beauty Industry and the Construction of the "Modern" Indian Woman'. In *Images of the 'Modern Woman' in Asia: Global Media, Local Meanings*, edited by Shoma Munshi, pp. 78–93. Richmond: Curzon.

Pal, Jiban K. 2010. 'Social Networks Enabling Matrimonial Information Services in India'. *International Journal of Library and Information Science* 2 (4): 54–64.

Parham, Angel Adams. 2004. 'Diaspora, Community, and Communication: Internet Use in Transnational Haiti'. *Global Networks* 4 (2): 199–217.

Pepper, Daniel. 2007. 'Indische Heiratsportale. Per Mausklick zum Eheglück.' *Spiegel online*, 15 April. Accessed on 14 January 2013 at http://www.spiegel.de/netzwelt/web/0,1518,477062,00.html

Puri, Jyoti. 1999. *Woman, Body, Desire in Post-Colonial India: Narratives of Gender and Sexuality*. New York, NY: Routledge.

Rajan, Rajeswari Sunder. 1993. *Real and Imagined Women: Gender, Culture and Postcolonialism*. London: Routledge.

Rajewsky, Irina O. 2002. *Intermedialität* [*Intermediality*]. Tübingen: A. Francke.

Runkle, Susan. 2004. 'Manufactured Beauties: India's Integration into the Global Beauty Industry'. *Manushi* (143): 14–24.

Sahlins, Marshall. 1999. 'What is Anthropological Enlightenment? Some Lessons of the Twentieth Century'. *Annual Review of Anthropology* 28: i–xxiii.

Schneider, Nadja-Christian. 2005. *Zur Darstellung von 'Kultur' und 'kultureller Differenz' im indischen Mediensystem. Die indische Presse und die Repräsentation des Islams im Rahmen der Zivilrechtsdebatte, 1985–87 und 2003* [*About the Depiction of 'Culture' and 'Cultural Difference' in the Indian Media System. The Indian Press and the Representation of Islam during the Civil Law Debate, 1985–87 and 2003*]. Berlin: Logos-Verlag.

———. 2007. 'Medienpluralismus in Indien. Fernsehen, Presse und Hörfunk entwickeln sich dynamisch' ['Media Pluralism in India. Television, Press and Radio Develop Dynamically']. *Bundeszentrale für politische Bildung* [*Federal Center for Political Education*]. Accessed on 23 October 2013. http://www.bpb.de/themen/IBDE4P,0,0,Medienpluralismus_in_Indien.html

———. 2012. 'The Medialisation of Post-Colonial Indian Society: National and Transnational Dynamics'. In *India in the World since 1947: National and Transnational Perspectives*, edited by Andreas Hilger and Corinna R. Unger, pp. 236–58. Frankfurt am Main: Peter Lang.

Schneider, Nadja-Christina, and Bettina Gräf. 2010. 'Tagungsbericht. Zeit für Medialisierung. Medien und transkulturelle Kommunikation in den Islam- und Regionalwissenschaften. 10.04.2010–12.04.2010, Berlin'. *H-Soz-u-Kult*. Accessed on 23 October 2013. http://hsozkult.geschichte.hu-berlin.de/tagungsberichte/id=3148

Sonawat, Reeta. 2001. 'Understanding Families in India: A Reflection of Societal Changes'. *Psicologia: Teoria e Pesquisa* 17 (2): 177–86.

Techie buzz. 2010. 'Times Internet Launches Spiritual Social Network'. *Techie Buzz*, 15 December. Accessed on 2 September 2011 at http://techie-buzz.com/india-tech/times-internet-launches-spiritual-social-network-speakingtree-in.html

Titzmann, Fritzi-Marie. 2011a. 'Medialisation and Social Change: The Indian Online Matrimonial Market as a New Field of Research'. In *Social Dynamics 2.0: Researching Change in Times of Media Convergence. Case Studies from the Middle East and Asia*, edited by Nadja-Christina Schneider and Bettina Gräf, pp. 49–66. Berlin: Frank & Timme.

———. 2011b. 'Matchmaking 2.0: The Representation of Women and Female Agency in the Indian Online Matrimonial Market'. *Internationales Asienforum: International Quarterly for Asian Studies* 42 (3–4): 239–56.

Uberoi, Patricia. 2001. 'Imagining the Family: An Ethnography of Viewing Hum Aapke Hain Koun … !'. In *Pleasure and the Nation: The History, Politics and Consumption of Public Culture in India*, edited by Rachel Dwyer and Christopher Pinney, pp. 309–51. New Delhi: Oxford University Press.

Whitty, Monica T., Andrea J. Baker, and James A. Inman, eds. 2007. *Online Matchmaking*. Basingstoke: Palgrave Macmillan.

Matrimonial Websites and Related Internet Sources

Community Matrimony TV Commercial. Accessed on 12 December 2012 at www.communitymatrimony.com/site/index.php?act=tv_commercial

Elitematrimony.com TV commercial. Accessed on 7 September 2013 at http://www.youtube.com/watch?v=EfauOhHtyo4

HumTum. Accessed on 10 January 2013 at www.SimplyMarry.com/matrimonial/humtum

Shaadi.com True Stories (cited version). Accessed on 17 September 2011 at www.shaadi.com/introduction/true-stories.php

Shaadi.com True Stories (new version). Accessed on 10 January 2013 at www.shaadi.com/introduction/index/true-stories

Soulmate Matrimonials. Accessed on 12 December 2012 at www.SimplyMarry.com/matrimonial/soulmate

www.40plusmatrimony.com (accessed on 23 October 2013)

www.abilitymatrimony.com (accessed on 23 October 2013)

www.bharatmatrimony.com (accessed on 23 October 2013)

www.brahmakshatriya.com (accessed on 23 October 2013)

www.communitymatrimony.com (accessed on 23 October 2013)

www.divorceematrimony.com (accessed on 23 October 2013)

www.elitematrimony.com (accessed on 23 October 2013)

www.glagna.com (accessed on 23 October 2013)

www.gujaratimatrimony.com (accessed on 23 October 2013)

www.gujjumatch.com (accessed on 23 October 2013)

www.indianmatrimonials.com (accessed on 23 October 2013)

www.jeevansathi.com (accessed on 23 October 2013)

www.kapumatrimony.com (accessed on 23 October 2013)

www.klassicmatch.com (accessed on 23 October 2013)

www.kutchilohana.com (accessed on 23 October 2013)

www.lifepartnerindia.com (accessed on 23 October 2013)

www.marryagain.com (accessed on 23 October 2013)

www.matrisearch.com (accessed on 23 October 2013)

www.merasathi.com (accessed on 23 October 2013)

www.nikah.com (accessed on 23 October 2013)

www.nrigujarati.com/matrimonial/index.php (accessed on 23 October 2013)

www.parinay.com (accessed on 23 October 2013)

www.parivarthan.com (accessed on 23 October 2013)

www.patelvivah.com (accessed on 23 October 2013)

www.pavitravivah.com (accessed on 23 October 2013)

www.privilegematrimony.com (accessed on 23 October 2013)

www.punjabimatrimony.com (accessed on 23 October 2013)

www.pyar.org (accessed on 23 October 2013)

www.rastogiworld.com (accessed on 23 October 2013)

www.secondshaadi.com (accessed on 23 October 2013)

www.shaadi.com (accessed on 23 October 2013)

www.shadi.com (accessed on 23 October 2013)

www.sikhingyou.com (accessed on 23 October 2013)

www.simplymarry.com (accessed on 23 October 2013)
www.trinitymatrimony.com (accessed on 23 October 2013)
www.usashaadi.com (accessed on 23 October 2013)
www.vichola.com (accessed on 23 October 2013)

Online Community Portals

BangaliNET, a home away from home. Accessed on 10 January 2013 at www.bangalinet.com

Columbus Tamil Sangam. Accessed on 10 January 2013 at www.columbusthamilsangam.org

Gujarati Arya Association Leicester. Accessed on 10 January 2013 at www.gaa-leicester.com

NriGujarati.co.in. Accessed on 29 September 2011 at www.nrigujarati.co.in

Odia Khatti. First social networking site of Odisha. Accessed on 10 January 2013 at khatti.fullorissa.com

Punjabi Community Halle e.V. Accessed on 10 January 2013 at www.punjabi-community.de.tl

Tamil Community Housing Association. Accessed on 10 January 2013 at www.tamilhousing.org.uk

Uttarakhand.org.in, connecting uttarakhand worldwide. Accessed on 10 January 2013 at www.uttarakhand.org.in

Uttaranchal.ws, community on the web. Accessed on 10 January 2013 at www.uttaranchal.ws

Part IV

Pictorial Politics

9

A Museum, a Memorial, and a Martyr: Politics of Memory in the Sikh Golden Temple[1]

Radhika Chopra

In May 2013 a memorial was inaugurated within the Darbar Sahib complex. Ostensibly devoted to memorializing the carnage during Operation Bluestar, the inscription on the entrance suggests clearly that this is a memorial dedicated to the memory of the controversial Khalistani militant, Jarnail Singh Bhindranwale. The significance of this memorial lies in its location within a sacred space. The tussle for prestige between the sacred complex and the memorial indicates that it is not the sanctity of spaces that is at issue here—it is their ability to secure memory and therefore their pre-eminence as mnemonic spaces that remains unresolved. The discord that preceded the unveiling of this memorial lays bare the politics that continue to haunt remembrance of the Khalistan movement and its key militant-martyr.

Ruckus in Punjab House over memorial

(*The Tribune*, June 22, 2012)

Punjab assembly adjourned twice over Bluestar memorial.

(*Times of India*, June 22, 2012)

The overwrought language of newspaper headlines and television news coverage are often an indication of the controversial nature of events. The occasion for the 'ruckus' in the legislative assembly reported by local and national dailies was the announcement of a plan to build a memorial within the sacred space of the Darbar Sahib complex and its eponymous Golden Temple—an ostensible shrine within a shrine. Bricks were ritually laid by the head priests of the five *takhts* or 'seats' of Sikhism, to denote intent. Many claimed that building the memorial within the Darbar Sahib would destabilise the hard-won peace finally achieved in the aftermath of militancy. The Punjab Chief Minister responded to the uproar against the plan assuring agitated legislators that 'the memorial will be just like a *gurudwara* where a Granth Sahib will be placed and there will be no photographs of anyone' (*The Pioneer*, June 22, 2012), and it would be dedicated as a *yadgar*—a memorial—to all those who died during Operation Bluestar, the Indian Army operation within the sacred space of the Darbar Sahi.

The Chief Minister's statement specifically demarcated two objects of anxiety—the style of the memorial and what would be placed inside. The swiftness with which he responded indicated the more generalised anxiety that surrounds memorials and remembrance of a particularly violent period in the modern history and politics of Punjab—and indeed of the Indian nation state—popularly known as the Khalistan period or the militant decades and the need to stabilise the memories of that troublesome period. The fear that this memorial would undermine authorised memories clearly lay at the root of the ruckus in the legislative assembly. Despite the vociferous objections, less than a year later the structure was completed and the 'inaugural' ritual was performed. The anticipated photographs were not there; but an image of the militant leader Bhindranwale appeared on the face of a clock placed within the memorial (quickly removed by the Gurudwara authorities), and his is the only name carved on a legend above an archway. The legend indubitably orients the memorial towards 'Shaheed Sant Giani Jarnail Singh Khalsa Bhindranwale', and only secondarily commemorates the '*samuh shahidan*', all those who had died during the army assault (Figure 9.1). To understand why the face on the clock and the martyr named in the inscription are thought to be particularly problematic, it is important to unravel—at least in some measure—the 'pre-history' of this memorial. Why has this memorial created such a stir?

Memorials, such as this one, that are erected to mark contentious events become controversial because they dispute official narratives of events (Young 1993) and expose 'the tension between established commemorative practice and emergent political concerns' (Zerubavel 1995, 147). Controversy and commemoration walk hand-in-hand during rituals performed at the site of these memorials, so that ritual performance and physical layout conjointly become a chronicle, enunciating what is to be remembered or eclipsed (Blair 2004). As a manifestation of the past a memorial is deeply entrenched in the present and its meanings

Figure 9.1

Inscription at the entrance to the new martyr's memorial, Darbar Sahib, May 2013

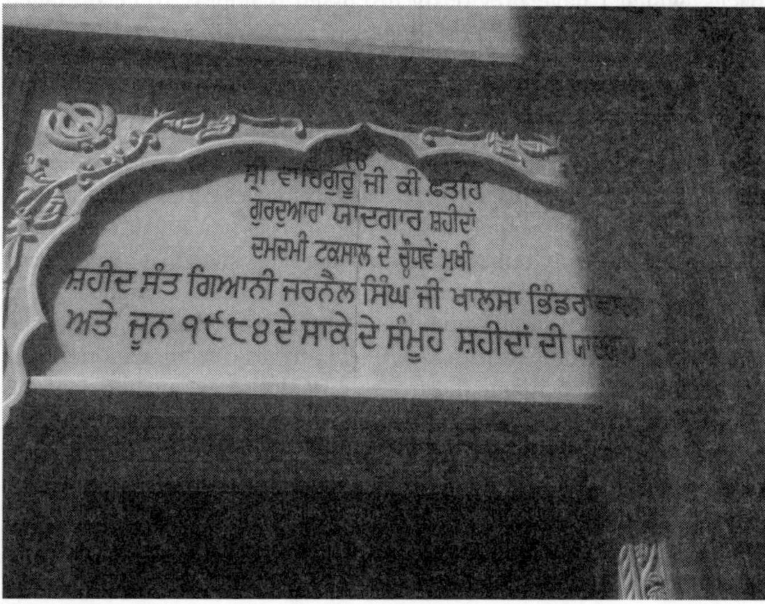

Source: Photograph taken by author.

are continuously 'opened' through the dialectics between flexible pasts and volatile presents that reconfigure them (Battaglia 1992). Rituals of commemorations aside, there is also the materiality of a memorial. A plaque, a shrine, a festschrift or a memorial lecture are purposive and 'active', but also distinctive in the manner they evoke or elide memory. As a mode of inscription, the laying of bricks for a memorial *gurudwara* within the Darbar Sahib complex in 2012 actively sought to orient builders and believers towards two sets of sacred spaces, but also to weave these spaces together. As an imagined architectural text, the controversial memorial *gurudwara* is tethered to the built environs of the Darbar Sahib and its treasured memories. But it is also disruptive because it exceeds the space within which it is located. The uproar generated by the mere act of brick laying gestures towards the capacity of the 'forbidden' and the controversial to alter and transcend its own idiosyncrasy subvert the terms of debate and vigorously reorient remembrance and forgetting.

I would argue therefore that commemorative performances of *Ghallughara Dihara*—or day of carnage—across local and transnational spaces, which I have previously discussed (Chopra 2011), presaged the act of brick laying for this *yadgari* or memorial. The *Ghallughara Dihara*, a post-1990s commemorative ritual inserted into the ceremonial calendar, produced the Darbar Sahib as a memorial space enfolding an entire community. The act of brick laying diluted this claim, disputing the inclusiveness of commemoration, seeming to contend that *ghallughara* as enacted is in fact a 'partial account' that accentuates certain memories of loss as vital while deliberately casting out others as unwanted. The charge of the partial quality of remembrance and the suggestion that *ghallughara* was 'not enough' to commemorate the carnage generated demands more comprehensive memorialisation. Quite apart from remembrance at the specific location of the Darbar Sahib, other forms of commemoration in spatially distinct mnemonic theatres projected discrete memories of the event and the period. The charge of incompleteness emanated not only from among the supporters of Khalistan, but also from the Indian state, which in its turn configured particular memories as paramount. Both the memorials for Indira Gandhi, at her home where she was assassinated and at the cremation site along the banks of the Yamuna,[2] make legible a wholly different rhetoric of remembrance, literally pitting these memorial spaces and anniversaries against the memories evoked within the commemorative ritual of *Ghallughara Dihara*. Equally, widows of men killed in the Delhi riots of 1984 professed a victimhood that could not be encased with Bluestar memorialisation.[3]

Here, my focus is on the controversies around the commemorations for Khalistan's key leader, Jarnail Singh Bhindranwale, and the uneasy but compelling charisma he embodied. The commemorations enacted in the first week of June within the Darbar Sahib complex that 'remember' Operation Bluestar, make little reference to Bhindranwale who was killed during the army operation, along with other supporters. In part, this may have had to do with the fact that for a number of years following his death in 1984 the Indian state prohibited any construction of a memorial in his name. Even more than state prohibition, however, the continual allusion to the destroyed *Akal Takht* in *ghallughara* commemorations and the simultaneous eclipse of Bhindranwale suggest that remembering him posed a dilemma for many within the Sikh community as much as it did for the state. Within the Darbar Sahib, remembrance of the destruction of the sacred complex was enunciated in a familiar language of ritual and in museum portraiture. No one, however, seemed quite certain what constituted Bhindranwale's or legacy or how to remember him. Uncertainty produced idiosyncratic commemorative forms—a protest against the head of a sect, Ram Rahim of the Dera Saccha Sauda, for example, was an occasion to circulate CDs of Bhindranwale's speeches; demands for political asylum in the UK have projected his image as an embodiment of political dispossession. His uncertain legacy produced an ambient sense of fear about the repercussion of memorialising him, so that when the bricks for a memorial were laid in the Darbar Sahib in 2012, over a quarter of a century after his death, chaos reigned. A contest over commemoration, overtly focusing on 'styles' of remembrance but underwritten by apprehension of unrest, seems germane to this controversy. Legislators feared that evoking Bhindranwale would be inflammatory, and having his photograph within a protected sacred space would confer upon his memory the potential to legitimate militant violence and convert it to heroic history. The Chief Minister's publicly announced prohibition of photographs in the proposed memorial needs to be understood as a recognition of the complexity of remembering Bhindranwale, and also perhaps as a declarative challenge to the priests who laid the bricks that they could go so far but no further and the state still retained the right to forbid specific objects and artefacts from being placed in the memorial *gurudwara*. The statement vacillating between warning and appeasement might also be construed as an acknowledgement of the problem of asserting secular and state control within a sacred space that still retains marks of the military assault and remembers the bloodshed.

The assurance that photographs would be prohibited in the new memorial seems to signal an unwitting acknowledgement of the popularity and power of photographs of Bhindranwale already circulating in the bazaars of Amritsar. The possibility of such images moving from bazaar spaces to sacred shrines is clearly unsettling, for the bazaar view of the sacred is unlikely to follow prescribed paths of memory. The challenge this memorial offers therefore exists at various registers. For the Indian state, the challenge is how to allow remembrance without putting itself in the dock for a state supported pogrom against Sikhs in Delhi; for the orthodox establishment of the Darbar Sahib, the test is how to contain Bhindranwale within a non-toxic discourse of martyrdom and to restrain the act of commemoration within predictable limits, by merging him with all other Bluestar martyrs and denying him an exclusive place in collective memory. For believers of the faith, commemoration is itself the challenge, for it poses the question of how to move beyond the experiences of a violent past and still celebrate militant passion embedded in the tenets of Nanak's game of love espoused in the scriptural verse—*Jau tau prem khelan ka chao. Sir dhar tali gali mori aao* (If you want to play the game of love, approach me with your head on the palm of your hand; Guru Granth Sahib 1412; Fenech 1997, 630); 'O people, death is not called bad if one knows how to die, blessed is the death of heroic men' (*maranu munasam suridm hakku hai* Guru Granth Sahib 579; Fenech 1997, 631).

Forms of Remembrance

Germane to anxiety is material form. The fact that the memorial took the shape of a *gurudwara* is central to the issue of remembering Bhindranwale. Evocative of usurpations that Weber spoke of so eloquently in his discussions of illegitimacy and domination, the usurpation of sacred space and seizure of memory set apart the birth of this memorial from other formally sanctioned sacred structures—for in its material form this is a *gurudwara* within a *gurudwara*, a shrine within a shrine. In the scriptural religion of Sikhism, sacred texts are housed within *gurudwaras*—or 'gateways' (*dwara*) to the divine. The most well known is the Darbar Sahib, in the city of Amritsar, with its eponymous Golden Temple. *Gurudwaras* and *takhts*, as seats of religious authority, are also places for acknowledged *shaheeds* or martyrs, who have a special place in Sikhism. As a religion born in ferment and resistance to the imperial Mughal state, its medieval *gurus* or spiritual spokesmen were deemed saint soldiers, a key concept in Sikhism since the fifteenth century (Fenech 1997, 2001; Macleod 1995). In the same vein, Sikh *shaheed* who died in defence of the faith provide testimony of their *sahadat,* their faith, and with their blood. Sacred space shared by scripture and *shaheed* imagine the latter as endowed with a powerful commitment to the Sikh faith, its doctrines, symbols, and its Gurus (Fenech 1997). Commemorative days and memorials are important sites for remembering *shaheed*; for Sikhs the *Ardas,* the prayer to divine authority that marks the end of any religious occasion is the most spectacular form of remembrance. The grace and virtues of Gurus and martyrs alike are 'remembered' in *Ardas*. Collectively recited in a ritually specified fashion, facing the scriptural text with folded hands, etymology links the prayer to the Persian *arz-dasht* or petition, so that the *Ardas* is simultaneously supplication and application. While some aspects of the recitation are mandatory, variant versions exist and within them 'personal or community intercessions are offered. They are usually brief and follow no set text' (Mcleod 2009, 19). Speculatively speaking, I would imagine that part of the unease generated by the memorial *gurudwara* centres on the possible evocations and petitions of the *Ardas* offered within this memorial shrine, to rival the formality of the *Ardas* recited in the forecourt of the *Akal Takht*.

While Sikh Gurus and martyrs are both linked to histories of religious persecution and political resistance, the critical difference between Gurus and martyrs is the closure of the line of succession of Gurus in 1699 and the transference of religious authority to the scriptural text.[4] With the closure of succession, martyrs, along with Babas, Pirs and Sants, and other religious heads of sects and institutional *deras*, or places of worship constitute the mobile terrains of religious observance as producers of piety. Highly valued in Sikhism well beyond the medieval period, martyrs continue to be created in response to contemporary politics or social conditions. Like Guru Janamsakhis, chronicles of martyrs, become critical texts, with carefully assembled images and symbols that hark back to recognisable historical landscapes, while incorporating newer events. Some visual representations approximate the *mazhbi tasveeran* or religious portraits of *sants*, *babas*, and *pirs*. It is possible to argue perhaps that just as in *janamsakhis* or hagiographies Guru Nanak becomes synecdoche for all gurus who appear in scriptural referencing as 'Light of Nanak' in the visual idiom of religious portraits or *mazhbi tasveeran*, some historical figures like Baba Deep Singh became synecdoches for martyrs in general. Even more interestingly, it is possible to argue that the images of shrines appeared as the synecdoche for the martyr. Representations of martyrs draw on this manufacture of charisma in the printed medium of the poster, or other pictorial representations, posed against the place of their martyrdom (Bilu and Ben-Ari 1992; Frembgen 1998). *Mazhbi tasveeran* in their printed or painted form become objects of veneration, creating a close relationship between devotee and martyr, who touch the *tasveer* with their foreheads or hang them in homes in special set apart spaces on walls. Sold at shrines or during days of commemoration, chronicles, posters, artefacts, and souvenirs become the stuff of pious observances to tangibly demonstrate belief. As symbolic and sacred objects, such representations acquire the power to bestow blessings and create an animation towards specific local events or places. Not necessarily organised, this *bricolage* of mementoes reconfigure unconnected memories into utterances of social disaffection (Margry and Sanchez-Carretero 2011, 4). Well before the bricks were laid, images of Bhindranwale in posters, calendars, and vinyl transfer graphics for windows and vehicles unfolded across various public spaces as 'grassroots memorials' (Margry and Sanchez-Carretero 2011) circulating during transnational commemorations or distributed as pamphlets denouncing the sectarian head of the Dera Saccha Sauda (Baixas and Simon 2008) creating aural and pictorial chronicles for Bhindranwale as martyr.

Grassroots memorials are not the only form of chronicles and pictorial representations of martyrs; nor are street corners the only places where they are found. *Tasveers* of *pirs* and *shaheeds* are also present in the museum within the sacred complex of the Darbar Sahib, sharing gallery space with paintings of events in the lives of the 10 Gurus. Given its location and its holdings of sacred art, this museum is treated as sacrosanct space, a home for revered beings and sacred things. It approximates a memorial of sorts since it houses chronicles of Gurus and of martyrs who died defending the *Akal Takht* and the Darbar Sahib in medieval and modern history, and those who died defending other places of their faith. The museum therefore is a space where belief and historical events are woven together into a visual chronicle of an embattled community and its defence against suppressive states. The various images in the museum suggest that these paintings are more than exhibits—they are *mazhbi tasveeran* meant to be viewed as devotional objects evoking belief, memory, and history all at once. The fact that the many different sites of sacredness appear in the paintings of the museum, with images of different martyrs who died defending them, does not in any way disturb the pre-eminence of the Darbar Sahib, the *Akal Takht*, and the Harmandir: quite the reverse. The veneration is a continuous process, but it seems to culminate towards a specific architectured space of sacredness, the Darbar Sahib and the Harmandir within.

At the same time, walking through the Darbar Sahib and its museum, it seems as if the holdings of the museum herald the coming of the memorial *gurudwara*, and those memorialised within. As a commemorative space, the museum was—and remains—subordinate to the sacred space within which it is encompassed. But it is by no means clear to me that the pre-eminence of the Darbar Sahib will remain as unassailably fixed *vis-à-vis* the newly constructed memorial *gurudwara*. The uproar in the political assembly denotes the tussle for prestige between the sacred complex and the memorial. It is not the sanctity of spaces that is at issue here—it is their ability to secure memory and therefore their pre-eminence as mnemonic spaces that remain unresolved. The museum was never intended to pose a challenge to the space that houses it; but as a rough draft, it presaged the shrine within the shrine, which now seems to have become the decisive text of memory.

Unravelling the Past of a Memorial

As I said earlier in the paper, and elsewhere (Chopra 2011), the ritual of *Ghallughara Dihara* emphatically emphasises the mutilation of the Darbar Sahib complex in the Bluestar operation as the hurt remembered and the loss to be commemorated. Almost 30 years have passed since that catastrophic week, and there are as many accounts of the event as there are story tellers. Though the death of pilgrims is mourned, collective memory is haunted by the destruction of the sacred complex and the mutilated Takht has become emblematic of the destruction unleashed by Operation Bluestar, its dome repeatedly reproduced in magazine, book covers, posters, calendar art, and poetry, like the fragment of verse reproduced below:

Aaj tappdi bhatti ban gayi,
Mere vehreh di har eenth,
Jithe duniya matha tek di,
Uthe bootan chaddi bhit.
Mere burj munare dha ditte,
Dha ditta Tak-hat Akal…

(Stanza, 'June 1984' n.d.)

Commemorations mourn the death of the Takht and the mass death of pilgrims who died during Operation Bluestar. For years, however, collective commemorations ignored Jarnail Singh Bhindranwale, said to have died sometime during the night of the 5–6 June. Well after the construction of the double sited memorial for Indira Gandhi, an official embargo prohibiting the construction of a martyr's memorial for Bhindranwale remained in place. The official restriction was matched by the subtle sidelining of Bhindranwale in commemorations enacted within the Darbar Sahib that underscored the destruction of the *Akal Takht* as the fundamental loss (Chopra 2011). Elisions within formal commemorations did not remain unnoticed. For almost 20 years following Bluestar, functionaries at the Damdami Taksal, the seminary of which Bhindranwale was head before he fled to take refuge in the Golden Temple complex, produced an alternate interpretation for omitted remembrance—they refused to concede Bhindranwale's death insisting that the Sant was *chardi kala*—in an intensely energised state of high spirits, and repudiated all rituals of mourning (*The Tribune*, May 17, 2001).[5] Cliques within the seminary positioned their refusal to mourn as a counter to state prohibitions. Perhaps the refusal was a denial of normalcy, a rejection of the closures suggested by ritual commemoration that the orthodoxy embraced and the seminary disputed.

I want to delve further into the material manifestations of erasure that whittle away at the exhibits of the Kendri Sikh Ajaib Ghar, the museum within the Darbar Sahib. I turn to the displays and displacements of exhibits and objects within its galleries of the museum to 'see' the acts of remembrance. If the ritual of *Ghallughara Dihara* is a way to remember a traumatic event (Chopra 2011), the reconstruction of the museum throughout the late 1980s and 1990s is a way of restoring history to community. Most writings on sacred art pay attention to the curatorial practices that treat sacred spaces and objects as special, recognising the significance of these objects vested with emotion or the 'spirit' of sacredness, simultaneously recognising that contemporary communities have active relations with their sacred objects, laying claim to them as signifiers of community.[6] Many contemporary museums that house or display religious and sacred art are mindful of 'living' quality of these exhibits. Sometimes, curators of exhibitions consult religious experts or anthropologists to draw up codes of ethics for the treatment and display sacred objects. An exhibition of sacred art in a museum, for example, may evoke, even mime, the spaces of the sacred, harnessing threads of memory that convert the museum gallery into a set apart space (Mauzé and Derlon 2003; Greene 1992; Seligman and Monroe 2006). What is of particular interest to me is the fact that this museum, the Kendri Sikh Ajaib Ghar, is part of a sacred complex already imbued with sanctity.

Beyond the issue of sanctity, objects possess the quality to 'be political' and display authority; they are active in creating and producing cultural, social, religious, and political landscapes. For me, it is both the artefacts and the museum located within the mnemonic space of the Darbar Sahib that demand attention. Location denotes its own understanding of boundaries between the sacred and the political and a reviewing of how things or persons appear as concurrently sacred and political while the act of viewing becomes expressive of belief and political engagement at once. The location of the museum within the sacred complex seems to charge the Ajaib Ghar with a mission—to continue to remember the destruction of sacred things and spaces. Within the complex as seen today, the *Akal Takht* presents a facade of calm continuity. It is the paintings in the museum that keep alive the memory of its mutilation. The Ajaib Ghar is therefore simultaneously museum and memorial, synchronising the pedagogical and the emotive aspects of both. The recitations of *Gurbani* and *Ardas* soar through the museum as an auditory canopy to remember and rehearse sacred history. Visitors enter the museum as believers, barefoot and head covered, as they would Harmandir Sahib, the eponymous Golden Temple, to consolidate a version of Sikh political history that contests the Indian state's narratives of Operation Bluestar. Contemporary politics ricochets off a medieval past, to reappear quickened by the ecstasy of persecution.

Paintings in the museum are an assortment of 'event' and 'biography'. The death of individuals across four broad periods of Sikh history creates a visual narrative of the carnage of pilgrims, beginning with the massacres by Ahmed Shah Durrani in the two *ghallughara*[7] of medieval Sikh history, followed by images of resistance to the colonial state, including the bloodbath at Jallianwala Bagh, deaths during Punjabi Suba agitations organised against the linguistic reorganisation of states in independent India, and finally Operation Bluestar. Paintings of deaths in medieval warfare or historical event are viewed conjointly as *shaeedi tasveeran,* representations of martyrdom; some are hung just below depictions of two major 'battles' in Sikh history, the *Vadda* and *Chotta Ghallughara* (the major and minor carnage) fought against invading Afghans, as well as exhibited below paintings that visually depict assaults on the Golden Temple throughout medieval history. In concert, these 'war paintings' create a visual storyline to present a remembered history of persecution of the faithful, assault on sacred buildings, and martyrs as embodiments of faith and community, where images of torture of the medieval period become the frame and the story of the present (Chopra 2009). Viewing is charged with a purposive intention of remembrance and commemoration, and the viewer converted to witness and storyteller of a particular version of history.

Post-1984 objects and paintings are clearly signposted in an earmarked gallery, including what I call the '1984 wall'. Down the centre of a long gallery, empty tank and bullet shells used in the '*fauji hamla*' (army assault, the popular term for Operation Bluestar) recovered from the walls and debris of the ruined *Akal Takht* are displayed in glass cabinets. They establish the context for the battle of Bluestar. At one end of that gallery, the facing wall, framed by glass cabinets of shells, is dedicated to a 1987 painting of the destroyed Takht, with a caption that unequivocally states '*Sri Akal Takht fauji hamleh toh baad* (6 June 1984)' (The *Akal Takht* after the army assault, 6 June 1984). Painted at the moment of its mutilation, the Takht represents the primal wound to the *sangat*, the community of believers (Covington 2009). The painting is the visual heart of the display, framed by portraits of men who died during Operation Bluestar or were put to death by the Indian state as traitors or assassins (though the captions below describe each man as *Shaheed*). The collective *sangat* of *shaheed* enclose and set apart the wounded Takht as a focal point, centring a viewer's grief, which must not be deflected away from the Takht as the primary corpse. The museum display mirrors the spatial and architectural enclosing of the Harmandir, the sacred centre of the *gurudwara* complex, framed and set apart by a pool of water, still bearing the bullet marks of the Bluestar battle. Within the sacred landscape as we see it now, the living Takht soars as a protective shield of the Harmandir;[8] in the museum we see the wounded Takht, a metaphorical *muh dikhaiyi* or final viewing of the corpse at the moment of death. Displayed at the site of its destruction, the portrait of the Takht provides the story of Bluestar. The portraits and captions of Bluestar martyrs, if I may use the term, are stylistic distinctive, set apart from earlier depictions of martyrdom (Chopra 2009). Death embraced in allegorical laughter, evident in captions, is the story of these martyrs further signified by the fact that while the year of birth is noted without a day or date, the exact date of each man's death is meticulously recorded in the caption because this is the day to remember each by as the day when each displayed their *shahadat*, their commitment to the Sikh faith and its key shrines.

In June 2007, when I first began doing fieldwork in the complex and its museum, Bluestar martyrs framed and protectively enclosed the painting of the mutilated Takht, acting almost as metaphoric pall bearers of this primal corpse. But later that same year, on 29 November 2007, a portrait of Bhindranwale was installed in the museum in what was reported in newspapers as 'a low key ceremony' (*The Tribune*, November 30, 2007). I saw the newspaper and television reports and went back to the museum two years later to see the display. The most striking aspect of the November installation was the displacement of the portraits of Bluestar martyrs away from the central portrait of the Takht. Over the course of the few years since I have been following the museum displays, some of the Bluestar portraits have literally turned the corner away from the Takht—and it is this 'movement' that to my eyes signifies the controversial *tasveer* of a troublesome *sant* that now centres the display.

Like memory, my discussion of remembrance does not follow a neat chronology or move down a clearly demarcated pathway. It cuts through different moments of remembrance and their material manifestations not only because I came upon them at different points in my research, but also because the mnemonic objects did not remain static. Some moved; others came up in discrete corners or were visually centred within the complex and the museum. Simultaneously, the display of Bhindranwale in shop signage grew to dominate the bazaar spaces that surround the sacred complex. Small vinyl images circulated in the streets on the backs of taxis or stuck onto petrol tanks of motorbikes. It is hard to establish whether street art was a response to the installation of the portrait or circulated in sync with the debates generated prior to the installation. In either event, street art had a way of exerting itself on the more formal displays within the museum, particularly upon the singular disposition of the portrait.

Re-entering the spaces of the sacred, it is clear that however elaborate or emotive the museum displays or ritual commemorations of *Ghallughara Dihara* that followed Operation Bluestar, for years a feeling of incompleteness remained. The question 'where is Bhindranwale' hovered remorselessly over the museum exposition. For more than 20 years no paintings of Bhindranwale were exhibited in the Museum; no rituals enacted specifically in his name; and nowhere was his name listed. He is briefly mentioned in the captions detailing the death history of Amrik Singh (Bhindranwale's close associate) and General Shabeg Singh (whose body was found in the forecourt of the *Akal Takht*). These tangential almost muted references were clearly unsatisfactory evocations for a person many identified as the embodiment and animating spirit of Khalistan. The refusal to acknowledge the death sat awkwardly within the larger rituals of post-Bluestar remembrance and memorialisation. Finally, in 2001, a group calling itself the Shahid Sant Jarnail Singh and Holocaust Commemoration Committee announced that it would perform his *antim ardas* at *Akal Takht*, 'in a dignified and peaceful manner' (*The Tribune*, May 17, 2001), countering what they called the 'illogical' refusal of the Damdami Taksal (of which Bhindranwale was head before he fled to the Darbar Sahib) to declare the death of Bhindranwale. The group may have been prompted by the widening circuits within which images of Bhindranwale circulated, including posters, car stickers, calendars, and entrances of Diaspora *gurudwaras*.[9] In 2003, within two years of performance of *antim ardas*, the ritual head of the *Akal Takht* declared Jarnail Singh Bhindranwale a martyr and formally presented a '*siropa*' (a gift for piety) to his eldest son as part of the commemorative rituals in the Darbar Sahib complex, an event widely reported in the local press and some national dailies (*Times of India*, June 6, 2003).

Even after the ritual recognition of his stature as martyr in 2003, it took some years for an official portrait of the slain militant to enter the Kendri Ajaib Ghar, the Central Museum, another delay that suggests the continued disquiet surrounding his memory and the undercurrent of foreboding vis-à-vis the pressure of street art dictating exhibits in sacred space—and its seems to me, the problem of housing him in the Darbar Sahib complex. Nothing was openly stated; but the changing displays in the galleries convey the anxiety about the potential 'living quality' of a portrait, comparable to the sacred potency of religious objects and sacred art, treated as 'culturally sensitive' living things (Mauzé and Derlon 2003; Greene 1992; Seligman and Monroe 2006). From what I could establish, through the period of the post-Bluestar reconstruction of the sacred complex and its museum (which I have discussed elsewhere; Chopra 2011), the image of Bhindranwale lay low in the library adjoining the museum. In a replication perhaps of the state-funded institution, the Nehru Memorial and Museum Library in Delhi, the official memorial of the first Prime Minister of India, the Ajaib Ghar Museum has its own library, though for almost 20 years there seemed to be very little to put in there perhaps because so much of the art and artefacts had been burnt during Bluestar. In the winter of 2006 when I did the first round of fieldwork the library holdings consisted primarily of pamphlets, political tracts, and newspaper or magazine reports, some in Gurmukhi and some in English. For example, the coverage of 1984 in the newsmagazine *India Today* and Raghu Rai's[10] photographs of the aftermath are preserved in the library. It is in this assorted collection that a photographed image of Bhindranwale's corpse was (and is) to be found, available for view only with special and very restrictive permission (Figure 9.2). It seems to be the official portrait of the corpse. In this reproduction present in the museum library, the caption reads: *Shahadat paun toh baad, Sant Jarnail Singh* (Sant Jarnail Singh, after attaining martyrdom).

Figure 9.2

Photograph of a photograph: Bhindranwale's corpse, June 2007

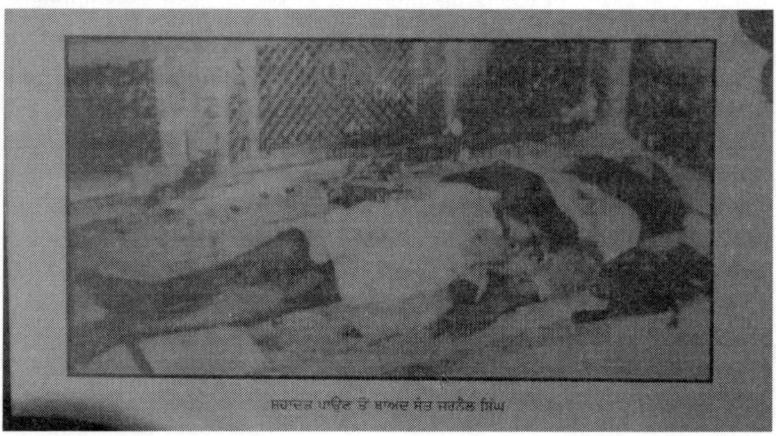

Source: Photograph taken by author.

Portrait of a Martyr

Through the period when the politically charged corpse was unavailable for display of any kind, the fact of death was necessary to establish. The fact also needed a witness. Mr Apar Singh Bajwa, a retired Superintendent of Police and the Chief Investigating Officer in a criminal case against Bhindranwale, was the states key witness to Bhindranwale's death. It is in his witness report that the wounds of the corpse are recorded; the body, Bajwa reported was 'injured on the right side of the face and had bled profusely in the abdomen' (*The Tribune*, Chandigarh, May 20, 2001). In the unattributed photograph in the library, the corpse is formally laid out on a sheet, a ritually mandatory performance of laying the corpse on the ground, but then photographed, which itself is unusual, for corpses are displayed but rarely photographed. In this photograph, the damaged side of his face noted in Bajwa's testimony is not visible to the viewer. This visual elision suggests that it was very likely photographed by army personnel who would have had access to the corpse but would have needed to show it without signs of injury for the treatment of enemy dead has always been an issue in all situations of war and conflict (Neff 2004). It is possible that Bhindranwale's corpse would have been treated with ritual respect by the army under the command of Lt. Gen K.S. Brar, a non-*keshdhari* Sikh, and the photograph taken as evidence of this 'deference' towards enemy dead. Though wounded corpses abound in museum portraiture, each identified in their contextual resistance either to imperial Mughal rule or the colonial state, this is one corpse that makes no reference to 'the enemy'. Despite the evident care taken in photographing and captioning the image, not many museum visitors saw the photograph. Perhaps there was a fear that viewing Bhindranwale's corpse would be too emotive an event, and heighten the commitment to martyrdom and resistance, simultaneously positioning the Indian state's project as an 'imperialist' imposition upon Sikhs, and his body as a metaphor of the wounded Sikh nation (Covington 2009). Perhaps too, this is a photograph that remained hidden because of what images could do—an apprehension voiced by the Chief Minister in 2012, without making any reference to which photograph would be prohibited within the newly cast *gurudwara* memorial.

In late November 2007, supporters of Bhindranwale made concerted attempts to hang his portrait in the Ajaib Ghar. Finally—as mentioned above—the portrait was installed on 29 November 2007 by the Shiromani Gurudawara Prabandhak Committee, in the Ajaib Ghar amidst intense controversy reflected in news reports. The gesture to mute the ceremonial installation was read as an attempt to pre-empt radical Sikh organisations from mounting a portrait depicting Bhindranwale armed with a revolver and other modern weaponry. A newspaper report noted that the low-key ceremony was a way of keeping radical organisations at bay (*The Tribune*, Friday, November 30, 2007). Emerging from 23 years of seclusion into a history of valorous martyrdom, Bhindranwale's formal portrait clearly could not be an image from an army archive. The painting that now hangs in the museum draws from a popular image of Bhindranwale, most evident in street art in which he is shown looking away from the viewer, into the far distance dressed in the attire of a saint soldier. But it is also markedly different from popular photographed images. The portrait painted in 2007 is distinctive at various levels: Bhindranwale stands barefoot on a bank of clouds, in white *choga* and blue *pag* (knee length garment and turban) attire most commonly associated with members of the Damdami Taksal, the fundamentalist seminary of which he was head for a period of time. He bears the *kirpan*, one of the key symbols of Sikh identity, but also touches the hilt of the sword in its elaborate scabbard, a weapon revered for its signification of authority.[11] Across his body he holds a *barsha* or arrow, a weapon he was frequently photographed carrying. Floating in celestial sphere, from where Gods in Indic paintings beam blessings upon mortals, are images of the Harmandir and the *Akal Takht*—the latter edifice shown in its state of pristine wholeness. Between the Takht and the Temple are the triangular saffron flags—*nishan*—that demarcate sacred space. The flags are a critical inclusion; on the face of it they denote the two scared structures that hover on either side of the central figure. But whether intended by the painter or not, they flag not just the religious structures as sacred but, it seems to me, signify the portrait itself as sacred space (Figure 9.3).

The visual elements within the portrait reference a series of portrait styles that have wide circulation. On the one hand, the portrait references the *mazbi tasveerain* of *pirs* and *sants* with key shrines appearing in the visual frame to suggest location and venerations. But the other set of aesthetic styles that are evoked in the painting are images of Sikh Gurus. A brief excursion into the portraiture of gurus is vital to understanding the *bhava* of Bhindranwale's portrait. Seventeenth-century Sikh painting that has become the template for Guru portraiture followed the Mughal miniature stylistics in positioning the Guru as a central figure in profile, with a halo.[12] Medieval painters drew on a range of sources to 'authenticate' their representations. The later Guler or Pahari styles painted many years after the death of the Guru attempted to portray the personal

Figure 9.3

Bhindranwale's portrait, January 2011

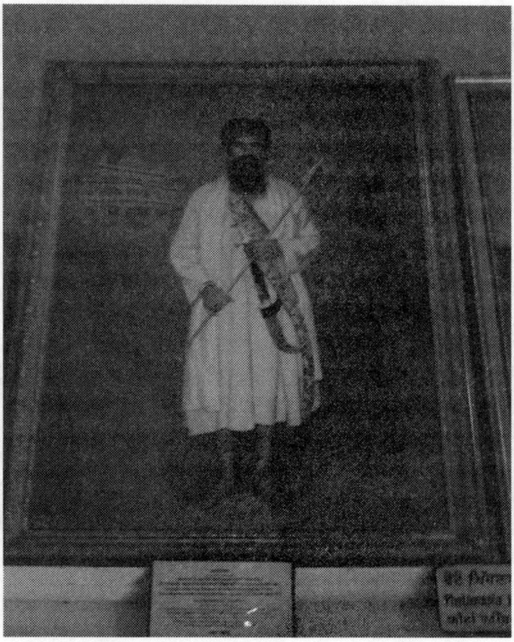

Source: Photograph taken by author.

traits and attributes of Gurus culled from literary and oral traditions. Sometimes the face of the Guru bore a resemblance to the patron who had commissioned the painting (Verma 2002), an element of realism in the portrait that suggests the consonance of power and spirituality. A series of different imageries and knowledge were drawn upon when painting the Gurus, and continue in representations of today. Modern montages and poster art, for example, follow Mughal and Guler styles to align the printed poster with painted portraits.

When the 10 gurus are painted as a collective they are often represented in action as it were, passing on legitimate authority to the Granth Sahib, the Book which is now anthropomorphised as the eleventh guru. The book is treated in all respects like a sacred and royal person, referred to as Sahib, carried in a palanquin, fanned by a *chaur*, a fly whisk, awakened at dawn and put to rest every evening. In the printed image below, the transference of authority and legitimacy upon the book is depicted in the

Figure 9.4

The 10 Gurus and the Granth, Souvenir in Guru Bazaar, Amritsar, May 2013

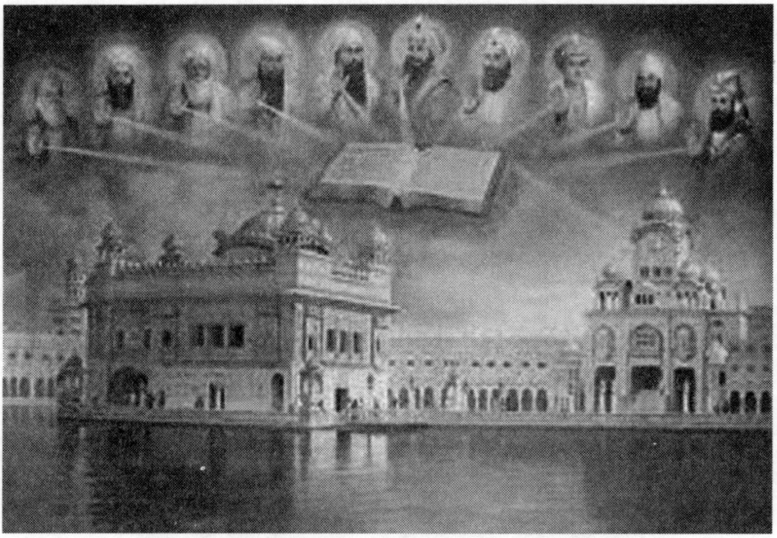

Source: Photograph taken by author.

rays of divine light emanating from the palms of the 10 gurus placed in an arc in cosmological space, rays that suggest the lineage of divinity and authority. The book, journeying between the Harmandir and the Takht in rituals of *prakash* and *sukhasan*, awakening and repose, is the guru housed in the *gurudwara*, the sacred being in sacred space (Figure 9.4).

The portrait of Bhindranwale is a composite of *pir* and *guru* images, drawing on elements of both. Gurinder Pal Singh, the painter of the portrait, seems to have drawn on medieval painters and contemporary printers and possibly on oral accounts and newspaper images, to deploy all the symbolism at his command to suggest the spiritual significance of the man whose portrait he painted. He could not have shown him with a halo for he was neither explicitly a Raja nor a Guru. What he does instead is to displace the halo as divine light onto banks of clouds to suggest a non-mortal, celestial sphere, upon which he places the central figure. Nor, it seems to me, could the painter have depicted him wearing the dual crossed swords of *miri-piri* (temporal and spiritual authority) in mimetic resemblance of Guru Hargobind. That would be overtly sacrilegious. Instead, the painter subtly suggests the two swords by the scabbard of the sword crossed at the centre with the arrow; a weapon Bhindranwale was photographed carrying during his occupation of the *gurudwara* complex from 1982, when he fled to take shelter, to 6 June 1984 the night of his death. Together, the clouds, the placement of the sacred buildings where he died (or died protecting, depending on the viewer's point of view), and the crossed weapons leave the viewer to decipher the *bhava* of this image, and understand the import of the painted message. The line of succession from Guru to Granth apparent in poster art is extended by the painter's placement of the key sacred buildings, linking the lines of cosmic blessing with a further layer—from the Harmandir to the person upon whom cosmic blessings are bestowed. The transference suggests a further movement but this time in reverse: the clouds below the feet seem to elevate the central figure to cosmological space and significance, into the sphere of those occupy divine space—the 10 Gurus.

The portrait is also markedly bigger than any of the other portrait of martyrs, certainly larger and more elaborately framed than any of the Bluestar martyrs. In fact, it is as large as the portrait of the wounded Takht. And it is placed next to it. The display of portraits of the *sangat* of Bluestar martyrs have moved, and then moved again, some turning the corner onto an adjoining wall, accommodating the insertion of the *ustad*, the master, in their midst. One way of interpreting the coupling is to pair the portraits of the man and the monument as a joint sacred centre. And perhaps the way the two portraits are displayed seems to suggest that this juxtaposition was one way museum authorities hoped to effect a containment of memory. In specifying prohibitions of guns and 'modern' weaponry in the commissioned portrait, perhaps the orthodox *gurudwara* establishment hoped to normalise remembrance, making Bhindranwale the defender of the Takht, but the shrine as the emotional centre of remembrance. Any visit to museum makes it clear, however, that Bhindranwale's portrait arouses greater interest. Like emotions aroused by sacred things, the *rasa*[13] of this image sets it apart. An anxious sign at the corner of the portrait fixed some years after the installation prohibits photography in three languages. It is a peculiar sign that forbids one visual form, while permitting another, suggesting an acknowledgement of a hierarchy of pre-eminence between the two images. It does seem to me the sign is a vain attempt to restore a balance between the two images, but the marked concentration of viewers attention unequivocally suggests the relegation of the Takht as mere 'evidence' of Bhindranwale's *shahadat*, and his death as the primal wound suffered by the Sikh nation. The panic provoked by the viewer's photograph reflects the fear of street art and internet communications creating an unpredictable crossing of passion with politics, a destabilisation of authorised memory. The truth of the sign, like the image portrayed, is that it triggers transgress.

Conclusion

The question remains whether in deflecting attention away from commemorations of the destroyed Takht, and converting the architectural mutilation as a metaphor for Bhindranwale's death, the viewing accomplishes more than the *gurudwara* authorities ever imagined when they conceded the demands for installation. Does Bhindranwale remain enclosed within a collective *sangat* of martyrs? Or has he metaphorically stepped out of this collective and risen to another level? It is important to go back to the image once again to discover, in its language of symbols, the potential movement and transformation effected by *rasa* of remembrance. Unlike other Bluestar martyrs, Bhindranwale is 'in action' for while the figure is still, the other elements position the *man* as possessing an exceptional power to surpass other martyrs. It is the way he inhabits sacred space standing dead centre to dwarf the Takht and the Harmandir that is most spectacular. It does not need too much imagination to speculate that the transformation of a political figure to a divine person will require more than a portrait as a tribute; it was only going to be a matter of time for the man to move from being a photographed corpse hidden in an archive to a palpably emotive portrait to a spiritual figure in need to his own space—the memorial *gurudwara*, a shrine within a shrine.

A *gurudwara* within a *gurudwara*, a memorial within a habitus already resonant with memories, are unlikely to exist in harmony. The enclosed memorial is in fact a counter memorial within the memorial space of the Darbar Sahib that challenges and usurps interpretations of the commemorative ritual of *ghallughara* and its pre-2007 museum. Looking at the displayed portraits and their placements, it seems to me that this portrait and the memorial *gurudwara* will present a challenge even more elemental than the performative ritual of *ghallughara*. The portrait housed in a sacred centre might well transform a 'historical personality' (Anderson 1991, 209) into a divine figure. The ruckus in the assembly in 2007 was probably prophetic in voicing a fear about the future shape of memory, and its conversion to a rewritten sacred chronicle. Clearly, the memorial *gurudwara* and its architectural inscriptions will pull the memory of this martyr right out of its frame to violate the tenets of a faith that declares its Gurus fixed and its scripture inviolable. In and through the memorial, a militant will not remain a martyr, but will soar towards the cosmological ether, to craft a place among the chosen 10.

Notes

1. We would like to express our gratitude to Routledge, Taylor & Francis Group for their kind permission to reprint the chapter by Radhika Chopra, first published in 2013 in *Sikh Formations: Religion, Culture, Theory* 9(2): 97–114.
2. The two memorials are at Shakti Sthal, her cremation ground along the banks of the river Yamuna, and at her official residence, No. 1, Safdurjung Road, in the heart of Lutyens' Delhi.
3. In June 2013, a plaque for a memorial to the Delhi riot victims was installed—again amidst intense controversy—in the Rakabganj Gurudwara in central Delhi. The choice of Rakabganj as a place of remembrance of a particularly horrifying event is itself important to analyse, for the *gurudwara* literally faces the Parliament of India, and forces upon the Indian political imagination the right to mourn forgotten victims and their histories.
4. The Granth Sabib as a sacred scripture does not exhaust all forms of knowledge about gurus or those who are venerated within Sikhism. *Janamsakhis*, literally testimonies of birth, but more accurately, hagiographies (McLeod 1994) of Sikh Gurus are also martyrs, but the reverse it would seem, was never possible.
5. In 2001, a group calling itself the Shahid Sant Jarnail Singh and Holocaust Commemoration Committee decided to perform his *antim ardas* at *Akal Takht* on the 6 June, 'in a dignified and peaceful manner' (*The Tribune*, May 17, 2001), countering they said, the Damdami Taksal's 'illogical and ridiculous arguments' (*The Tribune*, May 17, 2001). The politics of this tussle is evident in the subsequent action of the Damdami Taksal; just four years later in June 2005, the Taksal decided to honour Mr Apar Singh Bajwa, a retired Superintendent of Police, who had identified the body of Bhindranwale and then witnessed the cremation in 1984 (*The Tribune*, June 2, 2005).
6. Robust social movements among people of the First Nations have encouraged museums and curators in Canada, the USA, Australia, and New Zealand to recognise the cultural claims of people on sacred objects (Greene 1992; Seligman and Monroe 2006; Mauzé and Derlon 2003). Recently, Tibetan sacred objects have become significant to the exiled community as a way to project their dispossession; therefore, the treatment of their sacred art in museums and exhibitions is of immense concern to community and curators alike.
7. The term *ghallughara* is translated as 'carnage' when referencing the two events of medieval history, the Chotta and Vadda Ghallughara. However, in modern discourse, the translation draws from Holocaust memorials and Operation Bluestar as well as the anti-Sikh riots are translated in the protest literature as 'genocide'.
8. In relation to the *Akal Takht* the Harmandir is the sanctum, while the Takht is the protective architectural and ideological layer. Aerial views of the complex accentuate this relationship admirably.

9. CDs of Bhindranwale's speeches were widely distributed in protest rallies against the unorthodox Baba Ram Rahim of the Dera Saccha Sauda.
10. Raghu Rai is a well-known photographer and photojournalist; he was also a protégé of Henri Cartier-Bresson.
11. We cannot forget the two swords of *miri-piri* worn by Guru Hargobind, who wore the crossed swords signifying twin sources of legitimacy and authority. While displays of weapons in the Keshghar Sahib and during Holla are well established ritual practice and the display of arms on a person's body signifies his exemplar status.
12. The halo was not confined to portraits of Guru; Maharaja Ranjit Singh is shown in profile with a halo, as a sign of his temporal authority, a concrete manifestation of the Sikh tenet of conjoined spiritual with temporal authority. But this is a rare inclusion—though I think an important one—more frequent in representations of gurus than of rulers.
13. Goswamy writes of *rasa*, or aesthetic delight, as an experience, belonging 'exclusively to the viewer or listener, who alone can experience it' (1994, 190). Its counterpart is the mood, or dominant feeling of the object—its *bhava*, that 'belongs to the work and can be consciously aimed at by its maker' (Goswamy 1994, 190).

References

Anderson, B. 1991. *Imagined communities*. London and New York: Verso.

Baixas, Lionel, and Charlène Simon. 2008. From protesters to martyrs: How to become a 'true' Sikh *Samaj. South Asia Multidisciplinary Academic Journal* 2. http://samaj. revues. org/1532 (accessed September 2012).

Battaglia, D. 1992. The body in the gift: Memory and forgetting in a Sabarl mortuary exchange. *American Ethnologist* 19, no. 1: 3–18.

Bilu, Yoram, and Eyal Ben-Ari. 1992. The making of modern saints: Manufactured charisma and the Abu-Hatseiras of Israel. *American Ethnologist* 19, no. 4: 672–87.

Blair, William. 2004. *Cities of the dead: Contesting the memory of the Civil War in the south, 1865–1914*. Chapel Hill: University of North Carolina Press.

Chopra, Radhika. 2009. Visual mnemonics: Museum of martyrs. *South Asia Journal for Culture* 1, no. 3: 32–50.

Chopra, Radhika. 2011. *Militant and migrant: The politics and social history of Punjab*. London: Routledge.

Covington, Sarah. 2009. *Wounds, flesh, and metaphor in seventeenth-century England*. New York: Palgrave Macmillan.

Fenech, Louis E. 1997. Martyrdom and the Sikh tradition. *Journal of the American Oriental Society* 117, no. 4: 623–42.

Fenech, Louis E. 2001. *Martyrdom in the Sikh tradition: Playing the 'game of love'*. Oxford: Oxford University Press.

Frembgen, Jurgen Wasim. 1998. Saints in modern devotional poster portraits: Meanings and uses of popular religious folk art in Pakistan. *Anthropology and Aesthetics* 34: 184–91.

Goswamy, B.N. 1994. Another past, another context: Exhibiting Indian art abroad. In *Interpreting objects and collections*, ed. Susan Pearce, 188–92. London: Routledge.

Greene, Virginia. 1992. 'Accessories of holiness': Defining Jewish sacred objects. *Journal of the American Institute for Conservation* 31, no. 1: 31–9.

Margry, Peter Jan, and Cristina Sánchez-Carretero, ed. 2011. *Grassroots memorials: The politics of memorializing traumatic death*. New York and Oxford: Berghahn.

Mauzé, Marie, and Brigitte Derlon. 2003. "Sacred" and "sensitive" objects 2003, objects and societies, non-European components of European patrimony. http://www. necep.net/seminars2.html (accessed May 20, 2010).

McLeod, W.H. 1994. The hagiography of the Sikhs. In *According to tradition: Hagiographical writing in India*, ed. Winand M. Callewaert and Rupert Snell, 15–41. Wiesbaden: Otto Harrassowitz Verlag.

McLeod, W.H. 1995. Arjan's death. In *Historical dictionary of Sikhism, religions, philosophies, and movements, no. 5*, ed. W.H. McLeod, 40–1. Lanham, MD: The Scarecrow Press.

McLeod, W.H. 2009. *A–Z of Sikhism*. Lanham, MD: Scarecrow Press.

Neff, John. 2004. *Honouring the Civil War Dead: Commemoration and the problem of reconciliation Lawrence*. Lawrence, KS: University Press of Kansas.

Seligman, Tom, and Dan Monroe. 2006. Report of the AAMD Task Force on the acquisition and stewardship of sacred objects—June 1, 2006 Approved by AAMD Membership. *International Journal of Cultural Property* 13: 419–21. doi:10.1017/S0940739106060267.

Verma, S.P. 2002. Sikh painting: An appraisal. In *The Khalsa and the Punjab: Studies in Sikh history, to the 19th century*, ed. Himadri Banerjee, 160–83. New Delhi: Tulika Books. Young, James E. 1993. *The texture of memory: Holocaust memorials and meaning*. New Haven, CT: Yale University Press.

Zerubavel, Yael. 1995. *Recovered roots: Collective memory and the making of Israeli National Tradition*. Chicago, IL: University of Chicago Press.

10

Divine Order, Social Disorder: Debating the Visual Representations of Lalu Prasad Yadav

Ronie Parciack and Ilanit Loewy Shacham

This chapter addresses the ways the Indian visual media created a theological model to rationalise and condone political corruption in the modern Indian nation state. Specifically, it examines this model through a case study of Bihari Rashtriya Janata Dal (RJD) leader Lalu Prasad Yadav, and the way he was represented in a set of cartoons published by the Indian mass media between the mid-1990s and the early 2000s. Yadav, formerly Bihar's chief minister (1990–1997), a member of the 15th Lok Sabha and the Minister of Railways in the United Progressive Alliance (UPA) government between 2004 and 2009, lost the 2005 Bihar Assembly elections to the Janata Dal leader Nitish Kumar after a successful anti-corruption campaign launched by the latter, and was sentenced on 3 October 2013 to a five-year jail term following his conviction in the Fodder Scam. The Fodder Scam involved the embezzlement of about ₹9.4 billion (equivalent to US$420 million in 2014) from the Bihar treasury during the early and mid-1990s.

Despite being one of the first major politicians to lose his parliamentary seat on criminal grounds, he was released from jail after only two and a half months, and in 2015, facing the unprecedented dominance of the Bharatiya Janata Party (BJP) and prime minister Narendra Modi in the central government, he allied himself with Nitish Kumar and the Congress Party—a grand alliance that won by a landslide in the Bihar 2015 Legislative Assembly elections.

Corruption was an open secret in the mid-1990s' Bihar when Yadav was extremely popular as a leader. At the height of his popularity, Yadav was considered a controversial politician, and was identified with a number of scandals, with aspects of disorder and a style known as *Goonda* (bully) politics.

For nearly 17 years, until late 2013 when a special Central Bureau of Investigation (CBI) court convicted him and disqualified him from serving as a Member of Parliament (MP) for the next 11 years, Lalu Prasad Yadav became a living example of political resilience against all odds. Yadav's political survival has mostly been explained in terms of the social context of caste politics and especially the rise of the Other Backward Classes (OBCs) in the Hindi Belt from the 1980s onwards. This chapter, however, presents another perspective that is deeply rooted in Hindu theology as expressed through the vernacular plane (as defined by Michelutti 2009: 1) of visual culture. We argue that the core of Yadav's political resilience was an identification with the Hindu God Kṛṣṇa. This identification was created, articulated and sustained via channels of mass media, especially, by cartoons published in the Indian printed press and Internet websites. Kṛṣṇa, particularly as depicted in *purāṇic* (a literary tradition composed in the first centuries AD) tales, is identified with elements of disorder. However, as a divine essence, this apparent disorder becomes authoritative and hence stands for an order that is both defiant and simultaneously highly esteemed and valid. In this respect, it serves as a theological model that places antinomic conduct within an authoritative and non-democratic framework.

Religion and Politics in Contemporary India

The theoretical discourse on nationalism is frequently linked to features of secularisation. Nationalism is considered to be the product of the Enlightenment, the fruit of modernism and humanistic thought where man has replaced God as the centre of the universe. From this point of view, the nation state of modern India is regarded as a special case in that it has incorporated religious dimensions within its political discourse. This model of Religious Nationalism was formalised by Peter van der Veer (1994) and Nikki Keddie, who referred to it as the New Religious Politics (NRP; 1998).

Although sovereign India is, by definition, a secular and democratic state, one of the prominent discourses on nationalism and citizenry amalgamates the religious and the political. The discourse or ideology of Hindu Nationhood or *Hindutva*, as framed under the British Raj by V.D. Savarkar (1923), linked religious and national identities, nationalised Hindu concepts, wove Hindu features into the sociopolitical order, and proclaimed the Sanskrit/Aryan/Brahmanic culture as supreme (Bhatt 2001: 85, 94–95; Nandi 1970: 57; Ramaswamy 1999: 346). Although this is not the sole discourse;[1] despite the constitutional definition of the Indian nation state as a secular democracy (Singh 2005) and despite the all-embracing Nehruvian policy that prevailed in the first decades of Independence, *Hindutva's* high symbolic status and the powerful rise of the Hindu right as of the 1980s significantly impacted public culture and space. Hindu sensibilities are the foundation of Indian political arena and public culture and bring together the theological and the political.

Theological Models of Rulership in India

The confluence of the political and the theological is an old and well-established notion in subcontinental public culture. It may be rooted in the Vedic notion of *bandhu*, which denotes the ties and reciprocal dependence between all strata of reality. This ancient concept constitutes the basis for a range of models of conjunction and mutual affiliation between the phenomenal world and its metaphysical layers. It is widely developed in post-Vedic traditions, and extends to contemporary national discourse, where it may be most powerfully embodied in endowing a leader or a politician with the status of *svarūpa*; i.e., the incorporation of divinity. The identification of a ruler with divine and trans-empirical features was also part of the Indian epics, and first and foremost the Rāmāyaṇa (200 BCE–200 CE). In his essay devoted to the status of the king in epics, Sheldon Pollock writes: 'The King is functionally a god because like a god he saves and protects. He is essentially, ontologically, a god, because he incorporates the divine essence' (Pollock 1984: 524).

David Shulman traced expressions of a similar rapport in the Chola era in medieval southern India. There, the king, the focus of political power, was considered 'as embodying the cosmic centre and thereby encompassing, as the central Brahman-power, the entirety of creation' (Shulman 1985: 9–11, 75). The theological paradigms of ideal rulership are discussed mainly in relation to the exemplary, *dharmic* (orderly), brahminical governance model as encapsulated in the character of Rāma in Vālmīki's Rāmāyaṇa. Rāma, the protagonist of the epic, a perfect man, virtuous warrior and god,[2] embodies a value system, which is totally committed and subordinated to the codes of proper, exemplary, disciplined *dharmic* order whose significance transcends the phenomenal. His rule, considered as prodigious and utopian, was termed *Rāma-Rājya:* Rāma's Rule.[3]

In his seminal 1993 essay, Pollock demonstrated how, as of the twelfth century, the Rāmāyaṇa has functioned as an organising narrative in the Indian political imagination, and the ways in which Rāma became essential to enunciating the ideal of rule and ruling.[4] The concepts of both Rāma and the Rāmāyaṇa were resurrected in pre-Independence era, as well as in the last decades of the twentieth century, with the rise of the Hindu right and its drive to strengthen the Hindu dimension in the national consciousness. One of the most significant events in this respect was the *Rath-Yātrā* (Chariot pilgrimage), a series of campaigns and meetings initiated in the late 1980s by the BJP leader, Lal Krishna Advani. During these *Yātrās* (pilgrimage-style campaigns), Advani publicly posed as an archer,[5] imitating the well-known posture of Rāma, the bow-drawing warrior.[6] This manifest use of Rāma's iconography as *kodaṇḍarāma* (Rāma with the bow) was intended to directly equate Advani and Rāma, thus endowing him and the BJP with a clear, trans-empiric authority that promoted a utopian, prosperous age of welfare, harmony and Hindu religiousness; in short, a *Rāma-Rājya*.

The ideal of Rāma as an exemplary ruler, representing the appropriate social order, *dharmic* conduct and a religious Hindu stance, is not only shared by the Hindu Right but can also be found in the presumably secular Congress Party, perhaps because Gandhi himself referred to Indian sovereignty in this way (Udayakumar 1996: 980). The Gandhian significance of *Rāma-Rājya* denoted the abstract ideal of an independent Indian nation that championed the ideals of *satyāgraha* ('adherence to truth', a philosophical and practical path accomplished through an integral value system stressing non-violence), which differed considerably from the way it was defined by the Hindu right.[7] Nevertheless, the rivalry between the Congress Party and the BJP during the 1990s and early 2000s, together with the status of the *Hindutva* ideology as a symbolic asset that attracts voters, led to recent appropriations of the iconographic model of Rāma by Sonia Gandhi, Manmohan Singh and the Congress Party. For example, the important daily *The Hindu* published a photograph of Congress president Sonia Gandhi (like Advani years before) mimicking the bodily gesture of *kodaṇḍarāma* while launching the 2007 election campaign for the Gujarat state assembly.[8] She was photographed in the same posture in a 2011 Dussehra function that was covered by *Hindustan Times*; more recently, in 2013, during the Dussehra celebrations in New Delhi, Prime Minister Manmohan Singh showed the same posture.[9] These photographs suggest that the two opposing parties indeed share an ideal of governance, and both wish to be identified with the quintessential, brahminic codes identified with Rāma as shaped in Vālmīki's Rāmāyaṇa.

The visual arts also reflect these stances. The appended link leads to a popular Bazaar Art or Poster Art (popular posters ranging from devotional/ religious themes to depictions of national heroes, landscapes, etc.)[10] whose iconography draws mainly on *purāṇic* accounts. These posters are usually sold in local bazaars and are used for domestic rites, as well as for creating ritualistic foci in Hinduised public spaces such as street corners, cars, auto rickshaws, buses, etc. The appended image presents Rāma in the well-known *kodaṇḍarāma* iconography.[11] The next two links show images of L.K. Advani positioning himself as *kodaṇḍarāma* during the 1998 campaign and Sonia Gandhi in the same stance.[12] It is no wonder that while building his public image as a candidate for prime ministership, the recently elected BJP Prime Minister Narendra Modi also posed with a bow and arrow.[13]

Thus, a theological model underpins the notion of the ideal ruler in modern, secular, democratic India. As Arvind Rajagopal puts it: 'Hindu nationalists in recent times represented an attempt to create a populist language of politics, appealing to authoritarian, rather than democratic values' (Rajagopal 2001: 1).

However, even though the model of the ideal ruler is based on the figure of Rāma (Bhatt 2001: 172), and despite its salience in the contemporary political sphere, it is not the only model.[14] Rather, we show here that Indian politics employs another contrasting theological model of a deviant, defiant and antinomic ruler. This model is based on Rāma's counterpart, Kṛṣṇa, a deity who is endowed with opposing sets of values to those of Rāma. Kṛṣṇa's 'biography' is extremely detailed and diverse. The image of the young Kṛṣṇa was that of an order-breaching child and youth, as depicted mainly in *purāṇic* traditions (which differ from Kṛṣṇa the *dharma*-oriented teacher of the Bhagavad Gītā). The case study of Lalu Prasad Yadav illustrates the ways in which the image of a god closely associated to *adharmic* (chaotic) conduct and perhaps even to *adharma* in general could be channelled to rationalise and eventually legitimise a leader promoting an antinomic set of values. To fully develop this argument, we shall give a brief summary of the opposing sets of values with which each of the gods came to be identified.

Rāma and Kṛṣṇa: Opposing Sets of Values

Traditionally, both Rāma and Kṛṣṇa are considered *avatāras* (manifestations) of the God *Viṣṇu*. Their origin therefore is shared, but their characters, conduct and biographies, especially as shaped in the Rāmāyaṇa vis-à-vis *purāṇic* accounts, are polar oppositions, as is their power to attract different populations.[15] Rāma was born a prince destined for the throne, while Kṛṣṇa, although a descendant of the ruling class (*Kṣatriya*), was born in jail and brought up in the country amongst cattle herders. Rāma is thus associated with the upper class, whereas Kṛṣṇa is part of the common people. Rāma is described as adhering to the exemplary codes of good (read: *dharmic*) conduct such as discipline, stability, responsibility and most notably truthfulness in the brahminic sense. This may be the reason why in the Rāmāyaṇa (and in other literary and oral traditions) Rāma's childhood remains obscure: none of its 25,000 stanzas are dedicated to Rāma*'s* childhood. The first time his exploits are described is when he goes with Viśvāmitra into the forest to help safeguard his sacrificial rituals, which are being disturbed by demons. Thus, Rāma becomes literally and perhaps ontologically substantial only from the moment he can be counted on to help enforce or protect the *dharma*.

Accounts of Kṛṣṇa's childhood, however, are abundant and detailed. These depict him as a mischievous, butter-thieving child and prankster youth.[16] Later on, whereas Rāma marries the ideal, submissive, beautiful and famously chaste wife (Sītā), Kṛṣṇa's early adolescence is filled with eroticism that potentially challenges the normative strictures of the *dharmic* world. In stark opposition to Rāma's unique monogamy, Kṛṣṇa goes on to marry more than 16,000 wives.[17] The sociopolitical implications of these traits and tales culminate in associating Rāma with the political sphere dominated by brahminical ideology, as well by Brahmins and the forward castes, whereas Kṛṣṇa became popular among protest movements against brahminical order and elitist power hubs (as in the case of Gauḍīya Vaiṣṇavism, a late medieval religious protest movement that originated in Bengal).

The set of values associated with Rāma make him a favourable ruling model: this may explain images such as that of Advani drawing Rāma's arrow. 'Because it aspires to govern, the BJP strives to project an image of discipline, stability and responsibility', wrote James Lochtefeld (1996: 102). However, the characteristics associated with Kṛṣṇa—mischievous, thieving, luring, lawbreaking—could not make him into a model that the patriarchal, hierarchical, *dharmic*, brahminical world would tend to adopt.

Quite the contrary, Jürgen Lütt stresses that both Dayananda Saraswati and Mahatma Gandhi laboured to eliminate the mythology and set of values associated with Kṛṣṇa from the public sphere and discourses of nationalism that were crystallised in the late colonial era.[18]

However, Kṛṣṇa did not vanish from the political order or the public arena. Rather, Kṛṣṇa himself, together with Kṛṣṇaite values, constituted a model of the antinomic ruler that has been especially attractive to the non-brahminical electorate or populations who aspire to symbolically subvert brahminical codes, orders and sets of values. This has proved to be an attractive model for a wide swath of the population that has anti-brahminical and anti-establishment stands and most notably the OBCs whose power increased from the 1970s during the 1980s, and paved the way for a political counter-culture. Within OBC politics, a major role was played by the Yadav caste, which became a significant factor on the Indian political scene.

The Yadav Caste and the Rise of Minority Politics

Since Independence in 1947 to the late 1970s, India was ruled by the Congress Party. Because it was historically composed of representatives aiming to represent the manifold sectors of Indian society, and also due to its identification with the successful combat for sovereignty, the Congress Party enjoyed a consensual status for two decades, with no significant opponent on the political scene. From 1967 onwards, the image of this party underwent significant changes: it became identified with the Nehru–Gandhi familial dynasty, which was perceived as a party representing the interests of forward castes/classes, and distanced from minority groups (Thakur 1998: 604).

Minority movements and parties began to emerge as of the 1970s. Within this framework, the rise of OBCs is considered to be one of the most important developments in Indian politics, as it successfully undermined the power of the stance of the forward castes/classes in the public domain, especially in the Hindi Belt (Jaffrelot 2000: 86–87). The term OBCs denotes the castes located beneath the three upper castes (Brahmins, Kṣatriyas and Vaiśyas) but above the Untouchables. Numerically, they are estimated to comprise about 50 per cent of the Indian population, although their past ratio in representational bodies (Parliament, cabinet and state assemblies) was akin to that of minorities. The significant political empowerment of the OBCs led to positions such as the chief ministership of the giant states of Uttar Pradesh and Bihar.[19] In these states and in other states of the Hindi Belt, the rise of the OBCs corresponds to the rise of the Yadav Caste, the caste of Mulayam Singh Yadav, the founder of the Samajwadi Party and the former chief minister of Uttar Pradesh in three non-successive terms between 1989–2007, and of Lalu Prasad Yadav, the former president of the Janata Dal Party, and currently the chairperson of the RJD. During his political career, Lalu Prasad Yadav has served as the chief minister of Bihar between 1990 and 1997,[20] and between 2004 and 2009 as the railways minister of the UPA government.

The agenda of the OBCs' politics emphasises the promotion of caste interests such as affirmative acts and quota politics. These may be interpreted as an enhancement of social justice and a more just distribution of the nation state's resources. As such, it could be perceived as opposing both the Congress Party, which failed to construct a pluralistic image, as well as the Right-wing BJP, since *Hindutva* ideology is symbolically associated with a strong support of caste hierarchy, and hence the interests of upper castes.

The rise of the OBCs is associated with a subversive, oppositional process that is aimed at removing the former elites from their positions of power. Alongside the concrete facets of this uprising, which can be deciphered in socio-economic terms, however, there is another, more symbolic facet, namely their symbolic resentment of brahminical codes and sets of values. These are associated with high castes and classes, *Hindutva* ideology and the political parties that directly promote it or indirectly rely upon it. These codes have become identified with Rāma in Vālmīki's Rāmāyaṇa. Against this backdrop, the OBCs and the powerful Yadav politics formed a symbolic antagonistic political culture that acquired its legitimacy through affiliation with the theological model of Lord Kṛṣṇa.

Yadav Pro-Kṛṣṇa Politics

Two features characterise Yadav politics. The first is populism, i.e., the appeal to the lower strata of society as a part of a well-intended social policy. The second is its use of 'bully' politics. Yadav politics does not adhere to 'proper' conduct and accepted (read: brahmnical, *dharmic*, bourgeois) concepts of law and order. These two facets are closely linked to the ideology embedded in the Kṛṣṇaaite model. Its accessible, anti-elitist, non-brahminical dimension reflects Kṛṣṇa who grew up among the common people and not the monarchic aristocracy. This accessible, populist dimension of Yadav politics is perceived as a contrast to the exemplary and haughty conduct ascribed to prince Rāma. The second difference is the breaches of law and order that also link Yadav politics with Kṛṣṇaite mythology and set of values.

Specifically, Yadav politics are described as reflecting *dadaism* and *Goonda politics*. Anthropologist Lucia Michelutti, who explored the Yadav community in the city of Mathura, Uttar Pradesh, noted that delinquency and a spectrum of illegal activities (such as usury, protection rackets, violence, threats of violence, political corruption and the empowerment of local criminals) are widely practiced among Yadav members and its leaders (Michelutti 2008: 78). Michelutti associates these patterns with Thomas Bloom Hansen's concept of *dada culture*: *Dada* literally means grandfather (in Hindi), but it is colloquially used to mean elder brother and also to indicate criminals. *Dadaism* is a style of exercising political and social power and protection and invokes the images of masculine, assertive and often violent local strongmen, whose clout lies in self-made networks of loyalty rather than in institutionalised action and discourse. In Mathura, the same concept of political style is popularly known under the name of *goondaism*. People generally refer to local and regional Yadav politicians as *goondas* (Hansen 2001: 72; Michelutti 2008: 78).

These *Goonda Politics* are also the way Yadav political institutions were perceived.[21] This style contrasted sharply with the brahminical ruling ideal, which promotes *dharmic*, disciplined and reserved conduct, identified with the ruling model of ideal Rāma. The deliberate bluntness, the provocative defiance of law and *dharma* as a symbolic undermining of brahminical order, all emphasise the Kṛṣṇaite dimensions of Yadav politics. However, the link between Yadav politics and Kṛṣṇa is directly constituted via the most prominent figures of Yadav politics: the controversial Lalu Prasad Yadav.

Lalu Prasad Yadav—A Contemporary Kṛṣṇa?[22]

Lalu Prasad Yadav, born 1948, is a first-generation politician in independent India. He was born in a small village in northern Bihar, one of India's poorest and most crime-stricken states. At young age, he moved to the capital, Patna, where he lived with his uncle, a milkman. He studied at Patna University, where he has said to have been humiliated by upper-caste students who claimed that it was improper for a Yadav to acquire higher education. Yadav began his political career as a student leader at Patna University. In 1980, he became a member of the Bihar Legislative Assembly and a member of the Lok Sabha. In 1988, he led the opposition in Bihar, and following the victory of the Janata Dal in the 1990 elections, he became the chief minister of Bihar.

From the start of his political career, he constructed an image of a politician with a distinctive presence and a deliberately different style from mainstream politicians. His speech sounded rustic and uncouth, he deliberately spoke in the *Bhojpuri* dialect rather than in formal Hindi, the issues he referred to were intentionally provocative. He refused to conduct his swearing-in ceremony as chief minister at the official residence, the *Raj Bhawan*, and moved it to the statue of Jayprakash Narayan, a popular venue for demonstrations against the Congress Party's rule. For several months, he refused to move to the official residence of the chief minister and remained in the same flat where he lived with his brother. The image of Lalu Prasad Yadav was different from previous chief ministers; rather, he was a common man, connected to the masses (Frankle 2006: 12).

This image of an informal and deliberately provocative leader was complemented by more extreme dimensions associated with symbolic impurity. He claimed to have eaten rats, thus connecting himself politically to the lowest caste in Bihar, the *Musahars*, whose name denotes 'rat-eaters' (Frankle 2006: 14). Thus, he positioned himself as the contrary of the brahminic ideal of purity and 'pure' set of values. The way he directed the Janata Dal Party can also be associated with symbolic impurity: no institutions were formed for maintaining order in the party. Yadav dissociated himself from any ideas of ordered, institutionalised, policised—*dharmic*—order and politics. He became identified with the idea of order-breaching (Frankle 2006: 14, 16). All these serve as the backdrop for the term *Lalu-Rājya*—Lalu's rule, or Jungle-*Rājya*, that codified Lalu and his rule in terms of disorder. These concepts also positioned Lalu and his rule at the opposite end of the spectrum from the specific term *Rāma-Rājya*, Rāma's rule that denotes the exemplary brahminical ruling ideal.

But the most distinctive challenge to these concepts of order were the numerous scandals involving Lalu and in particular the 1996 Fodder Scam, in which he was suspected of stealing more than ₹9.4 million from the Bihar Animal Husbandry Department. He was detained but not before appointing his wife, Rabri Devi, as the chief minister of Bihar, a move that enabled him to run the country from jail. Gradually, Indian media labelled him as corrupt and identified him with the idea of defiance. Despite the scandals for about a decade, Yadav did not lose his prominent position on India's public scene. He was re-elected after a lengthy jail term and was sentenced to five years in prison only in October 2013. Yadav's political survival was mostly attributed to the socio-economic interests of caste politics, as well as to his representation of the interests of the backward castes/classes, his insistence on putting social justice as his first priority over wider economic interests and the strong alliance with Muslim populations. However, Yadav's success also lies in the legitimisation that was endowed with him through his popular identification with Kṛṣṇa.

Lalu's possible link to the Kṛṣṇaite model is based upon several factors. The first is related to the ways the Yadav caste associates itself to Kṛṣṇa: its geographical location, traditional employment, etc. The second factor is more symbolic and refers to representations in the mass media that identified Lalu Prasad Yadav with features of Kṛṣṇaite mythology and theology. This also involves the ways Lalu was portrayed as Kṛṣṇa *via negativa*—i.e., through representations in which he is depicted as opposing brahminical concepts of order and ideal rule.

Kṛṣṇa and the Yadav Caste

Lord Kṛṣṇa plays a key role in the Yadav caste narrative and social orientation. The caste associates itself with the history and life of Kṛṣṇa in several ways. In the most concrete sense, one of its major areas of influence is the Vraj region and the city of Mathura, the areas where Kṛṣṇa's childhood and adolescence took place according to texts such as the *Bhāgavata Purāṇa*. In addition, one of the typical Yadav livelihoods is cattle-herding (as previously noted, Lalu Yadav's uncle was a milkman), which also adheres to a pivotal motif in the mythology of Kṛṣṇa who grew up amongst cattle herders craving for milk and butter. This can also be linked to the Yadavs' position regarding cow protection and their mass consumption of milk and dairy products to emphasise that this is the favourite food of Kṛṣṇa (Michelutti 2004; 2008: 80, 83).

The Yadav caste is not only associated with Kṛṣṇa in terms of location, diet and occupation. Kṛṣṇa also serves as a unifying ethnic symbol in the Yadav community (Michelutti 2008: 77; Michelutti 2009). He is considered by the Yadavs as their ancestor-king-god, and they trace their genealogy back to him (Michelutti 2004: 47, 50–51). The Yadavs link Kṛṣṇa in an organic fashion to each and every member of the caste. This idea has far-reaching significance. Given the immanent notion in Hinduism that the world is made up of interdependent layers that can permeate each other, the deity can and indeed is present and incorporated in each and every member of the community. The key notions of *avatāra* (incorporation) and *svarūpa* (a human taking on the deity's shape while the deity is present within the human body) also enter into play. *Avatāra*, which is prevalent in Vaiṣnava mythology, refers to the different forms taken on by Viṣnu to save the cosmos and cosmic order. The latter term is employed in ritualistic theatre traditions such as the *Rāma-Līlā*, *Rāsa-Līlā* and other traditions of the Vraj region. In this ritualistic theatre, episodes from the biography of Kṛṣṇa are retold and re-enacted.[23] These spectacles are perceived as the manifestations of the god's acts, which occur at the very time and in the space of the actual performance; the actor portraying the god is perceived as a *svarūpa*—a manifestation of the god, and as such becomes an object of worship. As Haberman, based on De, noted, this is not a symbol or an allegory but rather a mythic occurrence in religious history (De [1942] 1961: 223; Haberman 1988: 45).

Hence, what occurs frequently in the sphere of popular theatre also operates in the political sphere. Rulers are attributed a *svarūpa*; those who wish to reflect brahminical ideas are willingly shaped as incorporations of Rāma, whereas Lalu Yadav, aspiring to undermine the very same set of values, was often shaped and perceived as an incorporation of Kṛṣṇa.[24]

Visual Mass Media Gives Birth to a New Avatar: Lalu as Kṛṣṇa

The most significant arena in shaping the image of Lalu as Kṛṣṇa was cartoons published in the Indian print and Internet press, as well as on Internet websites.[25] It is no coincidence that this conflictual thematic which involved the shaping of the order-breaching as god was formulated visually since these are perceived as somewhat indirect (Jameson 1981: 63). The indirect feature ascribed to visual images, as well as the humoristic nature of cartoons in general, eased potential tensions, provided refined expressions of threats upon hegemonic historiography and lessened the threat of counter-hegemonic narratives. The comic status of the political cartoon serves to camouflage its potential radicalism.

The links appended in notes lead to images that were taken from several publications in which Lalu was represented as Kṛṣṇa or, alternately, as an opposition to the ideals associated with Rāma. Most of the cartoons that overtly represent Lalu as Kṛṣṇa were taken from the Internet press.[26] It comes as no surprise that the Internet press hosts the most radical expressions: the medium of Internet is an open arena enabling a multiplicity of voices; it does not require the massive economic resources needed in the case of the print press, and is not subjected to conscious or imposed censorship. The Internet easily enables expressions of non-hegemonic, subversive or radical voices (Warf and Grimes 1997: 26). Alongside the Internet cartoons that link Lalu Yadav with Kṛṣṇa himself or with the characteristics of Kṛṣṇa, cartoons published by prominent magazines addressing socio-economic elites such as *India Today* also denounced Yadav for manifest breaching of the good, brahminical order, thereby indirectly constituting him as Kṛṣṇa *via negativa*.[27]

Biographical Features: The Child and the Childishness

Kṛṣṇa's biography, as formulated in the *purāṇic* literature, includes many of Kṛṣṇa's childhood exploits. The childish nature of Kṛṣṇa's character is highlighted particularly as compared to other deities. The cartoons depicting Lalu also show that a widely used technique for identifying Lalu Yadav with Kṛṣṇa was to highlight his childlike features. Lalu was often depicted in a way similar to popular poster representations of Kṛṣṇa,[28] as a puffy, rosy-cheeked child and has even been called 'fat cheeks'.[29] He was often depicted as a child at play: a puff-cheeked child playing the drums[30] or—when acting as railway minister of the UPA government—playing with a train set.[31] Another example of his infantile image is the baby 'Laluji' Doll,[32] which was manufactured in Bihar in the late 1990s.

This childish dimension was crucial to eliciting affection, legitimacy and forgiveness for Lalu's defiant, order-breaching acts. In a roundabout way, this may also explain forgiveness as regards Lalu's corruption charges and leniency as regards his signature qualities of disorder: after all, children are generally forgiven for creating havoc and being mischievous. Though

Kṛṣṇa constantly got into trouble with his mother, neighbours and peers, he remained an adored child—and so did Lalu.

Another intriguing representation, which fits into this frame involves a famous *purāṇic* episode known as the waist tying (*dāmodara*). In this episode, Kṛṣṇa once again steals fresh butter from the churn, but breaks the pot and makes a mess. Yaśodā, his adoptive mother, tries to prevent him from creating more trouble by tying him down with a rope, which despite being relentlessly extended with more and more ropes, is constantly two fingers short. Kṛṣṇa, pitying his tired mother, eventually allows his mother to tie him to a post (*Bhāgavata Purāṇa* 10.9: 1–18). Below is a link to a popular painting of Yaśodā taking hold of Kṛṣṇa and an echo of this episode in cartoons showing Lalu with his wife, Rabri Devi, who is depicted as a mother who takes her mischievous son, Lalu, by the hand.[33] The other child in the cartoon is Akhilesh Singh (nicknamed *Aloo*–the potato), Lalu's former RJD ally, who was accused of crimes including murder and kidnapping.

Another iconographical trope connecting Kṛṣṇa and Lalu is their affinity to cows. Kṛṣṇa grew up as a cattle-herder and is known as the protector of cows (*gopāla*). Popular iconographies present Kṛṣṇa in the loving company of cows. Similarly, many cartoons showed Lalu's closeness to cows. This iconography adheres to the traditional livelihood of the Yadav caste as cattle herders, but also contributes to visually representing the claims to kinship with Kṛṣṇa.[34]

It is noteworthy that this iconography, which could be termed Lalu-*Gopāla*, was widely used when the 1996 Fodder Scam was made public.[35] At that time, Lalu faced overt accusations of corruption. The cartoons employing this iconography re-contextualised Lalu's deeds and placed them within an elevating framework enabling a parallel between Lalu and Kṛṣṇa's deeds, thus reducing their criminal ramifications.[36]

Another cartoon published during the Fodder Scam (1996) combines representations of the childish dimension of the Lalu–Kṛṣṇaite iconography with an overt construction of affection amongst his assumed audience. One cartoon shows the fat-cheeked (childish) Lalu and his wife seated on a cow with piles of fodder in the background as reference to the scam. The interesting part of this cartoon is the Hindi inscription—*dharti ka Laloo*: a pun on the proverb 'The son of the earth' where the word 'little son' (Hindi: *lal*), usually uttered affectionately, is replaced by the politician's first name Lalu.[37]

In the examples so far, the identification between Kṛṣṇa and Lalu was created indirectly by highlighting a particular characteristic shared by

Figure 10.1

Lalu Yadav as Kṛṣṇa

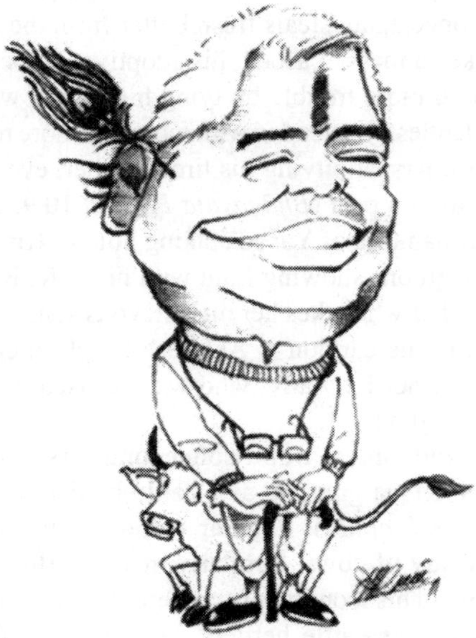

Source: See http://drishtikona.com/2004/05/05/laloos-bihar/ (courtesy of Indra R. Sharma).

both, namely, their childish appearance and mischief, their companionship with cows and so on. However, this does not mean that direct identification did not exist. In an intriguing cartoon published by the website www.drishtikona.com,[38] Lalu was portrayed with the classical iconographical attributes of Kṛṣṇa.[39] It shows a cow in the background, a peacock feather pinned in his hair, the glasses on a chain around his neck echo Kṛṣṇa's garland and even Lalu's walking stick appears to echo Kṛṣṇa's flute. Strikingly, the cartoon even imitates the style of some well-known iconographies of Kṛṣṇa in popular Poster Art tradition.[40]

The cartoon (Figure 10.1) presents the most direct identification between Lalu Yadav and Kṛṣṇa, and it has been in frequent use for some years in various Internet websites.[41] However, other cartoons published in established mass communication channels have linked Lalu and Kṛṣṇa negatively.

On the 7th of December 1997, *India Today*—one of the most highbrow magazines, published a cartoon in which Lalu (at that time in jail) appears as a prisoner preventing Jagannath Mishra (a former chief minister of Bihar who was also involved in the Fodder Scam) from reading the Bhagavad Gīta. The Gīta is part of the Māhabhārata epic and one of the most authoritative texts in the brahminic/*dharma* perspective;[42] the depiction of Lalu preventing Mishra from reading this text strengthens Lalu's image as a rude, uneducated man (read: of a backward caste) in contrast to the elite population as well as the brahminic set of values (that others even the jailed Mishra, a well-known Brahmin surname, accept or wish to be perceived as accepting). In any case, Lalu disturbs and troubles the reading of the authoritative, exemplary text, thus activating a set of associations that place him in overt opposition to brahmanic set of values. In fact, while serving as the chief minister of Bihar, Lalu Yadav prevented BJP's L.K. Advani from entering Bihar's capital Patna during his *Rath-Yātrā* campaign. During this campaign, Advani presented himself as an incorporation of Rāma which also supports the crystallisation of Yadav's image as 'anti-Rāma'.

Summary

The aforementioned examples associate one of India's most controversial political leaders with a much beloved, order-breaching deity. This association paved the way for rationalising and legitimising—even though for a limited time—the corrupt deeds Lalu Yadav was suspected of committing. Paralleling him with the deity-as-child enabled the development of a forgiving, loving attitude towards him and his deeds as though they had been committed by a beloved mischievous child. Furthermore, associating Lalu Yadav with a theological model of disorder anchored his acts within a framework that endowed him with a trans-empirical status. Similarly to Kṛṣṇa, Lalu Yadav was permitted to commit acts that infringed the socio-legal norms. The *purāṇic* literature views Kṛṣṇa's *adharmic* deeds as crucial steps taken for the sake of the cosmic order.[43] When employing a social perspective on Yadav's role in OBC politics, Lalu's deeds may be interpreted in a similar manner. The result is a new interpretation or a re-contextualisation of the notion of corruption within the Indian political sphere, especially within the complex symbolic scene of caste politics.

Indian politics has the image of a chaotic system due to the abundance of corruption scams that have occurred in the last few decades. Pradip K. Chibber, Subhash Misra and Richard Sisson called the issue of corruption as 'the problem of order' to describe the contending public norms resulting from the enormous heterogeneity of Indian society, a society divided by parameters of caste, class, communalism and other factors. This tension-saturated heterogeneity is closely linked to the issue of corruption, which has attracted growing attention since the 1980s. Unsurprisingly, this was also the decade marking the rise of the caste politics, and thus leaders who wished to undermine the political and economic power hubs traditionally dominated by upper castes gradually achieved ruling positions. These leaders protested against the existing order and challenged its perceived oppression of the lower socio-economical strata. This stand may have prompted leaders wishing to undermine old orders to act in a way that negated or breached the hegemonic order and norms. These actions were not interpreted as corrupt but rather as reflecting the subversive/anti-hegemonic interests of their voters. In this respect, Lalu's corruption may have been interpreted by his supporters as a legitimate protest against an oppressive system. The order-breaching leader could therefore be seen as an agent expressing his voters' protest and as redeeming his voters from the oppressive order. As Michelutti noted, Yadav caste rhetoric depicts Krishna as the first democratic leader of a secular republican government (Michelutti 2009: 224), in that he acts like a Robin Hood taking from the rich to give to the poor. A re-reading of corruption therefore suggests that the 'problem of order' was for a limited period perceived as a problem only from the perspective of the upper strata of Indian society; i.e., the urban population of high castes and classes (Chibber, Misra and Sisson 1992: 616) and not the lower strata. The 'good', 'appropriate' and *dharmic* order could therefore be perceived as a brahminical ideal and not as an ideal to which backward castes and classes aspire to be identified with. Possibly, there is no unifying concept of order in India.

This argument is reinforced by Ashis Nandi's interpretation of the concept of *dharma*, which traditionally served as a basis for legitimising power and authority in India (Nandi 1970: 67). During the first days of Independence, Nandi argues, politicians were expected to adhere to *sanskritic* concepts of brahminical rulership. However, the shift to mass politics with the fall of the Congress Party, the rise of small parties and the fact that especially between the 1980s and 2009 the parties that won the general elections were dependent on complex and unstable coalitions made this exemplary model (of a learned, urban, upper-caste politician) irrelevant. To sum up, the rise of caste politics and the emergence of new political forces have dramatically changed the Indian political map by challenging the dominant values of brahminic politics and by advancing antagonist and antinomic models. These relatively new models draw part of their legitimacy from a trans-empiric source associated with the mythology and ideology of Kṛṣṇa. This theological model formed the basis for an antinomic and antagonistic structure, which for more than a decade endowed a defiant leader with an authority relying on a non-democratic basis.

Notes

1. Indian democracy is considered to be a flexible mechanism with multiple notions of citizenship citizens can choose from. Shani lists four: Liberal, Republican, Ethno-National (*Hindutva*) and the discourse of the Non-Statist (Shani, 2010).
2. The question of Rāma's status as both human and divine is a complex matter thoroughly addressed by Pollock (Pollock 1984: 505–28).
3. The works of historian Romila Thapar and Sheldon Pollock help understand the historical development of this ideal. Thapar argues that the non-Brahminic *Rāma-Kath*ā and pre-*Rāmāyaṇic* Rāma tales were recited in public rituals and in kings' courts, thereby making them part of the public order (Pollock 1984; Thapar 1989: 5; Van de Veer 1994: 172–78).
4. This significance of the *Rāmāyaṇa* in the subcontinental political imagination is indeed twofold and extends to binary structures of Self and Other—Brothers and Others—in Pollock's words, the Other being the Muslims whose presence was no longer marginal in Indian history (Pollock 1993).
5. See http://indiatoday.intoday.in/story/1990-L.K.+Advani's+rath+yatra:+Chariot+of+fire/1/76389.html (accessed on 6 March 2017) and http://photos.outlookindia.com/default_vtl.aspx?pt=3&ptv=0&date=4/6/2006#TopImage (accessed on 6 March 2017). This position was repeated in the 2014 Lok Sabha polls; see http://ibnlive.in.com/photogallery/15724.html (accessed on 3 March 2014).
6. By doing so, Advani also referred to North Indian theatrical traditions, such as the *Rāma-Līlā*. For elaborate descriptions of Vaiṣṇavic theatrical traditions, see Haberman (1988, 1994), Kapur (1990), Schechner (1983) and Varapande (1982, 1983).
7. Gandhi also described this ideal as the Kingdom of God by using the term *Khudai Raj* (Urdu: the kingdom of God) which enabled the Indian Muslims to participate in the national ethos. There is a huge gap between the Gandhian use of this term and the way the Hindu right has used it (Udayakumar 1996: 981–82).
8. It is noteworthy that the reporter cited Sonia Gandhi accusing the BJP of wearing 'the mask of Mahatma Gandhi to hide its real ugly and unpatriotic face' (Dasgupta 2007). See also http://www.gettyimages.com/detail/news-photo/congress-president-sonia-gandhi-former-prime-minister-news-photo/494300902#congress-president-sonia-gandhi-former-prime-minister-manmohan-singh-picture-id494300902 (accessed on 6 March 2017).
9. See http://www.sun.mv/english/6838 (accessed on 6 March 2017) and http://latestnewspics.blogspot.co.il/2013/10/pm-sonia-set-ravana-on-fire-in-new-delhi.html (accessed on 3 March 2014).
10. See http://media.radiosai.org/journals/Vol_06/01APR08/05-avatars.htm (accessed on 6 March 2017). This medium has been investigated by Brosius (2007), Davis (2007)

Freitag (2002, 2007a, 2007b), Guha-Thakurta (2007), Jain (2003, 2007a, 2007b), Lutgendorf (2003), Neumayer and Schelberger (2008), Pinney (2003, 2004), Saeed (2007, 2011), Ramaswamy (2003, 2007, 2010), Roy (2003), Uberoi (2003, 2006) and others.

11. See a few examples in the following links: http://www.krishnasmercy.org/dotnetnuke/News/Blog/tabid/57/EntryId/398/The-Power-of-God.aspx (accessed on 6 March 2017), http://design-altruism-project.org/2012/08/09/330000000-superheroes/ (accessed on 6 March 2017) and http://www.krishnasmercy.org/dotnetnuke/News/Blog/tabid/57/EntryId/1139/Flying-Like-An-Arrow.aspx (accessed on 6 March 2017).
12. Dasgupta (2007). See also http://www.gettyimages.in/detail/news-photo/leader-of-indias-bharatiya-janata-party-l-k-advani-holds-a-news-photo/57265438#rajkot-india-leader-of-indias-bharatiya-janata-party-lk-advani-holds-picture-id57265438 (accessed on 6 March 2017), http://www.indiatvnews.com/photos/beautiful-pics-of-this-year-039-s-dusherra-1707.1691/6 (accessed on 6 March 2017, see picture no. 7) and http://www.thestatesman.com/photogallery/sonia-gandhi-c-holds-a-bow-and-an-arrow-as-dr-manmohan-singh-2-r-and-vice-president-hamid-ansari-take-a-glance-r-shahnawaz-khan-sns-805422.html (accessed on 6 March 2017).
13. NDTV (2012) and Nalapat (2014).
14. We refer mainly to this model, but the Indian political sphere offers other models connecting gods and political leaders. The identification of raging goddesses such as Durgā or Kālī and female political leaders such as Indira Gandhi, Jayalalitha and Mayavati is one of the most common examples. (See Jacob 2003; Lama Tawa 2001; Pinney 2004; Ramaswamy 2002, 2008, 2010; Waghorne Punzo 1999, 2001).
15. Though these differences between Rāma and Kṛṣṇa were part of their traditional biographies, they actually became pronounced only from the twelfth century. It is from this point in time, according to Pollock (1992), that Rāma was identified as the ultimate model of sovereignty. Interestingly, W.G. Archer notes that around the same time between the tenth and twelfth century, a shift in Kṛṣṇa's character occurs as well and he

    > […] is no longer regarded as having been born solely to kill a tyrant and rid the world of demons. His chief function now is to vindicate passion […] From this point of view, Krishna the prince was a mere pillar of boring respectability. Nothing in his conduct could arouse delight for everything he did was correct and proper. Krishna the cowherd on the other hand, was spontaneous, irresponsible and free. (Archer [1957] 2006: 78–80)

16. The biography of Kṛṣṇa can be found in the 10th book of the *Bhāgavatapurāṇa*.
17. Traditionally, Kṛṣṇa is believed to have married 16,108 wives. According to the *Bhāgavatapurāṇa*, (10: 54–58), he married 16,008.
18. 'Krishna as the God of erotic mystical love virtually disappeared from the public sphere of reformed Hinduism' (Lütt 1996: 152). The issue of Gandhi's use of the *Bhagavad-Gīta* and his attitude towards the figure of Kṛṣṇa in this text was recently addressed by Chakrabarty and Majumdar. Very succinctly, the authors discuss how Gandhi transformed the *Gīta's* message of action into a theory of non-violent resistance so that it fit his *satyāgraha* etiquette, while the figure of Kṛṣṇa in the *Gīta* is interpreted as embodying the Gandhian ideal of *satyagrahi* vigilance. Morever, Gandhi 'sought a series of routines by which the figure of the *satyagrahi*, as distinct from the modern political animal, could be both imagined and practiced' (See Chakrabarty and Majumdar 2010: 335, 346, 353).

19. 1977 was considered a turning point: for the first time, the ratio of forward castes' MPs dropped to less than 50 per cent. The rise of middle- and low–castes' MPs has not been consistent. After the Congress Party regained its power in the 1980 general elections, the ratio of forward castes in parliament rose again. In 1984, the ratio of OBC MPs decreased to 11.1 per cent, but it nearly doubled in 1989 (20.9 per cent) and kept on rising, prompting the major parties to form alliances with middle- and low-caste leaders. The OBCs became dominant in the Hindi Belt: Uttar Pradesh, Bihar, Madhya Pradesh, Rajasthan, Haryana and more (Jaffrelot 2000: 98).
20. Lalu Prasad Yadav lost power in 1991 but returned to power in Bihar between 1993 and 1995. In 1997, he was replaced by his wife, Rabri Devi, as he was imprisoned following the Fodder Scam.
21. For example, the Samajwadi Party, headed by Mulayam Singh Yadav, an ex-wrestler, is nicknamed the *goonda* party. This term was used mainly in relation to Yadav politics in Uttar Pradesh, but it can also refer to Yadav politics in other states such as Bihar. In both states, the Yadav caste is a leading political force.
22. India's Railway Minister Lalu Prasad Yadav milks a cow inside his residence before unveiling the 2009–2010 railway budget at the Parliament in a way suggesting a similarity between him and popular Kṛṣṇaite mythology and iconographies. See Lalu Prasad Yadav's Drama, photographed in Delhi, 13 February 2009. Available online at http://www.yohyoh.com/funny/all/all-countries//lalu-prasad-yadav-s-drama/41122 (accessed on 6 March 2017); and see also http://www.rediff.com/news/report/fodder-for-scam-lalu-prasad-yadav-and-his-cows-guilty/20130930.htm (accessed on 6 March 2017).
23. These theatrical traditions are usually based on episodes from the *Bhagāvatapurāṇa*, the *Viṣṇu-Purāṇa* and other texts like Jayadeva's *Gīta-Govinda*. For detailed descriptions of the *Kṛṣṇa-Līla*, *Rāsa-Līla* and other ritualistic *Vaiṣṇava* traditions, see Varapande (1982).
24. A similar argument was formulated by Michelutti who claimed that Mulayam Singh and Lalu Prasad Yadav are at times described by their caste supporters as *avatāras* of Krishna sent to Earth to protect 'the Oppressed' and promote social justice (Michelutti 2004: 60–61; 2009).
25. The figure of Lalu Prasad Yadav has been widely utilised by various sectors of Indian popular culture. He functions as a protagonist in popular jokes, as a model for commodities such as computer games, chocolates and even inspired and appeared in a Hindi film (*Padma Shree Laloo Prasad Yadav,* directed by Mahesh Manjrekar in 2007).
26. For a description of the Indian press, see Kumar 1999: 26–64.
27. This discussion focuses on visual representations of Lalu Yadav that link him or equate him to Kṛṣṇa in the mass media. However, these can also be found in other channels. Notably, Lalu is often referred to as the king of the Yadavs (echoing Kṛṣṇa's epithet *yādavendra*—the Indra/king of the Yadavs [*Bhāgavata Purāṇa* 10: 67, 90]). And see also IBN Live (2010). Lalu King of the Yadavs, New Delhi, IBN Live. http://ibnlive.in.com/videos/89509/kings-queens-2611-lalu-king-of-the-yadavs.html (accessed on 06.03.2017).
28. See, for example, the Bazaar Art painting of Kṛṣṇa on http://www.pbs.org/thestoryofindia/images/gallery/baby_krishna.jpg (accessed on 6 March 2017).
29. The cartoon depicting Yadav as a puffy-cheeked child is very popular. An example was published by *The Bihar Times* on 15 September 2004 and may also be downloaded from various websites: http://c2w.com/quizzes/26999-CARTOON-POLITICS/

questions?page=3 (accessed on 6 March 2017; open the link to question no. 21) and http://lalulaluyadav.blogspot.co.il/2007/07/laloo-prasad-yadav-tracker.html (accessed on 3 July 2014). Previously, it was accessible at http://o3.indiatimes.com/wildestdreams/archive/2005/12/23.aspx (accessed on 15 February 2010) and www.topmasala.in/jokes/celebrities-jokes/ (accessed on 6 March 2017). For the nickname 'fat cheeks', see Tewary (2005).

30. See http://caricaturecartoon.blogspot.co.il/2009/07/lalu-yadav.html (accessed on 6 March 2017).
31. See http://myagic.wordpress.com/2009/02/25/lalu-in-a-canadian-documentary/ (accessed on 6 March 2017).
32. See http://www.rediff.com/news/2005/jun/06look.htm and http://www.gettyimages.com/detail/news-photo/plump-doll-called-lalooji-is-pictured-on-the-shelves-in-a-news-photo/53025945#plump-doll-called-lalooji-is-pictured-on-the-shelves-in-a-toy-store-picture-id53025945 (both accessed on 6 March 2017).
33. See https://commons.wikimedia.org/wiki/File:Yashodha,_holding_a_toy_flute,_chases_the_naughty_boy_inside_a_Mughal-looking_palace_(bazaar_art,_1950%27s).jpg?uselang=de (accessed on 6 March 2017) Chowdhury (2006).
34. See https://plus.google.com/+BhaktiArtRenaissance/posts/2h7i3p8qDS4 and https://www.pinterest.com/pin/563231497119657118/ (both accessed on 6 March 2017).
35. The image of Lalu-*Gopāla* (with the bluish background) appeared in http://chauraha.wordpress.com/2008/06/19/lalu-hindi-english/as well as http://m.goanews.com/blog_details.php?id=40 (both accessed on 6 March 2017).
36. Interestingly, close to his 2013 conviction, the cow was turned into a raging bull in cartoons depicting Lalu. See http://www.indiabells.com/viewcartoons.php?c_id=539 (accessed on 3 July 2014), http://sheryartist.blogspot.co.il/2014/04/lalu-prasad-caricature-artist-shery.html (accessed on 6 March 2017) and http://www.apnewscorner.com/news/sports/details/2933/latest/Fodder-scam-Lalu-Prasad-jailed-for-5-years.html (accessed on 6 March 2017).
37. See http://caricaturecartoon.blogspot.co.il/2009/07/lalu-yadav.html (accessed on 6 March 2017) and http://www.indiantelevision.com/headlines/y2k5/jan/jan250.htm (accessed on 6 March 2017). Note that the affectionate dimension is further emphasised through the use of the long U. Using a short U instead of a long one would change the meaning to 'idiotic'.
38. See http://drishtikona.com/2004/05/05/laloos-bihar/ (accessed on 6 March 2017).
39. See the photograph made by photographer Dieser Datei here: https://commons.wikimedia.org/wiki/File:3_Hindu_deity_Krishna_on_ceramic_tile_at_Munnar_Kerala_India_2014.jpg?uselang=de (accessed on 6 March 2017); see also http://www.mygodpictures.com/beautiful-lord-gopal-sketch/ and http://www.glitters20.com/tag/janmashtami-images/page/4/ (both accessed on 6 March 2017).
40. See the representations of Kṛṣṇa at http://www.glitters20.com/tag/janmashtami-images/page/4/ (accessed on 6 March 2017) and similar designs at http://www.indusladies.com/forums/paintings/63844-tracing-designs-divine-pics-art.html (accessed on 6 March 2017).
41. Kṛṣṇa is one of the key figures of the *Gītā*. However, the figure of Kṛṣṇa as shaped by the *Gītā* is far removed from that of the *Purāṇas*. The Kṛṣṇa of the *Gīta* is an exemplary guru who embodies *dharmic* values, while the *purāṇic* one is the mischievous, order-breaching figure discussed here. The image of Lalu Yadav, as shaped by the mass media, refers to the *purāṇic* model alone and not to the one formulated by the *Gīta*.

42. Kṛṣṇa is one of the key figures of the *Gītā*. However, the figure of Kṛṣṇa as shaped by the *Gītā* is far removed from that of the *Purāṇas*. The Kṛṣṇa of the *Gīta* is an exemplary guru who embodies *dharmic* values, while the *purāṇic* one is the mischievous, order-breaching figure discussed here. The image of Lalu Yadav, as shaped by the mass media, refers to the *purāṇic* model alone and not to the one formulated by the *Gīta*.
43. Notably, every time Viṣṇu takes on an *avatāra*, this is to reinstate an interrupted cosmic order synonymous with *dharma*. However, Kṛṣṇa, more than the other Viṣṇu-*avatāras,* turns to *adharma* to do so. This is most apparent in the advice he gives to the pāṇḍavas during the Kurukṣetra war (Chakravarti 2006: 23–95).

References

Archer, William George. (1957) 2006. *The Loves of Krishna in Indian Painting and Poetry*. Charleston, North Carolina: BiblioBazaar.

Bhatt, Chetan. 2001. *Hindu Nationalism: Origins, Ideologies and Modern Myths*. New York, NY: Oxford-Berg.

Brosius, Christiane. 2007. '"I am a National Artist!": Popular Art in the Sphere of Hindutva'. In *Picturing the Nation—Iconographies of Modern India*, edited by Richard H. Davis, pp. 171–205. New Delhi: Orient Longman.

Chakrabarty, Dipesh, and Rochona Majumdar. 2010. 'Gandhi's Gita and Politics as Such'. *Modern Intellectual History* 7 (2): 335–53.

Chakravarti, Sitansu. 2006. *Ethics in the Mahabharata: A Philosophical Inquiry for Today*. New Delhi: Munshiram Manoharlal Publishers.

Chibber, Pradip K., Subhash Misra, and Richard Sisson. 1992. 'Order and the Indian Electorate: For Whom Does Shiva Dance?' *Asian Survey* 32 (7): 606–16.

Chowdhury, Amlan. 2006. '*Rabri takes Aloo and Laloo to New Home*'. Accessed on 23 February 2006 at http://ww1.mid-day.com/news/nation/2006/february/130208.htm

Davis, Richard H., ed. 2007. *Picturing the Nation: Iconographies of Modern India*. New Delhi: Orient Longman.

Dasgupta, Manas. 2007. 'BJP wears Mahatma's Mask to Hide its Ugly Face: Sonia'. *The Hindu*, New Delhi, 21 January. Accessed on 6 March 2017 at http://www.thehindu.com/todays-paper/tp-national/bjp-wears-mahatmas-mask-to-hide-its-ugly-face-sonia/article1785484.ece

De, Sushil Kumar. (1942) 1961. *The Early History of the Vaiṣṇava Faith and Movement in Bengal*. Calcutta: Firma.

Frankle, Francine. 2006. *India in Transition—Economics and Politics of Change—A Special Edition: Social Justice and Stalled Development: Caste Empowerment and the Breakdown of Governance in Bihar*. Philadelphia: Center for the Advanced Study of India—GE Foundation.

Freitag, Sandria B. 2002. 'The Realm of the Visual: Agency and Modern Civil Society'. *Contributions to Indian Sociology* 36 (1–2): 366–97.

———. 2007a. 'More than Meets the (Hindu) Eye: The Public Arena as a Space for Alternative Visions. In *Picturing the Nation: Iconographies of Modern India*, edited by Richard H. Davis, pp. 92–116. New Delhi: Orient Longman.

———. 2007b. 'South Asian Ways of Seeing, Muslim Ways of Knowing: The Indian Muslim Niche Market in Posters'. *The Indian Economic and Social History Review* 44 (3): 297–331.

Guha-Thakurta, Tapati. 2007. *Monuments, Objects, Histories*. New Delhi: Permanent Black.

Haberman, David L. 1988. *Acting as a Way of Salvation: A Study of the Rāgānuga Bhakti Sādhana*. New York and Oxford: Oxford University Press.

———. 1994. *Journey Through the Twelve Forests: An Encounter with Krishna*. New York and Oxford: Oxford University Press.

Hansen, Thomas Blom. 2001. *Wages of Violence: Naming and Identity in Postcolonial Bombay*. Princeton and Oxford: Princeton University Press.

IBN Live, 2010. 'Lalu King of the Yadavs', IBN Live. Accessed on 6 March 2017 at http://ibnlive.in.com/videos/89509/kings-queens-2611-lalu-king-of-the-yadavs.html

India Today. 1990. 'L.K. Advani's Rath Yatra: Charitos of Fire', *India Today,* New Delhi, 4 December.

Hindustan Times. 2011. 'Sonia Attends Dussehra Function', *Hindustan Times*, New Delhi, 6 December. Accessed on 3 April 2014 at http://www.hindustantimes.com/india-news/newdelhi/sonia-attends-dussehra-function/article1-754289.aspx

Jacob, Preminda. 2003. 'From Co-Star to Deity: Popular Representations of Jayalalitha Jayaram'. Women: A Cultural Review 8 (3): 327–37.

Jain, Kajri. 2003. 'More than Meets the Eye: The Circulation of Images and the Embodiment of Value'. In *Beyond Appearances? Visual Practices and Ideologies in Modern India*, edited by Sumathi Ramaswamy, pp. 33–70. New Delhi and London: SAGE Publications/Thousand Oaks.

———. 2007a. *Gods in the Bazaar: The Economies of Indian Calendar Art*. Durham and London: Duke University Press.

———. 2007b. 'The Efficacious Image: Picture and Power in Indian Mass Culture'. In *Picturing the Nation: Iconographies of Modern India*, edited by Richard H. Davis, pp. 144–70. New Delhi: Orient Longman.

Jain, Jyotindra, ed. 2007. *India's Popular Culture: Iconic Spaces and Fluid Images*. New Delhi: Marg.

Jameson, Frederic. 1981. *The Political Unconscious: Narrative as a Socially Symbolic Act*. Ithaca, N.Y.: Cornell University Press.

Jaffrelot, Christophe. 2000. 'The Rise of the Other Backward Classes in the Hindi Belt'. *Journal of Asian Studies* 59 (1): 86–108.

Kapur, Anuradha. 1990. *Actors, Pilgrims, Kings and Gods: The Ramlila at Ramnagar*. Calcutta: Seagull Books.

Keddie, Nikki R. 1998. 'The New Religious Politics: Where, When, and Why Do "Fundamentalisms" Appear?'. *Comparative Study of Society and History* 40 (4): 696–723.

Kumar, Keval J. 1999. *Mass Communication in India*. Mumbai: Jaico Publishing House.

Lama Tawa, Stephanie. 2001. 'Hindu Goddess and Women's Political Representation in South Asia: Symbolic Resource or Feminine Mystique?'. *Revue Internationale de Sociologie* [*International Revue of Sociology*]11 (1): 5–20.

Lochtefeld, James. 1996. 'New Wine, Old Skins: The Sangh Parivār and the Transformation of Hinduism'. *Religion* 26 (2): 101–17.

Lutgendorf, Phillip. 2003. 'Evolving a Monkey: Hanuman, Poster Art and Postcolonial Anxiety'. In *Beyond Appearances? Visual Practices and Ideologies in Modern India*, edited by Sumathi Ramaswamy, pp. 71–112. New Delhi and London: SAGE Publications/Thousand Oaks.

Lütt, Jürgen. 1996. 'From Krishnalila to Ramarajya: A Court Case and Its Consequences for the Reformation of Hinduism'. In *Representing Hinduism: The Construction of Religious Traditions and National Identity*, edited by Vasudha Dalmia and Heinrich von Stietencorn, pp. 142–53. New Delhi and London: SAGE Publications/Thousand Oaks.

Michelutti, Lucia. 2004. 'We (Yadavs) are a Caste of Politicians: Caste and Modern Politics in a North Indian Town'. *Contributions to Indian Sociology* 38 (1–2): 43–71.

———. 2008. 'We are Kshatriyas but we Behave like Vaishyas: Diet and Muscular Politics among a Community of Yadavs in North India'. *Journal of South Asian Studies* 31 (1): 76–95.

———. 2009. *The Vernacularization of Democracy: Caste, Class and Religion in India*. New Delhi: Routledge.

Nalapat, Madhavt. 2014. 'Modimatics: Minimum 240, target 300', *The Sunday Guardian,* New Delhi, 25 January. Accessed on 6 March 2017 at http://www.sunday-guardian.com/investigation/modimatics-minimum-240-target-300

Nandi, Ashis. 1970. 'The Culture of Indian Politics: A Stock Talking'. *The Journal of Asian Studies* 30 (1): 57–79.

NDTV. 2012. 'Zakia Case: "SIT Report Ignored Testimony against Narendra Modi", Says Retired Judge who Probed 2002 Riots', *NDTV*, New Delhi, 11 April. Accessed on 6 March 2017 at http://www.ndtv.com/article/india/zakia-case-sit-report-ignored-testimony-against-narendra-modi-says-retired-judge-who-probed-2002-rio-196167

Neumayer, Erwin, and Schelberger Christine. 2008. *Bharat Mata: India's Freedom Movement in Popular Art.* New Delhi: Oxford University Press.

Pinney, Christopher. 2003. *Photos of the Gods: The Printed Image and Political Struggle in India.* London: Reaktion.

———. 2004. *Photos of the Gods: The Printed Image and Political Struggle in India.* London: Reaktion.

Pollock, Sheldon. 1984. 'The Divine King in the Indian Epic'. *Journal of the American Oriental Society* 104 (3): 505–28.

———. 1993. 'Rāmāyaṇa and the Political Imagination in India'. *Journal of Asian Studies* 52 (2): 261–97.

Rajagopal, Arvind. 2001. *Politics after Television. Hindu Nationalism and the Reshaping of the Public in India.* Cambridge: Cambridge University Press.

Ramaswamy, Sumathi. 1999. 'Sanskrit for the Nation'. *Modern Asian Studies* 33 (2): 339–81.

———. 2002. 'Visualizing India's Geo-body: Globes, Maps, Bodyscapes'. *Contributions to Indian Sociology* 36 (1–2): 157–95.

———, ed. 2003. *Beyond Appearances? Visual Practices and Ideologies in Modern India.* New Delhi: SAGE Publications.

———. 2007. 'Maps, Mother/Goddesses and Martyrdom in Modern India'. *Journal of Asian Studies* 67 (3): 1–35.

———. 2008. 'Maps, Mother/Goddesses and Martyrdom in Modern India'. *Journal of Asian Studies* 67 (3): 1–35.

———. 2010. *The Goddess and the Nation: Mapping Mother India*. Durham and London: Duke University Press.

Roy, Srirupa. 2003. 'Moving Pictures: The Postcolonial State and Visual Representations of India'. In *Beyond Appearences? Visual Practices and Ideologies in Modern India*, edited by Sumathi Ramaswamy, pp. 223–64. New Delhi and London: SAGE Publications.

Saeed, Yousuf. 2007. 'Mecca versus the Local Shrine: The Dilemma of Orientation in the Popular Religious Art of Indian Muslims'. In *India's Popular Culture—Iconic Spaces and Fluid Images*, edited by Jyotindra Jain, pp. 76–89. New Delhi: Marg.

Saeed, Yousuf. 2011. *Muslim Devotional Art in India*. New Delhi: Routledge India.

Savarkar, V.D. 1923. *Hindutva*. New Delhi: Hindi Sahitya Sadan.

Shani, Ornit. 2010. 'Conceptions of Citizenship in India and the "Muslim Question"'. *Modern Asian Studies* 44 (1): 145–73.

Schechner, Richard. 1983. *Performance Circumstances from the Avant-Guard to Ramlila*. Calcutta: Seagull Books.

Shulman, David Dean. 1985. *The King and the Clown in South Indian Myth and Poetry*. Princeton: Princeton University Press.

Singh, Pritam. 2005. 'Hindu Bias in India's "Secular" Constitution: Probing Flaws in the Instruments of Governance'. *Third World Quarterly* 26 (6): 909–26.

Śrīmadbhāgavatam, with the Original Sanskrit Text, its Roman Transliteration, Synonyms, Translation and Elaborate Purports by Disciples of A.C. Bhaktivedanta Swami Prabhupāda. Tenth Canto, 'The Summum Bonum'. Los Angeles: Bhaktivedanta Book Trust, 1972–1989.

Tewary, Amarnath. 2005. 'Why We Should All Miss Lalu Yadav', *The Bihar Times*, Patna, 28 November. Accessed on 6 March 2017 at http://www.bihartimes.in/articles/amarnath/missinglaloo.html

Thakur, Ramesh. 1998. 'A Changing of Guard in India'. *Asian Survey* 38 (6): 603–23.

Thapar, Romila. 1989. 'Epic and History: Tradition, Dissent and Politics in India'. *Past and Present* 125 (1): 3–26.

Uberoi, Patricia. 2003. '"Unity in Diversity?" Dilemmas of Nationhood in Indian Calendar Art. Beyond Appearances?' In *Visual Practices and Ideologies in Modern India*, edited by Sumathi Ramaswamy, pp. 191–232. New Delhi and London: SAGE Publications.

———. 2006. *Freedom and Destiny—Gender, Family and Popular Culture in India*. New York and New Delhi: Oxford University Press.

Udayakumar, S.P. 1996. 'Betraying a Futurist—The Misappropriation of Gandhi's Ramarajya'. *Futures* 28 (10): 971–85.

Van der Veer, Peter. 1994. *Religious Nationalism: Hindus and Muslims in India*. Berkeley, Los Angeles and London: University of California Press.

Varapande, Manohar Laxman. 1982. *Krishna Theatre in India*. New Delhi: Abhinav Publications.

———. 1983. *Religion and Theatre*. New Delhi: Abhinav Publications.

Waghorne Punzo, Joanne. 1999. 'Chariots of the God/s: Riding the Line between Hindu and Christian'. *History of Religions* 39 (2): 95–116.

———. 2001. 'The Gentrification of the Goddess'. *International Journal of Hindu Studies* 5 (3): 227–87.

Warf, Barney, and John Grimes. 1997. 'Counterhegemonic Discourses and the Internet'. *Geographical Review* 87 (2): 259–74.

11

Amma Provides for All: Popular Devotional Aesthetics, Material Politics and the *Amman* in Tamil Nadu[1,2]

Jill Reese

In May 2011, the actress-turned-politician Jayalalithaa Jayaram was elected as the chief minister of Tamil Nadu for a third but not sequential term. News media widely attributed the success of the All India Anna Dravida Munnetra Kazhagam (AIADMK) party leader to campaign promises of material goods including fans, laptops, grinders and goats if the party were to be elected—what her critics gloss as 'freebies' equivalent to bribes for votes. In this chapter, I examine transformations in Jayalalithaa's public imagery beginning as her political predecessor's divine consort in the early 1990s to that of *Amma* (mother), an *amman* or mother goddess for the Tamil polity, and I provide a different reading of the turn to 'freebies' or campaign promises to garner votes. I argue that hers is an image regime that seeks to engage idioms of popular devotion to establish, maintain and reify corporeal and affective registers created through the consumption of items from what I broadly gloss as 'nutrition' schemes. The desired effect of the simultaneous consumption of her image alongside promised items is to sediment her persona in the public imagination as the benevolent *Amma* who provides sustenance for her devotees/public. This is done with the intention of not merely continuing governmental power at a state level, but for future national-level political achievement, where an iconic Jayalalithaa as *Amma* will be embraced nationwide.

This chapter is part of a larger intellectual project that examines how idioms of veneration are mobilised in a wide range of contexts in India and that the boundaries between the religious and the secular are rarely discrete. Further, it endeavours to enter an analysis of practices of veneration and governmental politics through its associated visual and material cultures, specifically, political imagery. Inherent in this is an understanding that image regimes are not mere representations to be 'read' as texts for meaning through surface-level aesthetics but that images also have the capacity to 'do'—to impact the viewer and generate knowledge (Losche 1995; Pinney 2004; Ramaswamy 2010), and that images can even be resistant to changes in aesthetic tropes.[3] This notion is borne out of an understanding of the agency of images and other 'things' to affect and be affected by the world around them (Appadurai 1986; Gell 1998). Inspired by a material turn in the study of religion that examines material dimensions of the relationships between objects and people in practices of devotion (Meyer 2008), this chapter proposes a turn to a 'material politics' that examines the materiality of political practices, including its associated visual culture, as well as the materials used in politics. A case study of the imagery of Jayalalithaa alongside what many consider her populist political practices illuminates the potential for a better understanding of the devotional and material aspects of her success.

A Brief History of Dravidian Party Politics

Before analysing the visual and material mechanisms engaged in Tamil politics and devotion, a very brief history of the origins and ideologies of the dominant Tamil political parties is necessary to understand Jayalalithaa's current place at the apex of Tamil politics. In 1967, the *Dravida Munnetra Kazhagam* (Dravidian Progress Federation, DMK) was the first party in India to oust the Indian National Congress in state elections. The Dravidian nationalist party was founded in 1949 by the Tamil screenwriter Annadurai, generally based on the ideologies of the Dravida Kazhagam (DK), a party that espoused notions that were a reaction to a perceived Brahman and North Indian cultural, religious and political hegemony. The platform of the DK, and later the DMK, was anti-Brahman, anti-North Indian and anti-Hindi, and supportive of atheism and a particular Tamil identity based largely on the language (Hardgrave Jr 1973). The DMK quickly utilised films as propaganda and incorporated popular cinema and theatre stars into the higher echelons of party leadership. While C.N. Annadurai led the party, the screenwriter M. Karunanidhi and the actor M.G. Ramachandran (MGR) vied for power. The first state-level electoral success in 1967 was driven by a political campaign featuring the charismatic MGR asking for votes from a hospital bed after being shot in the neck by fellow actor M.R. Radha (Pandian 1992).

After the death of Annadurai in 1969, Karunanidhi assumed DMK leadership, but the antipathy between him and MGR continued until MGR broke away to form the AIADMK in 1972, a party ideologically identical to the DMK. His party quickly overtook that of the DMK and he was elected the chief minister in 1977 and remained in power until his death 10 years later.

MGR's fan clubs served as regional party offices, and while many followed him to the new party, he also introduced fellow film stars to politics, the most prominent of whom was and continues to be Jayalalithaa. She played the heroine to MGR's hero in twenty films over a period of six years from 1965 to 1971 and is widely presumed to have been his mistress (Pandian and Geetha 1989; Vaasanthi 2006). In 1980, MGR incorporated Jayalalithaa into his cabinet, thus beginning her political career. She immediately bypassed many in the party who had spent years rising up the ranks and were dismayed by MGR's decision (Vaasanthi 2006). When MGR died, his wife Janaki, who had not previously been involved in politics, was urged by a faction of the party members to take over AIADMK leadership (Pandian and Geetha 1989). Meanwhile, Jayalalithaa claimed to be MGR's appointed successor and competed for party leadership. After a contentious battle, Jayalalithaa eventually succeeded in taking over party leadership. The DMK, still led by Karunanidhi, and the AIADMK continue to dominate Tamil politics and be alternately elected to power.

Jayalalithaa's Image Regime and the Aesthetics of Morality

An examination of the campaign imagery of Jayalalithaa, the state's most prominent female politician, provides an interesting case for the transformative potential of the image to counter perceived transgressions against social norms of morality through the amplification of distinct moral tropes; in this case, Jayalalithaa's personas as divine consort and later, *Amma*, to counter the negative perception of women in the public gaze such as film stars and politicians. The initial manifestation of

Jayalalithaa's image regime began during her first campaign as the leader of the AIADMK in 1991 and is important in distinguishing her political ambitions and responses by the Tamil polity. By 'image regime', I build upon Martin Jay's (1988) elaboration of Christian Metz's 'scopic regime'. Jay applies the term to examine European art in the modern era using aesthetic qualities such as perspective, spatiality, framing and tactility to define the boundaries of three visual subcultures. Here, 'image regime' is likewise used as shorthand to denote a body of images created by, for or in affiliation with a specific individual, group, movement or cause. The term incorporates the aesthetics, affects, rhetoric and, importantly in the sphere of Tamil if not all Indian politics, the public persona of the party leader. In the public images of Jayalalithaa, the image regime must be understood not merely as a publicity campaign that is a specific, orchestrated, visual and discursive message originating from one point—usually that of the party as designed, tested and marketed by an advertising or public relations firm or department, and disseminated from the top down. Instead, the image regimes of Tamil political parties derive from a fluid network of image-makers creating visual material using design motifs, slogans, photographs and film stills circulating in the public domain,[4] and who respond to the aesthetic successes of others while simultaneously noting the loosely sanctioned image-related standards coming from party leadership.[5]

When Jayalalithaa first contested a general election in opposition to the DMK, her claim to ascendancy was visually conveyed through specific choices of images of herself with MGR, as well as through a particular use of juxtaposition, scale, rhetoric and framing. As proposed by V. Geetha and M.S.S. Pandian (1989), the campaign imagery played upon the popular assumption that the unmarried and childless Jayalalithaa was MGR's mistress but repackaged the relationship as that of Jayalalithaa as the divine consort to MGR as god, an effective positioning given MGR's continued popularity and even a widespread veneration of him as a deity. This framing of their relationship was her claim to power but it also provided Jayalalithaa a method of assuaging concerns regarding her morality as a woman in the public sphere by providing the alternative benign persona of a divine consort.

Actresses, even those who portray on-screen deities, are generally not considered chaste due to their public lives.[6] The problem of their 'publicness' relates to actresses' historical association with prostitution that is also denoted in the Tamil language through the similarity of the terms for 'actress' and 'whore'.[7] Additionally, it is an actress' publicness and mobility that are considered outside social acceptability for women (Chinniah 2008; Seizer 2002). The virtue of her profession requires that an actress perform in public, either in front of a camera or a live audience, where she 'willingly exposes herself to the gaze of many unfamiliar men' (Seizer 2002: 120). The stigma is exacerbated by the fictive romances over her career with multiple men (Chinniah 2008). As the stigma makes it difficult to find a husband, historically, many actresses became mistresses.

The traditional ideal for Tamil womanhood is a moral persona attainable, and to a large degree expected, of every woman.[8] Regarded as a *cumankali*, or an idealised virtuous married woman, is most auspicious as a mother, especially of a son (Lakshmi 1990; Reynolds 1980). She is loving, kind and wise, a nurturer and upholder of Tamil culture and tradition. Her sphere is the private world of the home and she is submissive to her husband in all matters. Her *sakti*, or 'female generative force of the universe' (Wadley 1980: x),[9] is subdued and domesticated when she is married and yet it is assumed to be strong enough to protect her family from harm and death.[10] She remains a *cumankali* until her husband dies and her *thaali*, the sacred yellow thread tied around a woman's neck by her husband during their wedding ceremony, is the embodiment of her husband's protection (Ganesh 1990; Reynolds 1980).[11] For a woman without children, as long as she remains an unmarried virgin (*kanni*), she could eventually become an *amman,* which literally means 'mother', but in this context, refers to a type of unmarried and childless goddess whose *sakti* is unrestrained by a male partner (Ganesh 1990; Reynolds 1980). In traditional Tamil society, the *amman* is the only auspicious option for unmarried women of childbearing years.

Jayalalithaa asserted herself as MGR's political successor, but as a woman she faced multiple stigmas of being an unmarried actress who was now in politics—a very public position counter to the morally appropriate place of a married woman safely protected in the private sphere of the home. Such stigma was addressed by an inversion or rebranding of the assumed romantic relationship between Jayalalithaa and MGR, in that she became MGR's divine consort appointed to continue his vision. The claim that MGR chose her to be his heir was articulated in campaign speeches and articles published in her faction's newspapers, but especially in campaign imagery, many of which included film stills of MGR and Jayalalithaa as hero and heroine. In some political images, her body is turned towards MGR with head slightly bowed in deference, her hands placed together in respect—visually evoking her campaign statement that she would 'bring back MGR's rule' (Jacob 1997: 143). In others, MGR gazes down upon Jayalalithaa with beneficence, as if she were his perfect devotee. The connection with MGR was reiterated through the continuous circulation of their films throughout the state, decades after they were made

(Dickey 2008).[12] The campaign imagery often featured a much younger Jayalalithaa placed next to or below MGR, dressed in a white sari, while her body is gesturing towards his in supplication (Figure 11.1). It was her first positioning as a goddess, but attached and protected by MGR as god. Jayalalithaa needed to promote a culturally appropriate persona as divine consort to assuage the stigma of her public life. As reported by Sarah Dickey (2008), and also by my own informants, she won the election based upon her presumed appointment by MGR rather than on any of her own merits.

Figure 11.1

Images of MGR's induction of Jayalalithaa into the AIADMK are reprised for significant anniversaries such as this poster commemorating the party's founding, October 2013, Madurai, Tamil Nadu

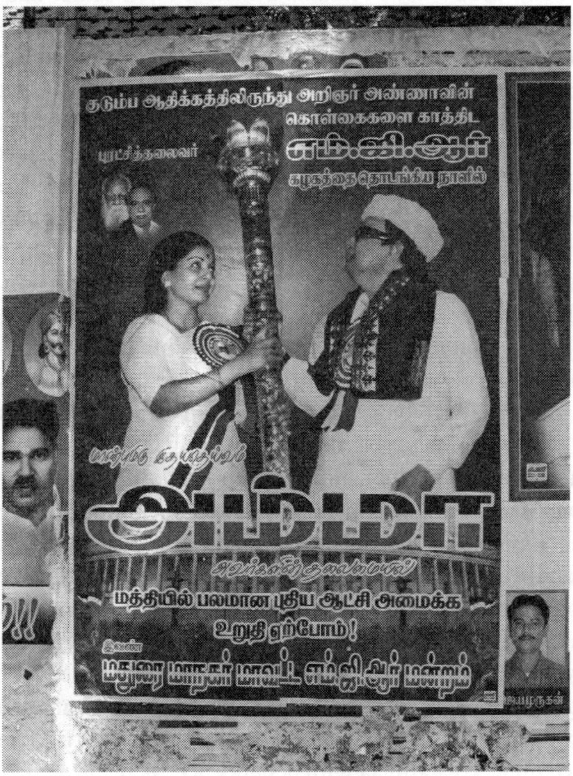

Source: Jill Reese.

The next incarnation of Jayalalithaa's image regime began after she achieved electoral power as the chief minister in 1991. Preminda Jacob (2009) documents the marked change in aesthetics of Jayalalithaa's image regime in which she now claims a majority of the image space rather than sharing equally with MGR. Jayalalithaa's forward-facing figure is solid with arms close to the body, always wearing a sari and a beatific smile, and has her hair pulled tightly back. She is christened *Amma*, aesthetically and semantically adopting the identity of an *amman*—the mother goddess whose children are her devotees. Jacob proposes that during this period, Jayalalithaa had so successfully solidified the claim of her *amman* status in imagery that her form reached a fixed state of iconicity where her body was in the static position of a religious idol with full frontality to the viewer, a half smile on her otherwise vacant face. Still, though, there remains reference to MGR who is the source of her power. Even while Jayalalithaa's image regime claimed her independent goddess-like status, MGR's photograph was usually stationed in the upper corners of the image.[13]

Aesthetics in imagery alone, however, have not been enough to persuade the Tamil electorate to widely embrace the beneficent persona of *Amma*. Sara Dickey (2008) provides ethnographic examples of how even AIADMK supporters considered her vindictive and unable to understand the plight of the poor. One man who admitted he voted for the AIADMK under Jayalalithaa's rule explained that MGR understood the suffering of the poor because he had experienced it himself, whereas 'Jayalalithaa doesn't know hunger because she was an actress, her mother was an actress, they were quite well off [...]' (Dickey 2008: 86).[14] At AIADMK rallies in early 2013, such sentiments were expressed to me from general party members who explained that even though Jayalalithaa was the leader, it was still 'MGR's party' and that they were 'MGR supporters'. Although Jayalalithaa transformed into *Amma* in the 1990s, even within her own party, members reported only voting for her based on their belief that she was directly appointed by MGR to continue his benevolent vision. Thus, her power within the party remained legitimised by the sustained veneration of the charismatic persona of her predecessor.[15]

While it is widely held that she was elected in 2011 based upon pledges of 'freebies', I argue that the electoral promises of material goods are more than mere pandering for votes. Instead, they are part of a grander design to connect with the Tamil populace on her own terms and in a way that simultaneously continues the *Amma* persona while also countering the perception that she does not understand the plight of the poor. Importantly, it demonstrates that Jayalalithaa as *Amma* had to be more than visual representation—that aesthetics as propaganda are not enough. Jayalalithaa must *demonstrate* benevolence to her subjects and thus engender the efficacy of her image.

Material Politics in the 2011 Election Campaigns

Jayalalithaa's failure to connect with the wider electorate as an aesthetic representation of a mother goddess, I propose, has in part prompted what I gloss as her 'nutrition schemes', a term used to encompass the various freebies and subsidised programmes aimed at providing sustenance for the mind, body and soul. These schemes are an effort to resonate with the affective registers of the Tamil body politic and spur the efficacy of her image regime as deity. The electoral promises are linked to her most recent image regime incarnation that includes touched-up photographs of her face on every item distributed, active images of her serving, giving and working rather than simply standing in iconic stasis, and proclamations that the items are given by her even when they are actually funded by state and local treasuries.

During the 2011 elections, Jayalalithaa promised voters everything from milch cows and food grinders to subsidised rice to gold for marriage *thaalis*. After entering the office as the chief minister, she established the Special Programme Implementation Department (SPID), a new and costly government office designed to coordinate the establishment of schemes and distribution of items from her election bid.[16] Depending on the project, it is paid for in part by the state treasury with local districts funding the remainder. Within her first year in office, the state government spent 250 million rupees under Jayalalithaa's directive on a national advertising campaign extolling her virtues as the chief minister with photographs that were uncharacteristically digitally altered to brighten her complexion and minimise wrinkles and other signs of aging (Rajan 2012). The AIADMK Propaganda Secretary recognised these as the official photographs of Jayalalithaa and a select few chosen to emblaze items doled out under the nutrition schemes.

Jayalalithaa's nutrition schemes are differentiated here under three broad categories, those of the mind, the body and the soul. To begin,

Figure 11.2

A government-issued laptop with original plastic covering to protect Jayalalithaa's image, August 2013, Madurai, Tamil Nadu

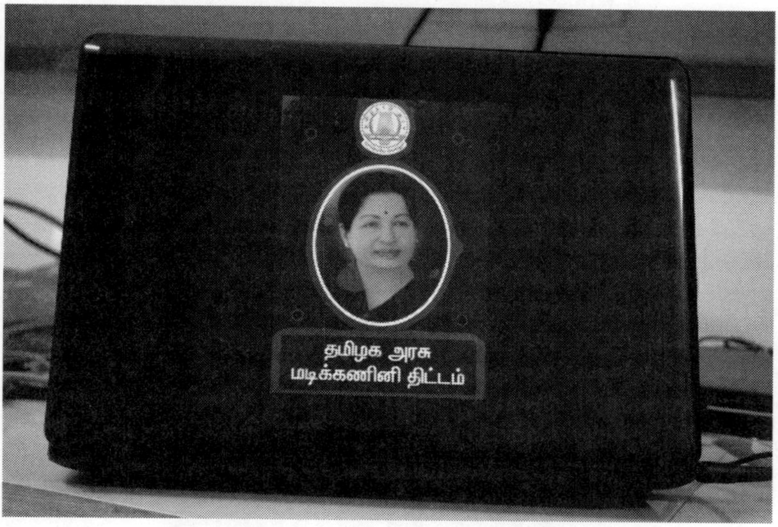

Source: Jill Reese.

Jayalalithaa's schemes pertaining to the enrichment of the mind include her most popular programme—free laptops for all university, and, later, secondary students regardless of caste or financial need. The distribution of laptops to college students began in early 2012 and was followed by the 11th and 12th standard students later that year. By the end of the first year of distribution, the SPID endeavoured to distribute nearly one million laptops (Rangaswami 2011). As seen in Figure 11.2, the cover of each laptop is dominated by one of the touched-up photographs of Jayalalithaa from the national advertisement campaign along with the Tamil Nadu government's logo and the words *Tamilaga Arasu Madikkanini Thiddam* (Tamil Government Laptop Programme). Each laptop is accompanied by a black backpack with a matching photograph screen-printed onto the canvas.[17] Other schemes for the enrichment of the mind include backpacks, notebooks, pencils, colour pencils, atlases, protractors, uniforms and shoes for children attending government schools, a broadening of funding schemes to help pay college tuition and bicycles for students from Scheduled Caste/Scheduled Tribe (SC/ST) communities to help them get to school.[18]

Figure 11.3

A woman holds a new 'Amma fan', March 2014, Madurai, Tamil Nadu

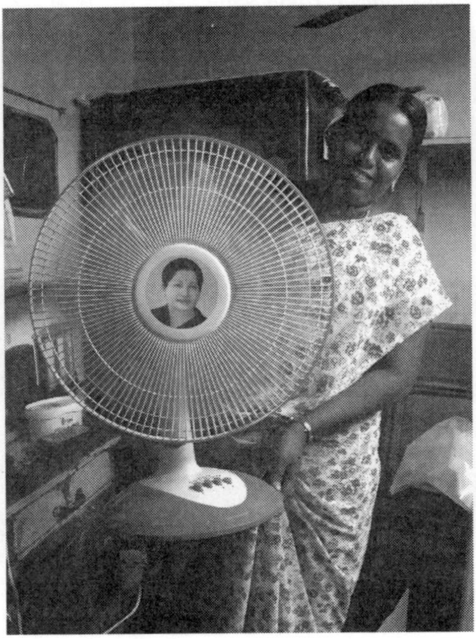

Source: Jill Reese.

By far, the largest nutrition scheme is that of the body, especially those dealing directly with food and its preparation. Jayalalithaa's campaign promises included free goats, milch cows, sheep, safe drinking water, fans, mixers and grinders mostly for SC/ST communities but also many other groups, as well as highly subsidised rice and other food staples. These promises were implemented and every item features images of her face either on the object itself or on a bag accompanying it, as seen in Figure 11.3 of a free fan. Jayalalithaa's face is printed onto the plastic centrepiece of the fan cover as if she watches over her subjects as they are cooled by her beneficence. Grinders and mixers also have her image with the Tamil Nadu government logo. In addition to free drinking water for some communities, bus terminals and railway stations began offering subsidised bottled water for 10 rupees each. Each bottle has the word *Amma* in English and Tamil moulded into the plastic and wrapped with a label featuring Jayalalithaa's photograph (Figure 11.4).

Figure 11.4

A vendor sells 'Amma water' that is decorated with Jayalalithaa's image, November 2013, Madurai, Tamil Nadu

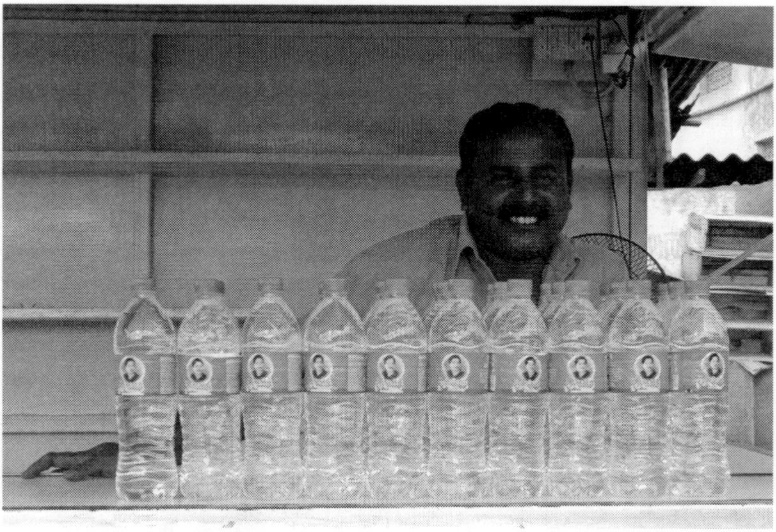

Source: Jill Reese.

Another highly successful food scheme is *Amma Unavagam* (*Amma* Canteen), a chain of hundreds of government-owned restaurants selling Tamil food such as idli, sambar rice, curd rice, lemon rice and chapattis at prices greatly below market value. The seed for the idea began under the DMK administration when they proposed that privately owned canteens and restaurants serve certain communities discounted food items,[19] but under Jayalalithaa's scheme, the plan was greatly expanded and heavily rebranded as her project to feed the poor.[20] Beginning with a couple of locations in Chennai, the restaurants feature 'healthy' food made in a kitchen with high sanitation standards and are run solely by women employed through local women's self-help groups. These restaurants have been set up in most of the major cities of Tamil Nadu since their introduction in late 2012, with more planned in other localities. The restaurants run at an annual deficit, partially made up by state coffers but mostly funded by district governments. The project is billed as one of empowerment for women, an effort to feed healthy food to the poor at affordable prices, and all under the

Figure 11.5

Women serve patrons at Amma Unavagam, *the state-wide restaurant chain selling government-subsidised food, November 2013, Madurai, Tamil Nadu*

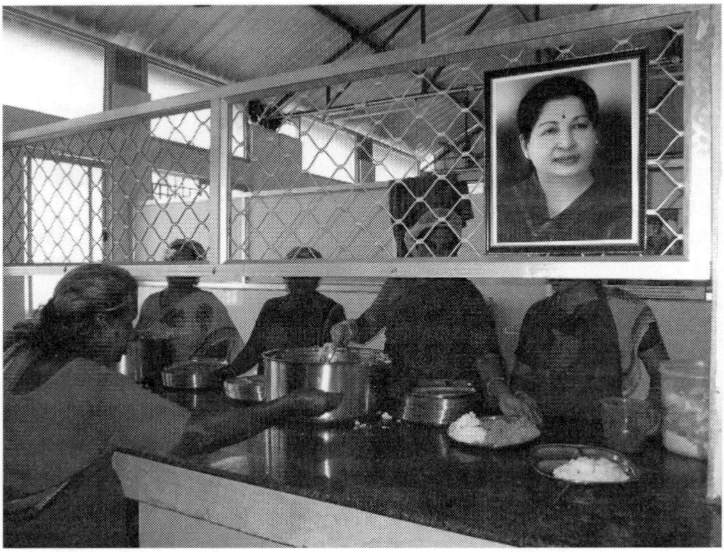

Source: Jill Reese.

gaze of Jayalalithaa whose face adorns the interiors and exteriors of every location (Figure 11.5).

Finally, Jayalalithaa has implemented several government schemes and projects aimed at nourishing the souls of her devotees. First, to make marriage more affordable for SC/ST women, Jayalalithaa promised four grams of gold to be used for each woman's wedding *thaali*. While such a scheme is not explicitly religious, it is considered here within the purview of soul nourishing because marriage is an essential part of identity and morality in Tamil society, especially for women. Providing gold for the *thaali* helps disadvantaged women afford marriage given that dowry continues to be widely practiced. Jayalalithaa also assists in the successful commencement of marriage by periodically hosting and presiding at mass weddings in Chennai where she bestows blessings upon the couples (*India Today*, Chennai, 18 June 2012).

A much more costly project is the founding and maintenance of large monuments of religious and cultural figures. In an effort to claim credit and authority over the realm of public monuments, Jayalalithaa has initiated the remodelling and extensive upkeep of statues, temples and buildings throughout the state but especially the monuments in Kanyakumari, a place notable for its location at the apex of the convergence of three bodies of seawater (the Lakshadweep Bay, Indian Ocean and Bay of Bengal). In 1979, MGR's AIADMK administration laid the foundation stone for an enormous statue to Thiruvalluvar, the revered Tamil poet, on a small island just off the coastline. The DMK, however, takes credit for the project because the statue was constructed while Karunanidhi was in power. In March 2013, Jayalalithaa began an 8.7 million rupee renovation project to protect the statue with chemical coating. She publicly reminded Karunanidhi that MGR began the project after Karunanidhi criticised Jayalalithaa for neglecting the statue during her previous two terms as chief minister (*Times of India*, Kanyakumari, 3 March 2013). Jayalalithaa also initiated projects to restore other buildings and temples within the notable city.

In going beyond ascribing herself credit for existent statues and temples, Jayalalithaa announced in 2013 that she would erect a statue of the mother goddess *Tamilttay* (literally Mother Tamil) in the city of Madurai that will be taller than the Kanyakumari statue of Thiruvalluvar. *Tamilttay* is the language personified as mother, goddess and queen—a modern invention of the embodiment of the Tamil language at a time when it was considered under threat by the central government's proposed implementation of Hindi as the official language of India (Ramaswamy 1997).[21] This in turn fuelled the anti-North Indian rhetoric espoused by Dravidian parties. To those who praised *Tamilttay*, she linked the Tamil language with an imagined glorious pre-colonial past where she was 'patronised by great Tamil kings' (ibid.: 19) and thrived on the devotion of her subjects. Additionally, during the anti-Hindi agitations, it was Karunanidhi who popularised *Tamilttay* through poetry and chants (ibid.). Installing a statue in her honour would allow Jayalalithaa to minimise Karunanidhi's historic devotion of *Tamilttay*. The location of Madurai is essential because for many Tamilians, especially in the south of the state, it is considered the home of Tamil culture and thus the most suitable residence for the mother of the language. Another motivation for Jayalalithaa's selection of Madurai may be because the city has historically been more supportive of the DMK.

Jayalalithaa's choice of *Tamilttay* for a towering monument is revealing. She could have chosen a number of figures important to Tamil history and culture, the most pertinent to her political trajectory being MGR. She inaugurated several of his hundreds of statues throughout the state (all on a scale of miniature to slightly larger than life-sized) and a visualisation of Jayalalithaa's future inauguration of an enormous statue of her benefactor would be most consistent with the earliest phase of her image regime in which she gazes towards MGR in supplication. It would continue his place in the party hierarchy and serve as a reminder that he is her original and primary means to power. However, for these reasons, an inhumanly scaled MGR in comparison to Jayalalithaa would instead complicate, if not thwart, her greater political ambitions because they prevent the solidification of an iconic stance of her own. To get out from under MGR's shadow, Jayalalithaa needs to choose a figure in line with her desire for independent political authority. *Tamilttay* becomes an appropriate choice to visually represent Jayalalithaa's ambitions because she already embodies, in the truest sense, the form Jayalalithaa wishes to achieve—that of mother, goddess and leader of the people, or queen.

Beyond that, *Tamilttay* is a particular kind of goddess—one who is independent and childless, nurturing and protective to her devotees who are her children, but powerful in her own right. She is essentially an *amman* without the potential for capriciousness and volatility, and not clearly defined within a particular Hindu tradition—thus, the very figure Jayalalithaa's image regime asserts for the party leader. Interestingly, this brand of female divine power has its corollary in the urban middle-class trend of reterritorialising powerful but volatile village goddess within the walls of mostly privately funded neighbourhood temples in Chennai. Often originally smallpox *ammans*, they are made benign through the removal of capricious characteristics that make them volatile and potentially vengeful, and are legitimised with Agamic authority through the institution of Brahman priests as ritual intermediaries (Waghorne 2001). They retain the essential functions characteristic of *ammans* such as fertility, healing and protection of devotees (Ganesh 1990). *Amma*, as presented by Jayalalithaa's image regime and with the schemes implemented by her administration, reflects this trend towards reterritorialised village goddesses in urban centres who continue to look after the health, prosperity and spiritual well-being of their devotees. In the 2000s, Jayalalithaa's image regime projected her as an *amman*, but it was considered superficial because the common opinion was that she did not look after the well-being of her subjects. Thus, the image regime was not widely embraced by the general population, let alone her party members. While retaining the aesthetics of the *amman* imagery, Jayalalithaa has implemented schemes to address the needs of her subjects.

Importantly, her current image regime includes the circulation of party images depicting Jayalalithaa *demonstrating* the actions of caring for her electorate. In one photograph, Jayalalithaa stands alongside *Amma Unavagam* workers and is moments away from delving a ladle into a large pot of curd rice to scoop onto a waiting plate. In another, Jayalalithaa is handing a large bag of rice with her face printed onto the bag's fabric to an eager female recipient in the state capital of Chennai. In addition to the many photographs of her bestowing items upon enthusiastic recipients, there are a small series that feature her seated at a desk while wearing large reading glasses, pen poised over paper and (we are to presume) putting her schemes into effect. Each of the photographs are regurgitated throughout the state on posters pasted on public streets, recreated in hand-painted murals, printed in the party's newspapers, used to decorate *Amma Unavagams* and included in installations created for Jayalalithaa's birthday on 2 February 2014. These installations were put up at bus stands, railway stations and party offices throughout Madurai, and the city's mayor V.V. Rajan Challappa travelled to each location for their individual ribbon cuttings along with other party dignitaries. Not only is Jayalalithaa a static icon accessible in print, she is also an active *amman* performing the functions essential to her subjects' care.

Aesthetics of Popular Devotion and the Sedimentation of *Amma*

What role does Jayalalithaa's imagery play in the continuation of state-level power and future national politics? What is it that her image regime as iconic goddess seeks to activate? This section explores the mechanics engaged in the entanglement of image regime, material goods and the Tamil polity. I will argue that the efficacy of her image regime as *Amma* is mediated by corporeal image practices and the aesthetics of popular devotion. There is a sensuous dimension to the interaction between people and images in South Asian visual practices, a tactile and embodied 'looking' that links the materiality of images with the beholder. The basis of this is *bhakthi* or loving devotion (Bate 2002), an active and direct relationship with the divine without need of an intermediary such as a priest. In order to activate the exchange of gazes to create a connection with a deity, the deity's image, icon or representation must be invested with divine agency through ritualised worship, thus 'activating' the image (Jain 2007).

Located within the practices of *bhakthi* is *darshan*—the reciprocal gaze between deity and devotee, the process of seeing and being seen by the divine (Babb 1981; Eck 1981) 'that moves the devotee to merge with the divine through one's flesh, not by transcending it' (Ghosh 2011: 82). Thus, at its most basic level, image relations and actions with the divine in India are visually *and* corporeally situated. Jayalalithaa was not the first ruler to attempt to mobilise *bhakthi* practices with subjects in an effort to solidify political power. There is a long history of local devotion to certain politicians through the practice of 'taking *darshan*' with leaders and even the dedication of temples to them (Jacob 2009; Pandian 1992). Sandria Freitag (2001) stresses the importance of the gaze between South Indian kings and their subjects for the symbolic and materials transactions of patronage relationships.[22] The public exchange of gazes served to unite, even if only temporarily, the various groups and constituencies of the ruler within an assembled whole, thus helping to form a community. Freitag writes that 'only the ruler could trigger the exercise of the gaze, but without the audience's physical proximity, he could not put the expected action into play' (2001: 41).[23] The street became a space where the public participated in ritual life through the exchange of gazes with not just deities on procession but with kings on procession as well, and legitimised regal authority through visual transaction. Even Jayalalithaa sought direct street-level *darshan* earlier in her political career by posting timings in which she would appear on her balcony for her subjects to 'take' *darshan* (Vaasanthi 2006). The public spaces of the street continue to play an essential role in the projection and contestation of political power, and thus, it is imperative that Jayalalithaa's image regime (and not just Jayalalithaa herself) be invested with *darshanic* efficacy if she is to present herself as an *amman*.

To clarify on the idea of image efficacy, Christopher Pinney proposes a somatic approach to the visual with 'corpothetics', a neologism for 'embodied, corporeal aesthetics' (2004: 8).[24] This is in stark contrast to a Kantian understanding of aesthetics that is de-somatised where the mind, as disembodied, gazes disinterestedly upon an object. Corpothetics in Indian visual practices stresses the *efficacy* of an image over what it 'looks' like to a viewer. The initial offering of *Amma* by Jayalalithaa's image regime offered the visual aesthetics of an *amman* with the iconic status of her solid form in a fully frontal position and the beatific smile on an otherwise blank face. It failed to resonate with the public because the imagery was inefficacious—*Amma's* image was not corporeally linked to her devotees because she had not demonstrated loving care for their minds, bodies and souls. The nutrition schemes were introduced in an effort to address that failure.

In returning to the mechanics of visual and material relations, images have the ability to work upon the body through affect—a corporeally based zone of intensities, a resonance experienced at a pre-subjective, and hence pre-social, level (Massumi 1995; Mazzarella 2009). Affect differs from emotion in that emotion is an abstraction that is socially qualified. For example, affect is indeterminately registered within the body, but emotion is felt, acknowledged and qualified based upon socially constructed ideas of what that particular emotion feels like and what it signifies. The difference between affect and emotion is one of 'resonation or interference, amplification or dampening' (Massumi 1995: 86). If the nutrition schemes are successful, Jayalalithaa's image regime will be efficacious with the affective registers of the general Tamil public who will associate her image with being fed, educated, cooled, protected and otherwise nourished by *Amma*.

In solidifying the link between *Amma's* image and the nutrition schemes, Jayalalithaa's face accompanies every item offered under the schemes by being directly printed or pasted onto either the item or the materials that accompany it such as the bags containing rice. This contributed to the continuation of her current political power and future political ambitions because the combination of the circulating imagery of Jayalalithaa as an *amman*, the nutrition schemes and the branding materials with her face and the name stabilises her narrative as a leader who cares for her subjects and sediments the icon of *Amma*. Bishnupriya Ghosh (2011) proposes the analytic device of the 'corporeal aperture' of an icon to understand the materiality of such circulating imagery and the mechanics of how icons operate. She employs 'aperture' because it is an apparatus within an image device that mediates the amount of light moving from the lens to the film or sensor plate. For Ghosh, icons likewise operate as a mediatory apparatus between subject and image object, allowing the subject to 'enter' a then and there, or place and time, projected or contained by the icon such as the so-called Tank Man photograph from 1989 in Tiananmen square where a single man faces multiple approaching tanks. Globally syndicated via news media, the image evolved to evoke not merely the defiance of one individual against a militarised autocratic regime but also a supposedly 'universal' ideal of democracy experienced by the majority of those who had access to the photograph, but desired by those who are not yet living in democratic freedom.[25] Ghosh incorporates 'corporeal' into her term based upon the sensory and bodily dimensions of 'looking', where the beholder is never disengaged from their own corporeal bodies as fields of power nor detached from affective sensations activated through human–image interactions. As Jayalalithaa's nutrition schemes unfold and the Tamil population consumes the material goods offered along with her image, the icon of *Amma* works upon the corporeal and affective registers of the beholder to transport them to a time when they were cared for by Jayalalithaa as *amman*.

This returns us to the most recent incarnation of image regime of Jayalalithaa. I argue that the aesthetic evolution of Jayalalithaa's image regime to *Amma* and the introduction and implementation of 'nutrition schemes' during and after the 2011 elections is motivated by her larger national political ambitions that necessitate a solidification of her persona to enable her continuation in state power and perception of her ability to implement beneficial socio-economic development to those outside Tamil Nadu. The mechanism for doing so rests upon engaging embodied visual practices through the deification of Jayalalithaa as *amman* not just through representational aesthetics in campaign imagery but through the corporeal and affective registers created through associations of being fed, educated, cooled and spiritually supported by Jayalalithaa through her nutrition schemes—thus, creating a feedback loop between image and embodied sensations. Through such reification, her image regime accrues positive symbolic associations within its density to finally become sedimented (Barthes [1957] 1972; Pinney 2004) with the solid and stabilised narrative of *Amma*, the *amman* who nourishes the Tamil polity. With aspirations of national power, the image regime seeks to project the sedimented icon of Jayalalithaa beyond states' borders to present a leader who has successfully developed her state and who has the skills to develop the nation. Never too early to unveil what could be the next phase of her image regime—christened here as that of *Amma*, Goddess of the Nation—the AIADMK commissioned party images for the 2014 Lok Sabha elections featuring Jayalalithaa framed by India Gate, the archway on the Rajpath facing Sansad and Rashtrapati Bhavans (Figure 11.6). The structure is adorned with the two-leaf icon of the party, and MGR and Annadurai's portraits are affixed on either side of the 'India Gate' nameplate. A giant atmospheric Jayalalithaa gazes out from each side of the monument as if she were watching over her subjects, which extends to all of the citizens of India.

Figure 11.6

Imagery created for the 2014 Lok Sabha elections depict Jayalalithaa framed by India Gate with photographs of MGR and Annadurai positioned above her, May 2014, Madurai, Tamil Nadu

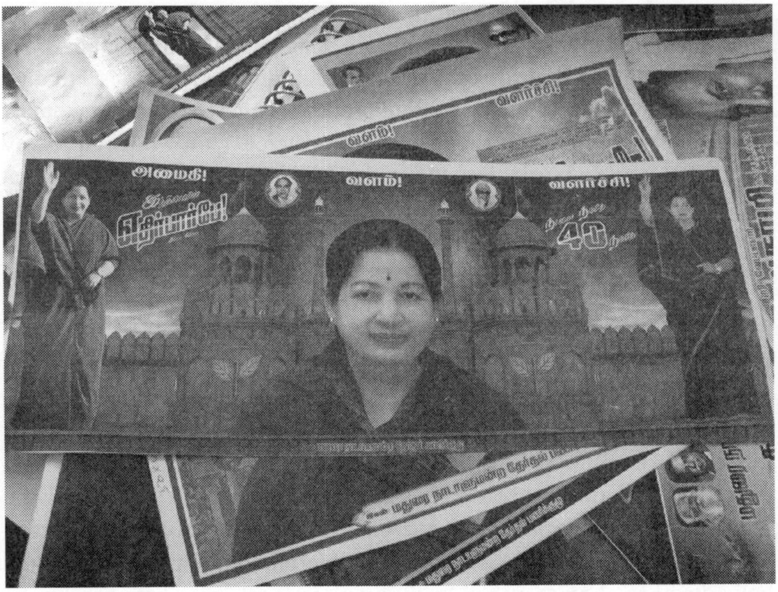

Source: Jill Reese.

Conclusion

In conclusion, there has been an intimate, albeit at times antagonistic, relationship between politics and religion in the history of the Indian state of Tamil Nadu, with nearly a half century of dominance by Dravidian nationalist parties founded on ideologies that espoused atheism and anti-Brahman, anti-North Indian hegemony, and with the aim of preserving a distinct Tamil identity. This chapter examined the idioms of devotion at work in the political imagery and recent government schemes of Jayalalithaa who rose to power within a Dravidian party although she is a devout Hindu Brahman woman not of Tamil origin. Despite much contestation, the former Tamil actress asserted herself as heir to the party after the death of its founder, MGR, the charismatic actor-cum-politician whose persona continues to be venerated throughout the state. Jayalalithaa's claim to ascendency was articulated mostly dramatically in widespread campaign materials perpetuating the popular perception of her as MGR's divine consort, including images from religious films, known as mythologicals, in which Jayalalithaa played consort to MGR as deity. There was a transition in the political imagery of Jayalalithaa once her claim to ascendancy was legitimised and she gained party power. As other scholars have noted, Jayalalithaa's image was transformed into that of *Amma*, playing the role of a revered *amman* who is either a 'mother goddess' whose children are her devotees or a chaste childless woman, and the only auspicious position for an unmarried adult woman in Tamil society, and a role Jayalalithaa is seemingly suited to fill as an independent former actress who has never been married. I aimed to go beyond the aesthetics of transformation in physical form to propose a corporeally based image regime that works to bind patrons to the goddess through the corporeal and affective registers resonating with the intake of the nourishment she provides in the form of government schemes implemented in the past two years of her current administration. These included the distribution of food preparation goods, new laptops for students, subsidised rice, a state-wide chain of government restaurants that offer nutritious meals well below market price and other schemes to provide sustenance for the body, mind and soul, all of which are financed by the state and municipal treasuries. Through the distribution of material items always emblazoned with her beatific smile, the image regime seeks to work upon idioms of popular devotion through embodied visual relationships with divine images, and resonate with the corporeal and affective registers associated with the consumption of *Amma's* benevolence in the form of nutrition scheme items.

Notes

1. An earlier version of this chapter was delivered at the 2013 Annual Conference for the British Association for the Study of Religion on the panel Bodies of Veneration: Motion and Change as Devotional Aspects in India, organised by Urmila Mohan. I am grateful for the many helpful comments and feedback from audience members, participants and the editors of this volume. Any errors or omissions are my own.
2. On 5 December 2016, while the chapter was in the process of being submitted to the publisher, suddenly news broke that Jayalalithaa had passed away. However, the arguments of the chapter remain valid despite *Amma's* death.
3. For example, Christopher Pinney (2007) demonstrates such resistance in the imagery of the cult hero Ramdev.
4. Public domain is used here to explain that creative elements are derived from sources that have been published or posted in media and are accessible to the public at large, rather than as intellectual property available without copyright restrictions.

5. The DMK has less of a reputation for attempting to moderate party imagery than the AIADMK, while under the leadership of Jayalalithaa, however, Karunanidhi has publicly reprimanded artists who have made 'mistakes' in poster design.
6. Female politicians also face stigmas associated with public identities outlined in this section. See C.S. Lakshmi (1997) on how women in the 1920s' Self-Respect Movement in Tamil Nadu reconceptualised male party members as family members (brother, father) in an effort to assuage prejudices about their activities outside the domestic sphere and thus justify political involvement. See also Uwe Skoda (2004) on the contrasting uses of kinship relations to alternatively identify or condemn two female politicians in the 2004 electoral contest between Sonia Gandhi (Indian National Congress) and Sushma Swaraj (Bharatiya Janata Party).
7. Susan Seizer notes that this affiliation is conveyed in the Tamil language in words such as *taci, tevatiyal, kutti,* and *kuttiyal*, all translate as 'actress' but also as 'dancing girl', 'prostitute', 'concubine' and 'whore' (2002: 117).
8. What is presented here is the traditional moral code in simplified form, the terms of which are negotiated in the lived experiences of women.
9. Men also possess *sakti*, but it is assumed that it is substantially less than that possessed by women (Reynolds 1980).
10. Traditionally, there is the assumption that a woman's chastity, i.e., morality, is tied to her ability to protect her family so that if some illness or tragedy were to befall them, her moral character would be in question (Egnor 1980).
11. Morality is considered materialised in the *thaali* (Reynolds 1980).
12. Their films continue to be regularly shown in Madurai and elsewhere in Tamil Nadu.
13. This is a popular image convention throughout India whereby a religious or political figure is placed in the upper third of the frame, and often in a corner, so as to convey benevolence, authority or legitimacy over the figure(s) in the bottom two-thirds of the image. See Sumathi Ramaswamy (2010) for numerous examples of this convention in images containing both religious and political figures positioned in relation to *Bharat Mata* (Mother India).
14. Although many studies, such as that conducted by M.S.S. Pandian (1992), have demonstrated that MGR's policies largely favoured the economic elite, the idea that he provided for the poor continues to be widely popular.
15. This chapter was written before the judgment in the nearly two decade-long disproportionate assets case against Jayalalithaa in which she was accused of possessing and spending well beyond the assets she had previously claimed, and for which she was sentenced to four years in prison. During the 18 months of fieldwork ending in June 2014 that informed this chapter, few people, regardless of political affiliation, specifically mentioned the ongoing case against Jayalalithaa when they spoke of her legitimacy as leader of the AIADMK. Instead, she was generally included in broad statements about corruption in politics such as 'All Tamil politicians are corrupt' or 'People enter politics to get rich.'
16. See http://www.tn.gov.in/rti/proactive/spi/handbook_spi.pdf (accessed on 21 May 2012).
17. The first distribution of laptops and backpacks featured stickers affixed to each, which many students quickly removed. Since then the images have been screen-printed onto the object to make extraction more difficult. Several students I spoke with had tediously applied nail polish remover to the backpacks to remove the image or had covered the photograph with a larger sticker. Additionally, it is now a crime to resell the laptops, though the practice continues to be frequent and widespread.

18. See www.tn.gov.in/schemes (accessed on 12 October 2013).
19. As told to me by *Amma Unavagam* workers and DMK party members.
20. It should be noted that anyone regardless of economic status is allowed dine at the restaurants. Based on interviews with patrons and restaurant staff, the majority of customers in Madurai tend to be male daily-wage earners. It is not uncommon for some patrons to consume both breakfast and lunch at an *Amma Unavagam* each day.
21. For a comparison of *Tamilttay* to *Bharat Mata*, see Ramaswamy (1997). For an extensive analysis of *Bharat Mata* images and history, see Ramaswamy (2010).
22. See Pamela Price (1996) for a more extensive history of royal–patron relationships in pre-colonial South India.
23. Freitag writes that in early modern India, there was 'a gaze that simultaneously shaped and reflect' because it was both 'panoptican' [sic] and mobile, where the gaze of the government was 'quite successfully *contested* by the surveillance exercised by civil society' (emphasis by Freitag 2001: 50).
24. The term is based upon the root of aesthetics, from the ancient Greek *aisthitikos*, a word meaning something akin to 'corporeal, material nature' (2004: 19).
25. Another example offered by Ghosh is the forward-looking aspirations of 'hope' and 'change' associated with the iconic image of Barack Obama created for the 2008 election campaign, where the then and there to be entered through the icon is a post-election period of American progress, liberal ideals and racial and economic equality.

References

Appadurai, Arjun. 1986. 'Introduction: Commodities and the Politics of Value'. In *The Social Life of Things: Commodities in Cultural Perspective*, edited by Arjun Appadurai, pp. 3–63. Cambridge: Cambridge University Press.

Babb, Laurance A. 1981. 'Glancing: Visual Interaction in Hinduism'. *Journal of Anthropological Research* 37 (4): 378–410.

Barthes, Roland. (1957) 1972. *Mythologies*. Translated by Annette Lavers. New York, NY: Hill and Wang.

Bate, Bernard J. 2002. 'Political Praise in Tamil Newspapers: The Poetry and Iconography of Democratic Power'. In *Everyday Life in South Asia*, edited by Diane P. Mines and Sarah Lamb, pp. 308–25. Bloomington: Indiana University Press.

Chinniah, Sathiavathi. 2008. 'The Tamil Film Heroine: From a Passive Subject to a Pleasurable Object'. In *Tamil Cinema: The Cultural Politics of India's Other Film Industry*, edited by Selvaraj Velayutham, pp. 29–43. New York, NY: Routledge.

Dickey, Sara. 2008. 'The Nurturing Hero: Changing Images of MGR'. In *Tamil Cinema: The Cultural Politics of India's Other Film Industry*, edited by Selvaraj Velayutham, pp. 111–23. New York, NY: Routledge.

Eck, Diana L. 1981. *Darśan: Seeing the Divine in India*. Chambersburg: Anima Books.

Egnor, Margaret. 1980. 'On the Meaning of Sakti to Women in Tamil Nadu'. In *The Powers of Tamil Women*, edited by Susan S. Wadley, pp. 1–34. Syracuse: Maxwell School of Citizenship and Public Affairs.

Freitag, Sandria B. 2001. 'Visions of the Nation: Theorizing the Nexus between Creation, Consumption, and Participation in the Public Sphere'. In *Pleasure and the Nation: the History, Politics and Consumption of Popular Culture in India*, edited by Rachel Dwyer and Christopher Pinney, pp. 35–75. Delhi: Oxford University Press.

Ganesh, Kamala. 1990. 'Mother Who is Not a Mother: In Search of the Great Indian Goddess'. *Economic and Political Weekly* 25 (42–43): WS58–64.

Gell, Alfred. 1998. *Art and Agency*. Oxford: Clarendon Press.

Ghosh, Bishnupriya. 2011. *Global Icons: Apertures to the Popular*. Durham: Duke University Press.

Hardgrave Jr, Robert L. 1973. 'Politics and the Film in Tamilnadu: The Stars and the DMK'. *Asian Survey* 13 (3): 288–305.

India Today. 2012. 'Extravagant Jayalalithaa Spends Rs. 4.5 cr of State Money on Mass Weddings'. *India Today,* Chennai, 18 June. Accessed on 7 December 2014. http://indiatoday.intoday.in/story/jaya-spends-rs-4.5-cr-of-state-money-on-mass-weddings/1/201271.html

Jacob, Preminda. 1997. 'From Co-Star to Deity: Popular Representations of Jayalaitha Jayaram'. In *Representing the Body: Gender Issues in Indian Art*, edited by Vidya Dehejia, pp. 140–65. New Delhi: Kali for Women.

———. 2009. *Celluloid Deities: The Visual Culture of Cinema and Politics in South India*. Lanham: Lexington Books.

Jain, Kajri. 2007. *Gods in the Bazaar: The Economies of Indian Calendar Art*. Durham: Duke University Press.

Jay, Martin. 1988. 'Scopic Regimes of Modernity'. In *Vision and Visuality*, edited by Hal Foster, pp. 3–23. Seattle: Bay Press.

Lakshmi, C.S. 1990. 'Mother, Mother-Community and Mother-Politics in Tamil Nadu'. *Economic and Political Weekly* 25 (42–43): WS72–83.

———. 1997. 'Bodies Called Women: Some Thoughts on Gender, Ethnicity and Nation'. *Economic and Political Weekly* 32 (46): 2953–62.

Losche, Diane. 1995. 'The Sepic Gaze: Iconographic Interpretation of Abelam Form'. *Social Analysis* 38: 47–60.

Massumi, Brian. 1995. 'The Autonomy of Affect'. *Cultural Critique*, No. 31, The Politics of Systems and Environments, Part II (Autumn): 83–109.

Mazzarella, William. 2009. 'Affect: What is it Good for?'. In *Enchantments of Modernity: Empire, Nation, Globalization*, edited by Saurabh Dube, pp. 291–309. New York, NY: Routledge.

Meyer, Birgit. 2008. 'Media and the Senses in the Making of Religious Experience: An Introduction'. *Material Religion* 4 (2): 124–35.

Pandian, M.S.S. 1992. *The Image Trap: M.G. Ramachandran in Film and Politics*. New Delhi: SAGE Publications.

Pandian, M.S.S., and V. Geetha. 1989. 'Jayalalitha: "Sworn Heir"'. *Economic and Political Weekly* 24 (11): 551.

Pinney, Christopher. 2004. *Photos of the Gods: The Printed Image and Political Struggle in India*. London: Reaktion Books Ltd.

———. 2007. 'The Accidental Ramdev: The Spread of a Popular Cult'. In *India's Popular Culture: Iconic Spaces and Fluid Images*, edited by Jyotindra Jain, pp. 32–45. Mumbai: Marg Publications on behalf of National Centre for the Performing Arts.

Price, Pamela G. 1996. *Kingship and Political Practice in Colonial India*. Cambridge: Cambridge University Press.

Rajan, M.C. 2012. 'Tamil Nadu Chief Minister J. Jayalalithaa on Image Makeover Spree', *India Today*, Chennai, 16 April. Accessed on 21 May 2012 at http://indiatoday.intoday.in/articlePrint.jsp?aid=184744

Ramaswamy, Sumathi. 1997. *Passions of the Tongue: Language Devotion in Tamil India, 1891–1970*. Berkeley: University of California Press.

Ramaswamy, Sumathi. 2010. *The Goddess and the Nation: Mapping Mother India*. Durham: Duke University Press.

Rangaswami, Anant. 2011. 'Tamil Nadu Kicks Off Freebie Season'. Accessed on 21 May 2012 at http://www.firstpost.com/politics/tamil-nadu-kicks-off-freebie-season-84444.html

Reynolds, Holly Baker. 1980. 'The Auspicious Married Woman'. In *The Powers of Tamil Women*, edited by Susan S. Wadley, pp. 35–60. Syracuse: Maxwell School of Citizenship and Public Affairs.

Seizer, Susan. 2002. 'Offstage with Special Drama Actresses in Tamilnadu: Roadwork'. In *Everyday Life in South Asia*, edited by Diane P. Mines and Sarah Lamb, pp. 116–31. Bloomington: Indiana University Press.

Skoda, Uwe. 2004. 'The Politics-Kinship Nexus in India: Sonia Gandhi Versus Sushma Swaraj in the 1999 General Elections'. *Contemporary South Asia* 13 (3): 273–85.

Times of India. 2013. 'Work on Thiruvalluvar Statue Begins'. *Times of India*, Kanyakumari, 3 March. Accessed on 7 August 2014 at http://timesofindia.indiatimes.com/city/madurai/Work-on-Thiruvalluvar-statue-begins.co.in

Vaasanthi. 2006. *Cut-Outs, Caste and Cine Stars: The World of Tamil Politics*. New Delhi: Penguin Books.

Wadley, Susan S. 1980. 'Introduction'. In *The Powers of Tamil Women*, edited by Susan S. Wadley, pp. ix–xix. Syracuse: Maxwell School of Citizenship and Public Affairs.

Waghorne, Joanne Punzo. 2001. 'The Gentrification of the Goddess'. *International Journal of Hindu Studies* 5 (3): 227–67.

Part V

Monumental Landscapes

12

Building 'Monuments' in a World-class City: Aesthetics and Politics of Contemporary Delhi

Sushmita Pati[1]

Introduction

Religiosity has reconfigured and redefined spaces, especially, city spaces, in ways that have lent new complexity to them. Instead of a progressive secularisation and disenchantment of the lived space, as many theorists following Max Weber would have liked us to believe, our experience has taught us otherwise. Religion has become of late increasingly and visibly important in public life. This chapter attempts at understanding the nature in which certain built structures in a city like Delhi become an important arena of public contestation and negotiations.

The first structure under analysis is the *Qila Rai Pithora,*[2] a structure which qualifies to be called a 'monument' without really being monumental. It was brought about by the state as a marker of Indian/ Hindu history and heritage, a history that contributes to the idea of an alternative form of nation building. The other structure discussed in this chapter is the gigantic but not 'magnificent' *108 Foot Sankatmochan Dham*, a temple with a huge and brightly coloured 108-feet-high concrete *Hanuman* Statue and a replica of the Vaishno Devi Temple (the original structure is a famous pilgrimage site in Jammu and Kashmir) which was completed in 2005 in Jhandewalan near Karol Bagh in central Delhi.

The purpose of this chapter would be to look at these two recently built structures with very different purposes, one a memorial and the other a temple; and to analyse how they come together at times and diverge at others. This chapter is located at the site of intersection of the visual, material and political culture that I am trying to probe in order to understand what underlies the recent proliferation of such monumental temples in the city of Delhi in the last two decades. In the context of Delhi, the urgency of understanding the logic behind such structures is grounded in the fact that this form of creation of temples/monuments is contemporaneous with a certain form of urbanity. Monuments have long been recognised as spectacles of state power in relation to urban spaces. The unmistakable insistence on the colossal size of these built structures, and more importantly their historicity, cannot be seen as, I would suggest, anything but deeply political. I would be looking at two monumental structures here and through them draw a broader analysis.

Through the *Hanuman* Temple, the attempt would be to unravel the ways politics configures the relationship between urban spaces and religiosity. I try to analyse how these structures have become a significant site for expressing new forms of modernity and community life. The two structures under review can be approached plainly as two examples of a similar wave of *Hindutva* ideological assertion. The attempt here, however, would be to go beyond this argument and see what these structures mean in a city which is being hailed as world class.

A Hindu King for the World-class City—The Case of *Qila Rai Pithora*

The Prithviraj Chauhan Memorial—also called the *Qila Rai Pithora*—is one of the most recent additions to the heritage of the city. The *Qila,* or whatever remains of it today, is widely acknowledged as the First City of Delhi.[3] An attempt to restore what was described as the capital of the Hindu Rajput king was initiated by Jagmohan, the then Minister of Urban Development and Poverty Alleviation with the Bharatiya Janata Party (BJP) government, in the Lok Sabha in December 2000. The figure of Prithviraj Chauhan becomes pivotal in this narrative because Chauhan holds a distinctive position in the Hindu history for having fought one of the earliest Turko-Afghan 'invaders', Mohammed Ghauri. The memorial structure was finally completed by the Delhi Development Authority (DDA) in 2002 and thereafter handed over to the Archaeological Survey of India (ASI). The precincts of the *Qila Rai Pithora*, after restoration, have come to spread over 20 acres of the DDA Conservation Park today. Paradoxically, the only traces here that remain of the past are the ruins of the ramparts. The rest is a vast expanse of manicured lawns and gardens with a structure that serves as a museum and library, adorned by an 18-feet-high statue of Maharana Pratap atop his famous horse *Chetak*. The 'Museum'[4] exhibits mainly the pictures of the 'seven cities of Delhi' and elucidates on the various restoration programmes specifically taken up by Jagmohan. It exhibits the pictures of sites like Jyotisar[5] before restoration and after, the Saraswati Project[6] in progress and the renovated Brahma Sarovar[7] as *Bharatiya Sabhyata ki Gaurav Gatha*.[8] The plaque explaining the site of Kurukshetra says:

> Kurukshetra symbolises the modern world, Arjuna the modern man and Krishna, the Great Perceptor, who offers a solution to the existential crisis through an integrated vision of the cosmos. Over the years, the sands of time and history had submerged the intellectual and cultural heritage of Kurukshetra. Recently, all the jewels of this heritage have been restored and reset in a radically upgraded environment. You have now, here in Kurukshetra, the eternal message of the Gita, through an artistically designed Sound and Light Show, lovely museums, panoramas, excavated sites—signposts of our vast and varied heritage [...] impelling you to visit Kurkshetra again.

At the site of the *Qila Rai Pithora*, a paved path goes around the central structure, which is mostly used by people living in the vicinity for jogging or morning walks. Evidently, the ideological investment behind this structure was hardly innocent. Historians like Sunil Kumar have forcefully contended that *Qila Rai Pithora* was never the capital of Chauhan and that his historical capital was Ajmer (Kumar 2010: x).[9] He further claims that rather this particular area fell within the capital of Delhi Sultans like Iltutmish and Ala-ud-Din Khilji, and it was only a governor of Chauhan called Govind Rai who owned a small fort near the Lal Kot. Mrinalini Rajagopalan also provides further evidence that the ramparts of the *Qila Rai Pithora* were actually rebuilt by Sultanate rulers like Ala-ud-Din Khilji (Rajagopalan 2011: 274; Figure 12.1).

Rajagopalan interprets this structure as an 'emergent rhetoric of masculinity and valour as a key element for citizenship in a robust Hindu nation' (Rajagopalan 2011: 273). Rajagopalan juxtaposes Jagmohan's initiative in the Lok Sabha for a commemorative monument for Prithviraj Chauhan and his passionate statement eulogising the inspirational past of *Qila Rai Pithora* having clear signs of affinity with the larger Hindu

Figure 12.1

The statue of Prithvi Raj Chauhan atop his horse Chetak placed on the roof of the building that serves as Prithvi Raj Chauhan Memorial

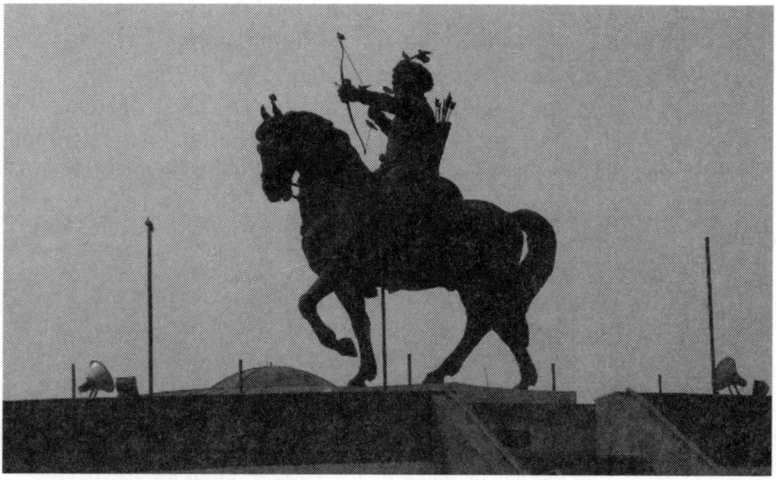

Source: Sushmita Pati.

nationalist project for celebrating Hindu history. The obliteration of the Muslim past is seen to be taking shape in these specific ways. The upshot of such a monument is this: a historically contested fact is established and given credence by not only the DDA but also by the ASI. However, there was a less metaphorical and more physical obliteration of Islamic past involved in this case. Tucked in the corner of the *Qila Rai Pithora* precincts lies this very dilapidated structure of a small, easy to miss *dargah*[10] called *Dargah Hazi Syed*. The officials at the Delhi Waqf Board informed me that that site was actually a Muslim graveyard with the *dargah* as a part of it. When the entire project to revive the old capital of Prithviraj Chauhan started, this plot of graveyard was acquired and covered over. Only the *dargah* remains today as it could not be demolished.[11] The coming up of the *Qila Rai Pithora* therefore was not only an onslaught on history at large but also a takeover of physical spaces that belonged to the Muslims of the city and which they regarded as sacred (Figure 12.2).

Though, the *Hindutva* agenda in this entire move is clear, Rajagopalan frames Jagmohan in this crucible of *Hindutva* too easily. She reads a certain intentionality and transparent deliberation in Jagmohan, which could be somewhat misplaced. Jagmohan here becomes a crucial figure to understand. This is not to deny that the sudden interest in the Prithviraj

Figure 12.2

The Dargah Hazi Syed *which remains in a dilapidated condition in the periphery of the* Qila Rai Pithora

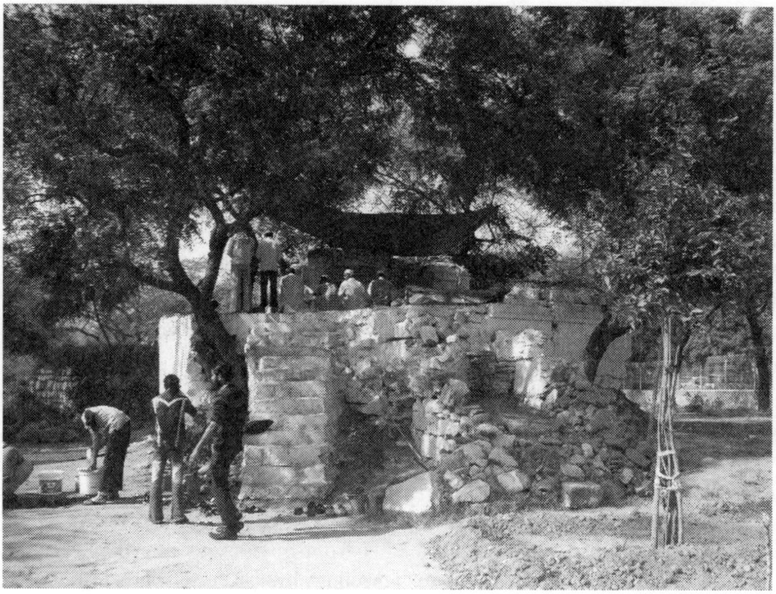

Source: Sushmita Pati.

Chauhan Memorial had to do with the *Hindutva* agenda. Yet, I would also want to argue that Jagmohan was a far more complicated person than what Rajagopalan draws him out to be. It has to do with a specific aspect of urban development which we see articulated here in the language of *Hindutva*. The dimension of the urban governance, the dimension of the larger city planning and regulating the aesthetics of the city space therefore becomes completely crucial to understand and explain this situation. The location of the Prithviraj Memorial is quite significant. From this larger perspective, located right opposite the DDA Flats and next to the Qutab Golf Club, and now a Metro Station right outside, brings an important dimension to this narrative; that of urban governance. The control of public culture and its deliberate projection in a specific way is, I would like to suggest, inherently linked with this kind of reordering of space. One can not only trace the contours of hinduisation of a certain city space in this case but also understand the modes in which state policies on conservation and heritage get interwoven with such politics.

While covering the unveiling ceremony of the Prithviraj Chauhan memorial, *The Tribune,* dated 9 June 2002, reported that several dignitaries including the then Lt Governor of Delhi, Vijay Kapoor, the ex-Chief Minister Sahib Singh Verma and Jagmohan emphasised on the need to project history in a 'proper light' which needed to focus on the great Hindu kings before the twelfth century. Jagmohan also repeatedly lamented the pathetic condition of the old forts and monuments. He said, 'there is an ideology and philosophy behind setting up projects like the Complex at this venue to preserve the heritage and make it relevant for urban needs' (*Tribune*, Chandigarh, 9 June 2002). He also argued that cultural complexes in memory of our national and historical heroes would be developed not only in Delhi but all over the country, and that this would help to weave history and heritage with the present and would create a centre of recreation for residents living close to such complexes (Jagmohan 2000).

Apart from this, he emphasised on the need for the vast patch of greenery for the low- and middle-class income group as well, which he would often define as the 'lungs'.[12] On the *Qila Rai Pithora* itself, *Indian Express* reported Jagmohan saying:

> Living in the metropolis, the benefits from open areas like these are incalculable. It is not just a question of meeting physical needs for recreation. There's also the need to stimulate thinking, give rise to ideas, provide the ambience to nurture the creative urge in people. (George 1999)

Turning the city green was admittedly a major motivation for Jagmohan. Speaking at a seminar on *Greening of Our Cities*, he curiously linked up the question of environment with the ancient culture. He was reported to have said that nature and trees have been an integral part of the Indian Civilisation and legacy since the Vedic times and that the same ethos needs to be recreated (Press Information Bureau 2000). Thus, we must remember that the conservation of the *Qila Rai Pithora* was also taking place in the backdrop of a radically greening of the city landscape.[13]

Jagmohan came into prominence with his stint as the DDA Chairman in the 1970s during the National Emergency. He went on to become the youngest Lt Governor of Delhi and then the Governor of Jammu and Kashmir. He also served as the Union Minister of Communications, Urban Development and Poverty Alleviation, Programme Implementation and Tourism and Culture. His proximity to the Gandhi family during Emergency years was also quite well known. However, later his distances with the Congress grew and he became the Union Minister for Tourism and Culture as a member of the BJP. At various points of his career, he appears to be a modernist figure par excellence, who perceived 'good governance' as the solution of everything, to the extent that he often referred to Indian Democracy as an Unskilled Democracy (Jagmohan 2007: 72). As the DDA Chairperson during Emergency years, he has been responsible for a massive attempt to restructure the city space. The widespread demolitions that Emergency is known for were happening to a great extent according to the Vision[14] that he had for the city. His passionate pieces of writings on the city of Delhi are replete with admiration for figures like Baron Haussmann and Le Corbusier and the way they could radically transform city spaces.[15] He would very often write of the city as a woman without lovers (Jagmohan 1975: 36) or a machine (Jagmohan 1975: 39) or a sick body needing 'green lungs' (Khandekar 2007).

As the Union Minister of Tourism and Culture in the year 2003, Jagmohan was accused of mining mythology and local superstitions in order to create a set of parks in and around Jyotisar in Haryana, where Krishna supposedly gave Arjuna the courage and conviction to fight his own brothers.[16] The 50 million rupees Saraswati Heritage Project was also intended to establish that the Harappan Civilisation was a continuation of the Vedic Civilisation which had little archaeological evidence (Bari 2003). He intended to develop 15 such sites stretching from the Adi Badri in Haryana to Dholavira in Gujarat as a part of this project along the banks of the River Saraswati whose historical authenticity itself is under question (*Indian Express*, New Delhi, 22 October 2003). Earlier that year, he had also sanctioned 8 crores to ASI to search for the river which is believed to have dried up millions of years ago (*Indian Express*, New Delhi, 22 October 2003). Significantly, he denied all allegations about this project being a part of the Sangh Parivar agenda. The Saraswati Heritage Project was for him a part of the 300 crore Regeneration India Project to boost 'cultural and spiritual tourism' all over India through similar projects as the Saraswati Heritage Project. For Jagmohan, as reported in the same article, the entire project was aimed at 'the synthesis of the spiritual and the aesthetic'. Though the Saraswati Heritage Project was abandoned later because of its unfeasibility, the debate it raked pushes us to understand Jagmohan very differently from what Rajagopalan would have us believe.

Jagmohan, even later in his career, shows strong continuities from his days as the DDA Chairman. 'Development' of the city was something he had always been very passionate about. His interest in the History and Heritage of the city was not new. However, his concerns regarding conservation of history and heritage were being argued with a different tenor—that of Hindu history. Comparing his statements during Emergency to his statements as a Union Minister in the BJP government almost 30 years later, one finds that the question of Heritage and History was not new to his vocabulary. But this question of History was by this time being articulated through concerns regarding promotion of Hindu culture and religion, which was not the case during the 1970s. His modernist credentials, however, remained uncompromised. As the Union Minister of Tourism, in a speech delivered on the National Tourism Day, he said:

> We have to learn to live in a disciplined, clean and healthy way. Look at the state of our cities, we need fundamental reform and reorganisation of the Indian mind, we have to think about creating a new dynamism, giving a new direction to society. (Khanna 2003)

The aforementioned statements from newspapers point towards a phenomena not unique, but surreptitious, and often overturn the way in which the arguments have been made so far. For Jagmohan, Hindu culture fed into the entire aspect of city beautification and encouraging tourism. It is here that we see the deployment of *Hindutva* sentiments to achieve extremely modernist aims of a cleaner and greener city and selling India in the tourism sector. Jagmohan is emblematic of this kind of governance. For this kind of governance, the utility of History goes beyond its historic value and converges with aspects of neo-liberalism and high modernism. Like *Akshardham* Temple,[17] Prithviraj Chauhan Memorial has been built as a representative of Hindu history, culture and heritage. Both have been built as spaces of consumption in a world-class city. The contrast, however, becomes apparent when we look at another Hindu temple but using absolutely different mode of spatial reordering, that is, the *108 Foot Sankat Mochan Dham*. It is definitely not accidental that the *Akshardham* Temple and the Prithviraj Chauhan Memorial are speaking the same language of the glorious past in terms of Indian Civilisation. While one is supposed to be a place of worship and the other a historic site, both resort to the same language of glorifying Indian Civilisation of a specific period. This leaves practically no difference between a temple set up by a new religious movement and a historical site created by the state. What, however, is difficult to pin down and say is whether the state is speaking the language of the new religious movement or the new religious movement is speaking the language of the state.

The Case of the Twisted *Hanuman*

The oddly sculpted 108-feet-tall *Hanuman*, standing at the Jhandewalan crossing near Karol Bagh, can be dismissed as one of the many idiosyncratic religious structures. Of course, at first glance, the tall, bright orange muscular figure of the *Hanuman*, which faces a roundabout at the intersection of the Link Road, Faiz Road, Arya Samaj Road, Sadhu Vasvani Road and Vandemataram Road, comes across as a major instance of *Hindutva* assertion in North India. The overground Delhi Metro flyover curves right around the structure, while the Jhandewalan Metro station stands right next to it (Figure 12.3).

The *Hanuman* has his hands folded close to his chest. Very prominent amongst this paraphernalia of jewellery is, however, the *janeu*[18]—a set of very prominent three white threads bunched together running all across his torso. The statue is a hollow structure made of concrete and painted in bright orange. It wears this curious attire, which seems like a pair of

Figure 12.3

The 108 foot Sankatmochan Dham from across the road, with the metro track running past it and the busy intersection of roads below

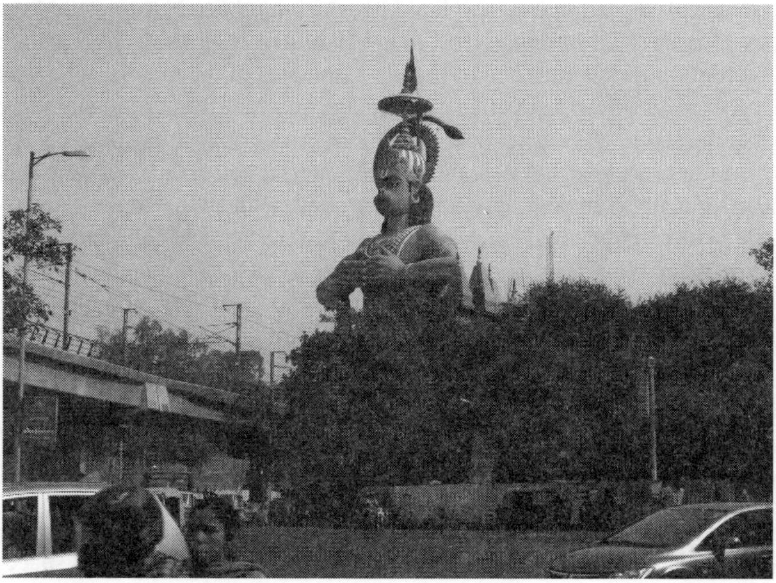

Source: Sushmita Pati.

bright red shorts with multicoloured stars with a green piece of cloth tied over it in a way to make it look like a short *dhoti.*[19] The statue is standing with its legs parted—which is the entrance to the temple. The entrance is also designed in a way to look like one is entering *Sursa's*[20] mouth. The posture in which the statue is standing appears strange because while the legs are straight, the torso is strangely twisted towards the right.

We need to note that Karol Bagh is a predominantly Hindu area, which used to be an area dominated by Muslims before Independence. Most of these local Muslim population migrated to Pakistan during the Partition. Subsequently, Punjabi refugees from Pakistan, who were mainly traders by occupation, took up residence in this place. Today, it is one of the busiest commercial areas in Delhi with busy markets in Ajmal Khan Road, Ghaffar Market and Bank Street. The BJP seems to enjoy a considerable support base in the area, as evident in the local elections. The local councillors from the Karol Bagh Zone for the past two terms have been from BJP. The Rajendra Nagar area, which is adjacent to Karol Bagh, is completely dominated by BJP. After a very long time, in the last elections, a Congress candidate was elected from Rajendra Nagar. Significantly, the Rashtriya Swayam Sevak Sangh Head Office is also located in the Jhandewalan area.

The *Hanuman* Temple occupies this broad pavement along the Link Road. The temple, due to lack of space, has grown vertically along the pavement. It is a three-storied building which has been constructed like a usual residential building. The statue stands right in front, like a huge facade. As Surendraji, one of the old associates of the temple, who was involved with the construction of the statue, informed me over an interview that the statue was earlier being built in a simple upright posture. By the time it was decided that it should face the intersection of the roads, the legs were already complete. It was turned around, with a twist at the waist of the fixture. Interestingly, it is attached with a mechanical contraption that is operated twice a week, at a precise time, when the *Hanuman* is shown to tear apart his chest to reveal gold-plated idols of *Ram* and *Sita.* The hands on usual days cover the chest, preventing the statues from being visible. On Tuesdays and Saturdays,[21] when this enactment happens, the fingers withdraw themselves back and the platform with the idols of *Ram* and *Sita* slides out. The bright orange skin around the hollow in the statue's chest, where the statues of *Ram* and *Sita* stay, is painted in red to resemble the blood. The tips of its fingernails have also been painted red. The statue is built so that its back is attached to the body of the temple and is placed in such a way that it does not occupy a lot of ground space, like rising from the facade, as noted before. Interestingly enough, there is an urban legend behind the *Hanuman* Statue in circulation. The legend behind the erection of a *Hanuman* Statue in what was formerly a Shiva Temple goes as follows: the founder of the temple, Baba Sevagir Maharaj, who arguably found the small temple and started meditating there, had a dream where *Hanuman* appeared and asked him to build a statue for him. It was decided in the beginning that the statue would be 52-feet high; this was later increased to 75 feet and then finally settled at 108 feet. The construction of the statue started in the year 1994 and took 13 years for it to be finished in entirety. Subsequently, we are told, Goddess Vaishno Devi appeared in this Baba's dream and similarly asked him to build a temple for her. Thus, a Vaishno Devi Temple also came up in the same structure in 2006. Located in the basement of the *Hanuman* Temple, this one is a crude replica of the Vaishno Devi Temple in Jammu and Kashmir. The devotees have to climb down a cave-like structure made of concrete which finally leads to the deity of Vaishno Devi presented in the form of *pindi*,[22] which, according to the believers, came up on its own (Figure 12.4).

Figure 12.4

The entrance to the Vaishno Devi Temple that announces 'Mother Vaishno's incredible Cave'. Next to it is one of the legs of the Hanuman *statue*

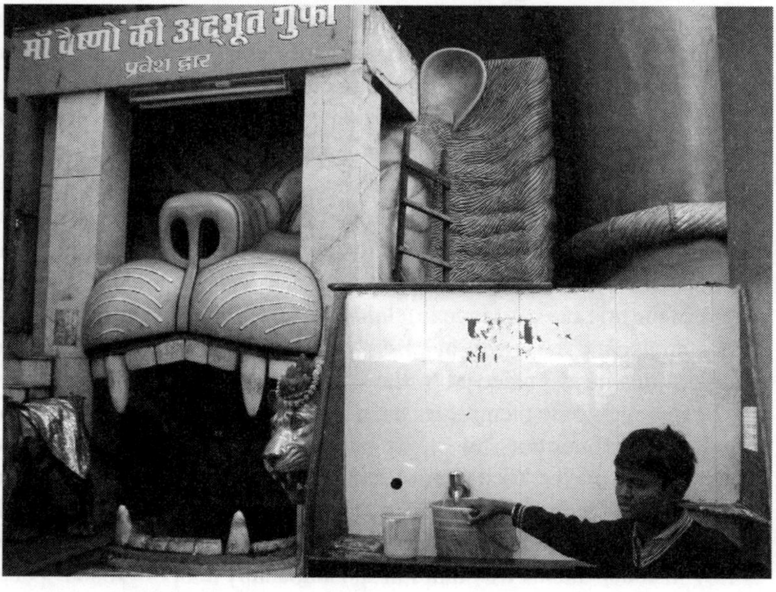

Source: Sushmita Pati.

The underground water that constantly seeps into the Vaishno Devi Temple is also considered holy. The *Hanuman* Temple claims to hold a record in the *Guinness Book of World Records* for continuous *ram naam jaap*.[23] The temple today is called the *108-Foot Sankatmochan Dham*. The Vaishno Devi Temple has a sacred lamp, or the *Akhanda Jyot*, lit by the Baba himself which is claimed to be continuously alight since 2006. The temple has grown in size and now houses not just Shiva and *Hanuman* but other gods like Radha–Krishna, Lakshmi–Narayan and also demi-gods like Sai Baba. Currently, the construction of a concrete diorama of the Kailash Mansarovar is underway on the open terrace of the temple. It has acquired such a popular landmark status that the title track for a tele-serial on Zee TV called '12/24 Karol Bagh' ends with a long shot of the characters of the serial playing a middle-class family on screen with the *Hanuman* Statue in the backdrop. Also, the recent popular Bollywood film *Band Baaja Baraat* which was released in early 2011 begins with a shot of this *Hanuman* Temple with a Metro passing by.

As it has been noted in the other cases, the 'copy' of the Vaishno Devi Temple and the Kailash Mansarovar not only allows the temple a certain degree of sacrality but also brings into it a certain logic of exhibition, a logic of spectacular display plugging into the popular realm of the Religious and Sacred. This is not to argue that exhibitionism and spectacles were not part of the Religious and Sacred before, but the precise modes through which this exhibition takes place by creating 'copies' is certainly very different (Tapati Guha-Thakurta 2014). However, despite creating a replica, the temple at Karol Bagh does not seek to merge with the 'original' and be identified as such as Guha-Thakurta's work goes on to argue. Despite erecting a replica of the Vaishno Devi Cave Temple, the attempt is at the same time to retain an identity that is its own. The host of other deities and forms of rituals the temple evokes is driven to create sacrality for its own, which is not borrowed or simply transmitted. The Karol Bagh case has only resorted to a crude replica of the original cave temple, claiming sacrality for the specific site in Delhi, through urban legends of *pindis* that allegedly emerge on their own and the *swapnadesh*[24] received by the Baba.

The members of the temple trust belong to a 'lower-caste' community called the *Gihara Samaj*.[25] It should be noted that the *Gihara Samaj* has been accorded a Scheduled Caste status in Delhi and Maharashtra.[26] The erection of a *Hanuman* Statue assumes an added relevance here in this case. While discussing the increasing popularity of *Hanuman* as a god worthy of independent worship, Philip Lutgendorf (2007) attributes this to the increasing influence of *Hindutva* on the 'lower-caste' communities.

According to him, the entire idea behind the formation of the *Bajrang Dal*[27] was to accommodate the subaltern population.

The period when the *Hanuman* Statue started coming up would seem to support Lutgendorf's contention. As we know, the demolition of the *Babri Masjid* in 1992 and the claim made by *Hindutva* forces on a specific site was not just an event of local importance. The event marked a watershed in ways that has become common knowledge today. Thus, the decision to build a *Hanuman* Statue need not be seen as an accidental move. The figure of the *Hanuman* itself gained a status after 1992 that was unprecedented. The utility of the statue does not seem to end at *Hindutva* assertion. The ritual practices which have come to define the temple like the *Ram Naam jaap*, the *Akhanda Jyot* along with the colossal *Hanuman* Structure come across as something that cannot be only understood simply as religious assertion. The attempt is also to establish itself as a unique place—a *dham* which is not just a place of worship but a sacred space in its own right. It is this concern to establish this site as Sacred that strikes one as odd. I have attempted to highlight this through a narrative I gathered from a number of small, insignificant stories circulating in the area about the making of the temple. Though my reading in this regard will remain constrained by a relative lack of evidence and absence of written documents and reliance on a public memory replete with the legends of the local Baba, I have tried to provide a narrative that is differently based on the critical use of the available material.

As already mentioned, the *Hanuman* Temple originally used to be a very small and obscure Shiva Temple in the past. In 1994, the construction of the *Hanuman* Statue was started by a local godman called Baba Sevagir Maharaj, who had been apparently staying and meditating there since 1931.[28] The temple is also attached to the adjoining Bhooli Bhatiyari Forest which still exists. It would appear that the temple was actually built on an illegal land. The expansion started in the 1990s and has happened only through progressive encroachment on public land. It is this aspect of illegality, I believe, that becomes most important in the story of this constantly growing statue and the diversifying temple. The strategy behind building a status of its own here, I believe, primarily comes from this aspect of illegality. Karol Bagh has always been a densely populated and extremely busy commercial area. Like many others, this area is prone to massive illegal construction. Since 2007, after the last spate of massive demolitions in DB Gupta Road, Saraswati Marg, Padam Singh Marg, Pusa Road and several others, Ajay Maken accorded Karol Bagh a special status along with places like Paharganj and Chandni Chowk so that no demolitions would take place in these areas until the chalking out of a new redevelopment plan.[29] Therefore, till very recently, Karol Bagh has witnessed both big- and small-scale demolitions. One such demolition drive had taken place in 1998 in order to connect the Ridge to Chandni Chowk. As many vendors sitting outside the temple informed me, a small and old temple known as the Sitaram Temple behind this particular temple was demolished at that point. Around that time, this temple couldn't be brought down as the statue was under construction and it is likely that the temple authorities developed a rapport with the officials in the local government. However, the massive construction and gradual encroachment on available land had already begun, which by then was only the pavement. The strategy to sacralise the site, to my mind, is inextricably linked to the narrative of demolition of illegal structures. An insignificant temple until 1994, the only way the temple could be made sacred was through monumentality and generating myths. Over the years, it managed to strike a rapport with influential businessmen and local politicians. The organisation which happens to be one of the biggest patrons of the temple is Bagga Links Motors Limited which also owns one of the most successfully running automobile dealerships in Delhi. The oldest of its showroom stands right next to the *Hanuman* Temple and also happens to be partly within the Bhooli Bhatiyari Forest.

Beyond the question of defence, it can also be looked at as a form of entrepreneurship. Another of their big patrons, Brijmohan Bhama, who contributed to the making of a gold *Hanuman* idol to be given to Barack Obama on behalf of the temple during the 2008 Election Campaign, is also a major Congress figure locally. Another trustee of the temple belongs to the BJP. When a structure like a temple is built, one can begin to mobilise a different register where the divine can intervene through dreams to ordain legitimacy to something that is potentially illegal. It is this legitimacy that is then used to counter governmental moves of demolition. It is able to reverse the process of primitive accumulation and create an exceptional status for itself. Here, we see a spectacle, which comes into existence as a strategy of defence.

After the erection of this statue, the temple's prominence has definitely gone up exponentially, including, strangely, a lot of middle-class population, which works in offices nearby and even foreign tourists staying in hotels in Karol Bagh. Many of the devotees here are regulars. Many believe that this temple fulfils their wishes, some come here because the 'service' of the temple is good. It is both the ubiquity and somewhat bizarre nature of cases such as the *Hanuman* Temple that can make us think about the various ways in which space becomes contested and the political strategies through which these contestations are settled. Perhaps, more importantly, it makes us rethink the modes through which we analyse the relations of space with politics. There is definitely more to it than meets the eye as these kinds of contestations are different from the Ayodhya issue. Unlike Ayodhya, the strategies deployed here, these contestations are therefore, not proclaimed. They are silent and thus hardly show themselves up as 'political'. These contestations therefore are not limited to the ownership of land. They go well beyond the question of ownership and often take the form of how the space is being practically used. The series of temples built along the pavement clearly becomes unacceptable to the governance, which is constantly reordering and regularising the use of space through demolitions. The temple authorities here could counter the threat to such an extent that around 2005, when the Delhi Metro tracks were being made, they had initially wanted to break down a certain number of steps of the temple, but later it had to give in and the tracks were made circumventing the temple. Some 60 odd families were resettled during this construction, but they could not touch the temple.

What, however, needs to be understood is that this *Hanuman* Temple, along with countering law, also fractures the easy conflation of Hindu history and Hindu culture as 'national' as we see in the case of *Akshardham* or the Prithviraj Chauhan Memorial. It is precisely this 'kitsch' culture and local myths and legends that the hegemonic idea of Indian culture would not have a place in the world-class city that Delhi aspires to be, despite being strongly Hindu. This form of Hinduism does not claim the historical, but the mythical. It does not make any claims on Indian culture, but only on the little space that they have somehow acquired. Therefore, the *Hanuman* Temple not just counters law but also counters this hegemonic idea of middle-class Hinduism that we see in *Akshardham* and the *Qila Rai Pithora.* It is precisely this uneasy fit between the two, in terms of the spatial practices these structures promote, that makes the relationship between them conflictual.

Conclusion

Dipesh Chakrabarty (2008) in his essay has looked into how the discipline of history is undertaken and how it is often in conflict with the public discourse of history. These structures in this chapter, under examination, can be taken to illustrate precisely what Chakrabarty may have meant by the public discourse of history. What we see here, therefore, is how this public discourse of history becomes inscribed on to the city space in the form of certain monumental structures. Both the structures loosely aim at a certain Hinduisation of the city space, but, at the same time, this process could not have taken place without involving internal contradictions. For, as we have seen, there is a different set of motivations in each case apart from the common marking spaces as dominantly Hindu. The investment of history into monuments and architectural structures thus become a political act with different levels of motivations at work. It is this aspect of performing and displaying history that ties up the three apparently unrelated structures.

If the strategic naming of modern structures as *peeth* and *dham*[30] comes to provide a means of gaining historicity and attaining a special public status as in the case of *Akshardham*, Hindu mytho-history also comes to be combined with a modern political and commercial enterprise to beautify the city and create Heritage sites. In the case of the *Hanuman* Temple, we see how certain 'fakes' and replicas themselves tend to be treated as authentic in their own right and redraw a new kind of sacred geography. These built structures are produced by layers of contestations and, most importantly, negotiations between contending demands in order to define a certain space—communities or religious groups, the politics of *Hindutva*, Hindu culture, the neo-liberal mode of governance and a high modern sense of aesthetics which perceives cities as ordered and beautiful spaces. Again, if we are to understand these built structures as not just inanimate objects but as actively constituting everyday life, structures like the memorial and the *Akshardham* reveal to us not merely the memorialisation of a Hindu king and valorisation of Indian culture but also a cosmopolitan middle-class ethos. While the *Hanuman* Temple can be seen lying at the other end of *Hindutva* spectrum—a subaltern domain that is created through contestations and collaborations with the state. There is no way one can pin down a single dominant pattern in the way these structures can be seen to have come into conversation with each other in their efforts to define space in a certain manner. These processes are highly context specific and, thus, also highly contingent. The very emergence of these built structures is underscored by somewhat discrete and shifting interests. Such representations cannot happen without negotiations or contestations. These structures, therefore, often do not represent any one strand but a curious combination of various factors. Perhaps, most importantly, these processes leave the pure distinctions between history-making and mythmaking blurred and problematic. At times, as seen in the case of the *Hanuman* Temple, the process seems to draw from the larger idea of a Hindu Nation, but it is the local character that becomes more and more important in terms of its construction on the ground. At the same time, we have the *Akshardham* and the Memorial, which borrow from the same set of ideas but converge with another idea that of the modern nation and creates a consonance between these two different ideas.

Contrary to the *Akshardham* Temple, the *Hanuman* Temple tries to attribute sacrality to itself by a very different modality. It takes the aspect of performance to an altogether different level. However, one does feel that the aspect of sacrality is way too muted compared to the aspect of spectacularity. Not surprisingly, therefore, the experience of inhabiting a space like the *Akshardham* Temple is very different from inhabiting a space like the *Hanuman* Temple. The monumental sizes of the structures are overwhelming in their own right. The common struggle is to establish themselves permanently on the map of the city. While one does it through sacralising the space, the other establishes its prominence not only on the city map but also in that of the nation. As is apparent, these structures are as much about redefining space as they are about controlling land and thereby creating assets.

A related but different kind of sacralisation is witnessed in the case of the Prithviraj Chauhan Memorial. Here, governance becomes one of the elements, which brings together Hindu mytho-history, a modern sense of aesthetic and a neo-liberal form of tourism. It also reveals the fact that these ideologies are so deeply ingrained in governance today that it is difficult to even recognise them as three different strands of thought, let alone being able to understand how the internal contradictions of these strands are getting resolved. Consider the way Jagmohan brings environment and the ancient Indian culture together, or how he uses the language of History, the utterances are deeply reflective of the way governance is reworking itself today. Thus, it is not only a memorial that we see but what also must become a park complete with a jogger's track, a museum and a library. We must also note, however, that such governmental ordering of space does not always translate or totally follow the intended pattern. A structure like that of the *Hanuman* Temple, on the other hand, stands at the other end of such moves, surreptitiously countering governance, for governance practically means the threat of demolition and displacement to them. Hence, the manufacture of popular sacrality is attained by resorting to God's command, creating new rituals and building 'fake' replicas to prevent demolition. What becomes interesting is that both depend on myths and legends for some kind of authentication or the other. But the difference crops up in the way one is elevated to the status of Heritage and treated as Historical, while the other remains purely in the realm of local legends, hearsay and faith, and is therefore only locally relevant.

One way of understanding these spatial contestations is to think about how they contribute to the act of creating subjects—subjects as upper-class citizens, as devout Hindus who are proud of their histories or as lower-middle class devotees for whom a temple, a *dham*, even when it is visibly fake, becomes important. This brings us back to the dichotomy of history and myth in public discourse. What is designated as history in public discourse is often a myth corroborated by the middle classes and several political organisations. Another way of looking at it may be to interrogate how history itself congeals around certain mythmaking processes. It evokes a sense of beauty, a sense of grandeur; which does not fit into the description of beauty and aesthetics of the middle-class sense of aesthetics that have increasingly begun to influence our urban experience today. Jacques Ranciere writes:

> Politics and art like forms of knowledge, construct fictions, that is to say material rearrangements of signs and images, relationship between what is done and what can be done. How political statements and literary locutions draft maps of the visible, trajectories between the visible and the sayable, relationships between modes of being, modes of saying and modes of doing and making. They take hold of unspecified groups of people adhere to a condition, react to situations, recognise their images. (Ranciere 2006: 39)

The *Hanuman* Temple becomes not only viewable but also extremely popular in an area that has been constantly subject to Delhi government's modernising impulse. What this temple therefore manages to do, by using religion, myths and legends in a specific way, is that it is able to reverse the process of primitive accumulation and create an exceptional status for itself.

Michael Warner (2002) has used the phrase 'publics and counterpublics' to elaborate on contrasts like this. He argues that a 'public' is more than a tangible group of people. A 'public' comes into existence very often by the virtue of being addressed. The imagined audience for discourses becomes the public (Warner 2002: 414). On the other hand, he describes 'counterpublics' as not merely subset of 'public' but constituted through a conflictual relation to the dominant public. They are structures by different dispositions or protocols from those that obtain elsewhere in the culture, making different assumptions about what can be said or what goes without saying. This form of cultural assertion made through space therefore is another form of making the 'counterpublic'. Warner describes the 'counterpublic' as beings socially marked by their participation in a kind of discourse which ordinary citizens would not want to be considered to be a part of. The *Hanuman* Temple does come across as exhibiting this notion of 'counterpublic'. The way these three places have been constituted show us how the temples and monuments like *Qila Rai Pithora* have come to constitute their own 'publics'.

The larger idea behind analysing these structures is to indicate the broader processes of politics at work than simply elaborating on the similarities and dissimilarities between them, located in different parts of the city. These structures are also in conversation with the state at each and every level. What is peculiar about these moves in contemporary times is the curious ways in which these monumental structures tie up with aspects of neo-liberalism. What these three structures together show us is how the aspects of religiosity, history and culture are inflected and connected by the new directions and forces of political economy. It is very apparent that its patronage has gone up ever since the statue has come up. The mornings in the temple are especially busy because of a host of working men and women shuffling in and out of the temple hurriedly on their way to work. Many have gradually come to believe in the credibility of the temple having the power of granting them their wishes. Some told me that they come here because of very good 'service' provided by the temple whereby nobody is made to wait for long, and that it conducts the worship and rituals on time. Nobody seems to enjoy a rooted, an invested relationship with the temple, including the people from *Gihara Samaj*. However, despite being able to attract the middle class to the temple, the temple's transformation from a Shiva Temple to a *Hanuman* Temple indicates that there could be an impulse to shift to a more liminal God popular with both the upper and the lower caste. The gradual diversification of the temple into Gods not just like Lakshmi–Narayan but also like Sai Baba indicates the temple's intention to be popular. It enjoys this every day, more popular kind of sacrality amongst people whereby it becomes possible to watch the bi-weekly spectacle of *Hanuman* tearing apart his chest standing on the road while eating *chole kulche*[31] bought from the street vendor on the pavement. The Vaishno Devi Cave also, while worshipped, is treated as a site for entertainment. This temple in a way brings the 'spectacle' and the everyday lives of the people in such a way that it blurs what we understand both by the spectacle and the everyday. The spectacles, which were made to be the bearers of divine providence, are made every day and mundane by the everyday practices of the devotees.

This temple when thought through questions of city planning, middle-class aesthetics, popular forms of religiosity, questions of inhabitation of space, histories and myths raises questions that might not always be very specific but rather very symptomatic of the ongoing in city spaces today. The attempt was not to point out the case of this temple as merely an 'exception' but to point out how these 'exceptions' are not really exceptional. It is a different mode of articulation of the political itself, well beyond the logic of radical politics. Deborah Cherry's work (2013) argues how monuments have an afterlife because of the multiple forms of interventions, which go on to attach meanings to the structure. She writes, 'afterlives are constructed in the corporeal, mnemonic, and sensory engagements between people—individuals, groups, institutions—and sites, objects, texts, and images. The concept holds the promise of survival, of living-on, through change' (Cherry 2013: 3). This article probes into the birth and the life of the monument in contemporary times and tries to do something similar. The specific deployment of space itself as the site of contestation brings us to an understanding of politics that might require us to use the tools of political analysis in more innovative ways.

Notes

1. Acknowledgements: I would like to acknowledge Dr Rajarshi Dasgupta for his valuable comments on this chapter. I would also like to express my gratitude to the 16th International Cultural Studies Workshop 2010 held in Jaipur and organised by the Centre for Studies in Social Sciences, Kolkata, Association of Social Anthropologists of the Commonwealth and the UK Conference, Jawaharlal Nehru University, New Delhi, 2012, where I presented different versions of this chapter. I am especially grateful to Professor Tapati GuhaThakurta, Professor Christopher Pinney and Professor Ghassan Hage for their extensive comments on the chapter.
2. *Qila* means Fort in both Hindi and Urdu, while *Rai Pithora* is another name for Prithviraj Chauhan. Throughout the chapter, I have used *Qila Rai Pithora* and Prithviraj Chauhan Memorial interchangeably.
3. Delhi's history is many a times chronologically ordered through the seven cities of Delhi. The 'first city' is the Qila Rai Pithora, arguably built by Prithviraj Chauhan, followed by Mehrauli, Siri, Tughlaqabad and Firozabad built by the Slave Dynasty, Shergarh or Purana Qila of Sher Shah Suri and lastly Shahjahanabad belonging to the Mughals. This version has come to be extremely important as it goes on to provide Delhi with a Hindu past that predated the Islamic rulers of the city.
4. I am using the quotation marks because though it is referred to as a museum, it is anything but a museum. It only has 'before' and 'after' pictures of restored sites and pictures of the seven cities. Its status as a museum is dubious to my mind.

5. Jyotisar in Kurukshetra, Haryana, is the place where Krishna supposedly instructed Arjuna through *Geeta* on the battlefield which was made into an archeological site.
6. Saraswati Project was again the brainchild of Jagmohan who wished to establish linkages between the Harappan and the Vedic Civilisation through this project. It was later discontinued.
7. Brahma Sarovar is a sacred water tank in Kurukshetra. In Hindu mythology, Lord Brahma, the creator, had himself created it.
8. The Glorious Tale of Indian Civilisation.
9. Another scholar who mentions this is Dasharatha Sharma ([1959] 1975: 69–71). The primary source, which gives a similar impression is Minhaj-i Siraj Juzjani, *Tabaqat-i Nasiri*, translated by Raverty. Similar assertions have been made by Hasan Nizami, *Taju-l Ma-asir*, written in the early thirteenth century.
10. A *dargah* is a shrine of some religious or spiritual person (Islamic).
11. This is definitely not the first time that such a case of demolishing Muslim graveyard was taking place in the city. Right after Independence, with the huge influx of refugees in the city, a lot of these graveyards and *dargahs* were simply destroyed and occupied by the refugee population. Delhi State Archives, High Commissioner of Pakistan (Letter No- F.32(2)/54-RRA) Vide File Number- 32(2)/54- R&R(A) dated 11 May 1956, the Under Secretary (Relief and Rehabilitation) to Delhi, P.N. Thukral, sent a big list of all the 'Allegedly desecrated mosques and religious places of muslims in and around Delhi'.
12. Jagmohan called the two parks right in front of Red Fort, the August 15 Park and the Chalo Delhi Park, as 'lungs' of the area. Nivedita Khandekar, 'ASI Permits Red Fort as Venue for Ram Lila, Heritage Lovers Protest' (Khandekar 2007).
13. Greening the city space has for Jagmohan been of a crucial concern. There was a plan of converting around 800 acres of land into seven patches of green spaces to be called the 'great greens'.
14. I am using Vision with a capital 'V' to emphasise on Jagmohan's high modernist perspective.
15. In his book, *Rebuilding Shahjahanabad,* he discusses these planners in depth and also his own role as an urban planner. He in that book chalked out an entire plan to create a second Shahjahanabad which would be an ordered and artificially recreated to have the 'feel' of erstwhile Meena Bazar with antique and handicraft shops, houses with latticed windows and a School for Oriental Studies (Jagmohan 1975: 60–81).
16. The demand to turn Jyotisar into a monument of national importance has been quite old. As early as 1954, there was a demand to bring the monument under government control in the Lok Sabha (Lok Sabha Debates, Vol. 5, Part I, 1954, pp. 1799–1800, question asked by M.D. Joshi). Maulana Azad, The Minister of Education and Culture declined saying that the monument was neither old nor considered to be of national importance.
17. Akshardham Cultural Complex was opened in the year 2005 by Bochasanwasi Shri Akshar Purushottam Swaminarayan Sanstha. It is built over 220 acres and consists not only temple but functions almost like a theme park for imparting 'value education' and knowledge on 'Indian culture' (see Brosius 2010; Srivastava 2009).
18. It is a thread worn over the torso by a Brahmin male to mark his ritual status.
19. *Dhoti* is a piece of cloth which is wrapped around the bottom half in various ways across North India.
20. In Ramayana, Sursa was a demon who asks *Hanuman* to enter her mouth and escape in order to test him.

21. Tuesday and Saturday are considered to be days for worshipping *Hanuman*.
22. A lump of stone, which is considered to have appeared on its own and is considered 'sacred'.
23. A ritual activity whereby the Lord's name is repeated over and over again in a tune. This can last for days, months or even years.
24. *Swapnadesh* refers to an instruction by God given to someone in a dream.
25. The temple authorities, however, do not proclaim their affiliation to this caste. The trustees have all changed their surname from Gihara to Giri. This temple, however, does not act as a community temple for people from the *Gihara Samaj*.
26. See www.giharasamaj.com (accessed 24 November 2012). Although Baba Sevagir Maharaj who erected the statue was a Brahmin by caste, he purportedly chose these three brothers as his successors.
27. It is a very aggressive wing of the Sangh Parivar, which was founded in 1984 as the Ram Janmabhoomi Campaign was catching pace. Even the term *Bajrang* means *Hanuman*.
28. There is no settled answer to how long he meditated and what was the form of the *tapasya*. The plaque in the temple does say something very vague as to how the place was made sacred because the Baba did *tapasya* for several years at that place.
29. Ajay Maken (Congress) became the Member of Parliament in 2004 from New Delhi Constituency after defeating Jagmohan, the BJP Candidate. Around 2006, he became the Minister of State for Urban Development when the city was under the onslaught of demolitions.
30. A sacred site for pilgrimage.
31. A popular cheap North Indian snack made of chickpeas and a bread.

References

Bari, Nishat. 2003. 'Lost World'. *India Today*, 10 November, New Delhi.

Brosius, Christiane. 2010. *India's Middle Class: New Forms of Urban Leisure, Consumption and Prosperity*. New Delhi: Routledge.

Chakrabarty, Dipesh. 2008. 'The Public Life of History: An Argument out of India'. *Public Culture* 20 (54): 143–68.

Cherry, Deborah. 2013. 'The Afterlives of Monument'. *South Asian Studies* 29 (1): 1–14.

Tribune. 2002. 'Stress Must Be on Medieval History'. *Tribune,* June 9. http://www.tribuneindia.com/2002/20020609/ncr1.htm#15

George, Nirmala. 1999. 'Rajput Fort Ruins to Make Way for Second Lodhi Gardens.' *Indian Express*, 30 November, New Delhi.

Guha-Thakurta, Tapati. 2014. 'Conceits of a Copy: Travelling Replicas of the Past and the Present'. In *New Cultural Histories of India: Materiality and Practices*, edited by Partha Chatterjee, Tapati Guha-Thakurta and Boddhisatva Kar. New Delhi: Oxford University Press.

Jagmohan. 1975. *Rebuilding Shahjehanabad: Walled City of Delhi*. New Delhi: Vikas Publishing House.

———. 2000. 'Statement Regarding Development of Prithviraj's Qila Rai Pithora'. *Legislative Assembly Debates*, 13th Lok Sabha, 22 December. http://164.100.47.194/Loksabha/Debates/Result13.aspx?dbsl=1876&ser=&smode=t#158

Jagmohan. 2007. *Soul and Structure of Governance in India*. New Delhi: Allied Publishers Private Limited.

Khandekar, Nivediata. 2007. 'ASI Permits Red Fort as Venue for Ram Lila, Heritage Lovers Protest'. *Hindustan Times*, 21 September, New Delhi.

Khanna, Vinod. 2003. 'Jagmohan: Clean Up, Get Rs. 1 Crore'. *Times of India*, 26 January.

Kumar, Sunil. 2010. *The Present in Delhi's Pasts: Five Essays*. New Delhi: Three Essays Collective.

Lutgendorf, Philip. 2007. *Hanuman's Tale: The Messages of a Divine Monkey*. New York, NY: Oxford University Press.

Press Information Bureau. 2000. 'Latest Press Releases'. Accessed on 3 November 2012 at http://pib.nic.in/archieve/lreleng/lyr2000/rjun2000/r29062000.html

Rajagopalan, Mrinalini. 2011. 'Postsecular Urbanisms: Situating Delhi within the Rhetorical Landscape of Hindutva'. In *The Fundamentalist City? Religiosity and the Remaking of Urban Space*, edited by Nezar AlSayyad and Mejgan Massoumi, pp. 257–82. London and New York, NY: Routledge.

Ranciere, Jacques. 2006. *The Politics of Aesthetics: The Distribution of the Sensible*. London: Continnum.

Sharma, Dasharatha. (1959) 1975. *Early Chauhan Dynasties: A Study of Chauhan Political History, Chauhan Political Institutions and Life in Chauhan Dominions from 800 to 1316 AD*. Delhi: Motilal Banarasidass.

Srivastava, Sanjay. 2009. 'Urban Spaces, Disney Divinity and Moral Middle Classes in Delhi'. *Economic and Political Weekly* 44 (26): 338–45.

Warner, Michael. 2002. 'Publics and Counterpublics'. *Quarterly Journal of Speech* 88 (4): 413–25.

13

Mayawati's Politics of *Sthals*: Spectacle of the Symbolic Landscape[1]

Upasona Khound

This chapter makes an attempt to explore the politics of *sthals* pursued by the erstwhile Dalit chief minister of Uttar Pradesh, Mayawati. She had taken up the task of iconising and memorialising the Dalit heroes, leaders, stalwarts and social reformers in the form of statues and memorials. The rapidly changing landscapes of the two cities—Lucknow, the capital city of Uttar Pradesh and the newly developed industrial area NOIDA (New Okhla Industrial Development Authority) bear testimony to this fact. Since the beginning of her stint as the chief minister from 2007 to 2012, it is witnessed that she had radically redesigned the public spaces of these two cities. In this context, the chapter tries to locate the shift in the politics of iconisation by the Bahujan Samaj Party (BSP) of the early phase of 1990s and the later phase under Mayawati's leadership. The chapter tries to show how the 'politics of statues' of Mayawati of the early phase has expanded, consolidated and regimented itself as the 'politics of *sthals*' during her recent tenure as chief minister. *Sthals* literally mean memorials. According to Gary Tartakov (1990), *sthals* refer to a sacred site, which is meant for deification of historic and contemporary figures. The *sthals* occupy large areas in terms of physical space in these cities. Thus, 'politics of *sthals*' is the new avatar of Mayawati's iconising politics. The chapter also tries to show how Mayawati's agenda is related to the broader issue of reclamation of public space for the subalterns. That is, to ask: Has such politics of iconisation through the construction of grand, majestic and palatial *sthals* been able to (re)configure the power relations of the Dalits at the symbolic level by empowering them through these iconic representations?

Mayawati's project of memorialising the subaltern leaders had already achieved a popular and controversial edge through media coverage and newspaper hypes. This chapter aims to sharpen the academic edge of approaching the phenomenon. In my view, the phenomenon should be spared due academic attention rather than dismissing it as a personal fetish of Mayawati. It cannot be gainsaid that the phenomenon has widespread implications on the sociocultural location of Dalits besides having political implications on the general electorate. Thus, keeping in view the repertoire of symbols that Mayawati has been able to enrich within two years after she had come to power in 2007, I want to locate this study in the broader domain of politics of representation by means of iconisation.

The structure of the argument will be put forward in the two sections that follow. In the first section, the changes and the shifts that are visible in the symbolic politics of Mayawati in her latest tenure will be focussed upon. A trajectory of the various efforts of statuisation and memorialisation of the subaltern leaders by the BSP right from its movement phase in the early 1980s to that of the recent phase under the leadership of Mayawati will be built up. Such a trajectory will not only acquaint us with the history of iconising in the state of Uttar Pradesh but will also help in pointing out the marked shifts that can be witnessed in the representations of the present phase. To substantiate the argument in terms of talking about the shifts and the changes of the present phase of symbolic politics, a brief description of the features of the memorial parks built by Mayawati after 2007 and an analysis of these features will also be taken up. In the second section, an attempt will be made to discern the important question—Have such grand and palatial memorials built by Mayawati been able to address the difficult yet pertinent question of physical space and its access to the Dalits?

As Stuart Hall (1997) has remarked, representation through a visual medium does not mean representing the meaning, which is already there and is static in nature. He argues that representation is rather a signifying practice within a particular discourse that helps in the formation of identity. If one embeds Hall's argument in the context of politics of representation by Mayawati, one can argue that these icons and memorials have really helped in the formation and assertion of identity of the Dalits. Thus, these memorials are not merely passive representations but have to be understood in their activating functions. These statues and the memorials which represent a particular community and help in the formation of their identity in turn help in institutionalising the memory of the leaders, heroes or the events whose authority is venerated by setting up these memorials. To argue in Dipesh Chakrabarty's words, memorials are mere objects unless and until 'certain practices to create rituals of remembering' are followed collectively to impart meaning to the memorials (Chakrabarty 2008: 49). This means that the importance of memorials can be conveyed only through the rituals of memorialisation, which are observed around these memorials. Thus, if we try to understand the memorials and the statues of Dalit heroes being put up by Mayawati in this context, it can be said that her symbolic politics has the inbuilt twofold strategy of both institutionalising the memory of the Dalit leaders and at the same time representing the Dalits through these memorials.

From the Politics of 'Statues' to the Politics of *Sthals*: Shifts in Symbolic Politics

In this section, Mayawati in her latest phase as the chief minister from 2007 to 2012 will be discussed. Unlike the other three stints as the chief minister, Mayawati returned to power in the 2007 Assembly elections with a commendable share of votes. This was the first time of her four tenures as chief minister of the state that the BSP was not heading a coalition government. With a view to enlisting and analysing the features of the memorial parks which are constructed throughout this tenure of Mayawati, I have decided to compare and contrast the same with the memorial-making endeavours of Mayawati in her earlier stints as the chief minister, as this comparison will be helpful in pointing out the distinguished features of her visual politics in the present phase. As such, I divide these issues in two parts—the *early phase* and the *later phase.* The *early phase* will include her attempts at constructing iconographies till 2002—right from the movement phase of the BSP till she had come to power thrice by heading a coalition of BSP–BJP (Bharatiya Janata Party) alliance. The *present phase* includes the symbolic politics during her recent tenure as the chief minister.

In the *early phase*, one could witness the short-lived nature of the coalition government and its impact on the visual politics of the BSP. Most of her agenda of setting up statues across the state remained unfulfilled because the political scenario of the state was in a state of constant flux due to the endemic short-lived coalition of the BSP with the BJP till 2002. And it is very difficult to take an accurate numerical account of busts and statues erected in the early phase as these mushroomed in various parts of the state as a part of the Ambedkarisation process and other mobilisational processes. However, keeping in view the political stability that has been restored due to Mayawati's commendable share of votes in the 2007 elections, her tactics of visual politics got an impetus. The victory of Mayawati with 206 seats out of 402 seats in the Assembly gave a boost to her endeavours. She had devoted herself to the completion of the unfinished tasks of statue and memorials installations, the foundations of which were laid in the earlier tenures but constricted by the nature of the coalition governments, the projects could not be completed. Thus, the political circumstances as we witness played a very important role in the symbolic politics pursued by Mayawati in both these phases.

The Early Phase

Scholars like Nicolas Jaoul (2006), Badri Narayan (2006) and others have shown that the sectarian political parties—the Republican Party of India (RPI), the Dalit Panthers and various other civil society groups started installing statues of Ambedkar and observed ceremonies around those statues from the middle of the 1960s, which continued unabated till the 1980s. In the western parts of the state, these activities took place as a part of the mobilisation activities of these parties through the Ambedkarisation process. In the 1980s, the Backward and Minorities Caste Employees Federation organised by Kanshi Ram took the lead of these Ambedkarite mobilisations, which were earlier in the hands of the RPI and the Dalit Panthers. It was at this juncture when the patchwork of sociocultural mobilisation in Uttar Pradesh gained momentum that the BSP was formed in 1984 and joined the process. Ambedkarite Committees were formed and made responsible for the setting up of Ambedkar statues in the remote areas and also their protection. After the emergence of the BSP in the scenario, the processes of sociocultural mobilisations around the Ambedkar symbols have intensified. In addition to these, BSP resorted to other innovative ways like disseminating myths through cycle squad (*jagriti dastas* [awareness shaft], *cycle dastas* [bicycle shaft]) to roam around villages through the cultural squads and so on. Hence, the BSP realised that such strategies, which have accumulated over a period of

20 years, could be harnessed by it when it came to power. Badri Narayan (2006) has rightly stated that under the leadership of Kanshi Ram, grass-roots mobilisation of the Dalits through a strategy of cultural politics was successfully harnessed by the BSP since its initial years.

So far as the significant features of the statues set up by the party activists and civil society groups were concerned, the features of the statues installed in official premises, say, for example, in the Parliamentary premises and any other official establishment were generally replicated on the statues; however, the latter ones bore livelier and brighter colours (see Jaoul 2006: 181). Generally, the small statues of Ambedkar represent his three-piece suit in bright blue colour with a red tie and black spectacles. Unlike the official statues, these statues are not carved out of bronze and are not of massive sizes. The framed pictures in Figure 13.1 on display at the occasion of Ambedkar's birth anniversary reiterate this fact. Placing Buddha's frame alongside Ambedkar's hints at some kind of deification of the Dalit leader and his enlightening role for the community.

The statues at the roadside, at the intersection of roads, in village slums and Dalit colonies were very small in sizes and made out of stone carvings, cement, plaster of Paris, etc. Thus, the relevance of the civil society initiatives and the grass-roots mobilisation efforts of sectarian parties of setting up of Ambedkar's statues, mobilisation of villagers around the Ambedkar symbol have contributed enormously to the acquaintance of Ambedkar's symbol in the villages of the poor and illiterate Dalits. The statues also empowered them symbolically and to a certain extent enabled the villagers to cluster their material and symbolic claims over

Figure 13.1

Pictures of Ambedkar on display on Ambedkar Jayanti, India Gate, Delhi. These are also replicated in the form of small busts and statues

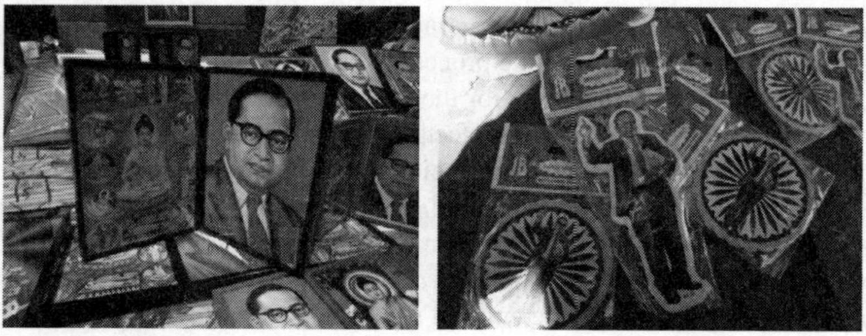

Source: Upasona Khound.

government-owned land as they sloganeered *Jo zameen sarkari hai, wo zameen hamari hai* (The land which is owned by the government belongs to us). In this, the BSP was quick enough to pick up the strategy and employ it as a successful mobilising strategy, right in its infant movement stage when it was more involved in the grass-roots mobilisation activities.

After Mayawati became the first Dalit chief minister of the state in 1995, during her brief tenure of two years from 1995 to 1997, she installed nearly 15,000 Ambedkar statues all over Uttar Pradesh. Not only many statues of Ambedkar were installed in this phase, but Mayawati also took up the efforts of naming institutions like universities, hospitals, sports complexes, roads and even districts after Ambedkar. Most notable among the Ambedkar statues set up during this period is the gigantic bronze statue set up at Lucknow in 1997. The most significant feature of this statue is that the statue was the replication of the Ambedkar's statue set up in the Parliament in the year 1967. However, the statue was quite different in terms of the materials used for the statues during the 1980s. Nevertheless, it seems that it was of the same material like the statue of Ambedkar of 1967 from which it was replicated. Thus, Mayawati's first official venture in the statue installation process was quite similar to that of the national commemorative process of statue and memorial installation. Another intriguing feature of memorialisation of Ambedkar during this period is that he was not only iconised in the statues but his presence was made almost all-pervading, which means that politics of naming was also an integral component of the memorialising discourse in this period.

Another interesting feature that Badri Narayan notes about the iconographies of this period is that apart from Ambedkar, Mayawati also undertook the task of memorialising leaders like Jotiba Phule, Pandita Ramabai, Ahalya Bai Holkar and Shahuji Maharaj. Earlier, when the party was active in its mobilisation activities, it also set up statues of 'vernacular' leaders like Jhalkari Bai, Udadevi, Bijli Pashi and so on.[2] The BSP in power tried to trace the complete lineage of the icons of the subaltern leaders who struggled against the caste discriminations at different levels in the society in pursuit of justice, right from the colonial period by acknowledging the leaders who have pursued the mission since then till the present. Therefore, it may be seen as a viable reason on the part of the BSP undertaking the memorialisation of all the leaders. Since Jotiba Phule had been one of the pioneers of the struggle since the late nineteenth century, iconising him must have been a prime emphasis of the memorialisation discourse. Besides this, in my view, the entire discourse would not be worth its cause of creating a full circle of memorialisation of the Dalit heroes unless and until it takes up the task of memorialising the leaders who took up the task of mobilisation in Uttar Pradesh. After 1995, Mayawati built statues of leaders and heroes all across the state. Towards the later part of the early phase, that is, after 2002, Mayawati started occupying large physical spaces for building these memorials.

Before discussing the memorials in present times, it would be interesting to note a brief description of history of memorial parks in Lucknow as a background. Lucknow has witnessed the evolution of memorial parks and statuaries since pre-colonial times, though the cartographic designs have changed through changing times. As Amita Sinha (2010) notes different typologies of parks—parks memorialising historic events, parks celebrating mythic cultural identity of the city, parks commemorating the state of Uttar Pradesh and the ones celebrating emerging political ideologies of post-Independence Lucknow are found in the city. She categorises three phases in which the parks can be divided: parks of the Nawabi period (1775–1856), parks of the colonial era (1856–1947) and parks of the post-colonial period (1947 onwards). According to Sinha, the iconographic programme from the colonial to the post-colonial period has witnessed the continuation of statuary in memorial parks, and while both the models of public parks—botanical and zoological parks and memorial parks—continued in the post-Independence era, the latter spawned. Sinha is however of the view that the contemporary parks built after 1980s have become overtly personality centric in nature and this has continued under Mayawati. The new memorial parks built by Mayawati are also 'reduced to spaces of political representation rather than area of civic engagement' (Sinha 2010: 68). A further discussion of Mayawati's agenda of statuary politics is presented in the following section.

The Later Phase

Before moving on to analyse the features of the statues and the memorials that are set up by Mayawati in the later phase, let us initially take a descriptive account of the majestic sites that appeared abruptly in the cities of Lucknow and NOIDA just within first two years of her resuming power. The most recent of these memorials that have been constructed during Mayawati's latest tenure as Chief Minister and would be taken up for the discussion are: (a) Dr Bhim Rao Ambedkar *Samajik Pariwartan Sthal* (Site of Social Change), Lucknow, (b) *Manyawar* (honourable/respected)

Shri Kanshi Ram Ji Smarak Sthal (Kanshi Ram Memorial Park), Lucknow (c) *Bauddha Vihar Shanti Upavan* (Bauddha Park), Lucknow and (d) *Rashtriya Dalit Prerna Sthal* (Site of inspiration of the Dalits), NOIDA. Instead of taking into account the features of these statues and memorials individually, let me point out the most distinctive features of these parks and memorials, which overlap all of these and are the most striking ones.

First and foremost, it needs to be pointed out that all the aforementioned parks and memorials have been christened with vernacular names. *Sthals* literally mean memorials. But when one witnesses the cartographic design of these *sthals*, it becomes clear that the gigantic appearances in terms of occupation of physical spaces, these convey much more than their literal meaning. These *sthals* are much larger than the national insignias like the *Rajghat* (Memorial of Mahatma Gandhi), *Shanti Upavan* (Nehru Memorial, where *shanti* denotes peace and *upavan* means garden), *Shakti Sthal* (Indira Gandhi Memorial, *shakti* stands for power), etc. Say, for example, Ambedkar *Sthal* spreads over a large area of 107 acres. The *Sthal* also accommodates the Ambedkar Memorial, Ambedkar *Samajik Pariwartan Sangrahalay* (*samajik* means social, *pariwartan* means change and *sangrahalay* literally means museum), Ambedkar *Samajik Pariwartan* Gallery, Ambedkar *Smarak Pratibimb Sthal*, Ambedkar *Smarak Drishya Sthal*, *Samajik Pariwartan Stambha*, *Samajik Pariwartan Prateek Sthal* and the *Samatamulak Chowk*. Other *sthals* like the Manyawar Kanshi Ram Ji *Smarak Sthal*, Lucknow, is around 86 acres of land, while *Baudh Vihar* and *Rashtriya Dalit Prerna Sthal* occupy 32.5 and 82.5 acres, respectively. These memorial parks occupy large acres of land and most of the spaces enclosed within them are carved out of *Makrana* marble and Bansi Pahadpur sandstone, which are rare in terms of geological occurrences. In fact, it can be said that the large areas within the boundaries of these memorials are exclusively made of marble, which impart a very palatial and sacralised view of the same. In addition to this, the names of all the memorial parks speak volumes of the social change that is sought after by Mayawati through the construction of these *sthals*, although symbolically these huge-sized parks are closed by high walls and have palatial gateways. Thus, these memorial parks are erected to be epitomes of social justice for the Dalits.

Regarding the statues inside the *sthals*, the parks and the memorials, it can be witnessed that unlike earlier when the BSP along with others like RPI and Dalit Panthers used to set up small statues made of cement and stone in the public squares, slums, etc., during its initial phase of mobilisation, the statues inside the *sthals* are made of bronze or marble

Figure 13.2

A view of one of the gates of Ambedkar Sthal, *Lucknow*

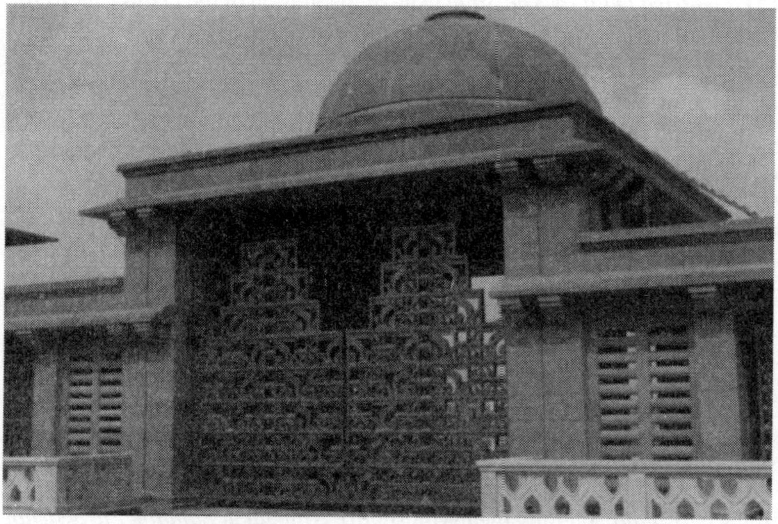

Source: Upasona Khound.

and their structures are mighty. It is important to note here that when BSP was formed, it joined the mobilisation strategy and later on changed its strategy after 1995. It has to be recognised that statues in the Parliament complex of India are made of bronze and it can be so that Mayawati wanted the statues built inside the *sthals* and the parks also to reflect the same officialdom and assertion in a statist way as the former do. In the Ambedkar Memorial inside the Ambedkar *Sthal*, Lucknow, the statue of Ambedkar is nearly of 71 feet placed on a pedestal and the other statues of the subaltern leaders are of 18 feet each.

A striking feature of the statues of Ambedkar, Kanshi Ram and of Mayawati herself is that the three amongst the icons of the other subaltern leaders in all the *sthals* represent the coming of a new-age modern and assertive Dalit. While it is true that Ambedkar's modernist imagery[3] has been superimposed overwhelmingly in the Dalit cultural landscape, the construction of Kanshi Ram's imagery and of Mayawati herself is very new. Nevertheless, a new posture of Ambedkar's statue has been innovated in the Ambedkar *Sthal*, where his statue is built in close resemblance of the Lincoln Memorial. The statue of Ambedkar is constructed in a sitting posture on a huge pedestal inside the main hall of the Ambedkar *Sthal*

Figure 13.3

Roadside statue of Dr Ambedkar, Lucknow, Uttar Pradesh

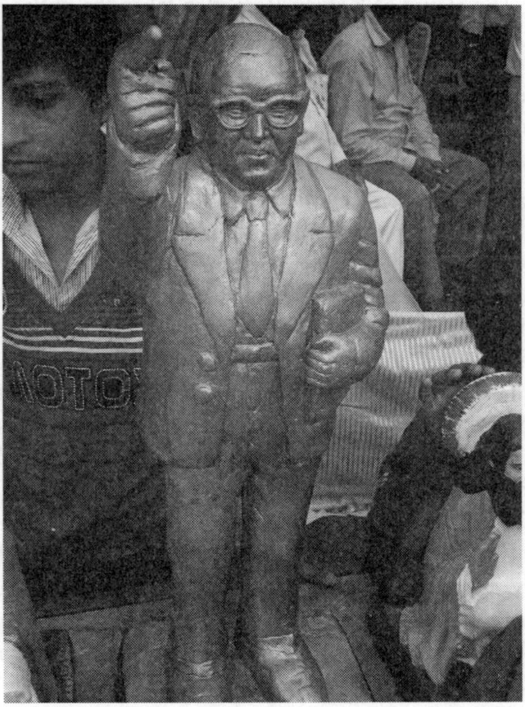

Source: Upasona Khound.

unlike the most popular statue of Ambedkar where he is standing holding the Indian constitution in the right hand and his left-hand index finger pointing to the sky (see Figure 13.3).

Kanshi Ram's statue is a new cultural resource for the Dalits. Mighty statues of Kanshi Ram have been erected inside the memorials, and, in fact, a *sthal* has been commemorated in his name also. His statues depict him as a modern man. The statues of Kanshi Ram also display a handkerchief in his right hand, which is considered to be one of the important articles that a modern man should carry as a part of his civil and social etiquette. Kanshi Ram's ideology emphasised that every Dalit should use his/her caste as a vehicle to uplift oneself, by educating themselves and becoming politically conscious. This is similar to Dr Ambedkar's call to Dalits of educate, agitate and organise. In other words, he prophesied that Dalits should strive to utilise the benefits of modernity and then by growing politically conscious should try to assert themselves as they are the *Bahujans* (majority) in the society. The statue of Kanshi Ram also takes the entire discourse of statuisation of Dalit leaders a step ahead in creating a legacy of subaltern leadership, which ultimately culminates with Mayawati.

The icons of Mayawati can be described as a modern avatar of a Dalit *virangana*.[4] The iconographies of Mayawati also depict her in a salwar-suit. Apart from that, she is portrayed holding a 'vanity bag' (leather handbag), which portrays the *viratwa* (courage) as well as the *rajatwa* (royal) quality of this modern Dalit *virangana*. While the vanity bag symbolises her economic independence as it holds economic resources, thus depicting the *viratwa* qualities which a modern female is expected to have; on the other hand, the prefix 'vanity' to the leather bag that she holds symbolises both her caste–class status. It is both an issue of caste and class for Mayawati being a daughter of the *Chamars*,[5] the leather workers who were originally deprived and alienated even from basic leather articles as these are considered to be very costly material. But holding a vanity bag depicts her ability not only to break the traditional barriers of caste but also the upliftment of her class. Kajri Jain (2010) has also tried to locate the symbolic value of the leather handbag that Mayawati's statue shows as empowerment of the *Chamars* symbolically, as earlier, this Dalit sub-caste used to engage in the profession of the leather works. By holding a leather bag, Mayawati empowers the *Chamars* who were never able to own the leather goods for themselves, but with the leadership of Mayawati it has been made possible.

Mayawati's statues form the newest and the most stunning feature of these memorials of the later phase. She must have built her own statue with a view to depict her as the Dalit leader of the present who completes the legacy of the leaders who are already statuised. In fact, in some of the recently constructed *sthals*, Mayawati's statue is placed at the centre, while the other heroes and leaders surround her in a semicircle in raised pedestals. The official interpretation of this iconography is that Mayawati's statue is placed at the centre to portray a welcome gesture to the visitors of the *sthal* and to acquaint them with the statues of all the leaders who have contributed to the upliftment of the Dalits.[6] In my view, this may symbolically represent a situation where the former leaders are gazing at Mayawati with the expectation that she will carry forward the struggle of the Dalits till she achieves transformation. Another way to look at this statue is that she is gazed at by the leaders because she has been able to carry forward the struggle of the Dalits to new heights and that it is because of her authority that she has been able to construct the grand memorial parks for the Dalits.

Figure 13.4

Elephant Gallery of Ambedkar Sthal, *Lucknow (Insight: Mayawati and Kanshi Ram flanking the cartographic design of the Park)*

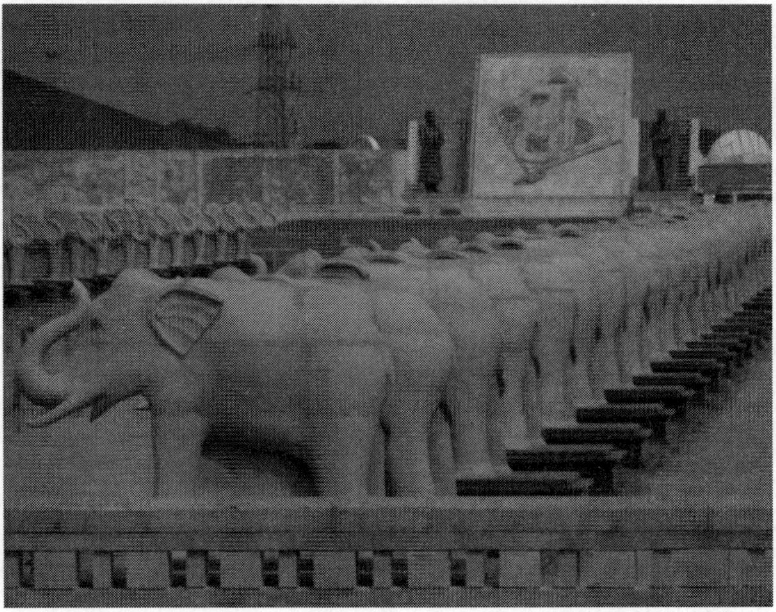

Source: Upasona Khound.

The constructions of/in the *sthals* embody both the elegance of traditional Buddhist architecture and the modern imprints, the latter characteristics mostly visible on the statues inside the *sthals*. The elephant icons are considered the representative style of the Buddhist architecture besides being the symbol of royal rule, which is also the symbol of the party. This style has been integrated to most of the *sthals* in the present phase as the 'Elephant Galleries' (see Figure 13.4). With the trunks of the elephants raised, the elephant icons represent a welcoming gesture to the visitors. Besides the elephant icons, the construction of the *Ashoka Chakra* on the *Samatamulak Prateek Stambh* also signifies the Dalits' empathy with Buddhism. The *Ashoka Chakra* is also the part of the national insignia, and by using it for the adornment of the *sthals*, Mayawati has shown the Dalits' access to the national symbols. A very innovative feature witnessed among these statues is the *Chahumukhi* (four-faced) statues of Buddha and other leaders—Ambedkar, Kanshi Ram and Mayawati (see Figure 13.5).

Figure 13.5

The Chahumukhi *(four-faced) statue of Buddha on the precincts of Ambedkar* Sthal, *Lucknow*

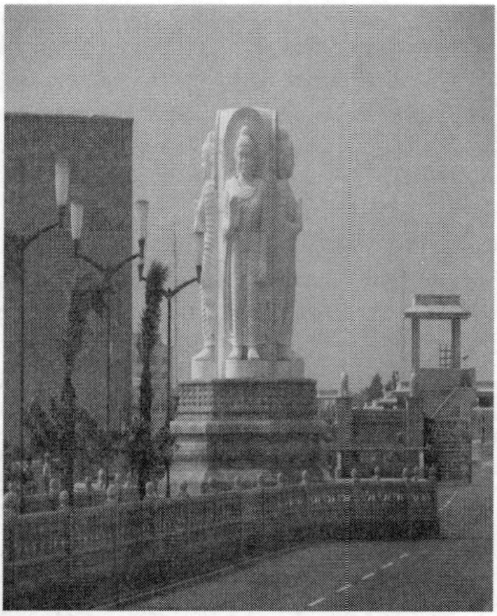

Source: Upasona Khound.

From the previous discussions of the distinctive features of the iconographies that have been constructed by Mayawati, it can be said that the politics of *sthals*, as I call it, is the new avatar of Mayawati's politics of iconising leaders and stalwarts. The grand iconographies are not only exquisite sites of monumental glory for the Dalits but have wider connotations for their sociocultural location in the Indian society. A case for reclamation of space by the subalterns through these monuments and statues has therefore been tried to be argued in this context in the next section.

A Case for Subaltern Reclamation of Space

After taking into account the majestic and grand statues and memorials built under the initiatives of Mayawati, a question worth asking is: Have such majestic and grand iconographies transformed the state of

Uttar Pradesh to a Maya Pradesh?[7] By observing the trajectory of how Mayawati's 'politics of statues' of the early phase has regimented itself as 'politics of *sthals*' in the present phase, the entire memorial landscape of Lucknow and NOIDA can be analysed in its light. Mayawati as a leader and representative of the Dalits achieved what no other leader has yet achieved. She has taken the Dalit politics to a new height. Given her stature as the chief minister of the state, she radicalised the landscape of the state at least at the symbolic level.

Hence, in this section, the issues of space and the (re)configuration of power relations due to the construction of such massive memorial parks will be taken up for discussion. It is to decide whether the memorials have really transformed the claims of the subalterns to the public space or not. Can we say that such reconfiguration of space has empowered the Dalits in the real sense of terms? Addressing these set of questions is the main aim of this section.

As noted earlier, a major distinction that can be pointed out between the iconisation of the early phase and the later phase is that the memorial parks of the present phase encompass larger physical space than the earlier ones. That is, in the early phase during her tenure as chief minister in 1995, 1997 and 2002, the iconographies were dispersed all across the state. Thus, the early phase signified the beginning of the symbolic assertion of the Dalits as envisioned by the Mayawati government. In the early stage, as we have already discussed, Mayawati was concentrating more on the setting up of statues in different regions of the state. The foundation of the redesigning of public space, which was started in the early phase, has reached its zenith in the present phase with the completion of the palatial and majestic *sthals*.

These *sthals* as it is noted occupy large areas in terms of physical space. As a matter of fact, the Dalit assertion through access to symbols encompassing large physical space seem to be almost complete with the majestic *sthals* having emerged in our sight just within three years of Mayawati assuming the office for the fourth time. Thus, when I say that Mayawati's 'politics of statues' has entered into 'politics of *sthals*', I don't mean that Mayawati's statue politics has become redundant but rather the statement connotes the expanding, consolidating and regimenting phase of iconising politics on the physical landscape in the present phase.

In her latest tenure, Mayawati focussed on the establishment of *sthals* in the two particular cities of Lucknow and NOIDA rather than installing statues all across the state. It can be because Lucknow is the capital city of Uttar Pradesh and redesigning of the capital city has its own long-term significance. It is captured in the public memory for a long time. On the other hand, NOIDA is close to the national capital New Delhi, and that her ambitions in national politics are not unknown, her efforts to redesign the city have a signalling effect. The endemic instability of the coalitional politics has hindered her symbolic politics since the 1990s to take a full-blown shape, and so she has taken up the unfinished tasks in the present phase. But this is not the sole answer to approach the entire discourse. In my attempt to link her symbolic politics to the issues of reclamation of space for the subalterns through the pursuit of 'politics of *sthals*' in the present phase, let us try to derive a comprehensive understanding of the shift in her politics from constructing mere statues to constructing *sthals*.

As we know, statues of Ambedkar have been used for the mobilisation of the Dalits in general by different political parties and civil society groups. Ambedkar statues and statues of other Dalit heroes were used by the BSP for mobilisation in particular. Importantly, these mobilisations have been successful as a part of the Ambedkarisation process, more so in the western part of the state. Notwithstanding this, the politics of statuary has undergone changes after BSP came to power. The mobilisation politics through statues were without any doubt successful, but it must be pointed out that in the 1980s, the BSP was a new entrant in the political scenario. It implies that it was necessary for the BSP, which was more a movement at its inception, to carry out mobilisation at the grass-roots level. So, corollary to the BSP being a movement, it can also be derived that the BSP was connected to the people in a constant manner due to its mobilisation activities, and thus the Dalits at the grass roots were continuously apprised of the symbolic importance of the statues, be it Ambedkar's or of the other heroes used for the Dalit assertion. The BSP was keen on garnering support of Dalits by inculcating the symbolic importance of Ambedkar and other heroes. Towards the later part of the 1990s and in its present phase, the BSP has arrogated itself into a political party more involved in the electoral calculations than in the grass-roots mobilisations.[8] While earlier, BSP took part in the 'symbiotic mobilisation' activities as part of the civil society, thus mobilising the illiterate, backward and poor Dalits; after 2007, the BSP captured power in the state and established itself to the Dalits through a state–citizen relationship. In this changed relationship between the BSP and the Dalits, the politics of statues of the BSP also took a new avatar. In fact, it can be said that without letting the statue politics degenerate into mere objects defunct of its symbolic values, Mayawati decided to rejuvenate the politics of statues in a new avatar—politics of *sthals*. After 2007, Mayawati continued to represent the Dalits symbolically by reclaiming the public space through a changed strategy, the essence of which remains the same.

In this sense, politics of statues and politics of *sthal* have to be understood as a continuum in Mayawati's statuary politics where the latter (*sthals*) have made its presence felt in a grander, majestic, mightier and in a palatial way in the present scenario. The installation of mighty *sthals* in the two big cities of Lucknow and NOIDA has helped Mayawati in retaining the Dalit spectacle of the memorial landscape. It also shows that a state which is represented by a Dalit leader has in her authority to confer memorialisation and inculcate symbolic values by redesigning space in a grand way. Over and above, the new form of politics of memorials of Mayawati also leads to the impression that she has rediscovered the mobilisation strategy of the Dalits in a new way, thus continuing with the same spree with which she began in the movement phase, throughout the 1990s till the present. With the same token, it can also be said that such an initiative on her part has also saved the commemorative icons from degenerating from their aesthetic and symbolic status.

Scholars like Maxine Loynd have shown how Mayawati's symbolic politics was on the verge of a change as early as 2005 when she inaugurated the *Bahujan Samaj Prerna Kendra* (Site of Inspiration for the Dalits) in Lucknow to commemorate the 10th anniversary of its first term as the state government. The Kendra is viewed by Loynd as 'production of spaces of empowerment' by the BSP under the leadership of Mayawati. In her views, the Kendra 'creates a separate territory—a semi private terrain that symbolically excludes the traditional power holders' (Loynd 2009: 470) Thus, in this study, I would like to take Loynd's work a step ahead and argue that what started with the creation of the opulent *Kendra* continued as the construction of *sthals* when she came to power in 2007. One can make a claim that the *sthals* she has constructed in the present phase are huge physical spaces enclosed by gigantic wall structures, which render the same palatial look. Inside the *sthals*, what the visitors find are the grander and larger than life statues of the Dalit leaders and heroes. Thus, I would like to contend that such adornment of the physical space with huge monument-like structures and the statues placed inside these get inculcated into people's vision and memory as symbolic markers, as heritage of the community. In the context of the *Prerna Kendra*, Loynd observes that:

> the Kendra is a project of the Dalit pride. The spatial arrangements in the Kendra contribute to evoking a Dalit imaginary. In addition the architecture and the internal arrangement of the building assume political and quasi-religious significance, rendering and producing it as a place

> of inner reflection and learning as well as imbuing it with an effective dimension, whereby serenity and introspection are required to move through the shining marble floors of this fortified structure. (Loynd 2009: 476)

In conclusion, I wish to argue that the *sthals* act as the sites of evoking Dalit imaginary by inculcating a sense of awe for the subaltern leaders. If historically Dalits have been denied the entry to the Hindu temples, the constructions of these iconographies by Mayawati have empowered them to reclaim the space that they were historically denied. These sacral iconographies stand out as exclusive sites of cultural and symbolic markers for the Dalits.

These spaces are inspirational for the Dalits, as these *sthals* encompass not only statues of the Dalit stalwarts and heroes but also murals, which highlight their life struggles. So, it can be said that Dalit cultural politics under Mayawati's leadership has entered a phase where she has helped the subalterns reclaim the physical space and thereby helped them not only to contest but also renegotiate their claims to space. In this sense, Mayawati has been successful in building a Maya Pradesh—a symbolic landscape, which has helped the Dalits empower themselves and assert themselves through such spaces. Nevertheless, her defeat in the 2012 state assembly elections has once again opened a range of questions regarding the mobilisation patterns through statues and memorials and its efficacy as a means of empowering the Dalits. Her reluctance to implement important policies like the Right to Education Act and other programmes effectively, which could have substantially empowered the Dalits, is cited by many[9] as one of the major reasons of her loss in the recent elections. Although such an argument has its own merit, yet her failure cannot be solely attributed to it. The politics of *sthals* of the present phase has its own specificities to be unlocked and studied not only because it has brought about spaces to venerate Dalit leaders exclusively but also because it has been a phenomenon in itself which has to be reckoned with.

Notes

1. This chapter is a part of my MPhil Thesis 'Politics of Iconography: Statues and Memorials in Uttar Pradesh (1995–2011)' submitted to the Centre for Political Studies, School of Social Sciences, Jawaharlal Nehru University in the year 2011.
2. Maxine Loynd has referred to the leaders who were indigenous to the state of Uttar Pradesh as 'vernacular' leaders (Loynd 2009).
3. The stances taken by scholars like Nicolas Jaoul (2006), Gary Tartakov (1990) and others.

4. The term *virangana* has been widely used in the alternative historical accounts, Dalit histories. The term is used to designate the heroic activities of the Dalit female leaders in the historical event of 1857 (Gupta 2008; Narayan 2006).
5. *Chamars* refer to the caste traditionally engaged in the occupation of shoe-making and leather work; also known as *Mochi*.
6. See *Uttar Pradesh Mein BSP Sarkar Dwara Desh Ke Anusuchit Jati/Janajati Evam Anya Pichde Vargo Mein Janme Santon, Guruonwa Mahapurushon ke Samman Mein Nirmit Mahatwapurna Sthalon Aur Gardeen/Park Adika Sankhipt Parichay* (2011).
7. Mayawati's attempts of iconising the Dalit leaders and herself have been satirised by the newspapers and magazines in many ways. One common way of satire is by adding 'Maya' as a prefix or after any other term. The idea of using terms like Maya Pradesh, Maya Land, Maya's Land in this chapter is derived from satirical writings like by Sharat Pradhan (2010) and Ajay Singh (2010).
8. Sudha Pai has argued that the BSP has transformed itself over time. She is of the view that towards the later part of the 1990s, the party has limited its mobilisation activities. The forms of grass-roots mobilisation that it undertook were, for example, the organisation of *Periyar Melas* and so on (Pai 2002).
9. See Verma (2012) where he argues that Mayawati lost because she failed to deliver welfare policies and failed to meet the expectations of better governance.

References

Chakrabarty, Dipesh. 2008. 'Remembering 1857: An Introductory Note'. In *1857: Essays From Economic and Political Weekly*, edited by Sekhar Bandyopadhyay, pp. 45–58. Hyderabad: Orient Blackswan.

Gupta, Charu. 2008. 'Dalit 'Viranganas' and Reinvention of 1857'. In *1857: Essays from Economic and Political Weekly*, edited by Sekhar Bandyopadhyay, pp. 193–212. Hyderabad: Orient Blackswan.

Hall, Stuart. 1997. 'The Work of Representation'. In *Representation, Cultural Representations and Signifying Practices*, edited by Stuart Hall, pp. 13–74. New Delhi: SAGE Publications.

Jain, Kajri. 2010. 'The Handbag that Exploded: Mayawati's Monuments and the Aesthetics of Democracy in Post Reforms India'. Paper presented at the School of Arts and Aesthetics, Jawaharlal Nehru University, New Delhi, 13 December.

Jaoul, Nicolas. 2006. 'Learning the Use of Symbolic Means: Dalits, Ambedkar Statues and the State in Uttar Pradesh'. *Contributions to Indian Sociology* 40 (2): 175–207.

Loynd, Maxine. 2009. 'Understanding the Bahujan Samaj Prerna Kendra: Space, Place and Political Mobilisation'. *Asian Studies Review* 33 (4): 469–82.

Narayan, Badri. 2006. *Women Heroes and Dalit Assertion in North India: Culture, Identity and Politics*. New Delhi: SAGE Publications.

Pai, Sudha. 2002. *Dalit Assertion and the Unfinished Democratic Revolution*. New Delhi: SAGE Publications.

Pradhan, Sharat. 2010. 'MegaloMaya'. *Governance Now* 1 (2): 26–28.

Singh, Ajay. 2010. 'Monumental Misgovernance'. *Governance Now* 1 (2): 29–30.

Sinha, Amita. 2010. 'Colonial and Post-colonial Memorial Parks in Lucknow, India: Shifting Ideologies and Changing Aesthetics'. *Journal of Landscape Architecture* 5 (2): 60–71.

Tartakov, Gary Michael. 1990. 'Art and Identity: The Rise of a New Buddhist Imagery'. *Art Journal* 49 (4): 409–16.

Verma. A.K. 2012. 'Why did Mayawati lose?'. *Economic and Political Weekly* 47 (18): 17–19.

Suchna Evam Jansampark Vibhag. 2003. *The Journey of Social Change. A Photobook of the Installation of Statues by BSP*. Lucknow, Uttar Pradesh: Suchna Evam Jansampark Vibhag.

Uttar Pradesh Mein BSP Sarkar Dwara Desh Ke Anusuchit Jati/Janajati Evam Anya Pichde Vargo Mein Janme Santon, Guruonwas Mahapurushon ke Samman Mein Nirmit Mahatwapurna Sthalon Aur Garden/Park Adika Sankshipt Parichay. 2011. Suchna Evam Jansampark Vibhag, Uttar Pradesh.

About the Editors and Contributors

Editors

Uwe Skoda is Associate Professor in India and South Asia Studies at the Department of Global Studies, Aarhus University. He is currently working on transformations of kingship in Odisha and is broadly interested in the fields of political anthropology and visual culture. He recently co-edited a volume on 'Contemporary Indigeneity and Religion in India' (*International Quarterly in Asian Studies* [1–2]: 2015).

Birgit Lettmann is Research Assistant and PhD candidate at Humboldt-Universität zu Berlin, Germany. In her PhD theses, she focuses on post-mortem photographs of pets, analysing the logics of representation and the human–animal relations, as well as setting them apart from other conservatory practices like taxidermy. Her research interest includes the cultural history of death and grieving rituals and the history of photography.

Contributors

Asunción López-Varela Azcárate is Associate Professor at the Faculty of Languages and Humanities, Universidad Complutense de Madrid. She holds a PhD on English Studies and an MA in Spanish Studies and Comparative Literature. Her research interests are Comparative Literature, World Literature, Cultural Studies and Intermedial Semiotics. She is the coordinator of the research program Studies on Intermediality and Intercultural Mediation (SIIM), https://www.ucm.es/siim. López-Varela has been a visiting scholar at different universities around the world. Currently, she is the president of the European Society for Comparative Literature and external evaluator for the EU research programs Horizon 2020, MSCA, and the Educational, Audiovisual & Culture Executive Agency EACEA. More information on her editorial activities and publications can be found at https://www.ucm.es/siim/asun-lopez-varela.

Rita Brara is presently at the Department of Sociology, Delhi School of Economics, University of Delhi, India. She is a Senior Fellow working on The National Green Tribunal. She is the author of *Shifting Landscapes: The Making and Remaking of Village Commons in India* (2006) and a co-editor of the journal *Contributions to Indian Sociology*. She researches in the areas of popular culture, ecology, rural development and kinship.

Roma Chatterji is Professor at the Department of Sociology, Delhi School of Economics, University of Delhi. Apart from having an abiding interest in folk culture, she has also worked on collective violence and medical sociology. She is the author of *Writing Identities: Folklore and Performing Arts in Purulia* (2009) and *Speaking with Pictures: Folk Art and the Narrative Imagination in India* (2012, 2016), co-author with Deepak Mehta of *Living with Violence: An Anthropology of Events and Everyday Life* (2007), editor of *Wording the World: Veena Das and Scenes of Inheritance* (2015) and co-editor with Deepak Mehta of *Riot Discourses* (2007).

Radhika Chopra is the author of *Militant and Migrant: The Politics and Social History of Punjab* (2011). She has published widely and presented conference papers on politics of remembrance, on migration and on masculinity. She has been Principal Investigator with projects for UNWOMEN and UNHCR and is on the Editorial Board/Collective of various journals.

Cécile Guillaume-Pey obtained her PhD in social anthropology from Ecole des Hautes Etudes en Sciences Sociales (EHESS), Toulouse, France. Her dissertation focused on the ritual practices of the Sora, a tribal group from Odisha–Andhra Pradesh border (Central-Eastern India). She is the author of several articles based on this work. Her other research interests include the anthropology of knowledge, the anthropology of art and the process of aestheticisation, the invention of writings and the learning of literacy skills. She is currently based as a Postdoctoral Research Fellow at the Institute of Sacred Music, Yale.

Malavika Karlekar is Editor of *Indian Journal of Gender Studies* and curator of *Re-presenting Indian Women: A Visual Documentary 1875–1947*, both at the Centre for Women's Development Studies, New Delhi. Educated at the Universities of Delhi and Oxford, since 2001, she has been designing and curating an annual calendar based on archival photographs of Indian women. For over two decades, Malavika Karlekar has written a regular column based on archival photographs for *The Telegraph* (Kolkata), and her recent books are *Re-visioning the Past—Early Photography in Bengal* (2005), *Visualizing Indian Women* (2005), *Visual Histories—Photography in the Popular Imagination* (2013) and *Memories of Belonging—Images from the Colony and Beyond* (2015).

Upasona Khound graduated from Hindu College, University of Delhi. She obtained her master's and MPhil degrees from Jawaharlal Nehru University (JNU), New Delhi, where she submitted her MPhil dissertation in 2011 on 'Politics of Iconography: Statues and Memorials in Uttar Pradesh (1995–2011)'. She then continued with two years of PhD at JNU till July 2013, after which she deregistered to join Assam Police Services. Currently, Upasona Khound is undergoing training as Deputy Superintendent of Police (Probationer) at Guwahati under the Department of Home, Government of Assam. Her areas of interests are Indian politics and political philosophy, and she has been engaged in research on political rhetoric in Indian democracy. She taught political science at Shri Ram College of Commerce (SRCC), University of Delhi, for a brief period.

Anusuya Kumar (Master of Arts in English Literature and Sanskrit) is a writer and researcher with years of experience teaching at the University of Pittsburgh in the USA, the University of Copenhagen and the University of Århus in Denmark. She is working on a book regarding the history of yoga and meditation practices in Denmark.

Ronie Parciack is a faculty member at the Department of East Asian Studies, Tel Aviv University, Tel Aviv, Israel, and a member of the Israel Academy for the Sciences and the Humanities Young Scholars' Forum. Her research interests include the visual language of Hindi cinema, the vernacular planes of political theology in India and the Indo-Islamic visual culture. She has published in several refereed journals and anthologies, and co-edited (with Dr Ritu Khanduri, University of Texas at Arlington) a special issue of *South Asian Popular Culture* on terror and media. Her book on the visual aesthetics of Hindi cinema *Popular Hindi Cinema: Aesthetic Formations of the Seen and Unseen* (2016) has just been published.

Sushmita Pati submitted her PhD at the Centre for Political Studies, Jawaharlal Nehru University, New Delhi, in July 2016. Currently, she is at the School of Policy and Governance at Azim Premji University,

Bangalore. She is interested in issues of urban politics at the intersections of Indian politics and political economy.

Jill Reese teaches courses on Material & Visual Culture in the Department of Anthropology at University College London, where she completed her PhD. Her research focuses upon the aesthetics, processes of making and display of political imagery circulating on contested streetscapes in Madurai, Tamil Nadu. She analyses the materiality of images and the productivity of spectacle in assertions of power, community and place-making, and demonstrations of patronage and respect. Prior to an academic career, she produced documentaries for broadcast television and taught video production, photography, and documentary history courses in India and the USA.

Ilanit Loewy Shacham completed her PhD at the Department of South Asian Languages and Civilizations, the University of Chicago, and will be joining the department of East Asian Studies, Tel Aviv University in October 2017. Her research interests include pre-modern South-Indian literature, especially second-millennium poetry in Sanskrit and in Telugu.

Fritzi-Marie Titzmann received her PhD from Humboldt-Universität zu Berlin, Germany, with a thesis on the Indian Online Matrimonial Market. Her research focuses on gender, new media and social changes in India with particular interest in digital phenomena. She is a faculty member at the Institute of Indology in Leipzig University, Germany.

Index